THE
SOUND OF MUSIC
STORY

ALSO BY TOM SANTOPIETRO

The Importance of Being Barbra

Considering Doris Day

Sinatra in Hollywood

The Godfather Effect:
Changing Hollywood, America, and Me

THE
SOUND OF MUSIC
STORY

HOW A BEGUILING YOUNG NOVICE,

A HANDSOME AUSTRIAN CAPTAIN,

AND TEN SINGING VON TRAPP CHILDREN

INSPIRED THE MOST BELOVED FILM OF ALL TIME

Tom Santopietro

ST. MARTIN'S PRESS ☒ NEW YORK

www.stmartins.com

The Library of Congress Cataloging-in-Publication Data is available upon request.

ISBN 978-1-250-06446-2 (hardcover)
ISBN 978-1-4668-7059-8 (e-book)

First Edition: February 2015

1   3   5   7   9   10   8   6   4   2

For Don and Anne Albino
and
S.B.

Contents

Acknowledgments

My first debt of thanks for help on this book goes to Ted Chapin, president of the Rodgers and Hammerstein Organization, and Bert Fink, executive vice president of R&H. This book would not have been possible without their support and expertise in all matters R&H, especially as regards *The Sound of Music.*

Particular thanks go to my agent, Malaga Baldi, and my editor, Michael Flamini. Their guidance proved invaluable throughout the entire process, and I feel fortunate to be in such good hands. Additional thanks go to Michael's associate editor, Vicki Lame, for her first-rate help with a plethora of details, as well as publicist John Karle for spreading the word.

I also want to acknowledge Michael Mattesino's excellent documentary *The Sound of Music: From Fact to Phenomenon,* which provided a detailed timeline for production on *The Sound of Music.* Although his focus on the film remains different from mine, his on-camera interviews provided fascinating and helpful material. As always, a special thank-you to film historian/author/professor Jeanine Basinger, whose knowledge and insight regarding film history remain unparalleled.

Although the majority of the key production personnel on the film are no longer alive, I was fortunate to interview several members of the team who proved extraordinarily generous with their time: Dee Dee Wood, Georg Steinitz, and Marni Nixon all spent a great deal of time answering my queries, and to them I extend my gratitude. Special thanks to the gentlemanly Dan Truhitte for his helpful, good-humored recollections, and a particular thanks to Johannes von Trapp, who provided extraordinary background information with his clear-eyed but very loving memories of his mother, Maria.

Special thanks to a host of friends who have been of invaluable assistance during the writing of this book for myriad reasons. Most especially I owe a big debt to Gary Horbar and Lon Weiner, as well as to my core of patient and tireless sounding boards: Steve Resnick, Peter von Mayrhauser, Dianne Trulock, Ara Marx, Yuriko Iwai, and Lauren Loizides.

Finally, thank you to a terrific group of friends and colleagues whose support and input during the past year have been extraordinary—and very much appreciated: Mark Erickson; Doris Blum Gorelick; Rheba Flegelman; Nina Skriloff and Dan Mirro; Beth and Alf Blitzer; Mary Gates; Nola Safro; Robert Albini; Katherine Aucoin; Ruth Mulhall; Mimi Lines; Kim Kelley; Peter Pileski and Bob Avian; Bruce Klinger and Frank Shanbacker; David Jackson; Rob Hudson; Marlene Beasley; Lynnette Barkley; Jan Heise; Joan Marcus and Adrian Bryan-Brown; Brig Berney; Steven Sorrentino; Bill Cannon; Alan Markinson; Tim and Karen Lernihan, Annie Smith; Anton and Almerinda Coppola; Brooke Allen; Eric Comstock and Barbara Fasano; Janet Strickland; Carol Strickland; David Jannone; Ed Nelson; Debbie Lamberti; Greg Galvin; Larry Katen and Philip Rinaldi; Steve Shapiro; Mark Henry; Mary Breilid; Simon and Nancy Jones; Michael Lonergan; Michael Wilkie; Russ Rosensweig; Scott and Jill Glenn; Tom Lynch; Wayne and Betty McCormack.

1.

A Very Good Place to Start

"I guess we did do something rather good."
—JULIE ANDREWS TO CHRISTOPHER PLUMMER IN
JULIE ANDREWS AND CHRISTOPHER PLUMMER—A REMINISCENCE

June 4, 1964: Julie Andrews was freezing. If this was spring weather in the Alps, what was it like in February?

With the sun rarely bothering to appear, weather continued to run roughshod over location shooting on *The Sound of Music,* and the unceasing rain had left one very small, unpaved road as the only way anyone could reach Mehlweg in southern Bavaria for the filming of the movie's title song. Which was precisely why the cold but ever-cooperative Andrews found herself arriving at the scenic meadow location by means of a decidedly unglamorous jeep.

Problems with the jeep, however, paled in comparison to the logistics involved with the rental of the helicopter that would swoop down to film Andrews as she launched into the world famous title song. Helicopter rentals were expensive—very expensive—and with the 20th Century-Fox front office firing off memos to director/producer Robert Wise to rein in the overbudget, much delayed filming, even the perpetually calm director felt the strain of completing the elaborate sequence. With only the first half of the number requiring the use of the helicopter, as soon as the shot was captured, the pilot would instantly fly to Obersalzburg for the filming of the movie's finale: the von Trapp family's escape over the Alps into Switzerland. There was no money for even one more day's helicopter rental.

The ever professional Andrews, a seasoned showbiz veteran at a mere twenty-eight, took an extra moment to prepare herself for the carefully staged rendering of the title song. This was no ordinary musical number, no song-and-dance routine laid down in the carefully controlled confines of the studio. Instead, in order to convey the sense of open-air freedom envisioned by Wise and screenwriter Ernest Lehman, a helicopter with storyboard artist Maurice Zuberano onboard would swoop in to film Andrews as she began her lilting vocal. With the helicopter weighed down by bulky equipment and cameraman Paul Beeson strapped precariously onto the side of the craft, the shot would prove difficult in execution—and potentially thrilling.

Wise and cinematographer Ted McCord knew that this opening not only had to look right, but would also establish the musical vocabulary for the entire film. If viewers did not accept the convention of Maria singing to herself while alone in the mountains, what would they ever make of a ten-minute montage set to the childlike "Do-Re-Mi"?

Wise had spent hours considering countless possible camera movements for this opening, only to discard every last one of them in favor of an overhead shot. Still, he hesitated. It would read onscreen just like the start of his own Academy Award–winning *West Side Story,* which began with a swooping camera that picked up dancers silhouetted against the New York City landscape. Well, the director figured, maybe it wasn't original, but at least he was stealing from himself.

McCord would be photographing the Alps—God's country—and the scene cried out for an omniscient, all seeing, from-the-sky approach, which is why the sixty-year-old Wise found himself perched halfway up a tree, waiting for the precise combination of light and wind speed that would allow Andrews to burst forth spinning into the title song.

But first, the shot had to be lined up and framed. There couldn't be the hint of another human being in sight: postulant Maria Rainer, momentarily freed from the stifling abbey, was singing precisely because she was basking in glorious solitude with nature. Andrews's slight figure would land smack in the middle of the frame, a speck against the wide open spaces until the helicopter zoomed in closer, still closer, and then—

From his perch halfway up the tree, Wise called out:

"Ready? . . . Roll camera."

Camera operator, soundman, and loader replied:

"Roll Camera."

"Speed."

"Scene one, Take one."

After the slate was clapped directly in front of the lens, Robert Wise paused momentarily and then commanded:

"Action!"

All eyes swiveled toward Julie Andrews. And waited. Until everyone realized that Julie could not hear any of that traditional start-of-scene checklist over the noise of the approaching helicopter.

Time to regroup. Choreographer Marc Breaux would now bellow "Go!" into his bullhorn, Andrews would charge forward, walking quickly in time to the music until at exactly the right moment she'd lean into her opening hillside twirl.

"Ready?"

Camera running up to speed, scene slated, and once again: "Action!"

Andrews strode purposefully across the meadow, throwing herself into a full-bodied twirl, arms outstretched as if to embrace the entire world, and launched into the film's opening words: "The hills are alive . . . "

Gone was the song's introductory verse beginning with the pensive "My day in the hills has come to an end, I know." Instead, bam! Right into the chorus—and right into Rodgers and Hammerstein's uncanny mix of music and faith. The song continued, and thirty seconds later there was Julie wanting to "sing through the night—like a lark who is learning to pray." Uh-oh, a praying bird? Was this all going to be too saccharine? Maybe—but thanks to St. Augustine, wasn't one of the von Trapp family sayings "When you sing, you pray twice?"

But for now there was trouble. Big trouble. And not with Andrews's performance. No matter the take, she lipsynched with pinpoint accuracy to her prerecorded vocal. The problem lay with the helicopter. With the nominal camera operator refusing to hang out of the plane, British cinematographer Paul Beeson assisted Wise and McCord by operating the camera himself while strapped to the side of the craft, the only way to capture the sought-after shot of Julie Andrews skimming along the meadow without the shadow of the craft falling on the ground. But each time the craft circled back to its starting position for another take, the force of the craft's downdraft proved so strong that Andrews found herself knocked over, sprawled in the grass while trying to avoid the mud. Pulling grass out of her hair and off her costume, makeup adjusted yet again, she would stride, twirl, sing, and once more find herself on the ground. Having been knocked down on fully half of the ten takes, even the placid Andrews "finally got so angry I yelled 'That's enough!' " Yell she did, but even Ethel Merman herself couldn't have been heard over the sound of the helicopter, and the pilot interpreted his star's hand signals asking him to please make a wider turn as a thumbs-up gesture of "You're doing great—let's go for one more." Was this any way to begin a multimillion-dollar musical? As it turned out, yes. And then some.

Wise, McCord, and Lehman had, in tandem with musical maestro/associate producer Saul Chaplin and co-choreographers Marc Breaux and Dee Dee Wood, worked to finesse every last phrase of this song, yet here they were, in the third month of shooting, and one question still lay over the entire enterprise: could any of this really work? Would people buy a nun bursting into song—and in the opening shots of an eight-million-dollar widescreen Todd-AO, stereophonic sound production no less? People expected reality from their movies now. Foreign films and the marked relaxation of production code taboos had changed the very nature of moviegoing. Religious pictures were no longer in vogue and musicals had fallen out of favor; how was any of this going to be received?

As it turned out, with a worldwide fervent devotion, five Academy Awards, vitriolic critical disdain, and a cultural impact that continues to resonate some five decades after the film's initial release. But for now, Julie Andrews just needed to pick herself up, dust herself off, and try her damnedest to channel the life force that was Maria Augusta Kutschera von Trapp, a woman whose complex real-life backstory made the Maria von Trapp found in *The Sound of Music* appear to be, well, Mary Poppins.

A nun turned governess, Maria von Trapp had married her naval hero employer, instantly inherited his seven children, given birth to three more, pushed the entire family to international singing stardom, outwitted the Nazis, emigrated to America, and morphed into a combination of Austrian relief dynamo, lodge owner, missionary, entrepreneur, loving family matriarch, and occasionally, family dictator. It all played out like a real-life fairy tale, and by the time Maria von Trapp died in 1987 at the age of eighty-two, thanks to the *Sound of Music* she had been turned into nothing less than a secular saint. Sainted not by her own claims, though she hardly shunned the attention, but by the millions around the globe who wanted to believe that someone—anyone—could be as good as the Maria von Trapp glimpsed forty feet high on the screen in the utterly winning persona of Julie Andrews. Maria von

Trapp, they reasoned, was proof positive that something good did indeed still exist in the ever-changing, ever-frightening world of the twentieth century. Was she really so good, so, well, perfect?

In the words of the John Ford Western masterpiece *The Man Who Shot Liberty Valance*: "When the legend becomes fact, print the legend."

2.

HOW DO YOU SOLVE A PROBLEM LIKE . . .

"I realized when I was a little girl, that to get her attention you really had to engage her. She had done these tremendous things in her life; met presidents and kings, and I could tell that she didn't have time for a lot of details."

—MARIA VON TRAPP'S GRANDDAUGHTER
ELISABETH, *VANITY FAIR*, JUNE 1998

The one overwhelming irony lying at the heart of *The Sound of Music*'s immutable status as a touchstone of childhood innocence is that Maria herself had anything but a storybook childhood. Far from security and happiness, Maria's formative years featured insecurity, neglect, and ofttimes downright cruelty.

Born on a train bound for Vienna on January 26, 1905, Maria was only three years old when her mother died. After first living with a father who was unable or unwilling to take care of her, the youngster was sent to live with foster parents. When, after her father died in 1914, nine-year-old Maria was forced to live with a relative known as "Uncle" Franz, the darkest years of her life ensued. Far from providing a welcoming home, the tyrannical Franz, a socialist and anti-Catholic atheist, had little time for his young charge, and, as detailed in Maria's decades' later autobiography, often beat her. Small wonder, then, that Maria's youngest child Johannes (the tenth and final von Trapp child, born in 1939) has publicly stated that his "complex" mother's exceedingly unhappy childhood had left her with "insecurities that plagued her all of her life."

Figuring that education could provide a way out of her unhappy circumstances, Maria worked to put herself through Vienna's State Teacher's College for Progressive Education. It was during those years that she began to spend increasing amounts of time wandering in the beautiful, mountainous Austrian countryside. These solitary journeys provided Maria with the sense of freedom and peace missing from her childhood, while also providing an ideal outlet for her boundless energy.

And energy she had. To burn. It's easy for audiences accustomed to the Maria von Trapp found in the figures of the trim Julie Andrews, or the petite Mary Martin who originated the role of Maria in the Broadway production of *The Sound of Music*, to forget the fact that Maria was a substantial woman whose sturdy frame proved ideal for her mountainside forays. Forthright, indeed blunt, and the possessor of a booming laugh, Maria remained a formidable figure well into her dotage, a no-nonsense, frequently tough woman full of boundless energy who registered as a rounder, Austrian version of Katharine Hepburn and her all-American no-nonsense practicality.

As to how Maria's life morphed from an unhappy childhood to that of a would-be nun, the answer, in Maria's view, lay in divine revelation. While still a teenager, she had joined a hiking group, and it was her suggestion that the club hike high into the Alps, to regions where snow remained even in summer. Surrounded by the literally breathtaking scenery, "suddenly it occurred to me—all this—God gives to me. What can I give him? I decided to go into a convent, which has perpetual enclosure."

It was this revelation, combined with a Palm Sunday service she attended while studying at college, that led her to the abbey upon graduation. Expecting nothing more from the Palm Sunday service than a chance to hear the music of Bach that she loved, Maria found something quite different: "Now I had heard from my uncle that all of these Bible stories were inventions and old legends, and that there wasn't a word of truth in them. But the way this man talked just swept me off my feet. I was completely overwhelmed."

Convinced that she would find the love and security so lacking in her everyday life within abbey walls, Maria traveled to Salzburg. Located between Munich and Vienna, and famed as the home of Mozart, Salzburg had existed as an independent church state for more than one thousand years before joining Austria in 1816. Perhaps with this history in mind, upon her arrival Maria, in an extraordinary display of naïveté, simply asked the first policeman she encountered for the name of the strictest abbey in all of Salzburg. "Nonnberg Abbey," the answer came back.

Founded in A.D. 719, Nonnberg ("Nun Mountain"), which is situated on an overlook outside of the city proper, was more than the strictest abbey in the area—it was also the oldest. After walking to the abbey, Maria announced that she wished to join the novitiate, and after meeting with the Mother Abbess, found herself beginning the life of a novice at age nineteen. Says youngest child Johannes: "She did everything 100 percent. Having found a religious belief in her late teens—after an hours' long confession—she wanted to dedicate her life to God."

In her autobiography, and of course in both the stage and film versions of *The Sound of Music*, that nineteen-year-old novice stands front and center throughout the life of the entire abbey. Such starlike stature may well have been embellished in recall by Maria herself. In an amusing anecdote recounted by *Sound of Music* screenwriter Ernest Lehman, when Lehman and the film's then-director William Wyler went to speak with the Mother Abbess in 1963 (with the aim of gathering background information about Maria), the Mother Abbess, in Lehman's recall, reacted as if to say, "Who's Maria?" "The Reverend Mother hardly remembered who Maria was . . . I think Maria exaggerated her importance at the Abbey enormously in the story."

In fact, the mention of Maria von Trapp could still cause decidedly mixed emotions on the part of Salzburg natives, with some going so far as to deny she had ever entered the novitiate at Nonnberg. Peter Husty, the head of exhibitions at the Salzburg Museum, went on record as suggesting that Maria's time at the abbey may have been grossly exaggerated, or perhaps even nonexistent, calling her relationship to Nonnberg Abbey "a little strange." Pointing out that she had been neither a teacher nor a nun, he emphasized the fact that unlike other novitiates, Maria left no trace at the abbey: no record of her birth, her mother, or her father; in his words she resembled "a will of the wisp." (Husty's viewpoint would seem undercut merely by the fact that when the family traveled to Salzburg in 1950, Maria held a personal reunion with the Mother Abbess.)

What was undoubtedly true, however, was that Maria was far more enthralled with the beautiful countryside outside of Salzburg than she was with life in the abbey. Possessed of great natural beauty, ringed by snowcapped mountains, and nestled in Austria's lake district, Salzburg, or more particularly the surrounding environs, provided a setting in which Maria immediately felt at home. Escaping to the mountains every chance she had, Maria first bent and then broke the strict rules of the abbey.

As the song "How Do You Solve a Problem Like Maria?" would have it, she actually did whistle and sing within the abbey walls, and the details of her personality paint her as a remarkably unpromising candidate for the quiet life of a nun in a cloistered abbey. Tales abounded of one nun who had not looked out the window at the outside world in fifty years. Fifty years? Maria couldn't last fifteen minutes without looking out of the window to drink in the surrounding natural beauty. Penance for looking out the window took the form of kissing the floor, and Maria would simply save time by kissing the floor first and then look out the window. This action found its way into *The Sound of Music* via Maria's confession regarding Sister Berthe: rather than follow Sister Berthe's instruction that she kiss the floor after committing a transgression, she figured she would break another rule sooner rather than later, so saved time by kissing the ground at the mere approach of Sister Berthe. In the words of Johannes von Trapp: "My mother was absolutely unsuited for a contemplative life in the abbey. I suspect the nuns were happy when the position opened up in our father's house."

Nonnberg would never be quite the same again thanks to the unruly Maria, who claimed that the nuns found her too coarse: "I had no manners. I was more boy than girl." She was not officially asked to leave the abbey, but it was thought that perhaps some time away might prove beneficial. Given her background as a teacher she was deemed just the right candidate to tutor Captain Georg von Trapp's young daughter Maria. (Maria's suitability as a teacher might have been recalibrated if the captain had ever been able to hear *The Sound of Music*'s assistant director Georg Steinitz, who held a nodding acquaintance with her; Maria had taught Steinitz's mother before entering the abbey, and in Georg's chuckling recall, his mother termed Maria "an awfully strict person—a dominating person. My mother felt her religious beliefs were close to what we would today call fanatical.")

A captain in the Austrian Navy and a decorated hero from his service during the First World War, by this time Georg von Trapp had suffered monumental losses in both his private and professional lives. When Austria lost the war it lost its entire coastline, and his job as a naval captain ceased to exist. Georg then lost his wife, Agathe Whitehead, to scarlet fever in September of 1922, leaving him sole parent to seven children: Rupert, Agathe, Maria, Werner, Hedwig, Johanna, and Martina.

Although well off financially (it had, in fact, been wife Agathe whose money buoyed the family's fortune; her grandfather had invented the modern torpedo), Georg was overwhelmed with his duties as a single parent and looking for assistance. While both the screen and stage versions of *The Sound of Music* depict Maria as governess to all seven children, she was hired simply as a tutor to young Maria, whose own bout with scarlet fever had left her too weak to walk the four miles to school every day. Perhaps because young Maria spent more time with her twenty-one-year-old tutor than any of the other six Von Trapp children, she was able, late in life, to offer up the sharpest, most clear-eyed assessment of her tutor turned stepmother: "She needed, all the time, excitement, so she created excitement. Sometimes it was too much for us, but she was a leader."

Maria's description of her appearance on the day of her arrival at the villa in Aigen in late summer of 1926 seems to mirror the film's depiction of a satchel-swinging, guitar-toting Julie Andrews so accurately that it seems to have directly inspired the film's costume designer, Dorothy Jeakins. Wrote Maria: "My satchel looked exactly like the bag of a horse-and-buggy doctor." Even Maria's unattractive dress in the film ("The poor didn't want this one") seems to have been inspired by Maria's actual garment; said daughter Maria: "She had a horrible dress on."

As to the actual first meeting between Maria and the Von Trapp family, it was, in her recollection, both low-key and not markedly different from how it is depicted in the film. The captain executed a slight bow toward Maria, took out a whistle, and blew signals to summon his seven children, who ranged in age from four to fourteen.

In contrast to the film's depiction of a whistle-blowing martinet, Captain von Trapp actually used the bosun's whistle only to locate his children on the grounds of his rather large estate. But the seven children really did wear sailor suits and, for moviegoers around the world who carry the image of seven children summoned by their father's whistle marching down the stairs to meet their new governess, Maria's recall of the event matches the film in surprisingly close fashion: "Led by a sober-faced young girl in her early teens, an almost solemn little procession descended step by step in well-mannered silence—four girls and two boys, all dressed in blue sailor suits." So ingrained was this childhood training of responding to signals that until the day she died at age ninety-nine, daughter Maria retained the ability to play every one of the seven signals. In Agathe's recollection: "We loved our signals."

In reality, Georg was a warm and loving if somewhat overwhelmed father. It was actually Maria herself (called "Gustl" by the children), with her emotionally stunted upbringing, who needed thawing. Starved for affection, a woman/child who had literally grown up without being kissed, she found herself willing putty in the hands of the youngest children. For those who find the film's connection between governess and children too precious for words, the reality actually proved even more deeply emotional: "I grew up without being kissed. . . . And then I came here to this house, and one of the little ones, Johanna—she was seven years old—she spontaneously came up to me one day, put her hands around my neck, and kissed me. I remember the sensation very well. It was the first conscious kiss of my life." Small wonder, then, that Maria later wrote in her autobiography: "Only one thing is necessary to be happy . . . and that one thing is not money, nor connections, nor health—it is love."

If it is a universal truth that every person alive has, at one time or another, felt misunderstood, underappreciated or in need of love, then in Maria's very real recollection of Johanna's kiss lies a key to the film's extraordinary success: more than the romance between Maria and the captain, the love story at the heart of *The Sound of Music* is the one between Maria and the children. Indeed, Maria herself publicly and repeatedly acknowledged that she fell in love with the children quickly, but only grew to love Georg after their marriage.

In that light, it makes sense that the captain's marriage proposal proved far more prosaic in real life than in the film's depiction of a moonlit song in a romantic, waterside gazebo. As related by her granddaughter, Maria was standing on a stepladder polishing a chandelier when the children ran in to the room crying out, "Poppa says he will marry you."

In the recollection of Agathe von Trapp, her father asked her: "Do you think I should marry Gustl? You know, she's quite pretty." Agathe answered: "I think if it is the will of God then you should marry her." It was, in fact, Agathe who late in life offered the most judicious explanation of Maria's marriage to Georg. Did Georg love Maria at the time of the marriage? Agathe responded thoughtfully: "I can't say I know it or I don't know it . . . but since he did what he did he must have liked her. But the way I saw it, I think she was providential, to be our second mother."

Said third oldest child Maria: "When she first came it was heaven on Earth. We took to her quickly. She sang, she knew new songs. . . . But I wanted Maria to stay a bigger sister. . . . I didn't want my father to marry her. I loved my mother so much I didn't want him to marry again ever. . . . But that was not possible. We never talked about this of course. We just let it happen."

If in the film Maria is thrilled when the captain finally declares his love, in real life her reaction proved far less sanguine. After the Mother Superior told Maria that marriage to the captain and mothering his seven children represented the will of God, Maria found "All my happiness shattered, and my heart, which had so longed to give itself entirely to God, felt rejected." First came a marriage proposal received in the middle of doing housework, not from one's intended, but rather, from his children. Next, the prospective bride displayed a less-than-thrilled reaction at the very prospect of marriage. Not exactly the stuff of Rodgers and Hammerstein songs. But the magic of any tale lies in the way it is told, and in the decades' later hands of Rodgers, Hammerstein, Wise, and Lehman, the lives of Maria and Georg von Trapp were turned into popular art that appealed to the entire world.

Did the family only begin singing after Maria arrived on the scene? The actual chronology here becomes a little fuzzy; it is unquestioned that Maria brought a guitar with her, but while some recollect that the children were already singing before Maria's arrival, in Maria's own words: "They didn't sing. I couldn't understand this. It was the first thing we did. We started singing." On the other hand, in daughter Maria's recollection, the Von Trapp villa was hardly the dour, music-less atmosphere depicted in the film: "Sometimes our house must have sounded like a musical conservatory. . . . You could hear us practice piano, violin, guitar, cello, clarinet, accordion, and later, recorders." Agathe von Trapp, in fact, specifies that father Georg was very musical, teaching Rupert and Maria the accordion, Johanna the violin, and Agathe herself the guitar. There was, in her recollection, no question about it: singing and the playing of instruments began long before the arrival of Maria. To the contrary, it was Gustl, she stressed, who joined in with an already singing family. "Thanks to our father, we already had a repertoire by the time Gustl arrived in our home."

Regardless of when the children actually began singing, after Maria's marriage to the Captain took place on November 27, 1927, at Nonnberg Abbey, the vocalizing remained an intrafamily affair until the mid-1930s, when the family's entire life was upended with the arrival of Father Franz Wasner.

In theory, Father Wasner had simply come to the von Trapp villa to live in a rented room and say mass in the family chapel. In reality, he ended up changing the lives of every member of the family. It all started simply enough when, after listening to the family sing, Father Wasner told them that they sounded quite good but could sing even better. Conducting from his seat, he insisted that the family repeat a motet until it sounded exactly right. Once the priest stated that what the family sang was very nice—"*but*"—the die was cast. Said Maria: "That 'but' was the decision of our lives. . . . None of us knew then just how lucky we were: this was the birth of the Trapp Family Singers." The entire *Sound of Music* global phenomenon had begun with one single word: *but*.

In the first movie version of the Von Trapp saga, the 1956 German language film *Die Trapp-Familie,* Father Wasner plays a central role as the musical taskmaster responsible for molding the Trapp Family Singers. By the time *The Sound of Music* hit Broadway three years later, he had been jettisoned by librettists Howard Lindsay and Russel Crouse, who decided that his presence would undercut Maria's role as musical tutor. In 1930s Austria, however, Father Wasner actually formed a very close alliance with Maria, with the priest dictating the family's musical direction while Maria rather willingly fulfilled the role of entrepreneur, cajoling and pushing the family to fame.

So intertwined did the twosome become that in 1935 they actually collaborated on a love song entitled "Zwei Menschen"—"Two People"—with Father Wasner the composer and Maria the lyricist. Exactly how close was their relationship? Sympatico enough to write a song with translated lyrics that prove decidedly unexpected from a collaboration between a priest and a former novice:

Two people walking under the starlit moon
The apple trees are in bloom
The petals are falling on their heads like snow
The bells are ringing in the distance

When interviewed for a 2012 documentary, Father Wasner's nephew commented on the fact that Maria and his uncle were genuinely kindred spirits; born in the same year and raised in similar hardscrabble circumstances, each was firmly dedicated to music and the church alike. The two wrote "Zwei Menschen" in the year they met, and in the words of Wasner's nephew: "They both probably had unfulfilled dreams. . . . It's an expression of something but we don't know what." Was it a love song? Were they in love? The answer will never be known.

Having openly and repeatedly criticized Hitler, Father Wasner found it necessary to leave Austria, accompanying the Von Trapps to the United States in the 1930s, where he continued as the driving musical force behind the Trapp Family Singers for two more decades. After the family stopped performing in 1956, Maria and Franz went their separate ways; Franz spent five years as a missionary on Fiji, followed by time in the Holy Land and a stint as rector of a seminary in Rome. Upon retirement, he returned to Salzburg where he lived until his death in 1992.

Maria and Franz were not reunited until 1983, when Maria made a final trip to Salzburg while the Vermont family lodge was being rebuilt after a devastating fire; the footage of their reunion reveals a duo so simpatico that it seems as if they are picking up a conversation they had finished five minutes earlier. As they finished each other's sentences and filled in missing bits of recollection, it was easy to fully comprehend Maria's statement: "He slowly but surely molded us into a real musical entity—an excellent musician. Seeing him again was so normal, so natural. He was very much a part of us."

Missionary work and reunion lay decades in the future however, and in those early years before the family began to sing in public, everyone involved felt content to simply practice, repeating phrases and passages over and over until the harmony was second nature, the entire family united by their love of music. In Maria's own nicely turned phrase: "We were intoxicated with music, drunk with the wonder of song."

Maria had given birth to daughters Rosmarie (1928) and Eleonore (1931), and with the family now numbering eleven in all, it became clear even in these earliest days of Maria and Georg's marriage that her keen eye would be continually trained on the family's finances. Having grown up with little and being practical by nature, Maria remained vigilant about savings, especially after September 1932 when the captain lost all of the family's money in a gallant but doomed gesture to keep his friend's Lanmer (Austrian) bank from failing. Georg had attempted to shore up the bank by removing the family money from his London bank and depositing all of it in the Lanmer bank in Zell am See. After the bank failed nonetheless, Maria dismissed servants, closed entire floors of the villa, and insisted that the family take in boarders to help with expenses. Boarders were fine, but after all the expenses were paid, their rental income did not prove very lucrative, and Maria soon saw a better way to recoup a bit of the family's fortune: a series of public concerts by the Trapp Family Singers.

Encouraged by opera singer Lotte Lehmann ("You have gold in your throats"), Maria enthusiastically pushed forward, but the captain remained appalled by the idea of his family singing in public. Payment for singing? How undignified. Even after the Von Trapps won the competition at a group singing festival, the captain still despaired at such an unseemly display. It seemed, Maria later wrote with a nicely judged sense of irony, that "only the solemn family resolution never, never to do such a thing again put his troubled mind at rest."

That resolution only lasted until the family won the top prize in the 1936 Salzburg music festival, after which they toured extensively throughout England, Italy, France, Holland, and Sweden. Said son Johannes: "He didn't like the idea of us performing for money at first. He got used to the idea. Necessity changes one's point of view in many ways." The Trapp Family Singers were now here to stay. Mixing sacred music with traditional Austrian folk melodies, the family's concerts struck a popular chord, coming as they did at the time of a significant revival of folk traditions.

As the family toured throughout Europe, they had an unanticipated firsthand view of Adolf Hitler at a café in Munich, a scene detailed by Maria in arresting detail. Hitler was, by the time of this encounter, fully entrenched in power, and the former artist was visiting Munich's "House of German Art" exhibit. In precise prose, Maria evokes a pre–World War II fürher who seems to embody, in Hannah Arendt's famous phrase, the banality of evil: "If one didn't know that Hitler was the all-powerful Führer of Germany, one wouldn't have looked a second time at him He seemed to be very, very ordinary, a little vulgar, not too well educated—no resemblance to the hero in silver armor on the wall."

In fact, while *The Sound of Music*'s depiction of the captain's decision to

forego service in the navy of the Third Reich is accurate, in reality, the cap-
tain's refusal represented the third time that the Von Trapps had defied the
Nazis. First, oldest child Rupert, a practicing physician, refused to work at a
Nazi-run hospital in Vienna where openings existed only because all of the
Jewish doctors had been forced to leave. Next, the family turned down the
German government's request that they sing on the radio in honor of the füh-
rer's birthday. Finally, when the captain refused a commission in the German
Navy, the necessity of fleeing Austria became clear.

It was not a decision undertaken lightly, but after Germany annexed Austria in 1938, and it became forbidden by penalty of death to sing the Austrian national anthem, the family, in Maria's words: "learned that the love
for your homeland comes even before the love for your family." (Defiance and
love of the homeland extended down to the youngest children, with Eleonore—
"Lorli"—proudly announcing to her first-grade class that her father had insisted, "He'd put ground glass in his tea or finish his life on a dung heap
before he would ever sing the German national anthem.")

Although, just as shown in *The Sound of Music,* family butler Hans joined
the Nazi party, he in fact warned Georg in August of 1938 that the Austrian
borders would soon be closed, a prescient piece of advice that allowed the
family to escape on the very last day before the borders were sealed. Nazi party
membership and all, Hans was, in the words of Agathe, "remembered with
gratitude." Packing one suitcase each, the family casually let it be known that
they were embarking on a "family vacation" for mountain climbing in the
South Tyrol, dropped off keys to the villa at a local religious order, crossed
the railroad tracks behind their property, and took the first train to Italy.

So casual was the family's appearance on the day of escape, that according to *The Sound of Music*'s Austrian assistant director Georg Steinitz, people
in Salzburg saw the family off at the train station. Appearing in the mid-1970s
on Julie Andrews's television show, Maria discussed how the necessary exile
had changed the entire future of the family on the most basic level: "We went
from being rich to being the poorest of the poor." The aristocrats were now
refugees.

Given the family's real-life escape to Italy, the film's lushly filmed finale
of their brave climb over the mountains into the safety of Switzerland was,
of course, a complete fiction. As many have pointed out, most particularly
Maria herself, if they had climbed over the Austrian mountain peaks, they

would have ended up in Germany, not Switzerland, and very close to the führer's retreat at Berchtesgaden at that. In Maria's typically blunt statement, "Don't they know geography in Hollywood? Salzburg does not border on Switzerland!" In fact, Salzburg lies 150 miles from Switzerland, but as canny old pro Robert Wise analyzed: "In Hollywood you make your own geography."

After the Von Trapps escaped, their villa became a headquarters for the Nazis, complete with bomb shelters built in the garden. Himmler himself made Maria (Mitzi) and Agathe's bedroom on the second floor into his own, and turned the family chapel into a beer parlor. Maria and Georg's rooms were converted into Himmler's private quarters and perhaps most disturbing of all, Father Wasner's rooms were converted into a private residence for Adolf Hitler when he visited. (After the war, the Americans returned the villa to the von Trapps, who sold the home to the Missionaries of the Precious Blood in 1947. The von Trapps used the money to pay off the mortgage on the property in Vermont, and their Salzburg home bore the name of Saint Joseph's Seminary; priests were now praying in the room where Himmler put his plans for the final solution into play. The Missionaries of the Precious Blood still own the property, but the villa itself reopened to the public in 2008 as the Trapp Villa Hotel. In 2008, the villa was converted to a bed and breakfast.)

From Italy the family traveled to England, and after signing a contract with Charles Wagner to sing in America, the family sailed to New York City. Although speaking no English the family enjoyed their stay, even if they all seemed bewildered by the modern life encountered in New York. In her own recollection, Maria reacted to the sight of her first escalator as if glimpsing an alien spaceship. When the family's visas expired in March of 1939, they returned to Sweden just before World War II erupted.

Contracts had been offered for another singing tour in the United States, but before signing off on the offers, Georg polled the entire family about undertaking another trip to the United States. The decision had to be unanimous: one vote of "no" and the move was off. As related by daughter Maria, after questioning each member of the family he opened the Bible and "It hit the passage 'God speaks to Abraham: Take your family and go into the land I have prepared for you.' " Speaking in her mid-eighties, Maria added: "I really believe everything was arranged by God."

The family's second arrival in the United States, in October of 1939, was not without a new set of problems however, thanks to Maria's outspoken behavior. Grateful to be back on the safety of U.S. soil, she exuberantly announced that she wanted to stay in the United States forever, and the American immigration service, wary of refugees from Europe, immediately sent the entire family into forced detention on Ellis Island. Eldest son Rupert was allowed to leave because he possessed an immigration visa, but the remainder of the family held only six-month visitors visas. Stranded and virtually penniless, the von Trapps did what they knew best—they sang for their fellow detainees. (The first draft of the script for the Broadway production of *The Sound of Music* actually dealt with the family's journey to America and ended with their arrival on Ellis Island. It was a smart decision to jettison scenes set in America; *The Sound of Music* represents the dream of happily-ever-after, one personified by walking over the Alps into freedom—not the reality of everyday life in Vermont.)

The FBI investigated the von Trapps before concluding, in effect, that a family singing religious and folk songs did not constitute a threat to U.S. security. After three days of detention the family was released, thanks to the combined efforts of Rupert, Bruce Mohler of the National Catholic Welfare Conference, and two friends the family had made in Merion, Pennsylvania. The von Trapps left Ellis Island penniless but happy to finally begin their new life in the United States.

Anxious to gain a foothold on the American music scene, the family auditioned for American manager Freddy Schang with a clueless, if talented performance any lover of backstage musicals would have been privileged to witness. His reaction to their sincere performance? An incredulously blurted out "A forty-five minute piece by Bach? Recorders? And you look too serious and have awful clothes. . . . And your name—The Trapp Family Choir— sounds too churchy. I am the manager of the Trapp Family Singers." Well, if the German-American Doris Mary Ann von Kappelhoff could become Doris Day, why not the Trapp Family Singers?

It was Freddy Schang who not only changed the name of the group but insisted that the family actually smile on the stage. He won the argument to have the women wear a bit of makeup on the stage, but definitively lost his suggestion that they wear high heels as well. Under the guidance of Mr. Schang the family now began to tour the country. It was a difficult existence in more ways than one, the unknown troupe drawing small (if enthusiastic) audiences.

Even the ever-optimistic Maria admitted: "It was difficult beginning with only four dollars. We rented a bus and practically lived in the bus for six months, touring and giving concerts."

Maria was happy, with the constant exposure to new cities and new people granting her the excitement she craved, but it was not an easy life for the children. Although Johannes was only four years old, he possesses distinct memories of the constant touring: "Traveling with the family, coming onstage, being introduced . . . The singing was hard work. There was a tremendous amount of discipline. We sang well as a group—we weren't soloists." Father Wasner's musical work ethic matched Maria's own drive for success, and in later years, his nephew Franz laughingly explained that during the twenty years that Father Wasner lived with the family, "He said mass every day and rehearsed them every day. The kids hated him for that!"

Slowly starting to acclimate themselves to their new homeland both off stage and on, the family now limited their religious music to the first half of the show, with the second act finding the family dressed in the garb of their homeland while singing Austrian folk songs and yodels. Local American songs such as "My Old Kentucky Home" were also worked into the repertoire at each appropriate tour stop. More relaxed on stage, the von Trapps learned to connect with the audiences in a more personal fashion—beginning with the night a fly flew into Maria's mouth and she stopped singing to announce that fact to the audience. The crowd loved such spontaneity and a new, more relaxed style of performing was born. When it was discovered partway through one concert that an instrument was missing, Maria told stories to the audience while Georg ran back to the hotel to retrieve the missing equipment. The audience was enthralled, chief among them the publisher J. B. Lippincott, who told Maria: "If you can tell stories, you can write a book." The end result was her 1949 autobiography, *The Story of the Trapp Family Singers*.

With their newly informal style of performance growing in assurance, the Trapp Family Singers began to acquire a national reputation. In their own way, they began to resemble a version of the Partridge Family three decades before that fictional family singing group hit the television airwaves, with the Von Trapps clad in lederhosen instead of groovy seventies bell bottoms and miniskirts.

Georg continued to work in the background, and if, on European tours, such work was limited to keeping the family scrapbooks and making travel

arrangements, in America he began to appear onstage shortly before the finale. Said Johannes: "My mother was the bundle of energy. In her relationship with my father, she was the engine and he was the governor who guided
it, controlled it, and directed it. They were very well matched in that regard.
My mother definitely needed someone to hold her down at times." Said daughter Lorli: "She had a volatile temper and I think she regretted the times she
blew up. She hadn't realized what quiet guidance he gave." Georg never did
grow comfortable in the limelight, and in hindsight, his granddaughter Kristina thinks that her grandfather suffered from depression: "My grandfather
didn't want to be in public in that way of touring the country. I think he
became increasingly sad. Now we call it depression. Then it was called
melancholia."

The Von Trapps were, in fact, a first-rate vocal ensemble, but their success also arose in part from being in the right place at the right time. As pointed
out by theater historian Laurence Maslon, they arrived in the United States
on the cusp of the American folk music movement, one that heated up during and after World War II, the attendant spirituals and folk songs "starting
to bubble up and pass the processed music of Tin Pan Alley." Against the back-
drop of the ongoing world war, the von Trapps' visible family togetherness
resonated strongly with audiences, and their immigrant saga of a large family arriving in the United States armed only with a fierce work ethic, struck
a chord with Americans of all backgrounds.

Because of their constant touring (from September through May of each
year, with a break only at Christmas) the von Trapps did not possess a real
home in the United States aside from the small farmhouse they rented in Pennsylvania from the Drinker family, who had helped rescue them from Ellis
Island. When a summer vacation in 1941 brought them to Stowe, Vermont,
however, the family fell in love with the Green Mountain area, which reminded
them of Austria. Ironically, Maria was in New York City conferring with their
manager when the other members of the family first spotted a ramshackle
old house with spectacular mountain views. When Maria saw the house for
the first time, she, too, fell in love with the mountainous countryside. Said
daughter Lorli: "My father saw the house. My mother saw the view."

Renovation of the wreck and the surrounding grounds became an all-
consuming project for the entire family. The old farmhouse was cleaned out
and new beams solidified; fields were plowed, crops planted and harvested,

clothes were sewn, gardens took shape, and everyone slept in either tents or the hay loft. There was no electricity for the first several years, and while free time was at a premium, a genuine home was slowly but surely taking shape. After the renovations were completed, the family moved into the Lodge, and without a formal plan in place, found that guests began arriving for overnight visits. In the words of Johannes, as guests, especially skiers, began arriving in increasing numbers over the years, "we sort of eased into it without formally opening a hotel—without making a conscious decision to go into the hotel business, we saw we were in the hotel business. We decided to formalize it by opening the Trapp Family Lodge in 1950."

Maria's energy proved limitless, and while such incessant activity would have exhausted mere mortals, it seemed to fit right in with Maria's worldview. In fashioning her new home Maria may have come to view herself as American, but writing in her highly successful autobiography (the book has had, to date, twelve printings) she made it clear that she followed no modern American trends; the modern age, Maria bluntly stated, had brought about too much sedentary behavior, such as watching movies. The antidote to such indolence lay in her wish for a leader who would unite people in a movement "like a forest fire from coast to coast, burning in its flames all this unhealthy sophistication . . ."

When money proved scarce—after agent fees and travel expenses were paid off, little remained in the coffers—Maria embarked upon another sizable project, starting a music camp for paying guests. An old Civilian Conservation Corps camp down the road from the Lodge was about to be torn down, so Maria arranged to buy and refurbish the camp; for a dozen summers, paying guests learned to sing in the von Trapp style.

So strong is the *Sound of Music*'s image of Maria as someone who gave up her religious vocation that it is easy to forget that even in Vermont, her faith continued as the dominant force in her new life as wife and mother. It also proved true on the family's musical tours, where she insisted, despite the understandable grumbling of the children, that the family give additional free concerts at abbeys and nunneries. In her 1975 book *Yesterday, Today, and Forever*, she forthrightly explains: "From then on only one thing matters in our life: to find out what Jesus would do, how He would react, what He would say in our stead as we go from day to day."

It wasn't just Maria who professed faith, but the children as well. Fully ensconced in American life, the new immigrants had experienced the same jolt as the rest of the country when Werner and Rupert received their draft notices during World War II. A disconsolate Maria was told by her sons: "Mother, remember the old saying 'If God closes the door, He opens a window.' . . . It seems to be God's will that we go." Seventeen years later, the same words would address another of Maria's fears in *The Sound of Music*, providing the cue for an inspirational song eventually heard round the world.

Maria remained fiercely devoted to her children and her faith in nearly equal measure—"No one can console like a mother, and no one can console and help better than this great mother of us all, the Church"—but she admitted that her own faith did in fact crack and weaken. At the bleakest of times she was operating on autopilot even during periods of prayer. Emptiness set in when she lost a baby because of her own weak kidneys, and health problems mounted. She began to suffer from fainting spells, high blood pressure, and convulsions, and she endured what amounted to an emotional breakdown. In her own words: "After the seven fat years the 'seven lean years' had come upon the Trapp Family, all compressed in ten months. Now they had to cope with sickness, breakdowns, death. At times it looked hopelessly complicated."

On Christmas Eve of 1947, Maria received the last Sacraments and her family was told that there was nothing left to do but pray. In that sad and troubling year, one that Maria dubbed "the memorable year," her life had begun to resemble the dark musical world of Stephen Sondheim a great deal more than it did that of Rodgers and Hammerstein, but she slowly and unexpectedly recovered. Her return to health, she was certain, could only be attributed to the prayers of friends in both Austria and America, and she approvingly quoted the words of her doctors that "this (recovery) cannot be attributed to medicine."

And yet, the children, and especially Maria herself, did not shy away from speaking or writing about the dark periods of their lives, times when belief fractured and barely held. In 1951, daughter Martina died in childbirth and Maria later wrote in moving fashion of surviving the tragedy only because the strength of her faith allowed her to draw upon an early Christian tradition that looked upon the death of a loved one not as an occasion of endless sorrow, but as the birthday of the loved one in heaven. It's a view remarkably similar to that of Oscar Hammerstein himself, whose words at Gertrude Lawrence's funeral included a baldly stated exhortation not to grieve endlessly: "Mourning is a surrender to the illusion that death is final."

Thanks to the stage and screen versions of *The Sound of Music,* Maria ultimately came to be viewed as an all-loving, benevolent earth mother, but perhaps because of the tribulations she and her family had experienced, she also possessed a moralistic worldview that pointed to a firm belief in the concept of hell: "the complete absence, and also forever and ever, of everything heaven is." It is no incidental point that in her autobiography Maria emphasizes the fact that Jesus mentions hell thirty-seven times in the Gospels: "One can go to hell not only for what one has done, but also for what one has not done."

Such a fire-and-brimstone view of hell was certainly not what had attracted the attention of filmmakers to the story of Maria's life. No, it was the sheer trajectory of her story, the trip from abbey to instant motherhood and singing stardom, that made her life seem tailor-made for the movies. According to family publicist Alix Williamson, Hollywood had first expressed interest in Maria's life story when *The Story of the Trapp Family Singers* was published in 1949, but Maria firmly turned down the offers, dictating that the film could only be made if she played herself. When, six years later, the German film industry came calling, Maria wanted an infusion of cash for the family coffers, and without ever consulting her lawyer, sold the rights for her life story to Wolfgang Reinhardt for $9,000—with no royalties. In Johannes's understated take on the sale: "My mother was never very good at business deals. She was too impatient and didn't like having an agent. It was a very bad deal."

She seemed content enough with the additional cash at the time of the sale—every bit helped when it came to the unending expenses accumulating from the Stowe, Vermont, farm. But when *Die Trapp-Familie,* starring Ruth Leuwerik as Maria and Hans Holt as the captain, grossed more than $1,000,000 and proved to be the hit of German cinema in 1956, that $9,000 began to rankle. After all, Maria wondered, whose story was this anyway? But, she reasoned, a deal was a deal, and when the film and its two years' later sequel, *Die Trapp-Familie in Amerika,* grew into two of the most popular German films ever released—thanks in no small part to the fact that little time was spent detailing the von Trapp's (anti-German) decision to leave their homeland—Maria contented herself with the ever-spreading fame of the von Trapp name.

The success of the two German films soon caught the eye of Hollywood, and Paramount Pictures optioned rights to the material with an eye toward filming an English language version. Hot new star Audrey Hepburn was pegged to play Maria, but although Hepburn went on to give a first-rate performance as the titular character in Fred Zinnemann's 1959 film *The Nun's Story,* she displayed no particular interest in Maria's life story. Paramount's option lapsed, and the rights reverted to the German production company.

There the matter might have rested, except for the fact that director Vincent J. Donehue, who was under contract to Paramount, happened to watch *Die Trapp-Familie* and became convinced that the story might prove to be a terrific stage vehicle for his good friend Mary Martin. Donehue envisioned a dramatic play about Maria's life, perhaps with the addition of an Austrian folk song to please Mary's musical fans. Were Mary and her husband/manager Richard Halliday interested in the project? Absolutely.

In the end it all turned out slightly differently than planned, because by the time Maria von Trapp's life story opened on Broadway, it had grown into a full-fledged musical written by esteemed playwrights Lindsay and Crouse and the greatest composer/lyricist team in musical theater history, Rodgers and Hammerstein. And in the hands of four very sophisticated New Yorkers, and one Texan singing actress who happened to be the queen of musical theater, the story of Austrian would-be nun Maria Kutschera von Trapp would soon grow into a story—make that fable—beloved around the world.

3.

BROADWAY AND RODGERS
AND HAMMERSTEIN

"The combined sales of the Broadway and movie recordings of The
Sound of Music *make it the most popular musical score of all time."*
—LAURENCE MASLON, *THE SOUND OF MUSIC COMPANION*

Having first worked with Mary Martin on the 1955 production of Thorn-
ton Wilder's *The Skin of Our Teeth,* Vincent Donehue had been eagerly
looking for another opportunity to work with the Broadway legend. After
her smash run in *South Pacific,* Martin had scored another triumph with *Peter
Pan,* and she was considered the closest thing to a sure bet where it counted
most on Broadway: at the box office. Although now well past age forty, Martin still possessed the winsome appeal that had first conquered Broadway in
the 1930s, and *Peter Pan* had proved Martin was a natural onstage with children.

Although the Hallidays quickly expressed enthusiasm for the story of
Maria's life, they continued to envision a dramatic play supplemented by actual von Trapp songs, rather than a full-fledged musical. Halliday and his
coproducer Leland Hayward now set to work on the task of obtaining per-
missions from both the sprawling von Trapp family as well as Divina-Film,
the German production company that had produced both *Die Trapp-Familie*
movies.

Tracking down all ten of the von Trapps proved a formidable and literally globe-trotting task, because after the family stopped touring in 1956,
Maria and daughters Rosmarie and Maria had embarked upon missionary
work in the South Pacific. Jet-age air routes had yet to reach much of the

South Pacific, rendering direct contact with Maria impossible, and written communication difficult at best. The isolated conditions may have frustrated Halliday and Hayward, but for Maria, the challenge of her work conditions proved invigorating, almost necessary. Said son Johannes: "My mother had a bit of a messiah complex. The musical mission was over . . . She felt a religious mission would replace it. . . . And it did—gradually."

Bounding from one locale to another in her missionary work, Maria would arrive in a new port only to find yet another letter from the pesky Hallidays. Having no idea who Mary Martin and Richard Halliday were, Maria would tear up their impassioned letters with nary a second thought. Refusing to take no for an answer, Richard Halliday finally hit upon the strategy of meeting Maria's ship in San Francisco when she returned from New Guinea. Maria granted permission for a theatrical version of her life story, but even after Mary and Maria struck up a friendship, obtaining Maria's final signature still proved difficult; the papers were finally signed only when Maria was recovering in an Innsbruck, Austria, hospital from the malaria she had contracted in Papua New Guinea.

With Maria's signature procured, the producers were able to obtain permission from the remaining von Trapps more readily, and by the end of 1957, they had succeeded in persuading all remaining family members to say yes to the production. To sweeten the deal producer Hayward granted Maria three-eighths of one percent of the royalties; when the sale of the film rights was negotiated by agent Swifty Lazar, 20th Century-Fox was coerced into granting Maria the same arrangement. Fifty years after the film's release, that clause still generates approximately $100,000 per year in royalties for the family.

For Hayward and Halliday, the negotiations with the German film company proved even more difficult than those with Maria, and ultimately required no fewer than six trips to Munich. The Germans refused to sell the rights for less than $200,000, a particularly hefty sum in 1957, so the producers found corporate support in the form of $200,000 from NBC television, a network that had a long-term deal with Mary Martin. The $200,000 was construed as an advance on Mary's future salary from the network, and with the money now in place, the Germans finally granted permission. Halliday and Hayward now held the rights to Maria's life story and both of the German language films, and took the first step toward production by signing the highly successful writing team of Howard Lindsay and Russel Crouse to begin work on the play. The working title? *The Singing Heart.*

As Lindsay and Crouse began to write, the question as to which music should be utilized acquired increasing importance. Maybe the von Trapp folk songs could be supplemented by one new song from good friends Richard Rodgers and Oscar Hammerstein II—or so the thinking ran. It was, after all, the Rodgers and Hammerstein team that had, along with Josh Logan, created Martin's career-defining role of Nellie Forbush in *South Pacific.* As it turned out, when Rodgers and Hammerstein were approached in the summer of 1958 about writing a song for *The Singing Heart,* they were aware that Frederick Loewe and Alan Jay Lerner of *My Fair Lady* fame had themselves considered musicalizing the story of Maria von Trapp, the project eventually faltering because Loewe did not share his partner's enthusiasm for the material.

Rodgers and Hammerstein, however, saw potential in the material and responded with a suggestion of their own: either shape Maria's life story into a play utilizing the von Trapps' actual repertoire, or turn it into a full-fledged original musical featuring a brand-new score by Rodgers and Hammerstein. Martin and Halliday instantly leaped at the possibility of a new musical written by their favorite team, but a formidable obstacle loomed: Rodgers and Hammerstein were busy completing their score for the upcoming *Flower Drum Song.* Would Martin and Halliday wait? The answer came back quickly: as long as necessary. Rodgers and Hammerstein were now on board, and not just as composer and lyricist; the duo joined Halliday and Hayward as producers of the show, culling many of the show's fifty-two backers from the ranks of their relatives and close friends.

By the time Rodgers and Hammerstein actually began work on the score for *The Sound of Music,* they had created an unparalleled body of work in the musical theater, a glittering run of hit shows that had begun in 1943 with their groundbreaking first collaboration, *Oklahoma!* With its blend of design, song, and dance all put to work in service of the story, *Oklahoma!* had revolutionized musical theater. With this one seamless show, Rodgers and Hammerstein had swept away both the fripperies of traditional European-style operettas, as well as the lighter-than-air star-driven American musicals in which plots existed solely to introduce the songs. Building upon the integrated approach pioneered by Hammerstein in the landmark 1927 musical *Showboat,* Rodgers and Hammerstein began writing musicals in which action and character formed such an essential part of the libretto that composer and lyricist were now free to delve more deeply into characters' inner lives, exploring subtext and psychological motivation in their masterful *South Pacific, Carousel,* and *The King and I.* By partnerships' end, they had produced eleven scores in a mere seventeen years.

In that bygone post–World War II era in which Broadway musicals produced hit songs and provided the musical soundtrack to accompany the nation's everyday life, no songwriting team loomed as large as Rodgers and Hammerstein. The bald statistics regarding their immense achievement illustrate the scope of their work: their musicals won thirty-four Tony Awards, ten Academy Awards, the Pulitzer prize for drama (a rare feat only managed by eight musicals), two Grammy Awards, and two Emmy Awards. A postage stamp in their honor was released in 1999, but perhaps most telling of all, in 1998 the duo was cited by *Time* magazine as ranking among the twenty most influential artists of the twentieth century. With their eye always firmly planted on what best served the show's story, Rodgers and Hammerstein emphasized a dramatic clarity that continues to provide the foundation for the frequent revivals of their shows. Cole Porter, Irving Berlin, and the Gershwins may be the equals of Rodgers and Hammerstein as composer and lyricist, but the flimsy books for their shows and the ensuing lack of attention to dramatic clarity preclude frequent revivals of their musicals in the twenty-first century.

Rodgers and Hammerstein, of course, possessed the additional advantage of timing: they were the right men, at the right time, and in the right place. In mid-twentieth-century America, Rodgers and Hammerstein's moral universe reflected the views of an American population that felt certain of its place in the world, a fit that lasted from their first hit, *Oklahoma!* in 1943, to their last, *The Sound of Music* in 1959.

By 1960, for the first time in U.S. history, more than fifty percent of all Americans could be classified as middle class. Having emerged from World War II a scant fifteen years earlier with their homeland physically unscarred, Americans had begun their, high-finned, wide-bodied automobile ride to the promised land of suburbia, all to the accompaniment of the show tunes that still topped the charts. The burgeoning revolution of television may have been changing the world, but sitcoms of the time still presented a superficially safe world of intact nuclear families where minorities remained invisible. Civil rights lay on the national agenda, but the movement was still gathering steam, and the feminist agenda had not yet come into focus. A Rodgers and Hammerstein musical featuring a singing nun and seven adorable children seemed a perfect fit for the popular culture of the day.

Hammerstein's emotional warmth seemed to make him tailor-made for *The Sound of Music*—in the words of his son James, "My father believed that nobility of man exists"—but Rodgers's more austere personality made his involvement in Maria's life story seem less of a natural fit. A melodic genius (in his own blunt phrase: "I can pee a melody"), Rodgers was most at home while composing or working in the theater, and he proved a distant figure even to his own children: not unloving, but certainly remote. His daughter Mary Rodgers Guettel, a noted composer in her own right (*Once Upon a Mattress*), mused that the act of composing "gave him the breath of life. It was the only thing he really enjoyed. There was an exuberance about him when he played." In her bluntly humorous manner she wrote in 1995 about her father's difficult personality: "Chemically depressed is what we'd call it now; then we didn't know what to call it, except tough to live with." It's a view echoed by Guettel's sister Linda Rodgers Emory, who simply noted: "He was never as happy as he wanted to be." It was left to Rodgers's music to provide him with that elusive sense of well-being, in much the same way that his music provided balm and uplift to the everyday lives of his audience.

By way of contrast, the altogether warmer Hammerstein could and did express affection, even if most frequently in his lyrics, but for all the differences between the two men, real and imagined, it was Rodgers who provided perhaps the truest and most loving tribute to Hammerstein after his death. Hammerstein's passing, noted Rodgers, proved harder for him to bear than did the death of his first notable partner, Lorenz Hart, because "almost to the day he died everything about Oscar was an affirmation of life. . . . He was infused with a faith and an optimism that only grew stronger as he grew older." Rodgers's words—life-affirming, faith, optimism—reflect the very attributes with which Hammerstein filled *The Sound of Music*. Rodgers never could have written *The Sound of Music* with Hart, whose irreverent and finely honed wit only partially hid a lifelong feeling of otherness, a bone-deep sadness due to his small stature and homosexuality. Hammerstein, a very different man, never feared open-hearted sentiment, and if the lyrics occasionally toppled over into the sentimental (what exactly is "a lark who is learning to pray?"), they were for the most part filled with genuine, honest regard for nature, family, and faith. A devoted father and husband whose love of nature dovetailed nicely with *The Sound of Music*'s overriding atmosphere, he was, in the recall of Julie Andrews, who worked with him on the 1957 television production of *Cinderella,* a "grave, quiet, very tall, terribly nice man."

Hammerstein's was a determinedly optimistic view of life, even if it occasionally toppled over into myopia. As related by his son William, Hammerstein would cross the street simply to avoid a blind person; in this manner he sidestepped both involvement and any related sadness. Explained William: "He always looked at the positive even when there was nothing but negative. . . . With his children he never knew when we were sick or had had an accident. He just put it out of his mind, and it worked!"

Hammerstein himself explained that he knew that the tragic existed, but felt it important to remind people that goodness and light persisted just as strongly: "We're very likely to get thrown off our balance if we have such a preponderance of artists expressing the 'waste land' philosophy." He would, one suspects, be discouraged by the nihilistic portrayals that pervade twenty-first-century popular culture, as well as by the deep sense of unease that bubbles just beneath the surface of modern-day American life. Then again, given his willed determination, he might very likely roll up his sleeves, search for uplifting material, craft a book and lyrics of deceptive simplicity, endure more than a few critical brickbats, and with his uncanny dramatic instincts, score another huge popular success.

As Rodgers and Hammerstein prepared to start work on the story of Maria von Trapp, one enormous change from the usual R&H production loomed on the horizon: with Howard Lindsay and Russel Crouse already signed to write the musical's book, for the first time in the R&H partnership, composer and lyricist would be creating their score from a story crafted by someone other than Hammerstein. It was a monumental shift in structure, but in working with Lindsay and Crouse, R&H were joining forces with the playwrighting equivalent of their own fabled partnership.

Lindsay and Crouse boasted a long string of gold-plated credits dating back to *Anything Goes* and *Life with Father* in the 1930s, *State of the Union* in 1945, and the more recent 1950 Ethel Merman hit *Call Me Madam*. For all of their renown, however, they were aware that it was the power of the Rodgers and Hammerstein names that was already driving the show, the musical having been instantly etched in the public's mind as Rodgers and Hammerstein's *The*

Sound of Music. Such public perception proved a source of frustration for the librettists, but seasoned veterans that they were, they accepted the slight with a rather bemused resignation. Book, writers, it seemed, remained invisible no matter how high profile the project; in December 1966, after the motion picture version of *Sound of Music* had turned into a box office phenomenon, Lindsay wrote to *The New York Times* in equal parts frustration and bewilderment to query: "Much has been written of the success of *The Sound of Music,* play and motion picture. Is it immodest of me to point out, because no one else ever does, that Russel Crouse and I had a hand in it."

As it turned out, the four creators worked well together, jointly envisioning that underneath the surface of a family-friendly sunny musical, lay a multitiered approach to the very idea of freedom: Maria herself both wanted and feared freedom from the abbey, the children desired a less regimented household, and everyone wanted to escape from a Nazi-ruled Austria. The creators were aiming for a musical play, no mere conventional musical comedy. As often proved the case with Rodgers and Hammerstein musicals, a romance of great passion would teeter on the edge of historical events that could readily crush the protagonists' dreams. If the war in the Pacific threatened the romance of Nellie Forbush and Emile de Beque in *South Pacific,* so, too, could the Anschluss undermine the love between Maria and Georg.

For the sake of dramatic clarity, changes would have to be made to Maria's actual life story. Lindsay and Crouse had only slightly over one hour—combined with one hour of R&H music—in which to tell the story of Maria's life. One after another, events were compressed or eliminated in the name of more efficient storytelling and dramatic momentum:

> *After the first draft, the family's emigration to America was jettisoned; keeping the action in Europe increased the sense of threat from the Nazis.*
> *There would be no discussion of Maria's difficult childhood.*
> *Her surname of Kutschera was eliminated, and her mother's softer sounding maiden name of Rainer employed instead.*
> *Maria would meet and marry the captain in 1938 at the time of the Anschluss, instead of eleven years earlier as had actually happened.*
> *By 1938, several of the von Trapp children were already adults, so birth order and names would simply be changed. Eldest child Rupert was already twenty-seven and finished with medical school at the time of*

the Anschluss. A singing intern? Forget it. Twenty-seven was too old to be adorable.

Exit Rupert.

Enter Liesl, the newest/oldest von Trapp child. No Liesl among the real von Trapp children? No problem—there would be now. And she'd have a teenaged romance with a good boy turned Nazi sympathizer. That'd increase the drama.

The essence of the family remained the same, but dramatic license could and would rule, so why stop at Liesl? With just a few stokes of the typewriter, not only did Agathe morph into Liesl, but Rupert became Friedrich, Maria was portrayed as Louisa, Werner changed into Kurt, Hedwig acquired the name Brigitta, and the two youngest children, Johanna and Martina, quickly grew into Marta and Gretl. The three children born of Maria's marriage to Georg? For purposes of the musical, Rosmarie, Eleonore, and Johannes simply did not exist.

It was only when Lindsay and Crouse had completed an outline of the book that Rodgers and Hammerstein began work on the score in March of 1959. Hammerstein utilized Lindsay and Crouse's first draft as a blueprint for his lyrics, as well as a guide for the placement of the songs. In some instances he plucked ideas directly from Lindsay and Crouse's own words; when crafting the lyrics for "How Do You Solve a Problem Like Maria," he lifted the phrases "curlers in her hair" and "whistling on the stairs" right from a scene that Lindsay and Crouse had penned.

The book writers were happy for R&H to lift ideas wholesale from their outline, and the writing of the show proceeded at a much faster pace than usual for Rodgers and Hammerstein, not only because Hammerstein could concentrate solely upon lyrics, but also because of the connection all four creators felt with the material. *The Sound of Music,* in Rodgers's recall, represented "the quickest job we've ever done."

In structural terms, it's the one Rodgers and Hammerstein show without even the trace of a dancing chorus, and the first that required musical research on Rodgers's part. In order to compose liturgical music, with which he had limited familiarity, Rodgers visited the nearby Manhattanville Catholic women's college in Purchase, New York. Attending a concert through the invitation of music department chair Mother Morgan, Rodgers struck up a friendship with the nun and was both surprised and delighted by her down-to-earth, humorous approach; arriving at a particularly exciting musical moment while conducting the concert, she, much to Rodgers's delight, exhorted the choir to "Pray it!" Inspired by what he had heard, Rodgers quickly began to compose the "Preludium" with which the stage musical opens.

Hammerstein wrote lyrics for the show in both New York City and at his farm in Doylestown, Pennsylvania. Ironically, for a show so closely associated with mountains and cool crisp alpine air, he also worked on the musical at his retreat in tropical Jamaica. Armed with Lindsay and Crouse's sixty-page treatment, he began mulling over lyric ideas for a tune Rodgers had supplied.

A first pass at words to match Rodgers's five notes of C-D-C-B flat-A produced: *"The hillside is sweet."*

"The hillside is sweet"—okay, but not quite right. "The hills are alive"?— yes.

Moving on: "(Today the air is) *sweet with summer music.*"

Fine-tuning each phrase, Hammerstein crossed out "summer music," and sketched in "sound of summer" before settling upon the phrase "sound of music." The "sound of music"—that, he felt, was right on the money.

The hills are alive
With the sound of music—

Exactly.
Now adding the phrases:

And my heart wants to sing
Every song it hears . . .

Hammerstein knew he had hit upon the precise uplifting tone he and Rodgers felt necessary for the entire score.

Hammerstein was an obviously sophisticated man of great intelligence, and while the homespun lyrics he began crafting were deliberately simple, they were never simplistic. His painstaking efforts to write lyrics that defined character while furthering story worked precisely because he genuinely believed in the show's sentiments. Love of nature, a rock-ribbed attachment to the land—these represented Hammerstein's core beliefs, and *"The hills are alive*

with the sound of music" represented nothing so much as another heartfelt iteration of lyrics found in *Oklahoma!*'s very first song:

"All the sounds of the earth are like music."

Writing while standing at a lectern, he continued to work on the lyrics,
constantly refining his word choices until the slightest of changes captured
an exact mood. Inspired by Mary Martin's friend Sister Gregory, who wrote
that a nun asks of herself: "What does God want me to do with my life? How
does He wish me to spend my love?"

Hammerstein began work on "Climb Ev'ry Mountain." First he considered:

Climb ev'ry mountain
High though it seem
Never be contented
Till you find your dream.

Close—yes. Serviceable—certainly. But Hammerstein was after a sense
of action, a feeling of determination. Making endlessly considered but very
slight adjustments, he added verbs for a sense of forward motion, only then
arriving at the lyric his perfectionist instincts would accept:

"High though it seem" became "Ford ev'ry stream" while "Never be contented" morphed into "Follow ev'ry rainbow."

Climb ev'ry mountain
Ford ev'ry stream
Follow ev'ry rainbow
Till you find your dream.

Here were images of nature joined with a sense of movement, their combination conveying the emotional uplift desired for the heart of the show.

While Rodgers and Hammerstein continued to refine the score, Mary Mar-
tin prepared for her role by spending time with Maria von Trapp at the von
Trapps' by now seven-hundred-acre family lodge. The sophisticated, petite
Martin struck up an easygoing friendship with the robust, high-energy

Maria, the two women finding that they shared an essentially optimistic can-do attitude toward life. During their time together, Maria taught Martin such small but telling gestures as the proper manner in which to cross herself, how to kneel properly, and not so incidentally, how to play the guitar. In the analysis of Johannes von Trapp: "Mary and my mother were very much kindred spirits."

As Maria grasped how willing Martin was to work ceaselessly in pursuit of conveying character, their genuine friendship deepened. Given their very different lives, they did not see each other often after the show opened, but the two were reunited in person decades later when Martin was a guest at the Lodge's January 1984 reopening, after a devastating fire in December of 1980 had destroyed the Lodge.

Playing the part of Maria required a great deal more skill than merely the mimicking of such small actions as kneeling and crossing, and because Martin and Julie Andrews made it look easy, it came to be assumed that the part was simple—in all senses of the word. In fact, as Martin pointed out, the part required great control: "I knew that my part required perfect pitch—and I'm not talking about music now. The treatment had to be very skillful, totally controlled. It was one of the most disciplined shows I ever did. You could never do a kidding thing, never play it broadly. I had to remember the character always, keep a tight rein on my emotions and my performance."

Rehearsals began in August of 1959, and by the time the musical began its pre-Broadway tryout in New Haven (followed by Boston), Martin's performance was already a crowd-pleaser, as was the score itself. Out of town audiences immediately responded with favor, humming "My Favorite Things" and "Do-Re-Mi" so readily that it seemed as if they were reacquainting themselves with old folk songs rather than hearing a new score for the first time. Of particular note was the response to "My Favorite Things"; for those who didn't like the show, Maria's list of beloved objects and images proved, in a word, cloying. For the crowds who grew to love the musical, however, the very act of enumerating the objects transmitted a sense of instant nostalgia, the "good old days" of security and comfort brought back by the idea of

> Raindrops on roses
> And whiskers on kittens
> Bright copper kettles
> And warm woolen mittens

It was Hobe Morrison, the esteemed critic for the show business bible *Variety,* who summed it up best, citing the "deceptive simplicity" of lyrics written by an artist of the first rank: "The lyricist seems increasingly to be writing about ordinary things, with an eloquence that lends universality and throat-catching impact."

Although the majority of Broadway musicals were traditionally top-heavy with music in the first act, Rodgers and Hammerstein's completed score proved to be even more front loaded than usual, with only three new songs (and three reprises) in the entire second act. Pleased with the audience response, the authors made few substantive changes during the show's tryouts, with one key exception: Rodgers insisted that the captain be provided with a solo in the penultimate scene in order to underscore his love of family and country. The result was "Edelweiss," the last song ever written by Rodgers and Hammerstein.

Diagnosed with cancer of the stomach at the end of the third week of rehearsals, Hammerstein had been too ill to attend most of the show's out-of-town tryouts, but when he felt well enough, he traveled to Boston and wrote this last lyric. The "bless my homeland forever" message of the song proved universal, managing to simultaneously strike a patriotic chord in nearly all audience members while deepening their understanding of the captain. (So effectively did the song come to symbolize Austria in the public's eye that when the president of Austria visited the Reagan White House, the director of protocol mistakenly thought that the song was the Austrian national anthem and instructed the Marine band to play the song upon the Austrian president's arrival.)

An expression of family love and national pride, the song's moving evocation of the eternal verities grew out of the dying Hammerstein's most deeply held emotions. The song was not only placed at exactly the right moment in the show, but the lyrics, in the analysis of Julie Andrews, "fit any homeland you are passionate about. The words and notes match each other so perfectly that they become timeless." In the recollection of Russel Crouse's widow Anna, when Hammerstein saw the show in Boston, his wife Dorothy said to Russel Crouse: "I have only seen Oscar . . . cry once in my whole married life . . . and he's been crying." Added Anna Crouse: "It broke your heart."

The addition of "Edelweiss" helped shore up the most glaring weakness of the show: given very little to do, Captain von Trapp resembled a stock figure out of an operetta. That die had been cast, however, back when the show first began to take shape; with Broadway's leading musical diva Mary Martin starring in a show written by her favorite composer-lyricist team, in a production headed by her own husband, it was quite certain from day one where the emphasis in storytelling would lie. Father Wasner was gone, Captain von Trapp remained peripheral at best, and while "Edelweiss" helped, the focus remained firmly fixed upon Maria.

When the show opened on Broadway on November 16, 1959, audiences cheered, and, in the recollection of Anna Crouse, when Mary Martin came out for her final bow, Maria stood up at the same time. For the actual von Trapp children, the opening of a smash hit Broadway musical based upon their lives simply brightened the spotlight they had known for many years. Said Johannes in 2014: "I don't remember when the family wasn't well known. A *Life* magazine spread in the 1940s had increased our profile. We had been primarily well known in baroque music circles—a fairly rarified atmosphere. We were comfortable with that level of notoriety. When the play opened, we became more of a media phenomenon. Of course the film's huge popularity made it that much harder again."

After the opening night cheers subsided, critics in the daily papers damned the musical with faint praise; coming two years after *West Side Story* and in the same season as *Gypsy, The Sound of Music* struck many critics as hopelessly old-fashioned; it was all too shallow and saccharine for words. As usually happened with musicals, the harshest words were reserved for the book writers, with critics particularly harping upon a libretto they deemed overly sentimental. Book writers, it seemed, received no respect, and in a damning, if cleverly worded pan, Walter Kerr's review in *The New York Herald Tribune*, found the show "not only too sweet for words, but almost too sweet for music." Librettists, it seemed, were dismissed even by actors associated with the property; when at the time of the movie's release, Christopher Plummer opined that "Practically anyone could write a musical about nuns and children and have it become a success," Russel Crouse acerbically replied, "I wonder why nobody ever did it?"

Some seemed predisposed to dislike the material on principle, granting the extraordinary score only mild praise at best. Kenneth Tynan bluntly termed the show "Rodgers and Hammerstein's Great Leap Backwards" and the entire score's reception, in fact, seemed to bear out Cole Porter's statement that with every show he wrote, the critics invariably stated: "Not up to his usual

standards." Rodgers, in particular, took exception to the carping notices, noting that a show concerned with a governess and her charges possessed a genuine emotion crucial to successful theater: "Anyone who can't, on occasion,
be sentimental about children or nature is sadly maladjusted."

What stuck fans of the show as the strengths of the piece—the music,
Maria's Cinderella-like journey from abbey to motherhood, the sense of hope
and happily-ever-after—proved to be the exact components that struck critics as weak and manipulative. Who, they wondered, were these nauseatingly
perfect children on stage? Maria's memoir actually provides the antidote to
the disgust some felt for those perfectly behaved von Trapp children, and in a
story that would have proven highly amusing on stage, she writes that one of
the younger (unnamed) girls told Maria that because it was Lent, she "would
not pinch Johanna and won't spit at Werner—until Easter." In a nice coda to
the episode, Maria wrote: "It was very hard to convince her that this was by
no means a superman's generosity."

Whatever their complaints about the book, in their disdain for the show
the critics missed one crucial point: Rodgers and Hammerstein had fashioned
a superlative score. Has any show ever boasted so many soon-to-be standards?
None come to mind, with the possible exception of R&H's own *South Pacific,*
but what makes *The Sound of Music* unique is the ease with which the songs
unfurl. Audiences responded to the entire story of the von Trapps as if it
were an Austrian folktale that just happened to arrive in the form of a
Broadway musical. In particular, audiences reacted to "Do-Re-Mi" as if it
was a nursery rhyme dating from their own childhood days, not a song written by two sophisticated men of the Broadway theater. So skillfully constructed is the song that it seemed to almost instantaneously exist—sui
generis—as a permanent part of the American landscape. In point of fact, as
the Broadway revival's cast album liner notes point out, far from a simple nursery rhyme with a three-note pattern, "Do-Re-Mi" represents Rodgers and
Hammerstein's successful efforts to utilize, and transform into the musical
language of Broadway, the work of the Italian music theorists Guido of Ar-
rezo and Giovanni Battista Doni, who invented a group of one-syllable words
for each note of the diatonic scale. A nursery rhyme it wasn't.

So strong were the individual songs in the score that many of them assumed lives in contexts completely unrelated to the show. "My Favorite Things"
was covered by artists ranging form John Coltrane to Barbra Streisand (who

turned it into a Christmas standard). "So Long, Farewell," "Edelweiss," and "The Sound of Music" all became part of the musical landscape, sung everywhere from television variety shows to concerts. Even the show's instrumental "Wedding Processional" grew in popularity to the point where it was utilized in hundreds of weddings: when another famous Maria (Shriver) married another famous Austrian (Arnold Schwarzenegger), she simply asked the Rodgers and Hammerstein Organization if she could walk down the aisle to the musical's "Wedding Processional."

Anchoring the entire score was the most famous of all R&H songs of inspiration, "Climb Ev'ry Mountain." A near identical twin to *Carousel*'s "You'll Never Walk Alone," and filled with the same hymnlike ascending chords and words of aspirational uplift, the song quickly grew into an all-occasions secular song of hope, a favorite of junior high school assemblies everywhere. At Hammerstein's funeral in late-summer 1960, nine months after *The Sound of Music* opened on Broadway, Howard Lindsay read the lyrics to "Climb Ev'ry Mountain" out loud. Spoken simply and with no undue emphasis, they remain extraordinarily effective.

Aided by the release of an original cast recording that won the Grammy Award and eventually sold three million copies, *The Sound of Music* grew into a Broadway box office smash. In its own way, the audience reaction played out as a theatrical iteration of "I may not know much about art but I know what I like," and audiences willingly, indeed gladly, suspended disbelief in their acceptance of Maria's Cinderella-like journey to happiness. Critical disdain didn't matter, and in the prescient words of Whitney Bolton in the *Morning Telegraph* the day after the Broadway premiere: "With better than two million dollars sacked up in the till . . . it couldn't matter less what a critic might think."

Nominated for nine Tony Awards, the show won five, including, in a tie with *Fiorello!*, the year's top prize, Best Musical. (In an interesting twist, Lauri Peters, who portrayed Liesl, shared a nomination as Best Featured Actress with all of the other children, including the boys, all of them losing the award to Patricia Neway, who won for her portrayal of the Mother Abbess.) Star Mary Martin won another Tony Award as Best Actress in a musical, beating out her good friend and rival Ethel Merman's star turn in *Gypsy*. Merman, a native New Yorker to the bone, responded to the loss in her best deadpan fashion: "How you gonna buck a nun?"

After sweeping the Tony Awards, the show settled into what eventually became a run of over three years, and even if jaded New Yorkers didn't particularly care for it, families and the out-of-town tourist trade did. Sniffing a potential crowd-pleaser, Hollywood came calling very quickly and in June of 1960, film rights were sold to 20th Century-Fox for a hefty $1.25 million.

Many studios would have expressed interest in *The Sound of Music,* but when Hollywood interest surfaced, it came in the very specific form of 20th Century-Fox, whose success with the earlier R&H musicals *State Fair* (1945), *Oklahoma* (1955) , *Carousel* (1956), and *The King and I* (1956), had given them right of first refusal on all R&H properties. As per the terms of the contract, once the show's initial Broadway run had been completed, *The Sound of Music* could head for the big screen.

Placing themselves in the hands of agent Irving "Swifty" Lazar, Rodgers, Hammerstein, Lindsay, Crouse, Halliday, and Hayward now found themselves the recipients of a very sweet deal. Thanks to Lazar's savvy negotiations, in addition to their producers' share of the sale, Rodgers and Hammerstein would receive the lion's share of the ten percent of gross granted to the creators after exhibitor costs had been met. Even if not quite on the same level as R&H, Lindsay and Crouse would also share nicely in the proceeds, especially if the film ever turned into anything resembling a hit; in hefting his muscle, Lazar had managed to insert a clause into the contract that granted the bookwriters a percentage of the film's net profit after the benchmark of twelve million dollars profit had been reached. Given Hollywood's notoriously creative definition of net profits, Lindsay and Crouse were not holding their breath for such a windfall. A twelve-million-dollar profit seemed beyond reach, but they appreciated the clause—and then quickly forgot about it.

The creatives were happy, Fox was excited—and yet by 1963 *The Sound of Music* seemed headed for oblivion. An expensive well-known property was gathering dust in the bottom of the studio's drawer for one basic reason: the fiasco known as *Cleopatra.*

It wasn't every movie that could switch legendary directors midstream, shut down production for months at a time, have its leading lady condemned by both the Vatican and the United States Congress, cause nervous breakdowns, and bankrupt an entire studio. But *Cleopatra* actually could. And did.

The studio in question happened to be 20th Century-Fox.

The Sound of Music was forgotten.

4.

20TH CENTURY-FOX—GOING, GOING, ALMOST GONE

~⌒~

When Joseph Mankiewicz replaced Rouben Mamoulian as director of the *Cleopatra* debacle, even his vast experience in Hollywood and his four Academy Awards for *A Letter to Three Wives* and *All About Eve* did not prepare him for the never-ending circus of Elizabeth Taylor and Richard Burton's *le scandale*. After spending months trying to rein in the movie's out-of-control shooting schedule and oversee the editing of miles of film, he had one goal in mind: finish the experience still alive. As the film lumbered toward its release date of June 12, 1963, his one consolation lay in the knowledge that it wasn't his money on the line—the tens of millions of dollars thrown at the out-of-control production were the sole responsibility of 20th Century-Fox. When *Cleopatra* belly flopped at the box office upon release (it would literally take decades before the film eked out a small profit), it was 20th Century-Fox that was in trouble. Big trouble. Not Mankiewicz, not Taylor, not Burton—but the entire studio.

The issue now being discussed in the executive suites of the Fox studios wasn't who was going to star in *The Sound of Music*; it was how to keep the studio doors open.

In truth, *Cleopatra* was merely the tipping point of a decades-in-the-making crash that dated back to the 1948 Supreme Court decision prohibiting the studios from owning their own chains of movie theaters. That decision had forever altered the way Hollywood conducted business; with the studios no longer able to control the distribution as well as production of their films, they faced an uphill financial battle. To make matters worse, such "block booking" of studio-produced films into studio-owned theaters ceased at the same time that the advent of television drastically cut into theater attendance. As people began to stay home in order to watch television, theater attendance dropped from a peak of ninety million per week in 1946 to forty million per week in 1960. Television had brought about a change not only in habit, but in mindset as well, one best summed up by studio mogul Robert Evans: "Today people go to see a movie; they no longer go to the movies." *Cleopatra,* it turned out, was the unanticipated disastrous final blow to the crumbling studio system model of film production.

As noted by Hollywood film historian Paul Monaco, beginning in 1960, studio employees who had grown used to long-term job security were being let go in droves: "During the second week of March 1960 alone, 3400 workers were laid off by the major Hollywood studios." In 1960, when *Cleopatra* was still in preproduction, Fox lost fifteen million dollars on actual film production, a then astronomical sum that forced the company to sell both stock and real estate; in April of 1962 chairman Spyros Skouras sold off the studio's fabled and valuable 260-acre back lot to make up the cash shortfall.

With Fox on the verge of shutting its doors, production at the studio halted to a trickle, and *The Sound of Music* was not at the top of anyone's "must film" list. Product needed to be down and dirty; quick Westerns and gritty dramas, not expensive Technicolor musicals, proved the order of the day. And hadn't *The Sound of Music* in effect already flopped at the box office? Back in 1960, when the studio had bought film rights to the musical, it also gained control of the rights to *Die Trapp-Familie* and *Die Trapp-Familie in Amerika* for a period of six years. Eyeing these two films as a test case for *The Sound of Music,* and hoping for additional money with a minimum of effort, Fox had combined the two films into one, dubbed the ensuing mashed-up movie into English, and released it as *The Trapp Family,* in 1961. The critical reaction to the film seemed to mirror the disdain that had greeted the Broadway show's opening two years previously, and did nothing to boost enthusiasm for *The Sound of Music* within the troubled Fox executive offices. Sneered *Variety* about the redubbed films: "Their uncompromisingly sentimental nature has a tendency to slop over into naivete." Box office verdict? A big fat flop.

Making matters even more complicated, in the three years between the sale of *Sound of Music* and the near collapse of Fox, the entire notion of suitable product had undergone an enormous change. Audiences were now drawn to edgier, more unconventional fare, a change spearheaded by the coming-of-age baby boomer audience. Alfred Hitchcock's *Psycho* (1960) symbolized a Hollywood cinema now driven by sensation rather than sentiment, and in its cultural impact, Hitchcock's masterpiece proved far more revolutionary than did the nine years later *Easy Rider* or any of its youth-oriented knockoffs. An astonishingly good film, *Psycho* also represented a first in Hollywood history: unlike *The Sound of Music,* it lacked any sympathetic characters, its thieving leading lady murdered within the first half hour of the film.

As the growing baby boomer population came of age, the groundwork was laid for a marketplace that ultimately came to be driven by the wishes of adolescent males with disposable income. When that growing purchasing power was combined with the fact that both young women and middle-aged matrons were beginning to reenter the workplace, old Hollywood notions of what constituted suitable material for filming were upended in rather spectacular fashion.

All of these societal changes seemed to accelerate at a bewildering pace with the assassination of President Kennedy in November of 1963. An event heretofore unthinkable in the post–World War II era in which America viewed itself as the world's good guy, the assassination seemed to trigger a nationwide change in attitude, as if, with this one tragic event, Americans had ceased to trust their own government. When, decades later, Stephen Sondheim wrote about the event in his extraordinary musical *Assassins,* he addressed the assassination in a song bluntly titled "Something Just Broke." The assassination may have represented nothing less than a national loss of innocence, and Sondheim's slashing dark style seemed worlds removed from that of his mentor Hammerstein. By way of contrast, when *South Pacific* had opened on Broadway a mere four years after the end of World War II, Hammerstein's heartfelt liberal pieties actually seemed au courant, indeed a bit cutting edge in their depiction of racial prejudice. For an America still deeply divided along racial fault lines, the lyrics

> You've got to be taught to be afraid
> Of people whose eyes are oddly made,
> And people whose skin is a diff'rent shade,
> You've got to be carefully taught.

stirred up talk, controversy, and even hate mail. Now, fourteen years later, in a country reeling from a presidential assassination and the escalation of an already unpopular war in Vietnam, a sweet-natured musical about nuns and children struck many as not just old-fashioned, but almost reactionary. Within certain hipster headquarters, in a mere sixteen years Rodgers and Hammerstein and their iron-willed optimism had morphed from theatrical revolutionaries to objects of derision.

Faced with these societal changes, increasingly unfathomable audience preferences, and a 1962 loss of forty million dollars, the Fox board fired Skouras even before *Cleopatra* was released, and turned for help to the very man they had previously dismissed as studio chief: Darryl F. Zanuck. After losing his job as head of production at Fox, Zanuck had started work as an independent producer, marshaling resources and spending considerable money to film the epic, all-star story of the Normandy D-Day invasion entitled *The Longest Day.* When the movie proved to be both a critical and commercial success, the board of directors felt emboldened to entrust Zanuck with the job of restoring the studio's fortunes.

Zanuck's surprising first move was appointing his son Richard, producer of *The Chapman Report* and *Compulsion,* as head of daily operations for the entire studio. The decision turned out to be a smart preemptive strike on the elder Zanuck's part. Every bit as intense as Darryl, Richard not only shared his father's diminutive stature, but also his instinct for story and a ruthless determination to bolster the bottom line. Wanting to buy time and stanch the flow of red ink, Richard's first decision proved bold and decisive: he temporarily shut down the entire lot, laying off all employees from executives to commissary workers. Parking lots stood empty, and what remained of the back lot resembled a ghost town.

With a handful of television shows still shooting, but no film projects in the pipeline, Zanuck began rifling through the files for a look at scripts fit for development. Settling upon low-cost comedies and action films (primarily Westerns and war films) as temporary fixes, Zanuck continued his search for more long-term solutions until coming across the by now years-dormant *Sound of Music.* The more Zanuck pondered the idea, the more puzzled he became by the property's demise. Even a mediocre religious film, he figured, always seemed to find an audience. Fox had made boatloads of money with 1953's inaugural Cinemascope feature *The Robe,* and Paramount's 1956 *The Ten Commandments* had proved to be a blockbuster. Granted, both of those successes had occurred in the previous decade—a lifetime ago in Hollywood years—but noting the lengthy run of *The Sound of Music* both on Broadway and in London's West End, he focused upon the extraordinary continued popularity of the score. Everyone knew and loved "Do-Re-Mi" and "My Favorite Things." The story was based on a real family and featured adorable children— Zanuck was sold and moved to reactivate the property.

Yes, he knew the story was sentimental, and he certainly acknowledged that critics had used the stage musical as a punching bag. But Richard Zanuck knew a good story when he read it, and his gut told him that with the right screenwriter the film could prove an actual success. There might even be some extra money to be made with the sale of television rights. So where was the right screenwriter? Who was an old Hollywood pro, possessed a solid list of credits, and actually understood the tricky genre of the Hollywood musical? In Zanuck's mind, only one man fit the bill.

Enter Ernest Lehman.

5.

THE SWEET SMELL OF ERNEST LEHMAN

"It would be unthinkable for a writer to tell a director how to direct. . . . But it is not at all unthinkable for anyone to tell a writer how to write. It comes with the territory."

—ERNEST LEHMAN, *AMERICAN FILM*

A freelance fiction writer who had first published stories and novelettes in *Collier's* and *Cosmopolitan* magazines, Ernest Lehman had begun his climb up the show business ladder by working as a copywriter for Broadway press agent Irving Hoffman. It was this firsthand experience in the world of New York City nightclubs and theaters that provided the grist for his tough, gritty novella *Tell Me About It Tomorrow.* Cynical, dark, and filled with an insider's knowledge, *Tell Me* marked the debut of a major talent, one with show business blood running through his veins.

After selling a story to television's *Playhouse 90,* Lehman signed a screenwriter's contract with Paramount Pictures in 1952, but his Hollywood career ignited when, two years later, he was loaned to MGM to write *Executive Suite* for director Robert Wise. Lehman and Wise hit it off immediately, the calm, solid director proving just the right foil for the intense, nervous Lehman.

After translating both *The King and I* and *Somebody Up There Likes Me* for the screen, Lehman's next adapted *Tell Me About It Tomorrow* into the 1957 film *Sweet Smell of Success.* The praise for Lehman's corrosive take on the dog-eat-dog world of New York City gossip columns ruled by the Winchell-like columnist J. J. Hunsecker (a first-rate Burt Lancaster) proved immediate and swift; nearly sixty years later, the film remains one of the very few as famous for its trenchant screenplay ("I'd hate to take a bite outta you.

You're like a cookie full of arsenic") as for its stars. With producer/star Lancaster throwing every last bit of his weight around onscreen and off, the process proved so stressful to Lehman that he ceded directorial duties to Alexander MacKendrick, with playwright Clifford Odets brought in to rewrite part of the screenplay. Just as an angst-filled collaboration with Billy Wilder on *Sabrina* had left him with a "doctor's prescription for fourteen days without Billy Wilder," Lehman now left town on a doctor-ordered vacation to Tahiti, and although acclaim for his script was instantaneous, he was not nominated for an Oscar; the snub represented the first, but not the last, slight he felt at the hands of Hollywood.

Lehman had instantly grasped *The Sound of Music*'s cinematic potential when he attended the show during the second week of its Broadway run, emphatically telling his wife that regardless of the critics, "someday this show is going to make a very successful movie." Lehman understood *The Sound of Music*'s bedrock appeal: the show concerned the eternal verities of faith, love, and family. It would, he felt, stand the test of time precisely because it was not concerned with catering to the attitude of the present day. However cynical Lehman could sometimes be, each time he saw the Broadway show he felt utterly captivated by the scene of family reconciliation in which the captain joins his children in song. That scene, he felt certain, could provide the film's emotional anchor, touching as it did on what he termed the universal "wistful yearning for more love."

Lehman knew that in real life parent-child reconciliations rarely unfolded in such a straightforward fashion, but audiences, he reasoned, would tell themselves that if the von Trapps could live happily ever after, maybe their own fractured families could be healed as well. Lehman remained so convinced of the musical's cinematic possibilities that shortly after the Broadway production opened, he made a point of telling his friend David Brown, then head of the story department at Fox, that *The Sound of Music* would make a very successful movie. So strongly did he believe in the musical that he repeated the very same message to heavyweight producers Buddy Adler (*From Here to Eternity*, *South Pacific*) and Richard Zanuck.

At the time of the Broadway musical's gestation, however, Lehman was concentrating on the only original screenplay of his career, his collaboration with director Alfred Hitchcock on the entertaining and witty *North by Northwest* (1959). By 1960, with a range now extending from *Sweet Smell* to multiple

story line sagas (*Executive Suite*) and Hitchcock, Lehman struck old friend
Robert Wise as exactly the right man to adapt the Broadway musical *West
Side Story* for the screen. By the time of this third collaboration between
writer and director, the pair had settled into a comfortable working relationship—or as comfortable a one as Lehman would ever allow himself.

Lehman understood the highly dramatic yet stylized demands of *West Side
Story,* and reasoning that nothing was sacrosanct, re-ordered the placement
of the songs "I Feel Pretty" and "Cool." He may have been dealing with the
work of Leonard Bernstein, Stephen Sondheim, and Arthur Laurents, but
trusting his cinematic instincts, Lehman felt certain that character development, tension, and the dramatic through line would be enhanced by placing
them at different parts of the story—and he was right.

When *West Side Story* opened to enormous critical and popular acclaim,
Lehman felt that he would at last achieve the recognition he deserved. It was
an assumption that proved partially correct. He received a third Oscar nomination for his work (the others being for *Sabrina* and *North by Northwest),*
but when the awards were handed out on the night of April 9, 1962, he remained the only one of the film's eleven nominees to go home empty handed,
losing the award to Abby Mann's screenplay for *Judgment at Nuremberg.*

He understood that the very nature of musicals meant screenwriters received the most criticism and least respect, but the frustration remained; in
the face of increasingly sophisticated screen fare, by the 1960s, most of the critical community now seemed to hold the entire genre of movie musicals in
low esteem. Regarding musicals as silly, lightweight entertainments, they neglected to fully credit the difficulty of blending song, dance, acting, and design in a hyperrealistic medium. It's a myopic attitude best summed up by
then *New York Times* film critic Vincent Canby writing that the re-release of
Singin' in the Rain showed that the film contained "at least five" first-rate moments. As film historian Jeanine Basinger wittily points out, "This is a situation roughly equivalent to a jeweler's stumbling across King Solomon's mines
and crying out 'My God! This stuff must be worth a hundred dollars!' " With
the passage of time has come the final verdict; six decades later, *Singin' in the
Rain* has worn a lot better than that year's Oscar-winning Best Picture, *The
Greatest Show on Earth.*

With his by now vast experience, Lehman understood every last one of
the pitfalls inherent in writing movie musicals, but when Zanuck called about

The Sound of Music, he immediately expressed interest. He clearly liked the musical, had a history with R&H through his screenplay for *The King and I,* and knew that the material called for the sort of straightforward narrative at which he excelled. Lehman, in fact, thought of himself as a craftsman of the "old-fashioned" three-act structure, one in which each character's journey is filled with a readily discernible beginning, middle, and end: "I think that much of good screenwriting is about carpentry. It's a juggling of beginnings, middles, and endings so that they all inevitably seem to be moving correctly together." Leaping at the chance for this high-profile, big-budget assignment, he figured why not shoot for the moon. If it flopped, well, why not flop big? And if, by some chance, *The Sound of Music* hit big, his deal called for two percent of the profits. Lehman was in, signing his contract on December 10, 1962.

When his deal was made public, it landed on the front pages of all the Hollywood trade papers, because *Variety* and *The Hollywood Reporter* deemed Ernest Lehman and *The Sound of Music* very big news. (Lehman later admitted that he wrote the publicity release detailing his signing.) Yes, the screenwriter was a big-name writer, and *The Sound of Music* a famous property, but Ernest Lehman landed on the front pages for one reason: his signature on a contract for *The Sound of Music* proved to Hollywood at large that 20th Century-Fox intended to reopen for business.

Acclaim for his choice of writing assignment was not, to say the least, universal, and Lehman was brought crashing back to earth when he ran into his friend Burt Lancaster, whose barbed comment was a terse, "Jesus, you must need the money."

Lancaster's disdain didn't matter. What did matter was finding a top-flight director, and what Zanuck and Lehman quickly learned was that no A-list director was knocking on the door for the job. Or, put in slightly different terms, most directors ran in the other direction at the mere mention of the property. Stanley Donen (*On the Town, Funny Face*) refused any involvement whatsoever—and he had actually invested in the Broadway show. Donen's erstwhile partner Gene Kelly offered the most pungent refusal of all when Lehman sounded him out about possible involvement: "He led me out the front door, and on the front lawn he said, 'Ernie, go find someone else to direct this piece of shit!' "

Where was the skilled, heavyweight director needed to shepherd the multimillion-dollar family musical to the screen? How about William Wyler? He of the dramatic, non-musical, *Ben Hur, The Best Years of Our Lives*, and *The Little Foxes*? The hard-of-hearing William Wyler who didn't particularly like musicals would now direct a Technicolor extravaganza featuring nuns, children, and a dozen songs? Why, the film industry wondered, would the seemingly very unsuitable Wyler direct a musical about singing nuns? He'd never even directed a musical before.

Which is precisely why *The Sound of Music* caught his interest.

6.

SIX CHARACTERS IN SEARCH
OF A DIRECTOR

⌒

It was only after Donen and Kelly made it clear that they had absolutely no intention of directing *The Sound of Music* that the legendary Wyler's name began to be floated with increasing frequency. (Lehman claimed that he was the first to suggest Wyler, asking Darryl Zanuck: "What about the greatest director in the world? Willie Wyler.") The Alsace-born Wyler had won Oscars for his direction of *Mrs. Miniver (1942), The Best Years of Our Lives (1946),* and *Ben-Hur (1959)* and proven his versatility in genres ranging from the Bette Davis dramas *The Letter (1940)* and *The Little Foxes (1941),* to the fairy tale–like *Roman Holiday* (1953).

The Sound of Music did not strike anyone as typical Wyler fare, but he was a gifted director, was intrigued by the idea of directing a musical for the first time, and after a phone call from Darryl Zanuck, allowed himself to be talked into seeing the Broadway production of *Sound of Music.* Wyler attended the show with Lehman on January 17, 1963, a theater outing that represented the screenwriter's third viewing of the show—his starting point for adapting any musical, he stated, was seeing the show four or five times. The outing with Wyler, however, proved to be his first experience seeing the show with someone who, in a word, hated it.

With plans already in place for Lehman and Wyler to chat with Darryl F. Zanuck immediately after seeing the show, Wyler and Lehman began their walk to the meeting. After walking several blocks, the ever blunt Wyler blurted out: "Ernie, I hated the show but keep talking. Explain to me why I ought to do it." Lehman talked fast, and although Wyler had disliked almost the entire show, he inadvertently threw Lehman a lifeline after admitting that one scene had, in fact, made a deep impression upon him: when Captain von Trapp began to sing with his children for the first time, even tough-guy Wyler admitted to fighting back tears.

Wyler was weakening but still not sold. In a conversation with his friend Robert Swink, the director expressed bafflement: "They want me to make this picture and I don't know what to do. The people in this musical are playing a scene and all of a sudden someone starts to sing. . . . Why the hell do they start singing?" But, the artistic challenge of directing in a new genre, along with the prospect of a high-profile assignment and hefty paycheck, seemed to pique his interest: "I knew it would be a success. The story was made in German, on stage and in film. In some other languages, too. I wrote the producer of the German film. He answered my letter. He said 'This cannot fail.' "

After repeated entreaties, Wyler pushed aside his doubts. "Lehman kept after me and I finally said yes . . . though I didn't like the story." (Ironically, when Lehman first told Zanuck how much Wyler had disliked the show, Zanuck responded: "That's your job—not writing the script, but talking Willie Wyler into directing the film.")

Wyler next met with Maria von Trapp herself in New York City. He was, he later admitted, startled by the sight of a nearly sixty-year-old woman arriving at a New York City hotel dressed in a dirndl, but the meeting proved cordial, and after Wyler asked three-time Academy Award–winning song-writer/producer/arranger Roger Edens (*Easter Parade, On the Town, Annie Get Your Gun)* to sign on for the film, Lehman quickly wrote a thirty-page outline of his proposed script. Edens, who already possessed familiarity with Salzburg, flew to Austria with the screenwriter on May 25, 1963, in order to scout locations, and Wyler joined the duo two days later. Interior scenes, and even some songs, could and would be filmed on soundstages back in Los Angeles, but all three men felt location shooting in the beautiful city and surrounding countryside was absolutely necessary for "Do-Re-Mi," "I Have Confidence," and the title song. Far from minimizing the musical backbone of the movie, the filmmakers should, Wyler felt, positively revel in the altered reality of a large-scale musical. In a memo to Lehman, Wyler wrote: "It is not to be a picture in which we feel slightly apologetic every time anyone sings. On the contrary, our aim is to be slightly apologetic every time anyone *talks*."

In the midst of their scouting excursions, Wyler and Lehman met with the Mother Superior of Nonnberg Abbey in an attempt to secure permission for filming at the abbey. Although separated from the Mother Superior by an iron grille, the duo plunged into a detailed explanation of their plans for the movie; in the recall of Wyler's wife, Talli: "It was hilarious to watch these two Hollywood characters convince the Mother Superior that they weren't mad."

Wyler, Lehman, and Chaplin next met with the Burgomeister of Salzburg, with Wyler pointedly telling the mayor: "We have a scene of the 1936 [*sic*] Anschluss in the picture. We want to stage this out in the open, with Germans marching, swastikas everywhere, and the whole population out cheering and throwing flowers. You know—the way it really happened." Replied the seen-it-all mayor: "We survived that, we'll survive this, too."

With location scouting completed, the trio returned to California, and at the behest of Richard Zanuck, the ever-professional Lehman very quickly turned in a first draft in order to ascertain just how interested Wyler was in actually directing the film. Lehman handed Wyler the script in September of 1963 and when Wyler professed to love the script, it was the first, and biggest sign of trouble dead ahead. The ever astute, always worried Lehman knew that "As soon as Wyler stated 'I can't think of a single suggestion to make,' " the director had no intention of involving himself with *The Sound of Music*. The opinionated, quasi-dictatorial Wyler, a man known for forty takes of one scene, saying there was nothing he could think of to improve the script? Highly unlikely. Instead, Wyler's original doubts about the material were returning post haste. He possessed no inherent feeling for, or interest in, the material, and, as his preproduction notes eventually revealed, his concept for the movie included emphasizing the onset of the Anschluss, a move guaranteed to disrupt the delicate fabric of the film's feel-good aura. Admitted Wyler: "I knew the movie wasn't really a political thing, but I had a tendency to want to make it, if not an anti-Nazi movie, one which at least would say a few things."

Wyler, it seemed, wouldn't be content photographing a handful of Nazis chasing the von Trapps at the abbey's cemetery. He wanted to film dozens of gun-bearing Nazis, with the camera closing in on the sight of tanks rumbling through Austrian streets. Conveying a genuine sense of menace would prove the order of the day, all of which made it abundantly clear that Wyler and *The Sound of Music* were not a director/musical match made in heaven. Wyler didn't just want another tone for the film: he envisioned a completely different texture and scale to the entire production design. In the recollection of Maurice Zuberano, Wyler's vision of the von Trapp villa seemed far grander than one appropriate to a mere captain: "Wyler wanted to do it as if they were the royal family!"

In retrospect, the tip-off to Wyler's unsuitability for the material lay in his very first scouting trip with Lehman and Edens. Lehman refused to set foot in the small private plane they had hired to fly over the Alps in search of meadows and scenic countryside, but Wyler and Edens hopped on board; after finding out that the pilot ferrying the two men around the countryside was an ex-Nazi, Wyler started a screaming match with the pilot while they were still in the air. Wyler, it seemed, agreed with the ever-cantankerous Billy Wilder, who stated in his typically jaundiced manner: "No musical with swastikas in it will ever be a success." (The overwhelming success of *Cabaret,* both in its repeated Broadway incarnations and in the Academy Award–winning film version, would subsequently prove both how wrong the great Wilder was, as well as how far the musical theater subsequently traveled on its path to social relevance.)

As the starting date for production loomed, Wyler grew more and more uneasy, brooding about a months' long commitment he didn't want to make. In the words of wife Talli: "Willy had all but signed. He was already working on the picture. But I would go into his den and he'd be sitting at his desk staring off into space. He was obviously miserable, just hating every minute of it." In response to Talli's query as to exactly what was the matter, he quickly muttered: "I can't bear to make a picture about all those nice Nazis."

Lehman began to grow suspicious about Wyler's intentions, and during a visit to Wyler's house, ostensibly to lobby the visiting Rex Harrison about playing Captain von Trapp, Lehman made a quick perusal of the director's desk. Wyler had scripts lying all over his study, but only one script was turned facedown: the screenplay adaptation of John Fowles's acclaimed novel *The Collector.* Lehman realized that the director planned to begin work on *The Collector* before even considering *The Sound of Music*, and when Wyler's agent asked Zanuck to postpone *The Sound of Music* until *The Collector* had been completed, the curt response was: "Go tell your client that I won't postpone this picture thirty seconds. Tell him to go make *The Collector.*" Wyler asked to be released from the musical.

Wyler was happy to leave the Austrian nuns behind, and in truth, Lehman and Richard Zanuck were just as pleased to see him depart. In the latter's recollection: "We all ranted and raved about how awful it was, what he'd pulled on us, but deep down inside, I was a bit relieved." Three years later, Wyler finally did make his musical directing debut with the hugely successful *Funny Girl,* shepherding newcomer Barbra Streisand to an Oscar-winning performance in her first film. Wyler felt more at ease with *Funny Girl* than with *The Sound of Music*; *Funny Girl* may have represented a whitewashed version of the Fanny Brice saga, but the rags-to-riches Jewish background of subject and star made for a more comfortable directorial fit than did Austrian nuns, and Wyler relished the challenge of guiding Streisand in her film debut, calling his star "a fascinating creature."

With Wyler's exit, the $8,000,000 production appeared rudderless, but in Lehman's recall, it was at this very time that he glimpsed Robert Wise sitting in the 20th Century-Fox commissary, rather glumly mulling the typhoon-induced postponement of his next film, *The Sand Pebbles.* Recalling their award-winning collaboration on *West Side Story,* and without Richard Zanuck's knowledge, Lehman called Wise's agent Phil Gersh and sent him the *Sound of Music* screenplay for his client's consideration. There was just one problem: not only was Robert Wise uninterested in *The Sound of Music,* but he had already turned down the film, having deemed the material too saccharine.

Lehman remained undeterred. Knowing that Wise was not a fan of the Broadway show, Lehman made certain to tell Gersh that just as on *West Side Story,* he had rethought the use of the already classic R&H score. Three million copies of the cast album sold or not, Lehman wanted changes made. This was film, not theater:

1. Gone were songs for the secondary characters Max and Baroness Elsa, and gone with them was the show's political commentary. Audiences wanted to hear Maria and the children sing, not the jaded adults; "How Can Love Survive" and "No Way to Stop It" would, the screenwriter felt certain, bring the dramatic momentum onscreen to a screeching halt and he cut them entirely. ("How Can Love Survive" did in fact make it into the film during the party the captain hosts in honor of Elsa. Once the baroness has, in the guise of friendly advice, firmly pushed Maria toward the exit door, she returns to the party, at which point, in a nice touch of irony, the orchestra plays "How Can Love Survive" for the waltzing party guests.)

2. "An Ordinary Couple": the declaration of love sung by Maria and the Captain would be cut. The song, in fact, was nothing more than ordinary in Lehman's view—passionless and bland. How about asking Rodgers for a new, more overtly romantic song to help reshape the chaste love story?

He might not have known it yet, but Lehman's desire to jettison "An Ordinary Couple" would be helped by Rodgers's own indifference to the song; what, the composer had asked, was ordinary about a romance between a former nun and a naval captain who had already fathered seven children? R&H had, in fact, even discussed replacing the song for Broadway, a plan that had been derailed when Hammerstein fell ill.

Rodgers granted his approval.

3. Nothing if not intrepid in changing the order of a highly regarded score, Lehman switched the placement and context of both "My Favorite Things" and "The Lonely Goatherd" in order to better serve the growing attachment between Maria and the children. Onstage, the boisterous "Lonely Goatherd" registered as a match in volume for the raging thunderstorm that scared the children. For the film, the song would appear much later in the story, with Maria's "Favorite Things" now serving as the welcome antidote to the frightening storm.

4. The screenwriter happily used many lines directly from the original libretto, but also invented several entirely new scenes in order to deepen the relationship between Maria and the children. On the night of her first dinner at the von Trapps, Maria would now sit on a pinecone deliberately placed on her chair by the children. Conflict between Maria and the children at their very first meal together would begin the relationship; audiences could then watch their relationship thaw before blossoming into all-out love. Because Maria did not tell the captain that the children had put a frog in her pocket and forced her to sit on a pinecone, there now existed an actual reason for the childrens' capitulation to her during "My Favorite Things." Maria would morph from foe to friend in one fell swoop.

5. In a newly invented "blueberry picking" scene taking place on the terrace of the villa, the children would try to cover up their attempt to visit the recently departed Fraulein Maria at the abbey. The captain's humorous interrogation of his children would illustrate the newly relaxed relationship between father and children, showing just how much their relationship had changed during Maria's time at the house.

6. Best of all, Lehman had figured out a way to top the one surefire scene in the play, which had appealed even to Wyler. After the captain joins his children in singing "The Sound of Music"—the emotional breakthrough for which everyone has been hoping—he sings a solo version of "Edelweiss." Although only heard once onstage, "Edelweiss" would be heard twice in the film: first as a solo for the captain that serves to underscore his love for his children, and then again as an emotional audience sing-along at the climactic music festival. With its moving evocation of family love and national pride, Lehman felt certain that the deceptively simple song could not only withstand repetition, but also buttress the emotional high points of the film.

By combining Lindsay and Crouse's Broadway script, Maria von Trapp's autobiography, and the two *Die Trapp-Familie* films, Lehman had actually managed to make the characters three dimensional, or, with the possible exception of the captain, close thereto. He had successfully avoided the trap of merely "opening up" the stage version for the screen. In the words of R&H president Ted Chapin: "What he did brilliantly was use many of the lines but he changed the humor a lot."

The final coup lay in Lehman's very opening to the film. Lehman guessed that Wise's creative instincts would be awakened by the visual possibilities found in the film's setting, and the screenwriter had written a grab 'em quick opening in which the visual dominated. Having conceived the opening number while literally sitting at his desk with his eyes closed, Lehman had simply typed the words: "This is what I want to see," before going on to describe the sights of the fairy tale–like wide open Austrian countryside, an enchanted-looking kingdom in which characters really could burst into song.

A sentimental, potentially sappy musical was now being shaped into a streamlined, cinematic screenplay, and Lehman thought Wise could be sold.

An at-loose-ends Wise decided to give the script one more try, and finding himself responding to the screenplay, he read through it twice and listened to the Broadway score repeatedly. Mulling over the possibilities, Wise sent the script on to Saul Chaplin, his trusted musical guru and associate producer on *West Side Story*. Pianist, songwriter, vocal arranger, musical director, and Academy Award–winner for *American in Paris, Seven Brides for Seven Brothers,* and *West Side Story*, Chaplin possessed decades of experience in helping to shape the great MGM musicals churned out by the studio's fabled Freed Unit. When Chaplin talked musicals, Wise listened, and Saul Chaplin found himself surprisingly touched by the script for a musical he had never much liked onstage. A professed admirer of the score, he had found the stage libretto much too sweet for his taste, but Lehman's script struck a chord; given the potential for saccharine overload, Saul Chaplin knew that *The Sound of Music* would sink onscreen without a realistic director like Wise at the helm. Wise, he felt certain, would bring the musical's underlying themes of personal freedom, dignity, and redemption to the forefront without being heavy-handed. He actually liked musicals, possessed the right skill set, and just the right firm but low-key personality. In Chaplin's estimation, it could all work, and when Wise told Chaplin, "If you say yes, I'll say yes," Chaplin pushed Wise to accept.

Phil Gersh told the studio that Wise was now on board as director, and an excited Richard Zanuck called Lehman to come down to the studio. In Lehman's amused recall, Zanuck blurted, "I've got a surprise for you—what would you say if I can get Bob Wise to direct this picture?" Faced with Lehman's knowing grin, Zanuck realized exactly what had transpired, and laughingly accused: "You son of a bitch! You slipped him the script, didn't you?"

Guilty.

ROBERT WISE

*"The best movies leave audiences feeling glad to be alive,
human, and reaching out to one another."*—ROBERT WISE, AFI
LIFETIME ACHIEVEMENT AWARD ACCEPTANCE SPEECH

Zanuck, Lehman, Chaplin—everyone involved felt certain that Wise's experience with films ranging from boxing biopics and melodramas to the stylized musical world of *West Side Story* uniquely qualified him for the challenges posed by this particular musical. He had directed in every possible genre and there wasn't a job on a film set that he couldn't perform. As it was, *West Side Story* hardly represented Wise's only musical credit; he had actually cut his teeth in the film industry as a sound effects and music editor on the Fred Astaire/Ginger Rogers films at RKO, and it didn't get any better than Fred and Ginger.

Great as Fred and Ginger were, however, the young and ambitious Wise certainly had more on his mind than a career in sound editing. He wanted to direct, and began methodically working his way up the ladder from assistant to full-fledged editor, overseeing the final edits of the very popular comedies *Bachelor Mother* (1939) and *My Favorite Wife* (1940). His career then took a quantum leap forward when he received an Oscar nomination in 1941 for his extraordinary and influential editing of *Citizen Kane*.

Over the years, even the patient Wise grew weary of talking about *Citizen Kane*, but his specific contribution to that unquestioned masterpiece, one often cited as the greatest film ever made, can be definitively ascertained in the highly influential breakfast table sequence. In a decades-spanning series of connected scenes, Kane and his first wife are shown eating breakfast together, their growing estrangement depicted literally and figuratively by the spatial placement and mannerisms displayed while sitting at the table. The sequence may have been conceived by Welles, but the pace and specific cuts that made the scene so effective were the work of Wise and Mark Robson (who himself went on to a commercially successful career as director of *Earthquake, Von Ryan's Express,* and *Peyton Place*). The two editors spent several weeks putting together this breakfast table montage until they had perfected the split-second timing of the introductory voice in each section of the segment, as well as "the speed of the whip-pans." In a brilliant film toploaded with memorable sequences, this artful deconstruction of a marriage may well reign supreme.

The lessons of *Citizen Kane* were to stay with Wise for the rest of his life. Said *The Sound of Music*'s assistant director Georg Steinitz: "I honestly believe that Robert Wise had the entire film in his head. He came from the world of editors and was so aware of always having total coverage—enough shots from all angles. He knew everything in every department. It's the unit production manager who has to keep track of the props, how many extras are needed, all the little details—but Wise himself knew every bit of that. It all comes from the general and Wise was our general. He was the ultimate pro."

After his extraordinary work on *Citizen Kane,* Wise's standing with the RKO brass had reached new heights; when reedits were demanded on Welles's *The Magnificent Ambersons* after a disastrous preview in Pomona, California, and the director was in Latin America filming the ultimately unfinished *It's All True,* the studio turned to Wise. Wise grabbed the opportunity, a move that over the years earned him more enmity than praise from those who consider *Ambersons* a masterpiece gone awry. Wise reshot the bedroom scene and added others, but the majority of his work (with his assistant Mark Robson) lay in the repositioning and reediting of scenes. Welles denounced the reedit, saying the film seemed "cut by the studio gardener," but Robert Carriger's 1993 book *Magnificent Ambersons Reconstructed* posits that Welles himself suggested even greater cuts than those made by Wise and Robson.

It was then, after hurriedly replacing Gunther von Fritsch as director on 1944's *Curse of the Cat People* partway through filming, that Wise's career as a director took off. Working under the aegis of legendary producer Val Lewton, but handicapped by the film's nonexistent budget, Wise achieved a heightened sense of menace through implication rather than graphic displays of violence. His strength as a director, it quickly became apparent, lay in his ability to transfer the written word into purely visual storytelling. In 1963's *The Haunting,* Wise was to present—or rather suggest—terror through a combination of sound and the terrific black-and-white cinematography of Davis Boulton. It's a frightening film in which atmosphere, not gore, proved all.

A solid pro beginning with his first feature, he displayed an ironclad willingness to cut any sequence, no matter how prized, if he felt it slowed down the film. The piece of advice he cited more often than any other was that given to him by director Richard Wallace, for whom he edited the 1943 film *Bombardier*: "If a scene seems a trifle slow on the set, it will be twice as slow in the projection room."

No matter the genre, Wise disdained stylistic flourishes, letting the material speak for itself. In films ranging from 1947's *Born to Kill* starring Claire Trevor as a decidedly nasty piece of work, to the racially charged *Odds Against*

Tomorrow, Wise let the script take centerstage. He could adapt to a "woman's film" like 1950's *Three Secrets,* the film on which he first worked with the talented and beautiful Eleanor Parker, but he was usually drawn to material that contained at least some hope for redemption, most notably in his 1951 triumph for 20th Century-Fox, the classic science fiction film *The Day the Earth Stood Still.*

He could turn lyrical, as in his 1953 adaptation of Edna Ferber's *So Big,* starring Sterling Hayden and Jane Wyman, but no matter the canvas—whether New York City in *West Side Story*, the grimy boxing milieu of *Somebody Up There Likes Me* (1956), or the oppressive submarine setting in 1958's Clark Gable vehicle, *Run Silent, Run Deep*—Wise consistently made a point of staging the most powerful emotional moments in small confined spaces. How would Maria and the captain finally express their love in *The Sound of Music*? Not in the expansive outdoor alpine countryside, but within the confines of the romantically small gazebo. Where would the Mother Abbess implore Maria to reach for the stars and climb every mountain? In her spare, one-room office rather than the soaring cathedral.

With his love of music, Wise had even managed to insert jazz-inflected musical statements into the award-winning and decidedly grim *I Want to Live,* and worked no fewer than six songs into the nightclub setting of *This Could Be the Night* (1957); *West Side Story* (1961), however, represented his first full-fledged musical film and was far from a sure bet for the movies.

Yes, the show had enjoyed a successful (732 performances), critically acclaimed run on Broadway (ten months after closing, it returned for an additional eight-month engagement), but it was never a smash hit of *My Fair Lady*–like proportions, and the musical's updating of *Romeo and Juliet* into present-day New York ran the risk of seeming ludicrous when blown up thirty feet high on movie screens. It was a brilliant, groundbreaking show, but it also, in the words of the show's librettist, the acerbic Arthur Laurents (*Gypsy, The Way We Were*), concerned "street toughs dancing in color-coordinated sneakers."

Signing on to produce the film as well as codirect it with Jerome Robbins, the Broadway musical's brilliant and notoriously demanding original choreographer and director, Wise took over as sole director halfway through shooting. In the view of United Artists, Robbins was spending too much time and money in an uncompromising quest to fulfill his perfectionist vision, in the process forgetting the all-important Hollywood dictum: this was show business, not show art.

By mixing the actual New York City streets with the stylized approach of shooting Manhattan's canyons straight down, Wise earned the audience's acceptance of a dramatically intense story told within the framework of the inherently artificial movie musical genre. He understood the musical's need to establish the basic vocabulary of the film within the first ten minutes: Will characters sing directly to each other? Do they express their passion in dance? Nothing if not bold in his choices, Wise gambled everything in those first ten minutes and won, opening the movie with gang members dancing on actual Manhattan streets. On the face of it, dancing gang members seemed ludicrous, but in the skilled hands of Wise and Robbins, the audience immediately accepted both the number and the basic premise of the film. More than any other genre, musicals represent the most delicate of juggling acts, a challenge Wise relished. Indeed, in the end, he seemed to take more pleasure from *West Side Story* than from any of his other films: "Taken from the original to the final film, I think *West Side Story* was more of a challenge, more of a creative accomplishment than any of my films."

Wise now said "yes" to *The Sound of Music,* and quickly struck a deal calling for salary plus ten percent of the profits. Repeating his dual *West Side Story* roles as producer and director, Wise would be involved in every aspect of *The Sound of Music,* from production right up to distribution and promotion. This would be a Robert Wise production in every sense of the word. If it didn't work, there'd be no one else to blame, a state of affairs that was just fine with him.

In October of 1963 Wise officially replaced Roger Edens with Saul Chaplin, brought in Boris Leven as production designer, Saul Wurtzel as production manager, and Maurice Zuberano as storyboard artist and second unit director. On November 1, the five men flew to Salzburg on a scouting trip, where Wise found himself so taken with the medium-size (population 150,000) Baroque city—dubbed "the Rome of the North" because of its plethora of churches and cathedrals—that he now made the decision to film in a way that would make Salzburg another character in the film. The Nonnberg Abbey . . . the cemetery at St. Peter's . . . Mirabell Gardens with its beautiful flowers . . . the Mozart Bridge crossing the Salzach River . . . the leaf-covered trellis arboretum . . . the circular wading pool . . . Neptune's Fountain . . . the

Festival Hall Rock Riding Academy—Wise saw possibilities everywhere he looked. All of these beautiful old-world settings could be displayed in musical numbers, and "I Have Confidence" and "Do-Re-Mi" would register as more than snappy show tunes: they'd showcase the charm of Salzburg and the overwhelming love the von Trapps felt for their native land.

For all the uplift inherent in the story, location shooting could also show characters simultaneously protected and dwarfed by the Alps, men and women shadowed by both the mountains and the ever-growing Nazi menace. The location possibilities seemed endless to Wise, but one seemingly insurmountable problem remained: where could they find the right mountaintop meadow visualized as the setting for the film's title song?

In order to answer this question, the five men found themselves trudging in the snow along with the film's location manager, before finally arriving at what the location scout deemed the "perfect setting" for the title song. The Hollywood veterans stopped, turned, and stared in dismay at their destination: a large field that was, in Chaplin's words, "knee-deep in snow and surrounded by tall, barren stalks, also heavily laden with snow." A green summer meadow seemed light-years away. Unfazed, the production manager confidently assured the dubious filmmakers: "Trust me." Seven months from now, he insisted, it would all be verdant and lush, the contrast with the snowcapped Alps all the more striking. Freezing though they were, the men took time to gaze at the spectacular view, and in their collective imaginations the meadow began its transformation into the ideal setting for the soaring title song. This could work. Now about getting out of the cold . . .

Those extra minutes spent gazing in wonder at the surrounding mountains would ultimately prove crucial. What the creative team now began to appreciate was the fact that the heightened reality of the setting actually dovetailed perfectly with the fairy-tale quality of the story: the extraordinary spectacle of meadows surrounded by towering mountains conveyed a sense of isolation, as if the entire story existed in a world of its own. The scenery was real, yet at the same time served to underscore the never-never land quality of the story.

Now back in the United States, Wise continued to juggle casting demands with the signing of his production designer, cinematographer, and editor. Turning to men with whom he had previously collaborated in winning fashion, Wise landed his first and only choice for each of those crucial jobs. Whatever else happened on the Technicolor musical's journey to neighborhood movie screens, the look of the film would be in the hands of the most talented professionals in Hollywood, because joining production designer Boris Leven would be cinematographer Ted McCord and editor William Reynolds. Oscar winners, team players, and amiable gentlemen. When to begin?

Yesterday.

7

DESIGNING *THE SOUND OF MUSIC*: FANTASY, REALITY, AND FOURTEEN SHOW TUNES

～♪～

BORIS LEVEN

"Boris was a tremendous asset. Every visual aspect
of the film was just superb."

—ROBERT WISE

The look, the physical settings, and the very texture of the film all began with one man: production designer Boris Leven.

An award-winning artist who by 1964 had already earned a reputation as one of the greatest production designers in the history of Hollywood, Leven was considered by Wise to be so essential to the film's success that the director contacted the designer as soon as his own participation in *The Sound of Music* was finalized. There would be no second choice for production designer; Wise wanted Leven and Leven alone, emphatically positioning his friend as the unquestioned "master at putting reality up on the screen."

Born in Moscow in 1908, Leven had studied painting in his native Moscow before unexpectedly emigrating to the United States in 1927. It was actually his brother who had secured a spot on the list of émigrés, but not wanting to leave his girlfriend behind, he ceded his place to Boris instead.

Upon his arrival in the United States, Leven enrolled at the University of Southern California, and after graduation, attended the Beaux Arts Institute in New York City. He would, he thought, make architecture his career, and began work as a sketch artist at Paramount Pictures just to tide himself over before beginning work as an architect.

With his extraordinary sense of detail and color, Leven quickly acquired the status of rising design star, and his burgeoning career led him to work with Samuel Goldwyn. In 1937 he parlayed that experience into a contract with 20th Century-Fox as art director and production designer, making his first big splash with 1938's *Alexander's Ragtime Band,* a musical epic for which he designed no fewer than eighty-six period sets.

Blessed with an extraordinary eye for the telling detail, Leven was able to blend the genuine with the theatrical; one look at 1941's *The Shanghai Gesture*— all lacquered furniture and "exotic" Asian motif—shows just how well Leven understood Hollywood's then prevailing vision of the Far East. In those far from multicultural times, where one of the film's leading characters was actually named Mother Gin Sling, Leven still managed to design a home for the leading lady that proved so detailed it functioned as another character in the film. A contemporary newspaper profile at the time of the film's production detailed that the walls of Mother Gin Sling's dining room comprised 3,000 square feet of mirror, on which actor Keye Luke painted no fewer than 750 Chinese figures. Whether the detail lay in Asian living rooms or in the cobblestones of an Austrian nunnery, Leven's gimlet-eyed vision enhanced the reality of the setting at hand.

Over the course of his legendary career, Leven was to be nominated no fewer than nine times for the Oscar (beginning with *Alexander's Ragtime Band* and *Shanghai Gesture*). His Academy Award–nominated work on *Giant* (1956) proved so powerful that in the decades following the film's release, the mere mention of *Giant* instantly called forth the image of the Leven-designed Victorian house silhouetted against the vast Texas sky. With his extraordinary range, Leven followed *Giant* with the gritty black-and-white *Anatomy of a Murder,* and two years later he garnered the Academy Award for his work with Wise on *West Side Story.*

In his Oscar-winning design for *West Side Story,* Leven smartly melded actual New York City locations with the stylized requirements of the musical genre. Reteaming with Wise in 1962 on the interior-centric small-scale black-and-white *Two for the Seesaw* (for which he scored another nomination), Leven found that his second outing with Wise proved even more enjoyable, their collegial temperaments and exacting work habits blending together very well. Wise functioned as the commander in chief, low-key but always in control, with Leven supporting him as his meticulous and gentlemanly lieutenant. What cemented their working relationship was a mutual belief in a team-oriented approach, both men eschewing a grab for glory in their trust that the work would speak for itself. Said Leven: "I have always enjoyed a complete rapport with the director and the technical personnel . . . each film on which I worked broadened my horizons, attitudes, and enthusiasm."

Excited to work with Wise for the third time, and with Saul Wurtzel finalizing the film's budget, in November 1963 Leven began sketching—with an avowed determination to avoid a stereotypical alpine world filled with castles and merry villagers. One false set, one phony detail, and the audience would be abruptly ripped back to the present day, far from the fairy-tale musical world depicted onscreen. Blueprints were drafted, location choices finalized, and with a total trust in Leven's vision, Wise now turned his attention to choosing the cinematographer for his widescreen, Technicolor musical.

First choice. Second choice. Only choice: Ted McCord.

Ted McCord

"Among his associates he was known for sharing his thinking with those with whom he worked, never keeping trade secrets to himself."

—*VARIETY*

In planning the palette of the film, how best to capture the sought-after balance between the romance of the gilded ballroom and the realism of the towering Alps, Robert Wise knew from the start that he would lean heavily upon Ted McCord. The two men had worked together on 1962's *Two for the Seesaw,* and while much of that black-and-white film featured the tight small spaces of Manhattan apartments, Wise knew that McCord's four-decade body of work featured multiple outdoor location shoots, particularly those found in a series of pictorially stunning Westerns. One look at the crystal clear detailed outdoor vistas in the 1959 Western *The Hanging Tree* told even a casual viewer that McCord understood it wasn't just a matter of capturing pretty pictures: the composition within the frame and the exact placement of the figures silhouetted against the stark landscape spoke volumes about the characters without a single syllable being uttered.

McCord began work in the industry in 1917, photographing dozens of films that ranged from Westerns to comedies. As his work evolved he began experimenting with the use of deep shadows, his expanding palette largely influenced by two disparate sources: the Dutch master Rembrandt, and the esteemed cinematographer Gregg Toland (*Citizen Kane, Wuthering Heights*). Having begun his long-term association with Warner Brothers in 1937, he joined the armed services during World War II and served as a captain in the U.S. Army Photography Unit. His work landed him in the forefront of troops entering Berlin at the end of the war, and he was among the very first cameramen to film inside Hitler's ruined chancellery.

The first peak of McCord's post-war work began with the black-and-white trio of *Johnny Belinda* (1948, Academy Award nomination), John Huston's *The Treasure of the Sierra Madre* (1948), and *Flamingo Road* (1949, directed by Michael Curtiz). His superb black-and-white photography for three ensuing Doris Day films not only demonstrated his understanding of the musical genre, but also his ability to enhance the allure of female stars, a fact of which Wise was certainly aware in planning the female-centric *Sound of Music*. McCord's photography of Day resulted in the best films of her seven-year stint at Warner Brothers: *Young Man with a Horn* (1950), *Young at Heart* (1954), and particularly, *I"ll See You in My Dreams* (1951). The last named, directed by Curtiz, featured a brilliant sequence in which Day falls asleep at a late-night jazz club and husband Danny Thomas slowly walks down the stairs, picks her up, and carries her out of the club. McCord lit the set so that Curtiz could film the sequence in one continuous take, and with the smoky lighting, late-night bar-closing atmosphere, and faintly dying music, the entire sequence registers as not only affecting but also downright beautiful. His sympathetic treatment of Day, emphasizing her strengths (the warmth of her eyes, the winning smile) and minimizing her flaws (the long-waisted figure) showed just how thoroughly he understood the photographing of actresses.

McCord's first Oscar nomination may have come with *Johnny Belinda*, but it was his gritty detailed work on *Treasure of the Sierra Madre* that so impressed director Elia Kazan that he requested McCord for his Technicolor and CinemaScope production of John Steinbeck's *East of Eden* (1955). Kazan realized that McCord's ability to manipulate focus and depth made him a natural for the color canvas he envisioned for the film, and McCord's ensuing manipulation of the shadows within the brothel hallway silently transmitted every last bit of necessary substance and texture.

Coupling McCord's background in Westerns with the fact that a great deal of *The Sound of Music* would be shot during the daylight hours, Wise knew that all of the difficult outdoor scenes, particularly in the "Do-Re-Mi" montage, could be handled with ease by McCord. In Wise's own words: "I felt he could bring the right touch of romanticism—not a harsh realistic treatment, but a soft focus feeling appropriate for all aspects." And on December 30, a deal was finalized for their professional reunion.

Who to edit?

WILLIAM REYNOLDS

"The only time I watch the editing of a film is when I'm bored."
—WILLIAM REYNOLDS

Born in Elmira, New York, in 1910, Reynolds came from a privileged background, but started out in the film business in the lowly position of prop mover at Fox Studios. Interested in a career as a film editor, he signed on at Paramount, and rose to fame within the industry by editing the 1938 Hedy Lamarr vehicle *Algiers*; after serving in World War II, he had the good fortune to enter into a long-term contract at 20th Century-Fox, where studio head Darryl F. Zanuck, a former editor himself, quickly realized the breadth of Reynolds's talent, and assigned him to a series of prestige pictures.

Those pictures eventually led to his first teaming with Robert Wise on 1951's *The Day the Earth Stood Still*. (Now considered a classic of the genre, at the time of its initial release, the film was accorded one of the more unusual honors in film history—a Golden Globe Award for the "Best Film Promoting International Understanding"; given that the plot of the film centered upon visitors from outer space, presumably that "international understanding" encompassed intergalactic brotherhood as well.)

Reynolds's first-rate body of work ranged from the hugely popular soap operas *Three Coins in the Fountain* (1954) and *Love Is a Many-Splendored Thing* (1955) to Rodgers and Hammerstein's *Carousel* (1956), and covered every genre from the first-rate Marilyn Monroe vehicle *Bus Stop* (1956) to the Fred Astaire musical *Daddy Long Legs* (1955). Having thoroughly enjoyed his collaboration with Wise in 1951, when Reynolds heard about the upcoming filming of *The Sound of Music* he seized the initiative and actually called the director in hopes of securing a reunion. As soon as Wise heard Reynolds's friendly greeting— "Let's work together"—the director knew that he had found the right editor.

Wise retained fond memories of Reynolds as both editor and "gentleman," and felt fully at ease with Reynolds's style and personality. As a former editor himself, Wise appreciated Reynolds's approach, one so instinctual that in the words of director Arthur Hiller, Reynolds edited "by feel, not by rote."

Never flashy in his style of presentation, Reynolds managed to consistently move the narrative forward, helping to increase the pace without resorting to attention-grabbing techniques. All of his choices were made in service to the picture: "Try to make the best possible version of what you as editor take to be the director's idea of the film. I'd like to think that when people see films, they're not aware of editing. The only time I watch the editing of a film is when I'm bored." Reynolds never evinced interest in the showy cut that drew attention to itself, instead focusing upon how audiences reacted to the actual structure and pace of the film; when attending previews of his films, he would, in the recollection of his former assistant Jim Langlois, deliberately sit in the middle of the audience, the better to hear where the laughs did or did not fall. It was, he felt, the best way to ascertain exactly where the story hooked—or lost—the audience.

Reynolds's low-key personality allowed him to collaborate beautifully not only with Wise, but with set designer Leven and cinematographer Ted McCord as well. Said Wise in his laconic Midwestern style: "I valued Bill's judgment more than I did anybody's. It's part of the editor's job to evaluate what he has and sometimes not use all of it. Bill had very good taste."

Leven was signed and hard at work, McCord had outlined his requirements for film stock and cameras, and with a deal signed on December 2, 1963, Reynolds was ready and raring to get to work. Which left only one key designer to be signed: who would and could realistically clothe nuns, naval officers, children, and Nazis?

DOROTHY JEAKINS

"Her special talent is to make costumes look real and not like costumes."
—ROBERT WISE

When moviegoers think of the onscreen von Trapp children happily tripping over the Austrian countryside, two sequences immediately come to mind: the

"Do-Re-Mi" travelogue, and the tree-climbing/boat-tipping sequence that immediately follows the number. In both cases, it's the costumes that provide instant recall: all seven children are attired in matching play clothes made from old curtains, the most famous drapes since Scarlett O'Hara turned green velvet curtains into a dress.

Mention Maria's wedding to the captain to even a casual viewer of the film, and the talk instantly turns to her dress and the graceful movement of the flowing train as she processed down the aisle. What curtains and wedding dress shared in common was the extraordinary attention to detail inherent in the work of designer Dorothy Jeakins, small but telling mixtures of colors and textures that went a long way toward providing character development. With her love of period detail, Jeakins proved the ideal designer for a musical film set in the "golden age" of 1930s Austria.

Recommended to Wise by Saul Chaplin, Jeakins enthusiastically signed on after Wise offered her the job in January of 1964. Given her own extremely difficult personal life, Jeakins's response to *The Sounds of Music*'s sweet-natured depiction of childhood and all-encompassing message that family love conquers all, seemed to represent a widescreen case of real-life wish fulfillment.

Born in 1914, Jeakins was abandoned by her parents at an early age; her father took the five-year-old Dorothy away from her mother and, over the next several years, proceeded to hide the youngster in a succession of foster homes. At one point young Dorothy was reduced to begging on the streets of Los Angeles along with her abusive foster mother. Said Jeakins at age sixty-seven: "To this hour I don't know what happened to my mother. She was a couture dressmaker. She made tea gowns." Describing herself as "pathologically shy and neurotically modest," Jeakins discovered her talent for drawing at an extremely young age: "I learned to read, write, and draw before I was six. In kindergarten I made a drawing of President Wilson, who had come to San Diego to speak at a war bond rally. They reproduced it in the newspaper. . . . That's the first time that I was aware that I had any drawing ability."

She began in the film industry by painting cells of Mickey Mouse for $16 per week, soon married, and then had two children. With her husband stationed in Paris during World War II, Jeakins was left on her own, suffering a severe post-war blow when her husband decided not to return home.

Jeakins was now left with sole responsibility for the care and upbringing of two small boys. Abandoned in turn by parents and husband, she understandably lacked any sense of her roots; in her own smartly turned phrase, she realized that she had "an affinity for the past" that began to manifest itself in her work. There she found a past she could design and control herself.

A first-rate portrait artist, after World War II she began work as a wardrobe illustrator at Fox, and when director Victor Fleming (*Gone With the Wind*, *Wizard of Oz*) looked through her portfolio, he was so impressed by her abilities that he instantly made her codesigner of his epic film *Joan of Arc*. Starring Ingrid Bergman, that 1948 film won Jeakins the Oscar for Best Costume Design in the very first year the award was ever given. She followed up that triumph by winning a second Oscar the next year for Cecil B. DeMille's *Samson and Delilah*. The designer's reaction to winning a second Oscar? She buried the award in a closet, stating, "I was part of the costume congress of Cecil B. DeMille. I didn't deserve to be included."

Having survived abandonment in her own childhood, Jeakins was especially sensitive to mistreatment of anyone else, and her experience with DeMille proved so painful that it caused her to later make her one publicly harsh critique of a coworker: "DeMille was the most vicious man. He indulged in that awful process of making people appear to be naked in front of other people. At the end of the day I would end up in the men's wardrobe, sobbing."

The range of her work continued to grow throughout the 1950s and she garnered particular acclaim for her work on musicals ranging from Broadway's *Peter Pan* (she won two Tony Award nominations for her theater work) to the film versions of *South Pacific* and *The Music Man* (the latter required hiring no fewer than seventy costumers). So prodigious was the designer's talent that her drawings and textile collages were regularly exhibited in galleries and museums, leading to a Guggenheim Fellowship in 1962 and an appointment as curator of textiles at the Los Angeles County Museum of Art.

With her eye for detail and inherent sense of style, Jeakins moved easily between the gritty black-and-white world of preacher con men in *Elmer Gantry* (1960) and the Technicolor splash of the Marilyn Monroe vehicle *Let's Make Love*, in the process acquiring a sterling reputation that found her in demand from golden age Hollywood giants John Huston, William Wyler, and Robert Wise.

Responding well to their perfectionist demands, she felt most at home with the period clothes that required the attention to detail she loved to provide. "I'll let my imagination work for me, seeing a character as a person I might know. . . . I'll place swatches of color around the floor, colors for background and foreground, and all the while I'm sifting for a unifying theme. To me, all the world's like a Cezanne painting, brimming with color." If the film in question was set in an era when the clothes were all made with buttons, then every garment she designed would be detailed with buttons. Never mind that no one else would ever be able to see time-saving, less-expensive modern zippers inside the garments. Jeakins simply would not utilize any materials that did not qualify as period authentic.

Throughout her career, the designer's understated personal style and sense of design meshed beautifully with stars of vastly different temperaments, and her collaborators ranged from the earthy Ava Gardner in *Night of the Iguana*, to the insecure Marilyn Monroe in *Niagara*. It was an approach that worked equally well with her leading men, from golden age giants like Gary Cooper to modern star Richard Burton. Actors felt safe with Jeakins, and in the words of actor/producer John Houseman: "She very seldom tries to impose her own quirks or ideas on the actors. She works for the script rather than the flash." Asked for her own philosophy of design, she murmured: "The canvas is the script and the designer is the painter." Jeakins intuitively grasped the need for understated clothes in the midst of *The Sound of Music*'s fairy-tale proceeding; in the blunt assessment of Saul Chaplin: "Dorothy Jeakins avoided fancy dirndls."

But Jeakins's final design choices still lay in the future for one simple reason: Wise had yet to finalize all of the casting on the film. He compiled numerous lists and held conferences with both Zanuck and his designers, but the final decisions would all be his. Nowhere was his choice more important—or delicate—than in casting the role of Maria. Without the right star, one who could anchor the film in reality, all bets were off. Not to mention the loss of $8,000,000 and the resurrection of a major Hollywood studio. Everything hinged on finding a young actress who could sing, dance, act, look attractive, make the love story believable, read credibly while dressed as a nun, strike the viewer as a totally appropriate nanny cum instant stepmother of seven, and appeal straight across the board to man, woman, child, and, not so incidentally, the Hollywood brass funding the entire extravaganza. Where did that fantasy figure exist?

In the person of Julia Elizabeth Wells Andrews Walton.

8

JULIE DOOLITTLE POPPINS VON TRAPP

*"The Sound of Music was the actual naked Julie Andrews
on the screen. . . . I don't think she ever quite again did what
she did in that film. She seduced the world."*

—CHRISTOPHER PLUMMER

In retrospect, the selection of Julie Andrews to play the role of Maria seems both inevitable and also the only possible choice that ever could have been made. It may now look like the easiest of decisions, but in the summer of 1963 as casting discussions got under way, nothing could have been further from the truth.

When those casting possibilities for *The Sound of Music* began, Julie Andrews was a completely unknown quantity on film. *Mary Poppins* had yet to be released and her second film, *The Americanization of Emily,* was only then starting production. Julie Andrews may have scored three consecutive Broadway hits with *The Boy Friend, My Fair Lady,* and *Camelot,* but that didn't mean she'd register on film as well. The powers that be wanted a real movie star with box office clout to carry their multimillion-dollar production. The problem lay in the fact that every single star-powered name floated as a possibility presented problems, and large ones at that.

Leslie Caron—*the French accent. Maria would sound like she'd arrived
at the Nonnberg Abbey via a Parisian finishing school.*
Grace Kelly—*retired from the screen and living her own fairy-tale life
as Grace de Monaco, Palais de Monaco. Her glacial beauty hidden in
a nun's outfit? In a musical?*

Anne Bancroft—*a gifted actress, but who was going to believe the woman born Anna Italiano as a singing Austrian nun?*

Angie Dickinson—*as a nun? Singing about her favorite things to children?*

Carol Lawrence—*and Julie Andrews wasn't considered a big enough name?*

Shirley Jones—*been there (Oklahoma!), done that (Carousel).*

And then there was Doris Day: she could sing and she could act, and not so incidentally, she also happened to be the biggest movie star in the world at the time casting was first discussed. After *Pillow Talk* and *The Thrill of It All*, Doris Day spelled success, but the freckle-faced superstar also read onscreen as the original all-American, girl, no matter what the role. *Teacher's Pet, The Pajama Game, Pillow Talk*—every last independent, high-energy career woman she played was American.

Richard Rodgers was not pleased with the idea of Doris Day as Maria von Trapp, and as far back as the days of Wyler's involvement, the composer had made his feeling known in a dismissive aside to the recently signed screenwriter Ernest Lehman: "I suppose you'll want Doris Day." Ironically, such disparagement actually seemed to contradict the composer's very public enthusiasm for Day's singing; after hearing her recording of "I Have Dreamed" from *The King and I,* he sent her a note stating that her rendition constituted the single best recording of his song that he had ever heard.

But Rodgers was right, if a little harsh, in his assessment that Day was wrong for the role. It was Day's Svengali-like husband/manager Marty Melcher who desperately wanted Day to snag the plum role, but the decidedly low-key Doris knew she was wrong for it, stating so in typically forthright fashion: "I'm too American to play a nun from Austria."

It was Andrews that Rodgers wanted, his knowledge of her powerful talent dating back to the mid-1950s when she auditioned for a part in Rodgers and Hammerstein's new musical *Pipe Dream*. At the end of the young actress's audition, Rodgers dryly commented: "That was absolutely adequate," and after Andrews realized that the legendary composer was joking, the up-and-coming singer/actress and the king of Broadway composers discussed the status of her career. Upon learning that she had been auditioning for Lerner and Loewe's proposed musicalization of *Pygmalion,* Rodgers stated: "If you're asked to do that show, I'd advise you to do it. If not, let us know." Said Andrews in later years: "I think it was the most generous piece of advice he could have given."

When that musicalized *Pygmalion,* now entitled *My Fair Lady,* opened in March of 1956, Andrews became the toast of Broadway, and landed on the cover of *Life* magazine. One year later, Rodgers and Hammerstein created *Cinderella* with the actress in mind. (The part of the king was played by *Sound of Music* librettist Howard Lindsay.) The resulting live television spectacular, watched by an estimated 107 million people on the evening of March 31, 1957, was, in the words of R&H president Ted Chapin, "the greatest screen test ever for *The Sound of Music.* . . . When you look at her doing Cinderella you now think 'Oh, I can see the beginnings of Maria von Trapp in that performance.' "

Andrews earned both an Emmy nomination and the admiration of Rodgers and Hammerstein for her extraordinary voice and clean acting style. Such was the nature of their developing friendship that Rodgers could even chuckle about the actress's spoof of *The Sound of Music* in her fabled 1962 television special *Julie and Carol at Carnegie Hall.* That satire found Andrews and Carol Burnett playing members of the squeaky clean, large-in-number "Swiss Family Pratt." Laughingly referring to the special in later years, Andrews recalled: "We thought we were so clever—of course it has come back to haunt me!"

Richard Rodgers thought Julie Andrews would make a terrific Maria. More to the point, so did Robert Wise and Ernest Lehman. The problem? The studio balked. Julie Andrews wasn't a name. She might not even photograph well; yes, they realized that she radiated warmth and understanding, and yes, she had a pretty face with a cute, upturned nose. She even seemed to possess a great figure if you could ever see it underneath all of those Eliza Doolittle and Queen Guinevere robes. By any standards Julie Andrews was in fact a very attractive young woman. But she wasn't a classic Hollywood beauty in the mold of Lana Turner or Grace Kelly, and $8,000,000 was on the line. Broadway acclaim wasn't enough. Ethel Merman and Mary Martin may have been the first ladies of musical comedy on Broadway, but neither was a great beauty and neither ever translated their onstage appeal into anything beyond pedestrian film careers. Carol Channing, a star since 1949's *Gentlemen Prefer Blondes*, never registered in Hollywood, and as for that brash singing newcomer Barbra Streisand? Well, she was so strange-looking, who knew if she'd even get to Hollywood? What, the executives wanted to know, made Wise certain that Julie Andrews was so right for the role?

For starters, Wise considered it a plus that Andrews was not cut from the standard glamour-girl cloth. Her fresh scrubbed beauty seemed ideal for the role of a postulant turned mother of seven. With her polite, friendly, yet slightly reserved personality, Andrews struck Wise as someone who would, even after all of her years on Broadway, instinctively possess an understanding of how to tone down her gestures, voice, and movement for the camera. Her work on television had taught her that less is more when there was no second balcony to reach, a basic lesson that the likes of Ethel Merman never seemed to fully grasp in her film roles.

It was an understanding Andrews had honed from a lifetime spent performing. After her pianist mother Barbara had divorced her schoolteacher father Edward Wells when Julie was age four, the youngster began a new life with her mother and stepfather Ted Andrews. Ted Andrews proved to be difficult and an alcoholic, but he was also the man who discovered Andrews's extraordinary voice and realized that hers was an exceptional talent. With her freakishly large voice, Andrews had begun performing as a youngster, and by age twelve she had already appeared on the London stage. As word spread of the youngster's singing, she garnered increasing attention, and her appearances in variety shows led to participation in a Royal Command Performance. Crossing the Atlantic, she repeated her success in New York, achieving Broadway stardom at age eighteen in *The Boy Friend* (1954), and following up that triumph with *My Fair Lady* (Tony nomination and New York Drama Critics Award) and *Camelot* (Tony Award nomination).

Having spent years onstage honing an ability to make the fairy tale–like aspects of *The Boy Friend, My Fair Lady,* and *Camelot* both believable and worthy of audience sympathy, Andrews, in Wise's eyes, possessed just the right mix of empathy and authority. At age twenty-eight, her particular combination of singing and acting seemed especially suited for characters whose spunk and energy provided the audience with an all-important sense of comfort— both that the job at hand would be accomplished with style, and that she'd sweep them along for an enjoyable ride right up to the task's completion.

Some might possess doubts as to Andrews's appearance or acting range, but to Wise, no one with a scintilla of common sense could have the slightest doubt about her voice. Ah, that voice: a God-given gift spanning four octaves, characterized by a crystalline soprano sound enhanced by perfect diction. When, in musical comedy land, the emotions grew so powerful that the characters could only express their pent up feelings in song, that was when Julie Andrews shone brightest of all, using her voice not just to comfort, but to tease, cajole, make happy, and set free.

Like all true stars, her own personality seemed to inform every role she played. Whether inhabiting the cockney flower-seller Eliza Doolittle or the queenly Guinevere, the essential Julie Andrews was always on display. She couldn't submerge her own persona under the protective cloak of dazzling technique, but instead, looked for aspects of a character within herself, finding that facet of the character with which she could most identify. In her Broadway stardom, she appealed to both women and men; to women, she seemed a confidante, a girlfriend but never a rival, while to men Andrews exemplified the woman one could bring home to meet Mom, all efficiency and fun, an ideal wife, helpmate, and mother.

Did she possess sex appeal? Did that even matter if the character started out as a would-be nun? Well, yes. Maria von Trapp may have begun the story clad in a nun's habit, but she also had to be attractive enough to catch the eye of a widowed naval captain/war hero. Sex appeal mattered, even when playing Maria von Trapp. As nicely put by Sam Wasson in his bestselling *Fifth Avenue, 5 A.M.*: "Whether it's a man or woman, boy or girl, the screen holds up mirrors to its audience, reflecting the shoulds and should-nots of family, love, war, and gender—sometimes knowingly, sometimes not, but always with an eye on sex."

As it turned out, Julie Andrews did indeed radiate a tamped down but discernible sex appeal. On the Broadway stage she radiated an appeal light-years removed from the overt eroticism transmitted by Hollywood glamour girls such as Lana Turner and Rita Hayworth, but a sex appeal it remained nonetheless. There was, especially in *Camelot,* the sense of a smoldering passion, buried but ready to burst forth. (James Garner, a veteran leading man of three decades, has publicly stated that two of the sexiest women he ever played opposite were Julie Andrews and Doris Day, girls next door possessing understated but undeniable sex appeal.)

Voice, looks, acting ability, and buried sex appeal: Andrews had it all in Wise's eye. She just had yet to be glimpsed on film. Yes, *Cinderella* had reached over 100 million viewers, but that was television, a one-night-only in-your-living-room-blink-and-it's-all-gone confection. *The Sound of Music* was to be a three-hour high-priced roadshow reserved-seat attraction, no changing of the channels possible. Did Jack Warner know something when he refused to cast Julie in the film version of *My Fair Lady*? Just what would Julie Andrews look like onscreen and in living color? There was only one way to find out: on October 30, 1963, Wise arranged a trip to Disney Studios with Saul Chaplin and Ernest Lehman in order to view footage from the still-unreleased *Mary Poppins*.

Wise, Lehman, and Chaplin settled into their seats, the screening room lights dimmed, and magical nanny Mary Poppins appeared onscreen in the person of Julie Andrews. After precisely five minutes Wise turned to Chaplin and announced: "Let's go sign her right now, before anyone else beats us to it."

In William Wyler's recall, it was he who first thought of Julie Andrews: "I had seen her play in *My Fair Lady* and I was very impressed. I went over to the studio and met her on the set (of *Mary Poppins*). Walt showed me some rushes and she was signed." In Ernest Lehman's recollection, however, Wyler had first suggested Audrey Hepburn for the role of Maria, and claims that in his role as screenwriter, it was he who first thought of Julie Andrews. Whether Wyler, Wise, or Lehman first thought of Andrews, the bottom line was obvious in a flash to an old pro like Wise: Julie Andrews possessed a star's personality, one that could shine "right through the camera, on to the film, and out to the audience."

Even better, Wise and Chaplin both saw the similarities between Maria von Trapp and Mary Poppins: the Maria von Trapp found in *The Sound of Music* screenplay resembled a somewhat more realistic Mary Poppins. She's an actual person, not a nanny who flies in from the sky, but both characters possessed the same energetic, well-scrubbed, comforting personality, one filled with exuberance, enthusiasm, and in Maria's case, a noticeable innocence. (One never thinks of Mary Poppins as innocent. All knowing, yes. Innocent, never.) Maria may not have possessed Mary Poppins's magical powers, but she came pretty close: she captivates seven children, causes their father to fall in love and marry her, teaches the whole family how to sing together, and outwits the Nazis. She doesn't fly away with a magical umbrella at the end of the film, but she leads her charges over the Alps into freedom, and the ideas informing the two characters struck Wise and Chaplin as remarkably similar.

Andrews certainly was familiar with *The Sound of Music,* having seen Mary Martin in the Broadway production back in 1959, but in her own words "never dreamed" that she would be asked to star in the film. If she ruminated about the film version at all, her thoughts had not progressed much further than an expectation that Martin would be asked to repeat the role on film, never pausing to dwell on the fact that Martin would have been over fifty at the time of filming.

Was Julie Andrews interested? Absolutely. "Having done *The American-ization of Emily* between *Mary Poppins* and *The Sound of Music,* I hoped that would show I didn't only play nanny roles! I wouldn't have turned down the role of Maria for anything." Andrews knew a plum musical role when she saw one, but a stumbling block remained: 20th Century-Fox demanded that the actress sign a four-film deal. Now it was Andrews's turn to balk. Four features meant too many films and too many unknown scripts. Instead, after both sides agreed to a two-film contract, Julie Andrews signed to play Maria for a fee of $225,000, without any share of the profits. Ironically, once the contract was signed, the studio never directly told Wise that Andrews's deal had been completed. Instead, in a last gasp of old-style Hollywood publicity, Wise and Chaplin learned that their first-choice leading lady was now a part of *The Sound of Music* team by reading about it in Louella Parsons's gossip column while overseas on their scouting trip in November of 1963. Wise, after all, was merely an Academy Award–winning director, but Parsons was syndicated nationally. . . .

Wise knew that he had chosen the right actress when, at a December 1963 prefilming luncheon at the Fox studios, Andrews leaned over to her director and quietly asked, "Now what are we going to do to take all the schmaltz out of this?" Terming the story "too mush," Andrews was understandably concerned. Here was a story that seemed to combine both the Bible and *Cinderella* in one fell swoop, with more than a dollop of *Sleeping Beauty* thrown in for good measure. Wise's answer to his star reassured her instantly; he intended to keep the film visually spare in order to counterpoint both the sentiment inherent in the story and the romance of the music. The headline of an article that appeared in *Variety* shortly before the start of filming cut to the heart of the matter: "Bob Wise Will Curb Schmaltz." In the words of film historian Jeanine Basinger, who worked with Wise on the Board of the American Film Institute: "He was just the right man for the film. He was very smart, a good man—a kind man. He understood the emotion of the piece without being a Pollyanna about it. Moviegoers were becoming more cynical by the mid-sixties and he knew how to tread the line. It was a proven entity that moved people and, yes, it contained nuns and children, but it also contained a real, credible threat. He was the right man for the job."

Her deal concluded, Andrews went to work months before shooting began. At the considerable peak of her vocal beauty at the time of *Poppins* and *The Sound of Music*, she began her preparation for the film by studying the entire score with her singing teacher Lilian Stiles-Allen. It was Allen who advised Andrews: "You must see the picture clearly and take the public into your confidence, so that they will see that same picture." The advice took hold: one need only listen to Andrews's controlled yet vocally exuberant take on the title song to realize that she conveys the entire essence and intent of the film even without the aid of the eye-popping scenery.

Most notably of all, however, Julie Andrews possessed the gift that only the truly great possess: even with all of the preparation, the studying of the script, and the careful analysis of the score with Stiles-Allen, she made it all look effortless. In her hands, breaking into song, dancing across a set, hitting marks, and lip-synching to a playback while trying to convey the essence of her character appeared as natural as breathing. The effort never showed, which ironically led people to assume that none of the required tasks were particularly difficult. Like Fred Astaire taking flight with devil-may-care ease, she made the difficult appear spontaneous, as if she were experiencing these musical emotions for the very first time.

Andrews's musical comfort level increased when, at her request, Saul Chaplin hired Irwin Kostal, with whom he had worked on *West Side Story,* as musical director. (Kostal's first ever film, *West Side Story,* had won him an Oscar.) Having worked closely with Andrews on both the television special *Julie and Carol at Carnegie Hall* as well as *Mary Poppins,* Kostal knew Andrews's voice inside and out, and inherently understood her preferred tempos and vocal placement. It would be Kostal's considerable task to orchestrate the Rodgers and Hammerstein songs and provide all of the film's underscoring, while scrupulously adhering to the contractual provision that the underscoring only utilize variations of Rodgers's original music. Recollecting the recording of the score under Kostal's supervision, Andrews smiled. "That seventy-piece orchestra. The sound was so thrilling and uplifting and enormous. There is very little else that is as exciting as that."

To complete the musical team, Chaplin and Kostal immediately hired another *West Side Story* alum, Bobby Tucker, as vocal coach. It would now fall

upon Tucker to shape the singing of the seven inexperienced youngsters portraying the von Trapp children, boys and girls who, aside from Julie Andrews,
carried the heaviest load of singing chores.

The musical triumverate of Chaplin, Kostal, and Tucker set to work with
one goal in mind: frame Julie Andrews in the best possible musical spotlight.
The musical success of *The Sound of Music* would rise or fall on Andrews's
shoulders, and providing her with simpatico arrangements and orchestrations
would go a long way toward achieving musical success. All three men possessed the highest regard for their star's musical abilities, with Chaplin placing Andrews's gifts on the same level of those of his MGM friend and
collaborator Judy Garland. Garland's voice throbbed with emotion, Andrews's
with an unearthly clarity; her voice seemed to belong in a cathedral as much
as a Broadway theater or Hollywood soundstage, but what the two women
shared, in Chaplin's view, was an uncanny ability to "learn music instantly,
as if by magic. They both made songs sound better than you imagined they
could."

To everyone's immense satisfaction, the casting of Maria had been solved,
but another problem acquired increasing urgency. Who was going to play Captain Georg von Trapp? If Andrews possessed no box office clout, then the
studio definitely wanted a name actor in the role of the captain, but what star
was going to stand around as nothing more than a handsome foil for the leading lady? Who could sing, act, and persuade audiences that he was worthy of
the saintly Maria? As it turned out, the answer was an actor who was not yet
a star—and one who wanted absolutely nothing to do with *The Sound of
Music.*

9.

CAPTAIN GEORG VON TRAPP

"I agree with W. C. Fields: children are fine as long as they're cooked."
—CHRISTOPHER PLUMMER, *THE SOUND OF
MUSIC* 40TH ANNIVERSARY EDITION

As time began to run short, Robert Wise rifled continuously through his roster of A-list actors. Surely one of them would be interested in a high-profile major Hollywood musical. But the problem didn't just lie with the actors' mixed feelings about the role of the captain. For all of their talents, each one of the proposed stars popped a caution flag in Wise's mind:

Rex Harrison—My Fair Lady *had proved he worked well with Julie, but was he too old?*

David Niven—*could he sing? Was he too British?*

Richard Burton—*great with Julie in* Camelot, *but of late he seemed more than a little preoccupied with Elizabeth Taylor.*

Yul Brynner—*he certainly wanted the role but the last thing he seemed like was an Austrian sea captain.*

Sean Connery—*James Bond romancing a singing nun?*

Peter Finch—*hmm . . . a definite contender in Wise's mind. Handsome, a fine actor—but not available.*

Bing Crosby—*a name, to be certain, but who was going to believe Bing as an Austrian naval captain? The singing would be a breeze, but Bing read onscreen as so resolutely American that his presence could throw the movie further off base than the casting of Doris Day as Maria. (Stated director Wise: "I felt we must go on the basis of the story and not bastardize it with just big names—say Bing Crosby and Kate*

*Smith." Which leads to the intriguing question: what role, pray tell,
would Kate Smith have played? The Mother Superior?)*

No, none of the names suited Wise, and he decided to screen test British
stage actor Keith Michel, whose test delivered the goods in spades. Onscreen,
the well-trained actor revealed a warm, masculine presence, one nicely suited
to the role of a stern yet loving father. In the end, however, Michel's screen
test registers like the fascinating screen test Robert De Niro underwent for
the role of Sonny in *The Godfather*: the actor hits all the right notes, fills the
frame nicely, and yet somehow doesn't fit the character closely enough. Talented though he was, Michel wasn't quite right, although certainly closer to
the role than Walter Matthau, whose January 1964 test landed wide of the
mark. No, Wise's first choice remained, as it had throughout the casting process, the highly respected but then relatively unknown stage actor Christopher Plummer. Said Wise: "I just knew he would give it an edge, a bit of
darkness."

Portraying a singing naval captain was definitely not a part of Plummer's
career game plan, but then again, he had never really counted on being an
actor. The young Plummer had envisioned a career as a concert pianist in his
native Canada, but the need for constant practice and the solitary nature of
the pianist's life did not suit his temperament, and he began casting about for
an alternative career. In the end he rationalized a change to theater with a
quick bit of self-analysis: "I'm a good mimic. I might as well go into the theater. I wasn't good at anything else, so in I went. . . . Sometimes being an actor
can be boring, but with one challenging bit it can be a joy for me and I wouldn't
trade it."

The switch in career proved propitious; possessed of good looks and a mel-
lifluous speaking voice, Plummer held a natural ability to submerge himself
in whatever character he was playing, After joining the Canadian Repertory
Company in 1948, he appeared in some seventy-five roles over the years, his
credits ranging from Synge's *The Playboy of the Western World* to Maugham's
The Constant Wife. He earned a Tony nomination for his role in Archibald
MacLeish's Pulitzer Prize–winning *J.B.* and scored a second major success
on Broadway in *The Royal Hunt of the Sun*. Roles in the Shakespearean canon
ranged from history plays (*Henry IV*) to the comedies (*Much Ado About Nothing*) and back again (*Henry V*).

The stage remained Plummer's focus, and by the time *The Sound of Music* began gearing up for production, he had appeared in only three films: *Stage Struck* (1958), *Wind Across the Everglades* (1958), and the recently concluded *The Fall of the Roman Empire* (1964). His scant movie experience didn't matter to Wise, who thought the actor would bring just the right mixture of gravitas, humor, and sex appeal to the role. The real problem remained with Plummer: of course it was flattering to be the first choice of any director, let alone the Academy Award–winning Robert Wise, but top choice or not, Plummer had little or no interest in the role. Play a man who resembled nothing so much as a stick figure in an operetta? Forget it.

Undaunted by the actor's recalcitrance, Wise remained so convinced that Plummer was right for the part that on the advice of the actor's agent, Kurt Friends—"If you fly over to London I think you can talk him into doing it"—he traveled to England in order to convince Plummer in person. It wasn't just the actor Wise would be sweet talking; the director also had to convince the studio that the relatively unknown Plummer was not only the right actor for the role, but also could look old enough to play the captain in realistic fashion. Born in 1929, Plummer was only six years older than Julie Andrews. Could he convince as a significantly older man who had a sixteen-year-old daughter?

It wasn't that Plummer was merely indifferent to the role. He actively disliked the stolid, one-dimensional nature of the captain. Ironically, Plummer recalled that Mary Martin had spoken to him about the possibility of playing Captain von Trapp on Broadway, but the idea proved a nonstarter: this supposedly older captain with seven children was in reality sixteen years younger than Martin, a state of affairs hardly conducive to the musical's archetypal story of a young girl falling in love with an older man.

As it was, when singer Theodore Bikel was cast as Georg for the stage production, he brought an unexpected, extra layer of actual experience to the proceedings; his own family had fled Austria after the Anschluss in 1938. During the run of the show, Bikel met Maria von Trapp, and although, unlike Martin, he did not become a good friend, he nonetheless managed to read the loving but overpowering Maria perfectly, dubbing her "a tyrannical saint."

Begrudgingly, Plummer met with Wise for an hour at the Connaught Hotel in London, with the director's straightforward approach managing to allay some, if not most, of Plummer's doubts. Yes, Wise admitted, the role was a far cry from playing Shakespeare and Molière. Yes, he knew that Plummer had just played Hamlet in a BBC production actually taped at Elsinore Castle. Wise would never claim that the role of Captain von Trapp rivaled Hamlet, and he certainly understood why the actor found the captain to be a bit of a one-dimensional bore. Changes, he reassured the actor, could be made to the screenplay. Plummer began to soften, but quickly balked when Wise broached the subject of a test. He'd allow his hair to be highlighted with streaks of gray in order to appear older, and still photos could be shot for the studio's approval, but beyond that, nothing.

Wise kept talking. Plummer respected the director's Oscar-winning track record and personal style ("Bob was the last of the gentlemen directors. He had a wonderful bedside manner"), and in strictly practical terms he realized that the film could increase his profile: "I love the stage but movies are good to spread one's name around a bit." Plummer weakened. It would, after all, be the leading role in a major Hollywood film. Finally, after the Fox executives responded favorably to the still photos of a gray-templed Plummer, the actor grudgingly acquiesced. Acquiesced, that is, under one condition: he wanted to work with screenwriter Ernest Lehman on injecting some depth to the role of the captain. Ten days after the announcement of his signing, Plummer outlined his goals in a letter to Wise: "As long as von Trapp remains extremely severe, clipped in speech, and relentless throughout the major part of the film—then, and only then, can the sentimental scenes, when they come, be played to their fullest without embarrassment." Georg von Trapp might never be mistaken for Henry V, but if Plummer had anything to say about it, and he did have plenty to say, the captain would prove to be a lot more than a cardboard leading man.

It may well be that the biggest of Ernest Lehman's substantial contributions to the film lay in putting aside his ego and working on the script with Plummer, because once the actor had signed his contract, it was the screenwriter more than anyone else who brought Plummer around to a grudging acceptance of his role in the film. Wanting to invest the captain with a sense of humor and a backbone, Plummer met with Lehman over four consecutive days in the screenwriter's office, the Academy Award–nominated screenwriter willing to examine every single line of the captain's with the actor.

Particular attention was paid to deepening the relationship between the captain and Baroness Elsa Schraeder, and truth be told, Plummer got a kick out of working with the esteemed screenwriter. Given his vivid imagination, and childhood memories formed by having watched many golden age Hollywood classics, Plummer had always fostered a yen for working in a smoke-filled room, hammering out a script with a hard-boiled writer by his side. His work with Lehman allowed Plummer to play *The Front Page* in real life, his Hollywood-influenced dream marred only slightly by Lehman's status as a nonsmoker.

Far from resenting Plummer's heavy input, Lehman welcomed the actor's thoughts, praising Plummer's intelligence and stating, "This guy was insisting that I be a good writer so he came off better than before. And he helped me!" Wise agreed: "Ernie said many times how much Chris contributed to the character." Plummer, in turn, grew into a fan of the screenwriter: "Ernie Lehman listened to my suggestions. He gave me some humor, darkness, irony. He was an enormous help. I just loved Ernie."

It was Plummer who stressed that given Georg von Trapp's position as captain in the Austrian Navy, he must have been sophisticated, well off, and cultured—a far more complex man than existed in Lehman's first draft. To Plummer's way of thinking, the captain was dissatisfied with his life; he was a widower, emotionally cut off from his children, and, given the post–World War I boundaries that had made Austria a landlocked country, a man without a profession. It was this state of affairs, Plummer felt, that caused the captain to "camouflage with a sharp mind and a sardonic wit . . . He must not appear, in any way, a pushover."

Plummer wanted the captain to have a definite, if droll, sense of humor— "The baroness had too much humor to have married a dull man"—but with typical cheek he also spoke of having met a nephew of the von Trapps who said his uncle was "the most boring man I ever met!" Condescending about the material Plummer was, but he was also sharp, savvy, and intelligent, and by pushing Lehman he helped transform the captain into a man whose ironic humor and flintiness seemed emblematic of a good man who, after enduring the pain of losing his wife, bottled up all of his emotions. "It was much more of a story than in the play—more of a relationship. In the play Mary Martin sang twenty-five songs and Theodore Bikel, who played the part beautifully and plays the guitar like a dream, had very little to say. The minute he finished Mary came on and sang another twenty-five songs." (Plummer proved less sharp in his analysis of the score, writing Wise: "I hope something can be done about 'Edelweiss' since it is very boring, schmaltzy, and trite. . . .")

Plummer grasped that the captain must appear to be at least as strong as Maria, an equal partner worthy of Fraulein Maria's love. The erudite actor went so far as to provide Lehman with an unexpected but fascinating frame of reference: "I suggested to him that he should think of the scene in *Dorian Gray* where Dorian Gray is saying good-bye to his old friend the Duchess. 'If you look at that and try to make *The Sound of Music* as sophisticated as that, I will kiss you forever.' " The resulting screenplay may not exactly bring Dorian Gray to mind, but Plummer did feel that Lehman succeeded in strengthening the captain's edge and sophistication. Genuinely grateful for Lehman's additional work, he openly expressed his thanks—presumably without the kiss.

In the end, Lehman, Plummer, and Wise all understood that while everyone involved wanted to cut down on the film's inherent sentimentality, the easy solution of writing the captain as an overt cynic would simply tilt the film out of balance in the opposite direction. Said Plummer: "We were in the middle—on that rope bridge. I wanted to be cynical as hell. Bob Wise kept saying, 'No—you've got to be straight with it. C'mon—stop that nonsense.' He was right."

Plummer was, if not happy, at least mollified. Julie Andrews was learning the score. Now about those seven children . . .

10

A Captain with Seven Children: What's So Fearsome About That?

⌇

The Sound of Music represented a multimillion-dollar production centering on Julie Andrews's onscreen relationship with seven children, all of whom had to sing, dance, act, and try to keep up with Andrews herself. These kids had to have the skill levels of professionals yet simultaneously fulfill Robert Wise's strictest tenet: absolutely no kids who reeked of professional showbiz.

The children had to be natural—but with incredible skills. And if they didn't seem credible as a member of a real-life family, then their skills didn't matter—out they'd go. Said Wise: "I selected those children very painstakingly. They had to be the right age, with enough basic family similarities."

Beginning in December of 1963, Wise plunged into two months of auditions for the roles of the seven von Trapp children. By the time auditions were finished, he had read or filmed more than two hundred children in London, New York, and Los Angeles. As it turned out, after two continents' worth of auditions encompassing hundreds of hours, all but one of the children—Nicholas Hammond—was cast right in Wise's backyard of Los Angeles.

Although more than two hundred children were in fact tested for their singing and dancing abilities, the music remained far from Wise's top concern: "I didn't worry so much about the singing—we could always dub that in." As it turned out, although the seven children did perform their own vocals, musical supervisor Irwin Kostal utilized the additional voices of seven children and five adults during recording sessions in order to achieve a more full-bodied sound. Ultimately, the only time the seven onscreen children sang without additional background vocals occurred when they try to sing "The Sound of Music" to cheer themselves up after Maria has left.

Perhaps the biggest casting problem with the children lay in finding the right young woman to play Liesl, the eldest of the onscreen children. Based upon Agathe von Trapp, the character of sixteen-year-old Liesl required an actress who was pretty, believably naive as a girl on the verge of womanhood, and fully capable of singing and dancing "Sixteen Going on Seventeen," the only nonensemble number written for any of the children.

The young women who passed the first round of auditions now screen tested:

Lesley Ann Warren—*talented, but not exactly naive.*

Teri Garr—*charming, if relatively inexperienced, but a bit shaky in the musical sections.*

Shelley Fabares—*a name, thanks to her starring role on* The Donna Reed Show, *and the owner of a hit single recording of "Johnny Angel." Possible, but not quite right on the money.*

Sharon Tate—*beautiful and sweet, but as an innocent pre–World War II Austrian maiden?*

Mia Farrow—*then on the threshold of great fame for her role in television's* Peyton Place *and just two years short of tabloid notoriety as the third, and thirty-years-younger, Mrs. Frank Sinatra. With her slightly ethereal aura and blond good looks, Farrow auditioned well and impressed Wise enough to read for the role three times. Her indeterminate accent actually seemed right for the role, but her singing, although not off pitch, seemed wan, lacking in the exuberance one associates with a naive sixteen-year-old in a Rodgers and Hammerstein musical.*

No one seemed exactly right and deadlines were looming. With none of the name actresses proving satisfactory, attention shifted to the unknown young women eager for the role. Deluged with names, Wise could not test everyone. Unknown was fine, but the line had to be drawn. Who, the powers-to-be wondered, was this Charmian Farnon? For that matter, what kind of name was that?

At the time she was called in to test, Charmian Farnon was working in a doctor's office while majoring in speech therapy at California's San Fernando Valley State College. Although she possessed no formal training as either a singer or dancer, her screen test revealed a winsome presence, and more important, a face the camera loved. With a nice figure and striking blue eyes that caught the light, she riveted attention. Could she act?

She had never acted professionally, but, along with her sister, had in fact been pushed into performing by her mother. Writing about her mother in her 2000 autobiography *Forever Liesl,* Charmian Carr offered a loving but clear-eyed view of a mother who sounds like the prototype for the grasping stage mother Mama Rose in *Gypsy.* "We ultimately realized that it was not our success that our mother desired, it was applause for herself." Having also dealt with a father who had deserted the family, Carr had grown up quickly out of necessity, yet remarkably enough, managed to retain an appealing sense of optimism and good cheer.

Wise liked Carr looks, charm, and screen test, but possessed one real reservation: her age. Although Carr had purposefully not stated her actual age of twenty-one during her audition, Wise could tell that she was older than sixteen, and remained concerned about her credibility as a teenager on the brink of her first love. The director wavered, but associate producer Chaplin, who had immediately gravitated toward casting Carr, continued to champion her case. It was Carr's genuine talent for singing and dancing that won Chaplin over (choreographer Dee Dee Wood similarly termed her a "solid professional" as singer, dancer, and actress), and Wise agreed to Carr's casting with one proviso: finding her surname of Farnon to be less than suitable, he asked her to change her last name to Carr. The idea struck an instant chord with the twenty-one-year-old: "Changing my last name would be a way to reinvent myself, to move past my father." The last of the children to be cast, Carr was hired without a contract in place: "They felt my eyes were too blue so they had to see me on film." Not signing her contract until March of 1964, she only began working with her fellow castmates after two weeks of rehearsals had already taken place. Recollected Duane Chase at a fortieth anniversary reunion: "Every day at rehearsal there was a different Liesl until Charmian showed up!"

Friedrich: the second oldest of the von Trapp children. Based on Rupert, the oldest of the seven von Trapp children from Georg's first marriage.

Fourteen years old, the oldest son, and desperate for his father's approval, trying to act grown up but still very much an adolescent.

The young men Wise auditioned seemed either hopelessly stage bound, projecting for the nonexistent second balcony, or too worldly to play a teenager in pre–World War II Austria. Just as the director wavered, in walked thirteen-year-old Nicholas Hammond, freshly arrived in New York City from his home in Virginia. With his arm in a cast (the result of a skiing accident), and faced with the sight of coolly professional blond Friedrich wannabes waiting to audition, Hammond figured he had little chance for the role. Feeling absolutely no pressure, he delivered a winning, natural reading. With a scant two previous credits on his résumé—one episode of the television series *The Defenders,* and a role in the 1963 film *Lord of the Flies*—Hammond fit Wise's demand for unstudied child actors. He could carry a tune, but best of all, could do so without show business bravado. Sold. Contract signed: February 14, 1964.

Louisa: the second oldest von Trapp daughter, modeled upon Georg and Agathe's daughter Maria. Wise and Chaplin could not find the right combination of charm and ease of manner until fourteen-year-old Heather Menzies arrived for her audition. She may have possessed scant experience, but her low-key personality and self-possession helped her win Wise's attention. Just how low-key a personality? Asked by a friend what movie she was testing for, she replied that she wasn't sure, but she did know that "it was something about musical instruments starring Julie Harris and it was going to be filmed in Australia."

Since Wise desired a mix of attitudes, heights, and hair colors like that found in a real family, Menzies also provided Wise with his token Aryan blonde. The director wanted to avoid the stereotypical operetta family of towheads, but one blond girl would do quite nicely. Menzies was cast to play the thirteen-year-old Louisa.

Brigitta: A direct young girl, third oldest of the von Trapp girls and decidedly the most outspoken. Addressing new governess Maria, Brigitta forthrightly states: "That's the ugliest dress I've ever seen."

Perhaps this part required a bit of actual experience—which arrived in the form of eleven-year-old English-born Angela Cartwright. Already a veteran of a Robert Wise production, thanks to her uncredited bit in the director's 1956 film *Somebody Up There Likes Me*, she had followed up her screen debut with appearances on seven television series, the most notable of which was her run from 1957 to 1964 as Danny Thomas's daughter on *Make Room for Daddy*.

While wearing a blond wig, the by-now thoroughly Americanized Cartwright actually first tested for the role of Louisa, but both Wise and Angela herself felt that she delivered a better, more relaxed audition in her natural brunette state as Brigitta. Although the only seasoned actor among the seven children, Cartwright exhibited none of the precocious style that would have irreparably harmed the sense of onscreen family. She remained, in Wise's view: "Lovely to work with."

Kurt: The younger of the two von Trapp sons and very much still a boy, proudly announcing to new governess Maria: "I'm Kurt and I'm incorrigible." The actor playing Kurt had to come across onscreen as "all boy" but still possess a tangible remnant of childhood gentleness. When thirteen-year-old Duane Chase came in to audition for the role, his experience was limited to a handful of commercials, the most notable of which had been a print ad for pancake batter. It was Chase's wide-open grin of delight at the prospect of eating pancakes that had actually captured Wise's attention. Hooked by that look of unadulterated boyhood exuberance, Wise auditioned Chase and found his persona on camera to be as natural as it had appeared to be in print. In Chase's recollection, Wise narrowed down the casting possibilities for the children to two different groups of seven. He would look over the lineup and then combine actors from the two different lines—all in order to arrive at a mix of looks and styles that resembled that of a real family.

Once Wise determined that Chase could carry a tune, his casting was assured, and the role was offered to him on February 19, 1964. Never one to waste a bit of business, Wise memorably featured Chase's ear-to-ear pancake grin in a through-the-bed-frame shot during "My Favorite Things."

Marta: Second youngest of the children. She needed to come across onscreen as a sweet little girl, shy, and very much in need of a mother. Like Duane Chase, when seven-year-old Debbie Turner came in to audition for Wise, her scant résumé featured only a sprinkling of commercials. The director, however, found himself very taken with Turner's gentle manner, one that made her a natural as the first of the von Trapp children to embrace Maria.

Gretl: The youngest of the von Trapp children, and the biggest potential trap for overacting. An "aww, how cute" audience favorite of a character, the role required a five-year-old who could sing, dance, act natural, take direction impeccably, and appear blithely unaware of the camera. Where was this 1964 version of Shirley Temple? Wise needed to look no further than Kym Karath.

Born in 1958, five-year-old Karath already possessed three professional credits by the time she walked in to audition for Wise and Saul Chaplin: a bit in the Henry Fonda/Maureen O'Hara *Spencer's Mountain*, a very small part in the Jack Lemmon vehicle *Good Neighbor Sam*, and most noticeably of all, a winning, naturalistic turn as Doris Day and James Garner's youngest child in the Larry Gelbart penned comedy *The Thrill of It All*. (Splashing in the bathtub, she firmly stated, "Mommy—I don't want that shampoo—it smells like the cracks in the playground. I want my hair to smell like my piano teacher's hair!")

Karath's hilarious audition for *The Sound of Music* played out like that of a good-natured version of the precocious Baby June in *Gypsy*. In walked the preternaturally self-assured youngster—"five going on twenty-five" in Karath's own words—at which point she addressed the august-looking Wise and Chaplin with a self-assured: "Good afternoon, gentlemen." The scene became even more humorous when, upon being asked what she was going to sing, she replied that she knew all of the songs in the musical and would now sing "Sixteen Going on Seventeen." Saul Chaplin later admitted to being nonplussed by the self-possessed Karath, but Wise was disarmed, figuring that her professionalism would prove an asset in a role requiring strenuous singing and movement. Amused by her youthful self-confidence, he added: "If I had not hired her as my little actress, I would have hired her as my secretary."

The five-year-old's hilarious antics weren't confined just to the audition room or *The Sound of Music* set. In later years she recalled that after her sister appeared in the 1962 film version of *Gypsy*, the family priest had come to the Karath house, only to have the very young Kym sing "Let Me Entertain You," Gypsy Rose Lee's signature striptease in the show. If a child can be said to be capable of registering as simultaneously savvy and innocent, the young Karath represented ground zero of that personality mix. (When Kym's mother was approached about having Kym appear in *Spencer's Mountain*, she referred the casting director to Kym, whose measured response immediately established her priorities: "If it doesn't take too long because I have a lot of dolls to take care of and I'm very busy.")

Casting of the children was now complete, but the biggest stylistic question of all remained: except for Cartwright, all the children were Americans, so with what accent were these supposedly German-speaking Austrian youngsters supposed to speak? Rationalizing that Julie Andrews spoke with a pronounced British accent, and that the Canadian-born Plummer spoke with a hint of the British Isles in his tone, Wise made the decision to have all seven children speak with a mid-Atlantic accent. Guided by voice coach Pamela Danova, the children set to work learning their lines with just enough of an English accent to make the vocal style consistent among everyone, children and adults alike.

With the children's roles now cast, Wise turned his attention to the supporting adult roles. He possessed ideas and short lists for each of the secondary yet plum roles: Max, Frau Schmidt, Rolfe, Franz, and especially the Mother Superior. But highest on his priority list: casting Baroness Elsa von Schraeder. Arch, sophisticated, the closest thing to a villainess, but one with a touch of vulnerability, the Baroness's combination of character traits made for a very long list of possible actresses. Robert Wise briefly considered each name before him, but his own list began and ended with just one name: Eleanor Parker.

11.

COMPLETING THE CAST

*"I loved Eleanor Parker. So extraordinarily
beautiful. And such a sweetie."*
—CHRISTOPHER PLUMMER

BARONESS ELSA The trick in casting the role of Elsa lay in finding a beautiful actress who also possessed the acting chops capable of turning the brittle-seeming baroness into a flesh and blood, understandable woman. Without a credible rival to Maria for the captain's affections, the upstairs/downstairs conflict between the baroness and Maria could easily collapse, and along with it, the appealing *Downton Abbey*–like mix of social status and unabashed romance.

Maria, of course, would win the battle; after all she had the children, not to mention the nuns and God himself on her side. The fun would lie in the contrast between Maria's natural quality and the baroness's gilded hauteur, with the Baronesss possessing an aristocratic air that would work only if the actress portraying Elsa allowed the audience to glimpse the woman beneath the veneer. While the audience would find the baroness unworthy of the captain's affections—she doesn't like children!—she needed to be portrayed with a depth sufficient to supply the audience with a genuine rooting interest.

On the list of possible actresses compiled by Wise and casting director Lee Wallace:

Irene Worth—*terrific stage actress but not a major player in the film world.*
Cyd Charisse—*beautiful, but a dancer.*

Dana Wynter—*solid, attractive, but not a star.*

Grace Kelly—*she'd make the movie an event. Decidedly unavailable.*

Eva Marie Saint—*beautiful, talented, and very American.*

Viveca Lindfors—*fine actress but not a name.*

Eva Gabor—*European, but did people still consider her an actress or just a perpetual guest on Merv Griffin's television talk show?*

No to all of them. It was Eleanor Parker who remained Wise's first choice for the role from start to finish.

A great beauty in her younger days, Parker still exuded a highly attractive, strikingly self-composed presence onscreen, and she had worked very happily with Wise in his 1950 female-centric melodrama *Three Secrets*. Wise knew that Parker's genuine vulnerability would grant the baroness actual dimension, as well as an unexpected touch of sympathy; in his own words, Parker "came to mind right away. I always liked and respected her for her beauty, the range of her acting ability. We talked about some other people but Eleanor turned out to be the right choice." Eager to work once again with Wise, the three-time Oscar nominee—*Caged* (1950), *Detective Story* (1951), and *Interrupted Melody* (1955)—happily signed on.

THE MOTHER ABBESS In casting parlance, the role of the wise, all-accepting Mother Abbess represented a plumb role for a "woman of a certain age" and the preliminary casting choices centered upon three well-known, highly acclaimed actresses:

Irene Dunne—*a five-time Academy Award nominee with an extraordinary list of credits ranging from comedy* (Theodora Goes Wild) *to drama* (Cimarron) *to musicals* (Roberta, Show Boat), *the versatile Dunne could handle any genre. She was, to boot, a devout Catholic who was a daily communicant, but she had stopped acting in 1962 and although Wise was interested, he wavered. Would she really come out of retirement? Was she the very best choice for the role?*

Jeannette MacDonald—*Hollywood's iron butterfly, a singer with a voice tailor-made for operetta and a far better actress than usually acknowledged, MacDonald, unfortunately, was already in failing health and her possible casting never moved beyond the discussion stage. She died two months before the release of* Sound of Music.

Edith Evans—*arguably the finest, most versatile stage actress of her generation, Evans had also scored on film in roles ranging from* Look Back in Anger *to* The Nun's Story, *and she had nabbed an Academy Award nomination for her turn in* Tom Jones. *The stumbling block? She couldn't sing.*

With the three leading candidates unavailable or unsuited for the role, and after testing Gale Sondergaard, Wise heeded a friend's suggestion that he consider Peggy Wood. Wood had sung on Broadway and had, in fact, been offered the role of the Mother Abbess in the Broadway production of the musical. She had turned down the part, not feeling up to the vocal demands required by the theatrical schedule of eight performances per week. Her own witty take on the Broadway requirements: "Getting my voice back in shape and performing eight times a week? It's a nun's life!"

Wise sensed that Wood's personal warmth would lend the Mother Abbess the air of a wise older woman, rather than that of a forbidding remote drillmaster. Most famous for her portrayal of matriarch Marta Hansen in television's *Mama*, Wood had never worked with Wise, but at their very first meeting, the director was immediately won over by her personal appeal and charm: "I looked up her background and met with her in New York and fell in love with her . . . one of the best bits of casting on the film. Very, very warm."

Wood voiced her concerns over the singing requirements, and reassured by Wise that she could be dubbed if necessary, she enthusiastically signed on for the role. As it turned out, as the time for prerecording approached, the actress still felt that her voice was not in top shape, and the Mother Abbess's rendition of "Climb Ev'ry Mountain" was ultimately dubbed by Margery McKay, wife of rehearsal pianist Harper McKay.

MAX DETWEILER If, in traditional musical plays, the romantic leads (in this case Maria and the captain) are supported by a more overtly comic secondary couple, then in *The Sound of Music* those supporting roles were appropriated by Baroness Elsa and her humorously cynical friend, the impresario Max Detweiler. Who would be the right match for the beautiful, skilled

Eleanor Parker? Who possessed the right blend of humor and sangfroid? Wise had an inspired idea—Noel Coward.

Playwright, composer, lyricist, actor, producer, director—Coward's theatrical range seemed virtually limitless, and his clipped, arch delivery seemed tailor-made for Max's cynical, witty lines: "I love rich people and I love how I live when I'm staying with them."

Ironically, Coward's diary entries from five years earlier reveal "The Master's" shrewd assessment of the Broadway production starring his friend and former costar Mary Martin; although he considered the play saccharine and too much like a fairy tale, he admired Rodgers's music and found the entire production possessed of a "professionalism" far beyond anything else he had seen on Broadway that season.

Perhaps as a result of Coward's unceasingly busy schedule, negotiations were never seriously pursued, and Wise moved down his list to another interesting and off-beat choice, pianist/comic Victor Borge. Borge had never acted in a movie before, but the Danish-born pianist was the right age for the role, and with his European show business background, understood the world of Max Detweiler. Borge, however, was used to his concert hall/television stardom, and his salary demands proved so excessive that negotiations never moved forward.

Louis Nye? A familiar face from appearances on television sitcoms ranging from *Make Room for Daddy* to *The Beverly Hillbillies*, Nye had, in his own words, begun in radio voicing the roles of "rotten Nazis and emotional juveniles." The problem, however, lay in the fact that he remained untested as a film actor, his work onscreen consisting of brief roles in *Who's Been Sleeping in My Bed?* and *Good Neighbor Sam.*

Uneasy with Nye's lack of experience, Wise focused his search on Richard Haydn, the British-born actor who had gained fame on the radio as Edwin Carp, self-proclaimed "poet and fish expert." Possessed of a deliberate, overly enunciated manner of speaking, and the veteran of dozens of films ranging from 1945's *And Then There Were None* to *Forever Amber* (1947) and *Please Don't Eat the Daisies* (1960), Haydn's bemused attitude seemed tailor-made for the ironic, self-possessed Max.

Director Wise did not know Haydn but had seen his work, and felt certain that the actor could bring a welcome note of light cynicism to the proceedings. Haydn accepted the offer quickly, and his casting proved propitious, not only for the acerbic wit he brought to the film, but also for his friendly on-set demeanor. He proved instantly popular with the seven children, all of whom gravitated toward his unstudied kindness. Such was the easygoing bond formed between the actor and all seven children that ultimately all of them simply referred to him as "Herr Dad." He also quickly endeared himself to both Andrews and Plummer, both of whom relished his often risqué show business stories, with Andrews in particular enjoying Haydn's warmth and humor: "I'd be exhausted and feeling a little sad. He'd make me laugh on purpose coming home in the car—just to make me feel better."

SISTER BERTHE—PORTIA NELSON The role of Sister Berthe may not have been a large one, but Wise knew it would prove to be a memorable one, the character's wit and sour disposition making her the most noticeable of the nuns aside from the Mother Abbess. When Portia Nelson was suggested to Wise for the role, he was unaware of her work, but after a bit of investigation, quickly concluded that she would bring just the right touch of tart relief to the sticky proceedings.

The first person ever to sing the soon-to-be-standard "In Other Words" (forever known as "Fly Me to the Moon"), Nelson went on to compose "Make a Rainbow" for the television special *Debbie Reynolds and the Sound of Children,* and that sweet anthem was sung at President Clinton's first inauguration in 1992. A more typical composition, however, was her cabaret standard "Confessions of a New Yorker," in which the singer mock complains of being in "Hate/Love with New York"—a tough, wry lyric that reads and sounds exactly like a song Sister Berthe would sing if she ever decided to enter the world of New York City cabaret. Nelson's dry quality, combined with Broadway acting credentials in such musicals as 1954's *The Golden Apple*, won her the role.

SISTER SOPHIA—MARNI NIXON *The Sound of Music* represented a big break for Nixon; after providing the singing voices for Deborah Kerr in *The King and I* and Natalie Wood in *West Side Story,* she had dubbed Audrey Hepburn's singing voice as Eliza Doolittle in *My Fair Lady.* Finally, with *The Sound of Music,* she would be seen, and not just heard, onscreen. Said director Wise: "We wanted to give Marni a chance to actually be seen on the screen—a way to pay her back for her work on *West Side Story.*"

Nixon, in fact, was put to work as soon as she was cast in the film. Long before actual filming commenced, Nixon, under the guidance of Saul Chaplin, recorded all of the songs that the character of Maria would sing in the film. Already casting an eye on the potentially lucrative foreign markets, the studio decided to have the songs recorded as a guide for singers who would eventually record the songs for the film's release in foreign territories. Said Nixon: "They wanted these foreign singers to hear the songs sung as intended— the words, the nuances. That way those singers could watch the film and match the translation to the words. I felt honored to be asked. I didn't memorize the songs—I was singing them from the lyric sheets. The only embarrassing part came when it turned out they filmed me recording the songs. I had to go through hair and makeup and then through the years people would say to me, 'I saw you recording *The Sound of Music*!' "

FRANZ—GIL STUART Recommended by another member of the *Sound of Music* team, Stuart was a familiar face to Wise although the two had not previously worked together. Stuart seemed to possess the right look and hauteur for the butler turned Nazi, and Wise quickly stopped his search and offered the role to Stuart in March of 1964, shortly before the start of filming.

ROLFE—DAN TRUHITTE The character of Rolfe posed a particular casting problem for the film: what young man was capable of portraying a Hitler Youth but could also believably sing and dance the sweet-natured paen to puppy love, "Sixteen Going on Seventeen"?

The contrast between teenage lothario and junior Nazi would prove especially important because of Lehman's decision to darken the character in the transition from stage to screen. In onstage productions of *The Sound of Music,* Rolfe often strikes the audience as a bit of a lightweight: he sings and dances and ultimately does not turn in the von Trapps—not exactly traditional behavior for a budding Nazi. Lehman and Wise knew that Rolfe and Liesl remained rather one dimensional, possessing none of the depth of R&H's secondary lovers from *South Pacific,* Liat and Lieutenant Cable. That budding interracial romance, played out against the ongoing war in the Pacific, carried a real sense of danger. Liesl, on the other hand, was simply a sweet, young girl, which meant that Lehman would try his best to generate additional suspense by having Rolfe willingly betray the family. Without the right actor, that action could stretch audience credulity to the breaking point, especially with the romantic "Sixteen Going on Seventeen" still fresh in the audience's collective memory.

After considering a not-yet-famous Richard Dreyfuss, whose musical skills remained rudimentary, as well as song-and-dance veterans like Danny Lockin (four years later he would play the role of Barnaby Tucker in the film version of *Hello, Dolly!*), Wise read Dan Truhitte, who had come to his attention through the casting office.

In Truhitte's recall: "My agent had sent me on a cattle call for the role. I rounded the corner to the soundstage and saw about five hundred blond-haired boys waiting! They filmed ten seconds of footage of all of us, no singing, no dancing. I heard nothing. Six weeks later my agent was at a party where he saw Pamela Danova, the dialect coach. He was talking to her about the role of Liesl and Pamela said that every role had been cast except Rolfe. My agent said, 'I have someone you'd be interested in,' and he ran to his car and retrieved a head shot he had of me.

"I met Pamela who sent me over to meet Robert Wise and Saul Chaplin. They gave me the script for the last scene, where Rolfe turns in the von Trapps. They had already started production and still didn't have their Rolfe. I read the scene at Argyle Production's house on the lot. Wise and Chaplin liked what I did and sent me over to see Dee Dee Wood and Marc Breaux. I could dance—I'd been offered a scholarship to Sacramento Ballet—and I danced for them. They wanted the "Sixteen Going on Seventeen" number to look like youngsters having fun. Fortunately I received an A for my dancing ability.

"The next day was a personality test—there were thirty people in the studio. Robert Wise talked to me in that very real, low-key manner of his and said, 'Dan, I want you to sit in front of the camera and just talk to me while I film you.' Then I asked him if he would mind if I sang for him. Mr. Wise said 'I didn't know you could sing—what are you going to sing?' Of course I said, " 'Sixteen, Going on Seventeen' " When I finished everyone was smiling—that really was the very best feeling of all for me—to see that they liked what I did. Boy was I glad I had taken singing lessons. That's because I had started out as a dancer in competitions when I was very young. I'd tap, do wings, flip-flops, I'd be killing myself and someone would just stand there, sing, and win every time. So I took singing lessons—good decision! I think I just had the sound they wanted—I had a kind of young Irish-sounding voice. They had already started filming and two days later I had a contract.

"They dyed my hair blond—even my eyebrows and eyelashes! Every week they'd have to touch it up so that I had that Aryan look, instead of my normal dark brown hair."

Thrilled to be a part of the production Truhitte remembers sitting directly behind Julie Andrews in a screening room while watching footage of the rushes: "At the end of the rushes she turned around and said, 'You must be Dan Truhitte—congratulations on getting the part!' What a wonderful woman: kind, hardworking, loving—a pleasure always."

Although Truhitte, at age twenty, was a year younger than Charmian Carr, he registered on film as someone who looked at least one year older, a key component in fulfilling Rolfe's lyrical mandate:

You need someone older and wiser
Telling you what to do
I am seventeen going on eighteen
I'll take care of you

Having been a singer and dancer since the age of six, his experience nicely complimented Carr's native but untested abilities, and contract in hand, Truhitte prepared to play Hollywood's first singing and dancing junior Nazi. In the decades-later words of Wise, "Dan Truhitte handled the part very, very well. He really looked the part."

FRAU SCHMIDT—NORMA VARDEN Only one significant speaking role remained to be cast—that of housekeeper Frau Schmidt. This time, however, no extensive wish list existed. Wise determined early on that he would cast Norma Varden, whose no-nonsense yet sympathetic personality and voice would precisely convey the housekeeper's brisk persona. Wise had directed Varden twenty years earlier in his second directorial effort, the seventy-minute low-budget quickie *Mademoiselle Fifi* (1944), and although the film was clearly a lesser effort in the Wise canon, Varden's practical, grounded portrayal of the wholesaler's wife resonated with Wise. Was she interested? Yes.

With Varden, Gil Stuart, Ben Wright as Herr Zeller, and all of the nuns agreeing to contracts in March, casting was now completed. With the budget approved, set construction under way, and below line personnel all in place, rehearsals with the children began on February 10. On February 20, Julie Andrews arrived at the Fox studios for the start of her own rehearsals, joined ten days later by Christopher Plummer. With makeup and wardrobe tests completed, and prerecording having finished on March 26, the six months of preproduction were over and the start of shooting was at hand.

After surviving a bankrupt studio, a first director who didn't like a single thing about the movie, a Nazi-sympathizing helicopter pilot, and a grouchy leading man, *The Sound of Music* was finally ready to begin filming.

March 26, 1964.

Soundstage 15 on the 20th Century-Fox lot.

Scene 23A

Maria's arrival at the von Trapp household.

"Roll Camera."

"Action!"

12.

LET'S START AT THE VERY BEGINNING

Robert Wise had a bad case of the jitters. He'd won an Academy Award for his one previous musical, possessed total faith in his leading lady, knew Varden was a total pro, and had spent fully half a year on preproduction, but it all still felt like the first day of school—"like a high diver taking the plunge into a pool far below." One false move as the captain of the ship and he'd set the entire production off on the wrong foot. Andrews shared his feelings of nerves: "All I could think of was 'I hope I'm doing this right.'"

Pros that they were, neither star nor director exhibited the slightest sign of nerves to anyone else. Too much depended upon their concentration, and even more important, on their ability to inspire confidence in others. The camera rolled and Andrews moved into her key light, her wide-eyed gaze at the von Trapp family villa conveying Maria's sense of wonder. Varden's crisp seen-it-all demeanor effortlessly conveyed Frau Schmidt's "You don't know what you're in for" attitude, and—cut! *The Sound of Music* was under way.

With one scene under the belt, production moved into the first musical number to be filmed: the complicated "My Favorite Things." But before a single piece of the number could be shot, a hair crisis had loomed. Because so many of the children sported dark locks—Hammond, Carr, Turner, Cartwright—Wise decided to add another blond child to the mix. Would one of the children wear a wig? Definitely not. Instead, Nicholas Hammond's natural brown hair would be dyed blond. Very blond. But the hair department went overboard, applying such great quantities of harsh dye to Hammond's hair that when he turned up for this first day of filming, the now blond-to-the-roots youngster sported a severely blistered scalp.

And Hammond did not actually represent the film's first blond disaster.

Although it had been deemed that Julie Andrews's basic appearance would remain unchanged for the film, all concerned agreed that a few blond highlights would nicely accentuate her appearance. Once again, the application of the dye quickly grew out of control, and in Andrews's own recollection, when her hair was dyed one week before the start of filming, it first turned orange. In the end, it was decided to bleach all of her short bobbed hair blond. Maria Rainer von Trapp was now a bottle blonde—and ready for action.

Hair crisis solved, "My Favorite Things" was ready for the cameras. Onstage, "My Favorite Things" is presented as a folk song and Maria and the Mother Abbess sing together before the Mother Abbess informs Maria about the position of governess in the von Trapp household. Lehman, however, decided to use the song as the means by which Maria comforts the children during a thunderstorm (a thunderstorm that had actually been the invention of the *Die Trapp-Familie* screenwriter George Hurdalek. With Hurdalek's screenplay providing structural support for portions of the film, he was ultimately rewarded with a stand-alone title card reading: "With partial use of ideas by George Hurdalek.") Now utilizing "My Favorite Things" as the musical means by which the growing bond between governess and children could be strengthened, Lehman further altered the sequence by having the captain arrive unannounced mid-song, his attendant disapproval lending an extra layer of conflict to the sequence.

As the first day of filming the number progressed, it was cinematographer Ted McCord who stepped to the fore. His adroit use of lighting traced the entire arc of the number by itself: he began with shadows and then layered in storm flashes, until the singing resulted in a literal and metaphorical lightening of mood before it all came to a screeching halt with the arrival of the captain.

A consummate team player, McCord even contributed to the number in a fashion having nothing to do with his work as cinematographer. As shooting dragged on, the painstaking and gentlemanly McCord realized that the inexperienced, tired, and generally out of sorts Duane Chase simply could not provide the necessary ear-to-ear smile required by Wise for one shot in the number. In stepped McCord, not with any change in lighting, but rather, with antics behind the camera that made Chase not just smile but grin. A veteran Academy Award–nominated cinematographer making an inexperienced child actor laugh for the sake of the shot—it all boded well for Wise's team-oriented approach.

Chase's grin had been successfully captured but that was just one shot among dozens required by the number. The much bigger problem lay in the fact that the number was designed to show Maria bonding with the children through music, yet having just met the seven young actors, Julie Andrews barely knew their names. To further complicate matters, it quickly became apparent that during each and every scene with the children, Julie Andrews would have to be at the peak of her game on every single take—no matter how many—in case the take in question should happen to be the one in which all of the children hit their marks and struck the right emotional notes. The children could and would stumble, overstep their marks, and miss their cues, but Julie Andrews needed to be letter perfect. Every time. Said Charmian Carr: "I never saw her make a mistake."

With Lehman having moved "My Favorite Things" to this earlier position in the film, it was Maria who would be filmed singing the entire song: at this point in the story, the von Trapp children have not yet learned to sing. Rather than have Maria burst into song right away, Lehman introduced the song as if Maria were simply having a conversation with the children. Scared of the thunderstorm, the von Trapp children need soothing, and Maria provides palpable comfort by speaking warmly of:

Green meadows—skies full of stars
Raindrops on roses . . . and whiskers on kittens

It is only with the next phrase of "Bright copper kettles and warm woolen mittens" that Julie Andrews begins to sing. There is no jarring rush into song. Maria simply moves from speech to song, making the song part of the story and quietly bringing the children—and the audience—along with her. By leading into the number in a way that captured the audience by surprise, Lehman had successfully solved what he considered the hardest part of starting a musical number: avoiding all suspicion that the dialogue is a lead-in to a song. Lehman may have written the dialogue for the film, but he understood that in a movie musical it was all about the songs: "Musical numbers are what you must get to—they shape your work. . . ." Said Robert Wise: "Ernie did a marvelous job of tailoring the dialogue to lead into the song."

The number proceeded in fits and starts, with Wise making sure to shoot the beginning of the actual song from a different camera angle than the dialogue leading into it. In the Wise playbook, the audience should always be presented with new visuals to keep them interested. Shoot the dialogue from one angle and then cut to a close-up as the song starts: "I tried to do that every time I could."

A new problem with "My Favorite Things" now emerged, and it lay in the staging of the number by husband and wife choreographers Dee Dee Wood and Marc Breaux. The duo had been rather unknown to Wise when first suggested as possible choreographers, so Wise and Saul Chaplin asked the Disney executives if they could view the "Chimney Sweep" footage the team had choreographed for the still unreleased *Mary Poppins*. Impressed by the exuberant number, Wise scheduled a meeting with the duo and took an instant liking to their upbeat personalities. The feeling was mutual. Said Wood: "Robert Wise was one hundred percent a gentleman. He would direct quietly, which makes you really listen. He kept a watch in the pocket of his jacket or vest; he was very aware of time, of wanting to get X amount done each day. I borrowed that idea from him for future work!"

After listening to the choreographers discuss their desire to impart a sense of movement to every number—even the nuns in full-length habits would move while singing "How Do You Solve a Problem Like Maria"—Wise was sold. He had found his choreographers.

Now, however, the husband-and-wife team found themselves under the gun. They had spent several weeks in preproduction meticulously planning out every musical moment before rehearsals began, but after a full five days had been spent filming "My Favorite Things," the number was not working properly. It needed to appear natural and instinctive, with no sign that the entire sequence was, in fact, planned down to the smallest musical beat. Yes, all that advance planning was playing out in smooth fashion, but it all proved too polished by half. As Ernest Lehman watched the filming he realized that the pillow tossing and childish high spirits precisely synchronized to prerecorded music looked overly choreographed and unnatural. Where was the sense of childish spontaneity?

After a quick conference, Wood and Breaux began to simplify the movements. Reconceiving the action, they took out all of the polish and a much better number began to emerge. Said Wood: "We solved the problem of the staging because Robert Wise was such a great leader—he made you want to work harder to solve any problem that arose. When we finished restaging it Julie and the kids had a ball with it."

In an amusing sidelight to the choreographed pillow fight, Charmian Carr recalled that the sound of the thunder that sends the scared children running into Maria's room for comfort was so loud that she consistently missed her cue to sneak into Maria's bedroom after meeting Rolfe at the gazebo. It was Andrews who came up with a neat bit of trickery to solve the problem; when Maria is shown praying for all of the children, she put extra volume into Carr's exact cue—the phrase "God bless what's his name"—so that Charmian could hear her cue over the crashing thunder.

The delays, the changes in blocking, the acting with seven potentially scene-stealing children—it all could have resulted in temper tantrums from most Hollywood divas. But temperamental displays were never a part of the Andrews personality. Cast in the role of a nun cum Cinderella figure who exudes nonstop good cheer, Andrews actually did just that, leading by example and setting the tone for the entire company. Complaints were never forthcoming, no matter how long the delays. Such was her professionalism that when speaking of her difficulty and dislike of learning to play the guitar, she allowed as how she did finally succumb to the long-dreaded guitar practice "rather sulkily." That was it for complaints—she sulked over guitar practice. It all constituted, one suspects, a sulkiness undetectable by anyone else. Even her sulkiness was leavened by a smile: "Playing the guitar was like touching your head and patting your tummy at the same time." Wise said: "Julie is so musical that she picked up the guitar quickly. It's hard to synchronize the playing and singing with the playback but she did it." (Perhaps dislike of the guitar proved to be another foundation of the genuine rapport between Andrews and Plummer. In Plummer's blunt phrase: "I loathe the guitar! The guitar hurt my fingers so much that they bled. I faked it and strummed away and someone else did all the magical work.")

Unlike Plummer, who maintained a distant, sometimes chilly relationship with all of his screen children except Charmian Carr, Andrews played games with the six youngest right from the start. Yes, Andrews's actions were partly calculated out of knowledge that she needed their trust to help the film and her own performance, but her willingness to enter into the spirit of fun arose out of her own genuinely down-to-earth personality.

The off-camera Andrews acted just like governess Maria herself; if the children were being filmed in close-up, Andrews would make silly faces off camera to help the children laugh, would tickle them for fun, and dispense hugs, which instilled a feeling of trust and safety that lasted for the next fifty years. In the admiring words of Robert Wise: "Julie was so great with the kids—warm to them, hugged them, kissed them. It was a joy to see how they loved her, how well she worked with the children. The warmth that was generated you now see on the film."

The young Nicholas Hammond had fallen under Andrews's spell when seeing her final London performance in *My Fair Lady,* and later confessed to already feeling a mix of awe and love on his first day of working with his idol. Debbie Turner remembers the hug Andrews gave her: "a motherly hug and I loved it." Turner and Hammond did more than hold Andrews in high regard; in the manner of youngsters with favorite teachers, they fell more than a bit in love. Said Kym Karath: "That love you see on camera is genuine. . . . I felt as much like I was in the heart of a family as I could have possibly felt. It was the happiest feeling for a five-year-old girl. . . . I couldn't have looked more adoring in 'My Favorite Things'—and it was genuine." In later years, Debbie Turner recalled Andrews as simply having a "magical way about her." The noticeable difference in Andrews's and Plummer's interaction with the children, even at this very early stage of shooting, was nicely summed up by Nicholas Hammond: "Every one of the children had to adore Maria and feel on his or her toes around the captain and that's exactly the way Julie and Christopher behaved with us, all the time."

With "My Favorite Things" completed, the company moved on to two further interior scenes: the climactic scene in which the family attempts to hide from the Nazis in the abbey's graveyard, and the staging of "Maria." Wise was particularly pleased with how the filming of the graveyard chase unfolded: "In the stage show Rolfe is a wimp. He doesn't turn in the von Trapps. In the film, we changed that. And I've always loved the marvelous piece of business Ernie cooked up with the nuns taking the carburetors."

In Dan Truhitte's recall, the graveyard chase may have been the penultimate scene in the movie but it represented the first scene he shot. "The tough part was that I had to start out playing Rolfe at his worst—he turns in the von Trapps!—and then I had to regress, so that the last scenes I filmed were Rolfe at his most naive, singing and dancing with Liesl. In the graveyard scene, the captain warns Rolfe 'You'll never be one of them' and Rolfe has to defy the captain. I was really happy about pulling off the scene.

"All credit to Robert Wise. He was so great—a true gentleman. Such a kind man, never angry, an incredible talent and always smiling . . . In fact, the only time I every saw him get upset was in the graveyard scene when the spot man couldn't seem to coordinate moving the spotlight with where the flashlight was going. They removed the man and got another man who did a better job. . . . He treated everyone with respect. He'd make suggestions, never orders, and just radiated an ambiance of goodness. A terrific director. His gentlemanly quality not only made him a good director but really informed the film—it was a very happy set and that shows on film."

The graveyard chase also figured in one of Marni Nixon's most humorous recollections of the filming. Knowing that she might receive a close-up during the scene of the nuns with the carburetors, she snuck back into the makeup room, hoping to change her appearance. "I had very light lashes and I didn't like the fact that nuns couldn't wear mascara and eyelash enhancer! They kept telling me I looked fine but I was embarrassed by looking so plain. I know I was playing a nun but . . . At any rate, my plan backfired. I sidled into the makeup room and put mascara on my eyelashes for the close-up I'd receive while standing by the abbey door dealing with the Nazis. Well, evidently I had a habit of batting my eyelashes too fast and on my close-up it was very obvious I had makeup on. Robert Wise just matter-of-factly, and gently, said, 'We'll cut that close-up!'"

Both of these abbey sequences depended greatly upon production designer Leven's exactingly detailed sets, whose construction he had been supervising for weeks. Of necessity, Leven had been forced to build all of the interior abbey sets when the Mother Abbess at Nonnberg Abbey forbade any filming in the abbey itself. She would allow filming in the approach to the abbey, but nothing more. (When, for design purposes, the production crew hung a nonoperational bell cord outside the abbey, the nuns liked the look so much that they asked to keep the cord.) Using photographs and drawings of the actual sites as his guide, Leven designed uneven, purposefully wet cobblestones for the abbey courtyard; one look at the pavement underneath the nuns' feet as they sing "Maria" reassured viewers that they had indeed entered the world of Austria in the 1930s. Said Marni Nixon: "It was like a print of the actual location in Salzburg."

Leven's perfectionist instincts, honed in the nearly twenty-five years since *Mother Shanghai,* found full expression throughout, whether in the von Trapp ballroom (inspired by the Venetian Room in the Leopoldskron Palace) or in the graveyard based upon that found at Salzburg's St. Peter's church. Said Julie Andrews: "It's amazing how real it all felt with steps and tombstones." Director Wise was so pleased with his friend Leven's work that he went on record as stating: "This will sound like heresy to the cinematographers, but I think the production designer, if he's creative, can contribute as much to the look of the film as the cameraman. Boris Leven was a brilliant production designer." Fortunately for Wise, Ted McCord harbored no such thoughts of heresy because of his own close relationship with Leven. Having previously worked together on *Two for the Seesaw,* the two low-key pros possessed a genuine friendship, and far from feeling territorial about their own contributions, the duo would take the time to confer every day after looking at rushes.

The "brilliance" of Leven to which Wise referred was most notably realized in his design of the gilded von Trapp ballroom. When Maria first explores the ballroom upon her arrival, its shrouded, somber affect symbolizes the shutdown, yesteryear quality of the family's emotional life. When, months later, the captain throws a ball in honor of the baroness, the gold-trimmed panels and shimmering lights reflect not only the happiness of the beautifully dressed dancers, but also the emotional and musical rebirth of the family. So expertly designed was the ballroom that upon completion of filming, it was donated to the Hollywood Museum.

With the filming of "Maria" taking several days on Leven's meticulously wrought set, the detailed preproduction planning by Breaux and Wood now bore full fruit; in order to simulate the requisite movements, the choreographers and their assistants had actually rehearsed the number while wearing nuns habits. Recalled Dee Dee Wood: "It's obviously not a dance number but it was meticulously choreographed. The number was storyboarded and the nuns were positioned very specifically. It was like painting a portrait. We really did wear those nuns' habits to rehearse—we wanted to know exactly how the material would flow. Somewhere there's a picture of me in the nun's outfit on a bicycle with my legs raised in the second position!"

Wood and Breaux's detailed instructions allowed the actresses to manipulate the unexpectedly weighty garments while synchronizing their movements in time to the music. Marni Nixon recalled the material as being heavy and realistic—"definitely no polyester!"—yet it still allowed the actresses to move smoothly "without a lot of jiggling around . . . The number had been so well rehearsed and thought through that it was easy to perform. Robert Wise—who was a total gentleman—never acted like a director lording it over you. He wasn't even there for the rehearsals. He trusted Marc and Dee Dee to do their job. He'd receive reports of course, but he trusted the people around him. His forte was a terrific insight into people working with him. He was at the camera when shooting took place, but during the preparation of the number he left the choreographers alone. He felt certain that he had chosen the right people."

In the end, the number actually turned out to be one of the few musical sequences in the film which unfolded as it had in the theater. Although it was sung in a lower key and the lyrics were partially spoken, in most details it was presented in the same manner, and still included the one Hammerstein lyric that Mary Martin's friend and religious adviser Sister Gregory had criticized as inaccurate back in 1959:

And underneath her wimple she has curlers in her hair

Although Sister Gregory had in fact urged the creators not to hem themselves in with an overly reverential approach, she had firmly pointed out that no novice would ever or could ever have worn curlers beneath her wimple.

This number also provided the first shared scene, however brief, between Julie Andrews and actress/singer Marni Nixon, here cast as Sister Sophia. With Andrews having been famously snubbed when the *My Fair Lady* movie was cast, and Nixon providing the vocals for the movie's Eliza Doolittle, Audrey Hepburn, rumormongers gleefully anticipated fireworks when the two actresses met. Would Andrews snub Nixon?

The truth proved to be exactly the opposite. In Nixon's recall, when the two women met on set for the first time, Julie "just walked right over, put out her hand and said, 'Marni, I'm such a fan of yours!' " That generosity of spirit carried over into the next week, when, a scant two weeks into filming, Andrews, with the weight of the entire multimillion-dollar production on her shoulders, took the time to help Nixon prepare for her audition as Eliza Doolittle for the New York City Center revival of *My Fair Lady*: "I said to Julie that I was having trouble with one of the scenes—that I didn't know how to perform it properly, couldn't find the proper beats. I was being so dramatic and too strong in the scene. Julie said 'I bet I know which scene it is'—and she was right. She knew exactly! It was so fortuitous—you just couldn't plan it better—that she was there and took the time to help me. I'll never forget Julie, standing there in her underwear, telling me how to throw that slipper!"

With filming of "Maria" completed, the sixty-person *Sound of Music* company flew to Austria in April of 1964 for location shooting in Salzburg. Cast and crew departed in high spirits for what they thought would be a brief and enjoyable six-week shoot, but seasoned Hollywood professionals and neophytes alike were about to learn a major lesson: the best-laid plans of Hollywood heavy hitters don't stand a chance in the face of a recalcitrant Mother Nature. Or, in the words of Julie Andrews, "Nobody told us when we went to Salzburg that it had the world's seventh-highest rainfall. . . ."

13.

SALZBURG, RAIN, AND NATURE'S REVENGE

"I looked like Orson Welles."

—CHRISTOPHER PLUMMER,
ON HIS FONDNESS FOR AUSTRIAN PASTRIES

The Sound of Music represented big-budget studio filmmaking at the tail end of the studio system, and the publicity shots capturing the cast's departure for what still seemed like "exotic" Austria sum up that vanished world with one snap: posing by the plane that would take them overseas, the seven children are dressed up as if for church. Today, child actors desperate to appear hip might sport ripped jeans and trendy designer clothes; then, Duane Chase and Nicholas Hammond wore sport coats and ties, and the girls dressed up in hats, gloves, and their best Mary Jane shoes.

It wasn't just the children who put on their best Sunday clothes for overseas travel. When Peggy Wood had downtime, she toured Salzburg with new friend Anna Lee, a noted veteran of many John Ford movies and here cast as Sister Margaretta. (Lee, in fact, was married to Julie Andrews's *Mary Poppins* director, Robert Stevenson.) One look at the candid shots of the twosome touring Salzburg is all that's needed in order to learn exactly how much Hollywood has changed since the tail end of the studio system. Standing on the streets of Salzburg, Wood and Lee are decked out in hats, pocketbooks, and furs—visual reminders of an era when stars never appeared in public unless fully decked out. Taking full advantage of their free time, Wood and Lee toured both Salzburg and the surrounding countryside, presumably without the hats and furs when out on the mountain trails. Said Julie Andrews: "I really envied them their ability to take advantage of Salzburg—the sights and sounds. I was just always so busy that I couldn't." Of course Andrews was several steps ahead of Marni Nixon, who laughed: "I was mad because several of the other nuns got to go to Salzburg and I filmed all my scenes at the Fox studios. I just wanted to go to Europe!"

In the recall of Georg Steinitz, by the time the cast arrived in Salzburg, the electricians had already been at work for three full weeks in order to start the complicated installation of cables. Steinitz, whose command of languages soon made him invaluable to the production, had actually secured his job by a fluke; hired as a driver for the head of the small film studio where the *Sound of Music*'s cover sets were installed, he had been crushed to see his dream job of location assistant director given to another man. When, however, 20th Century-Fox fired that man after one week, Steinitz went to the studio personnel and bluntly stated: "I'm the man you're looking for." With locations in both Austria and Germany, a camera truck arriving from Spain, and crew members hailing from multiple countries, Steinitz's ability to speak German, English, Spanish, Russian, French, Italian, and Arabic soon made him indispensible to the company. Still working as a driver for the head of the studio, he would finish his stint as chauffeur, rush to the *Sound of Music*'s night shooting, remain on set all night, sleep for one hour, and then head back to his job as chauffeur. "I was saved by the fact that Mr. Wise had scheduled a lot of night shooting at that time. I was exhausted but exhilarated— this was a big Hollywood film. I was twenty-five years old, it was my first big film, and I loved it. Mr. Wise was absolutely terrific. Such a gentleman."

While Wood stayed behind to monitor final rehearsals in Los Angeles— "We all knew what each department was doing; there were no surprises"— Saul Chaplin and Marc Breaux arrived in Salzburg a full week before the rest of the company in order to work on the musical numbers. Knowing that the filming of songs on location always proved substantially more difficult than in the controlled environs of a studio soundstage, Breaux and Chaplin mapped out the precise movements and timing required for the three songs to be filmed on location: "Do-Re-Mi," "I Have Confidence," and the title song. *Sound of Music* may never have been conceived as a dance-centric film, but in the planning of Breaux, Wood, and Chaplin, the continuous movement exhibited on-screen in these numbers would serve as the bridge between scenes, hopefully producing the sense of exhilaration, youth, and bursting of boundaries characteristic of the best musicals.

Unable to rehearse in the midst of the actual traffic flowing through the locations, the two men would measure out the distances called for by the choreography, wait for a red light, turn on their tape recorder and blast the music while Breaux timed the numbers by dancing down the streets. In Chaplin's understated take on the situation: "Unfortunately the lights had no regard for the length of our playbacks." The traffic signals would change, horns would honk, and as the last notes of "I Have Confidence" blared forth, Breaux would dodge furious drivers and jump to the safety of the sidewalk. Having rested between each traffic-dodging take, Breaux would wait for the lights to turn, Chaplin would blast "I Have Confidence," and as the choreographer once again leaped down the street, *The Sound of Music* began to take shape—and flight. (When a nearby Austrian policeman asked the duo what exactly they were doing, both men were rendered speechless; said Chaplin, "I couldn't explain it to the policeman in English, let alone German.")

When the full company arrived in Salzburg on April 18 and 19, 1964, it quickly became clear just how much of the workload was going to fall on the slim, sturdy shoulders of Andrews. Plummer, by way of contrast, would be called onto the set only sporadically, allowing him great chunks of time in which to explore the beautiful countryside he quickly grew to love. (Plummer also grew to love "the beer, the quiche, the schnapps. I put on so much weight Bob Wise said to me 'We have to get a whole new costume for you!' ") The children, parental guardians and tutors in tow, would be needed on set most days, but even their schedule paled in comparison to Andrews's.

Working nonstop—"I lost myself in work, work, work"—Andrews began filming *The Sound of Music* while coping with her own self-doubts about motherhood. Although only twenty-eight, the veteran performer possessed more than enough self-awareness to see the irony in portraying the super stepmother of all time while having to leave her one-year-old daughter Emma Kate in the care of others. Married to award-winning designer Tony Walton, but separated from her husband by the demands of work, Andrews in later years reflected that in these early stages of her film career, she would return home, "hug Emma Kate, and I would think—what am I doing here? What kind of life is this for you? A father thousands of miles away and a mother who is locked in a studio all day."

Starting each day at 6:00 A.M. in hair and makeup, and called upon to appear in nearly every scene, Andrews could not spare the time to pal around

with the other cast members on location, yet her energy and sheer professionalism never flagged; when she finally did have a day off toward the end of
the location shooting, she switched gears, hired a bus, and took *The Sound of
Music* company to the Royal Ballet Theatre in Munich, leading everyone in
the singing of show tunes along the way. All that was missing was a guitar
and a chorus of "Do-Re-Mi."

For now, however, on the night before her first day of shooting in Salzburg, Andrews spent the evening preparing; she may have spent very little
time with Christopher Plummer thus far, but tomorrow she'd be marrying
him, and in the beautiful and famed Mondsee (Moon Lake) Cathedral in front
of hundreds of spectators. Would the wedding come off as the culmination
of a shimmering fairy-tale romance, or would it appear a stolid affair in a
stately but noticeably dark cathedral?

In the end, the combination of Ted McCord's brilliant lighting, Dorothy
Jeakins's extraordinary wedding gown, and the beautiful, centuries-old cathedral added up to a visual statement that influenced the dreams of generations of young girls to come. The cathedral itself, in the words of both Andrews
and Dee Dee Wood, was "freezing," but such was the majesty of the entire
sequence that Wood, sitting in one of the pews watching the processional
"found myself in tears. It was just so beautiful."

Onscreen, the wedding unfolded seamlessly, but the end result represented
hundreds of detailed, painstaking decisions, all made by golden-age Hollywood
professionals working at the peak of their powers. In preparation for the
sequence, Ted McCord spent two full days lighting the cathedral while confronting two distinct interior challenges: how to enhance the ever-changing
light filtering through the church's stained-glass windows, and the best means
by which to light the entire middle aisle down which Maria would process toward the altar. Although there would be singing on the soundtrack, not a single
word of dialogue would be spoken throughout the wedding; McCord's ability
to tell the story of the ceremony solely through images would prove the key.

To prepare for the wedding, Wise and McCord attended an actual wedding at Mondsee Cathedral two days before the start of filming. The director
wanted to explore both the atmosphere within the cathedral and the details
of the wedding ceremony itself, while McCord spent his time studying the
intensity and different sources of natural light found throughout. (Although
most accounts point to a smooth working atmosphere between the two men,

Georg Steinitz recalls "a little bit of a cool atmosphere between them" during shooting, with McCord becoming upset when he offered a suggestion that Wise rejected. "However it certainly never got loud.")

Because of the different film stock utilized in 1965, it was not possible to film in very low light the way it would be today, so McCord utilized filters and hidden sources of light throughout the soaring cathedral itself. The first problem he had to solve arose from the cathedral's plethora of stained-glass windows, all of which caused the natural sunlight to bleed directly into the studio lights (which had been set up to enhance the intensity of the interior light). This mix of light sources resulted in an overly blue wash that threw off the visual effectiveness of the entire scene. In order to correct the problem, McCord placed color correction filters on the windows, thereby balancing the two sources of light. As detailed in an interview he gave at the time of the film's release, the cinematographer positioned a small light on the floor—in the lower left corner of the frame—which he then angled up toward the window. With additional natural light flooding the cathedral from the opposite direction, the end result resembled a warm bath of natural light entering the cathedral from the right of the screen and traveling until it grazed the steps leading directly to the altar.

To complete the effect, McCord placed a hidden series of floor-to-ceiling lights behind the proscenium arch in front of the altar. In this fashion he was able to create the illusion that the light flooding the altar poured directly from the large windows behind, as if the wedding of Maria and Georg had the full blessing of God himself. This entire lighting scheme had been worked out in order to enhance Wise's decision to shoot Maria's walk down the aisle as a side angle traveling shot. The side-on view would heighten the sense of a fairy-tale processional, with the walk toward the altar accompanied by a chorale reprise of "How Do You Solve a Problem Like Maria." (A more humorous note about the wedding was sounded by Andrews in her recollection that the man supposed to be marrying Maria and Georg "was the bishop of the abbey—I think he once in a while had an eye for the ladies and was not exactly as saintly as he's made out to be.")

It was Dorothy Jeakins's dress for Julie Andrews that proved the capstone for the sequence; commenting on the wedding gown, Andrews simply stated, "I've never felt as beautiful as when I wore that wedding gown. I've never felt prettier before or since. That dress was a miracle. . . . It was very simple—

just yards and yards of tulle—and the veil, very simple clasping on the head." Andrews's relationship with Jeakins started with respect for her talent, but grew into a genuine friendship: "She became a great friend—we kept each other company a lot."

It was Ernest Lehman's idea to further enhance the sequence's sense of majesty by having the camera pan up and up until it finally bursts through the ceiling to the ringing cathedral bells. It is only then, with the viewer exhilarated by the wedding, that Wise, McCord, and editor William Reynolds masterfully utilize one last rather sour-sounding bell to lead the viewer directly into the sight of Nazis marching across the plaza. Without one word of dialogue, Maria and Georg have been united in a marriage right out of "Once upon a time . . . " yet this same sequence has masterfully ended with a cut that propels the viewer directly into a new story line about the growing Nazi menace.

The decision to cut from the pealing church bells to storm troopers marching across the plaza also helped to solve a big problem looming over the film: how to depict the Nazi occupation of Austria without stomping on the delicate fabric of the story. Onstage, the Nazis had in fact been glimpsed during the Boston tryout of the show, but they were eliminated before the show arrived on Broadway, with Rodgers asserting that keeping the Nazis offstage made that particular plot element "even more harrowing, with the enemy unseen." The words "Heil Hitler" were never spoken on stage, the greeting purposely shortened to "Heil." For the very different medium of film, however, Wise and Lehman felt that the visual image of the Nazis would help ground the film in a bit of historical reality.

The fact that Hitler was welcomed with open arms by many Austrian residents at the time of the Anschluss was one that Austrian government officials preferred to forget. Georg Steinitz has recalled that the original plan for the sequence called for a big crowd of extras shouting and welcoming the large column of Germans marching by. In a handy bit of revisionism, however, Austrian officials informed Pia Arnold, the German production manager functioning as liaison with the Austrian government, that the people of Salzburg had never been Nazi sympathizers and therefore no Nazi swastikas could be depicted in the film. When Maurice Zuberano, speaking (through Arnold) on behalf of Robert Wise, replied that the government's refusal to allow the display of swastikas did not present a problem because the film would simply

utilize actual newsreels of Hitler arriving to cheering Austrian crowds, permission for a shot of Nazi troops crossing the Residenplatz in front of swastika
banners was granted very quickly.

In the sharp recall of Dee Dee Wood: "No townspeople would watch that
sequence. They were around all the rest of the time but when we filmed that
sequence they just disappeared. We actually had trouble getting people to play
those Nazis. Just to hear the sound of those boots marching was chilling. . . ."

Austrian native Steinitz ironically recollected that "The compromise
seemed to be that the Anschluss took place during intermission! After you've
had your food and drink the film starts again, and you see Austria conquered
by a few dozen Nazis who march by three banners, with a few uninterested
extras looking on." And yet, thanks to Leven's production design, all it took
were those three stark red and black swastikas draped from a building, their
startling colors contrasting with the somber brown-hued tones of the uniforms,
and the point had been made.

One unintended bit of controversy resulting from the sequence came when
the film crew did not take the banners down the instant filming had been
completed. The building in question was the site of an International Mail Congress, and when the delegates arrived for their meeting, the swastika flags were
still hanging. Said Steinitz: "Of course that caused a lot of controversy.
Everyone had to be calmed down, the situation explained, and needless to
say, the banners came down very quickly."

The stripped-down look of the scene fit Wise's credo of no preaching: "I
liked the fact that *The Sound of Music* . . . did have its point to make about
the Nazis. The main thing is not to pump away heavily at the theme. Let that
come out through your characters and the development of the story. That
would be my principle."

In the end, the sequence did in fact work, but it features Nazis who are
glimpsed without any guns, a fact that definitely undercut a necessary sense
of menace. The weapons appear to have been a casualty of compromise, Austrian style.

McCord equaled his extraordinary work on the wedding sequence during the chorale sequence in which the nuns, minus Maria, are filmed singing
the Rodgers-composed "Preludium" with which the Broadway musical had
opened. Delivering a striking mise-en-scène, with the interior lit so that the
whites of the nuns' habits stand out in stark relief against the muted interior

colors, the sequence forms a bookend to the vastly different light-filled wedding sequence in Mondsee Cathedral. These contrasting interior looks, in fact, are purposely mirrored in the outdoor musical numbers; Maria's film opening hymn to "The Sound of Music," all light and color, is diametrically opposed to the literally and metaphorically dark look found at the climactic outdoor music performance of "So Long, Farewell."

Here in the "Preludium" sequence, while the chorale music floats in the background, Wise's camera alternates between group shots and close-ups of weathered, beatific faces. (The older nun holding her hand up to the side of her face appears to be costume designer Dorothy Jeakins.) It's a musically stirring sequence, and further serves to underscore the difference between such quiet devotion and the immediately preceding scene of Maria's exuberant hillside singing of "The Sound of Music."

"I HAVE CONFIDENCE"—SORT OF

With the wedding sequence completed, attention turned to filming one of the film's two original songs: Maria's paen to self-reliance entitled "I Have Confidence."

The idea for this new song had originated with Ernest Lehman during preproduction, with the screenwriter deciding that a new song dramatizing Maria's boundary-bursting journey from the abbey to the von Trapp villa would propel the film forward with style and speed. In her autobiography, Maria had actually described her first trip to the house, and Lehman felt that it provided the perfect background for the new song, one expressing her exuberance and determination.

As envisioned by Lehman and lit by McCord, the number was structured to capture Maria's journey from the darkness of the abbey to the light-filled countryside, the determined novice striding across the Siegmundplatz, rushing past the famous horse murals, and even singing out the window of a bus, with all of the set pieces culminating in Maria's exuberant run down the road to the villa. Only then would Julie Andrews end her powerful vocal with one final belted note, the end of the song perfectly punctuated by her ringing the villa's bell to start her new life. (The song may have been a solo for Julie Andrews, but in the words of Ted McCord: "All told there were about fifty people involved behind the camera, all to photograph one little girl, happily rushing down a country road!")

Production notes revealed that in Wise's typically painstaking fashion, he considered the number from all possible camera angles; scribbling detailed notes to himself, he questioned every facet of the number, from the use of a concluding twenty-five-yard dolly shot to whether or not Maria's satchel and guitar case would read on film as both period accurate and suitable for an impoverished novice.

One major problem had emerged in the planning stage, back in Los Angeles, however: the new song Richard Rodgers delivered turned out to be brief, in a minor key, and most decidedly not the upbeat anthem envisioned by Lehman, Wise, and Saul Chaplin. What audience would want to make this somber journey with Maria?

At the start of the process, Saul Chaplin had written the composer a detailed letter outlining the very qualities of pluck and goodwill that he, Wise, and Lehman had hoped Rodgers would deliver in his melody. In the associate producer's frustrated view, the sober song the composer had delivered meant "Either he didn't want to write the new material, or he wanted me to offer to do it." In the end, Chaplin used music Rodgers composed, but changed the overall effect by mixing in several additional elements. First he created a new beginning for the song based upon a verse in "The Sound of Music" not being utilized in the film. He then followed this introduction with Rodgers's own version of the musical soliloquy, before ending with a reprise of Rodgers's music to which he added an extra chorus of lyrics.

It's startling for anyone, even Academy Award–winning Saul Chaplin, to change a Richard Rodgers composition, but after doing precisely that, Chaplin had Marni Nixon cut a demo record of the finished song for Rodgers's approval. The composer's lukewarm telegraphed response? "Prefer my version. Okay to use yours if that is the decision." In consultation with Lehman and Wise, Chaplin proceeded with his patched together version, which fit the good-natured determination so central to the Andrews star persona. The song works precisely because Julie Andrews can and does radiate confidence, but it's never overwhelming, as it can be with, say, Barbra Streisand. (Andrews is too well mannered to demand that the world not rain on her parade.)

Chaplin, however, was so concerned about telling his star that Rodgers had not fully composed the completed song that he did not tell her of the song's composition-by-committee until two years after the film's release. As it happened, Andrews liked the song, but admitted to never fully understanding the lyric "Strength lies in nights of peaceful slumber"; while filming the number, she attempted to make up for this less-than-ideal lyric by swinging her arms, clicking her heels, and deliberately appearing to be so nervous that the lyric in question would rush by unnoticed: "I tried to act dotty so that I conveyed Maria's nervousness. I think it actually helped the song."

The filming of "I Have Confidence" also provided the film with a big burst of publicity when, on May 22, 1964, Maria von Trapp visited the set. In its way, the visit actually constituted a peacemaking mission, given that before shooting began, director Wise had found himself politely but firmly rebuffing Maria's attempts to position herself as an adviser on the film. Having received one too many unsolicited pieces of advice from Maria, on March 20, 1964, Wise finally wrote her a letter emphasizing that *The Sound of Music* was neither documentary nor slavish re-creation and would simply be "based loosely" on the von Trapp family story. Wise, in fact, had gone out of his way not to learn all of the details of the actual Trapp Family story: "My job was to translate that play and if I had all that baggage about what had actually happened it would have been like a dead weight on me. . . . She was bossy and I was the one running things so I didn't like that about her."

This issue of control went to the heart of Maria's energetic, in charge, and occasionally domineering personality. Maria always remained the star in her own mind, and was bound and determined to remind the public of that stature. Said her youngest child Johannes: "My mother never quite accepted that she had sold the rights and that meant they could do whatever they wanted with the story. . . . My mother was used to controlling things. . . . She tried very hard to see my father was portrayed in a more gentle, kinder fashion than he had on the Broadway stage."

The issue of control having been settled, Robert Wise found the on-set Maria "charming and lovely," and he cast Maria and daughter Rosmarie as extras walking in the background—the far-off background—during "I Have Confidence." The ever-energetic and forceful Maria found the repetitive nature of filmmaking decidedly not to her liking; her seconds' long scene of passing by in the background required seven takes, after which she commented: "That's one ambition I'm giving up," before declaring that her film career had begun and ended in the same day.

Never shy around handsome men, the on-set Maria took one look at Christopher Plummer and blurted out a hearty, "You're so much more handsome than my real husband. Ho, ho, ho." Plummer recalled Maria's on-set visit as an occasion of boisterous laughter and flirtatious banter, from a woman he described as "buxom . . . bouncy, and bossy." Maria maintained a lusty appreciation for Plummer and when, many years after the film's release, she spied the actor at a gathering held by the governor general of Nassau, she cut through all of the diplomatic decorum in typically robust fashion by exuberantly crying out: "My husband! My husband!" before embracing Plummer. In the actor's own words: "We got on like a house afire . . . I absolutely adored her."

When Andrews and Maria did meet on the set, they struck up a cordial relationship, their goodwill granting Maria the opportunity to size up Andrews, while the ever-polite star found that she simply hoped to make a good impression: "I was kind of nervous because I'm sure she must have been very anxious about who this lady was who was portraying her. I like to think we took to each other instantly." In the words of the film's original production notes, Maria told Andrews: "I'm delighted you're playing it as a tomboy—because that's what I was." Maria, of course, was more than a tomboy: she was downright hearty, and although Julie Andrews was a trim five seven, when viewed next to Maria she seemed, in Plummer's view, "so slight by comparison."

Far removed from the 1964 publicity efforts of Fox, in 1977 Maria offered a blunter assessment of her stage and screen alter egos, baldly declaring that both Mary Martin and Julie Andrews were "too gentle—like girls out of Bryn Mawr . . . I was a wild creature." Whatever her reservations, Maria possessed a genuine fondness for Andrews, and they renewed their acquaintance years later when Maria was a guest on Andrews's television show. Their banter about the film may have been scripted but it nonetheless proved amusing:

Andrews: How was I?

Maria (with a smile): You were absolutely wonderful—but . . .

Whereupon Maria's caveat served as the lead-in to a musical segment in which she showed Andrews how to let loose with a genuine Austrian yodel.

All such banter between the two Marias lay well in the future, however, because as Wise attempted to complete filming of "I Have Confidence," the first few drops of rain fell, quickly growing into a steady downpour. Because rainfall must be very heavy before it will actually show on film, Wise managed to capture the final shots of Maria at the villa's gates before the rain turned torrential and put a halt to filming.

The issue of the gates to the villa had figured in the very question of how to depict the von Trapp home onscreen. What could be simpler or more authentic than utilizing the family's actual villa for the climax of the number? Well, plenty as it turned out; because although undamaged during the war, the villa had been commandeered by Henrich Himmler himself, who had ordered an impenetrable and forbidding wall to be built around the house (by slave laborers). The wall not only spoiled the lines of the house but changed the very atmosphere. The solution?

Knowing, in the words of Wise, that they all "wanted to stay away from castles—too cute, too pixie, too sweet," Leven, Wise, and Zuberano found two different houses that could be blended together to form one villa. A clean-lined and rather imposing seventeenth-century home at Frohnburg (now the home of Mozarteum University) would be used to depict the front of the house in two scenes: Maria's first arrival at the home and the post-honeymoon sequence in which the captain pulls down the Nazi flag hanging in front of the house. (In an amusing anecdote about the flag tearing, Georg Steinitz recalled that the special effects department had sewed the rip line in the flag a tad too strongly: "When Christopher Plummer tried to tear the flag, it wouldn't rip. He pulled and pulled and ended up hanging on it like Tarzan–it still wouldn't come off. It was resewn and then the sequence finally worked!")

Trees were trimmed to improve the view of the villa, the house repainted from "Schoenbrunner Gelb" (yellow) to the von Trapp villa colors of white and ochre, and the location was good to go—with, of course, just a few Hollywood improvements thrown in along the way. Johannes von Trapp's wry comment on the film's version of the family villa: "My family did live in a big house with a lot of servants and a big garden, but in the film we're in a palace, not just a comfortable villa. It was a little over the top." How best to convey the imposing aristocratic character of the villa? It was decided that Leven would install iron gates at the entrance; confronted with a home of forbidding grandeur enclosed by an imposing gate, Maria's gulped murmur of "Oh, help!" near the end of "I Have Confidence" would ring all the more true.

The problem regarding the front of the villa may have been solved, but the back of Frohnburg lacked both the terrace and lake necessary for the scene in which Maria and the children fall into the water in front of the captain and Baroness Elsa. Loathe to give up what they deemed their perfect front of house exterior, Leven and Wise scheduled the lake and patio scenes to be shot at Leopoldskron Castle, which was owned by a school of American studies. Everything required for the scene existed right at Leopoldskron: a (man-made) lake, a landing for the boat, and an expansive terrace facing the water. All set? Not so fast. The film company now found itself barred from shooting at Leopoldskron. Undaunted, the ever resourceful Leven re-created the setting at Bertelesmann—a property situated right next door and also owned by the school. The two different locations would be seamlessly edited into one villa by William Reynolds.

Leven's simple but clever solution of utilizing two locations required a bit of sleight of hand when it came to reverse point-of-view shots emanating from the house's interior. When Maria arrives at the von Trapp home for the first time, and is greeted by Franz the butler (Gil Stuart), the beginning of their exchange, which takes place from Maria's point of view as she stands in front of the villa, was filmed on location at Frohnburg. The reverse shot from Franz's point of view, however, was shot back in Los Angeles on an interior set. Two settings on two continents equaled one house.

A similar blend occurs when the captain and Maria return from their honeymoon; greeting their parents outside, the children hug Georg and Maria and then enter the house. The entrance to the house was photographed on location, but the ensuing sequence depicting the captain, Maria, and Liesl talking inside the house, was filmed on a Fox studio interior set. This interior sequence was subtly but notably enhanced by the work of Dorothy Jeakins; taking care to chart each character's emotional status during the scene, Jeakins deliberately designed a more stylish and mature outfit than had previously been glimpsed on Andrews. Maria's life has changed—she is now a wife and mother, and her style of dress reflects those new roles. Along with her clothes, Maria has also changed her method of addressing her new husband. Formerly greeted as "Captain" or "Sir," he is now "darling," with no stop in between for "Georg." (Never once in the film does Maria address the captain as Georg.)

In order to match the different locations accurately, Wise had still photographs and film footage taken of both the exterior sets and the approaches leading thereto, the photographs providing the necessary detailed blueprint for the blend. He further protected himself by asking editor Bill Reynolds to bring a movieola to the set, their joint scrutiny of the footage ensuring that no glaring continuity errors would leap out at them months down the road in the editing room.

With a second villa complete with terrace, lake, and dock secured, it was time to film the scene of seven happy von Trapp children cavorting in the boat with Maria before falling into the water. Just one large impediment to the scene's high spirits arose: Kym Karath's terror of the water.

With the screenplay calling for the unsteady boat to tip all of the children overboard, Karath of necessity would end up in the water. Unable to swim, the youngster was frightened, yet determined to play along: "Robert Wise definitely had a gift for making someone feel like they're part of a team. It brings out the best in people." Reassured by the fact that Julie Andrews would keep a sharp eye on her at all times, Karath settled into the boat, and prepared herself for the unwanted submersion. Andrews caught Karath, the take was completed, and Karath breathed a genuine sigh of relief. But Wise did not like the first take, and now wanted one long shot of the children falling out of the boat and wading to shore.

Needing a shot of someone bundling Karath out of the water, Wise told Heather Menzies to carry the youngster to dry land at the end of take two, and with that final piece of instruction in place, all of the actors took their places in the boat:

"Roll Camera."

"Speed."

"Action!"

The camera rolled and the boat tipped, but this time Andrews fell over one side of the boat and Karath the other, with the five-year-old swallowing water, and starting to sink to the bottom. With Karath's mother standing on the sidelines screaming, "My baby! My baby," Alan Callow, the son of assistant director Reggie Callow, jumped in and saved the youngster. (Reggie Callow himself actually appears in the film as the driver of the horse-drawn carriage during "Do-Re-Mi.")

When Menzies herself scooped up the by now very frightened youngster she was rewarded by the five-year-old vomiting all of the water she had swallowed over her castmate. The resourceful Menzies simply washed herself off in the water. Finally, on the third take, everyone fell out of the boat on the same side and Karath's ordeal was at an end. (It was the second take that was used in the final edit, and sharp-eyed viewers will note a jump cut to Menzies, a necessary means of eliminating the footage of cast and crew trying to save Karath.)

Minus the near drowning, the high-spirited boat tipping sequence nicely contrasted with the sharp exchange between Maria and the captain that immediately followed. After Maria and the captain argue strongly over his unrelenting style of parenting, Georg asks Maria to leave at once. However, when he hears his children singing to the baroness, he softens: in the words of Wise, it's the "key turning point in the story." Plummer and Andrews had meticulously rehearsed the arc of the scene in advance with Wise, carefully charting the increasing volume of their mutually voiced displeasure as well as Maria's forthright denunciation of the captain, and both actors relished the chance to bite into a scene of real confrontation. Said Wise: "I was really pleased with the way that turned out."

"Do-Re-Mi": Maria von Trapp and the World's First Music Video

When the attention of all departments turned to the musical centerpiece of the film, "Do-Re-Mi," the overriding question remained whether the song could actually work onscreen. Would it land as a high-spirited romp—easy to achieve when Mary Martin is strumming a guitar right in the very same room with you—or as a hopelessly dated reminder that in the real world nannies and children don't sing in the horse-drawn carriages known as fiacres? Conceived by Ernest Lehman as a musical montage in which the seemingly childish rounde would require multiple locations and split-second timing, in its dramatic conception the number would not just propel the story forward but also compress time and space by depicting the passage of an entire summer.

Easy enough to say "compress time and space through song" but exactly how could the number be staged? There were no complex Sondheim-like lyrics featuring subtext to be explored. This was simple and straightforward—and had to last for nine minutes onscreen.

In choreographer Marc Breaux's recollection, "They asked what we were going to do for the 'Do-Re-Mi' number. I thought about it for a day or two and said, 'As long as she's going to be their nanny, let's make it like a travelogue and take them to every part of the city.' I don't like to do that many cuts, but every eight bars or four bars they (the audience) had a new venue to look at. . . ."

Locations selected by Breaux, Wise, and Lehman included everything from the Mozart bridge to mountainside meadows—even the ice caves at Warfen that had so captured Wise's fancy would make an appearance. The children would not be seen in the caves, but Wise specifically devised action that found Kurt and Friedrich tossing a ball at the start of the number: the higher the ball, the more of the caves could be seen in the background. More than any sequence in the entire film, "Do-Re-Mi" was planned to maximize Wise's overriding directorial concepts: Salzburg would pop onscreen as another character in the story.

Fearing that the film's biggest production number might lie stillborn on the big screen if every single movement was not properly synchronized, choreographers Wood and Breaux had drilled the children relentlessly during the weeks of rehearsal in Los Angeles before location filming began. Over and over the children rode their bicycles down the streets and alleys of the Fox back lot; as one child sang "Do," he would sprint to the front of the pack, only to be succeeded by the next child singing "Re," the entire group anchored by Maria pedaling her bicycle with Gretl perched in the seat behind her. Aside from Kym Karath, everyone needed to learn how to ride at varying speeds, synchronizing their pedaling with musical rhythms while lip-synching the lyrics in an ever-changing bicycle game of follow the leader. Said Charmian Carr: "When we got to Salzburg we knew everything. We had rehearsed for two months."

Filming the number in nine different locations throughout May and most of June, Wise and cinematographer Ted McCord planned to begin the number in a mountainside meadow, with Maria strumming her guitar and teaching the children to sing. The aim was to present the characters as a seemingly inevitable part of the landscape, Maria's free spirit and zest telescoped into the image of her leading the children Pied Piper–style—heads thrown back in exultation as they gloried in the sheer beauty of the meadow and towering peaks. After this stunningly scenic opening, Maria would utter two words— "Now children"—and the number would cut to a new location on Winkler Terrace, with everyone seen in different clothes. With this one cut, weeks have flown by. By the end of the song, considerably lengthened from the show, the entire summer would have passed.

If it all timed out properly, Maria and the children would run, boat, and bike their way through the landscape, pulsating figures who by their unfettered movement would give audiences a sense of freedom and release. By grounding all of the von Trapps in the landscape, audiences would also be granted another level of understanding as to why the Austrian homeland mattered so much to all of them. Said Julie Andrews: "Filming the montage was the quintessential moment of the film because we were all over Salzburg—in the country, out of it up in the mountains, running around fountains. It was so clever to use it as the moment the children were freed and to see that they adore Maria because of it."

The aim was to leave the audience with the same sense of exhilaration granted by the sight of Frank Sinatra, Gene Kelly, and Jules Munshin gleefully extolling the virtues of "New York, New York" in *On the Town* as they romp all over the city expressing the sheer joy of being alive and on twenty-four-hour leave from the Navy. Like Streisand moving through space, pushing forward onboard a surging train and sailing triumphantly past the Statue of Liberty in "Don't Rain on My Parade," it was all about a burst toward freedom.

What Wise, Breaux, and Wood wanted to avoid were the pitfalls found in the film versions of *Brigadoon* (1954) and the R&H musicals *South Pacific* and *Carousel*. In the words of R&H chief Ted Chapin: "*South Pacific* is almost like three movies in one: a travelogue celebrating the beauty of the region, the musical numbers, some of which are great, some pedestrian, and the most successful part of the film—the war story. It's just that you can never quite move beyond all those colored filters. It's distracting. Even *Oklahoma!*, which possesses many great elements, has the seemingly stagebound 'Many a New Day.' Why are they dancing around that room? For a completely successful transfer to the screen, the musicals need to be in the hands of master filmmakers like Robert Wise. Fred Zinnemann, who directed *Oklahoma!*, was a great director but he also was dealing with Rodgers and Hammerstein as producers of the film. It makes for a very different dynamic."

Even in the hands of master filmmakers, however, classic Broadway musicals could suffer unexpectedly in the transfer to the screen. If ever a film had cried out for location shooting, it was Lerner and Loewe's *Brigadoon*; starring two of film history's finest dancers, Gene Kelly and Cyd Charisse, and directed by the great Vincente Minnelli (*Gigi, An American in Paris*), the movie featured a beautiful score with songs that lent themselves perfectly to dancing outdoors ("Heather on the Hill"). But, with an increasingly budget-minded MGM refusing to pay for overseas filming, the end result featured great dancing on fake studio representations of the Scottish highlands, and the audience instantly knew that it was all phony. Where the movie should have soared, it never did more than trot.

In exactly the same manner, the obviously fake studio sets seen in portions of *Carousel* denied audiences the natural beauty and texture Wise and McCord now hoped to capture in and around Salzburg. In translating a solid theatrical musical into the hyperrealistic medium of film, Robert Wise was willing to put up with any location hassles—torrential rain, freezing temperatures, even uncooperative farmers—in order to avoid a fatal sense of static phoniness. He was determined, obsessed even, that the "Do-Re-Mi" montage would manage to fulfill the dictum of Alan Jay Lerner: "A great song can take the place of seventeen pages of dialogue."

Filming the beginning of the song as a sing-along at a picnic in the mountains sounded like a great idea, and the setting of Werfen, above the Salzach Valley, was certainly inspiring. It was, however, also freezing cold on that mountainside, the altitude so extreme that the actors were, for all intents and purposes, inside of a cloud.

Over and over a shot would be prepared, only to have ominous clouds roll in and a slight drizzle turn to downpour. As the June temperatures dropped to unseasonable lows, the cast and crew would huddle in blankets, play cards, tell stories, and in more than a few cases, partake of a few belts of homemade schnapps to keep warm. True to form, Julie Andrews would pick up the guitar and sing to the children during the repeated breaks.

The continual cloud cover actually did prove a blessing in one specific way; with McCord and Wise having mutually decided that they did not want a bold Technicolor hue to the film, opting instead to increase the romantic feeling of the film by filming in soft focus, the different shapes and colors of the clouds and sky, from golden sunshine to gathering cumulous clouds, added drama and texture and actually helped to cut down on the goop factor.

When sunlight finally appeared at Werfen, the endless waiting transformed instantly into "Ready, set, go!" In Andrews's recall, "Ted McCord would continually look through his viewfinder, and all of a sudden state, 'In five minutes we might get a shot of sunlight'; you had to be very disciplined and very ready to film at any moment." In the end, the montage's opening shots where Maria leads the children in Pied Piper fashion were snagged during the only minutes in which the view had been visible for three full days.

Robert Wise expected everyone involved, cast and crew alike, to be set for action at all times, and for all of the joking and singing through the weather delays, cast and crew remained in a perpetual state of readiness. With his bespectacled Midwestern insurance agent looks, Wise appeared to be, and was in fact, a genial sort. But no one on a Robert Wise film ever forgot that his word was law on the set. He simply never felt the need to raise his voice to achieve the desired effect. If he felt an actor was not up to the task or not cooperating sufficiently, he would simply let him go, firing the formidable Spencer Tracy on *Tribute to a Bad Man* and replacing him with the more cooperative James Cagney. Where an Otto Preminger intimidated, Wise explained calmly.

That gentle but firm control served the entire company well during the filming of "Do-Re-Mi," with the entire number shot in increments: two minutes of picnicking in the Alps, ten seconds patting the head of a statue, nine seconds at the Mozart bridge. It was hard, indeed nearly impossible, to grasp the number's overall effectiveness in this piecemeal method of shooting, but the troupe forged ahead and even mistakes seemed to increase the song's effectiveness. When part of the number found Maria and the children skipping along a riverside path, Karath unexpectedly fell down. Wise and Reynolds left the unplanned fall in the final edit, feeling that it added to the naturalism of the scene. Karath's own assessment? "I was a klutz."

Because of her fussy eating habits, Karath also figured in another humorous "Do-Re-Mi" anecdote. Faced with foreign cuisine, the five-year-old would only eat bread and fried artichokes, a diet that guaranteed a sizable weight gain. As a result, one of Andrews's most vivid memories of filming the number centers around her recollection of straining to pedal her bike with a chunkier than normal Karath perched in the seat right behind her. Years later, appearing on *The Ellen DeGeneres Show,* Andrews recalled that she genuinely liked and enjoyed all seven of her onscreen charges, adding: "They were all lovely. However, the youngest one (Karath) was probably the most difficult for me, because she was just a tad heavy in those days. Today, she is this amazing, gorgeous-looking Monroe-esque young lady."

More than any other number in the film, it was "Do-Re-Mi" that benefited from the musical know-how of Saul Chaplin. A jack-of-all-trades on the film, Chaplin was by now serving as right-hand adviser to Wise, music coordinator with choreographers Dee Dee Wood and Marc Breaux, and all around cheerleader in charge of boosting spirits. To Wise's considerable gratitude, "Saul worked with Julie, supervised numbers for orchestrations on pre-scoring, and was instrumental in supervising all the voices—all the musical components of the film. He was involved with casting, made contributions to the script, and to every aspect of the film including costumes—he was very, very, creative." Said Julie Andrews: "Saul, Marc, Dee Dee, and myself—we formed a singing group called the Vocal Zones. We'd sing lusty, bawdy songs on the mountainside to keep ourselves warm. We were playing cards, naughty with the jokes—great fun. . . . The song we sang the most was the 'Hawaiian War Chant!' "

So genial a presence was Chaplin, so attuned to the children, that script supervisor Betty Levin at first found him noisy and, if anything, too overwhelming a presence on the set. Discovering a mutual love of chamber music, however, Levin and Chaplin began to attend concerts together in Salzburg, and their relationship underwent a noticeable thaw. Said Betty years later: "There was candlelight. You would swear you were back in the eighteenth century. . . . We had the most beautiful, romantic time. . . ." Friendship turned to love, resulting in a marriage that lasted until Chaplin's death in 1997. In Betty's laughing recall: "Where else could you find someone who loved chamber music and didn't smoke?"

Chaplin's friendly presence—"a very nice gentleman" in the words of Georg Steinitz—permeated the entire production and it was Heather Menzies who lovingly summed up Chaplin's winning personality with the econium: "Part of the love that's evident in the film is Solly up there. What a tremendous life force he was!" It's a view echoed by Dan Truhitte: "Saul was as great a gentleman as Robert Wise, and that's saying a lot. He was really a musical genius. So generous and kind on the set. Some years later I was on the MGM lot and Saul drove by in this car. He stopped the car and actually ran after me just to say hi and greet me—a true gent."

During rehearsals in California, while watching the seven children and Andrews swing their arms and hitch kick their way around a mock-up of the Pegasus fountain ledge, Chaplin, in a flash of insight, had realized that the eight nearby Mirabell garden steps could be utilized to correspond with the eight notes of the scale heard at the end of the song. Wise loved the idea, and

Wood and Breaux choreographed the children and Andrews to hop up and down the steps, until, as the song reached its conclusion, they all hopped up again as Andrews put a musical exclamation point on the song by leaping an entire octave on her final note. That exhilarating last note was Andrews's own idea: "I thought it would be fun to go higher and higher as I climbed the steps. I asked if I could do the big octave leap and everyone said 'Go for it.' "

Now, months later, the filming of "Do-Re-Mi" had finally been completed, but skepticism abounded as to exactly how well the number would hold together. Georg Steinitz, hired in part for his knowledge of the Salzburg locations, admitted as much: "We had no sense that 'Do-Re-Mi' would prove to be so extraordinary. To tell the truth, the Germans and Austrians on the crew thought the number would never be a success."

One person—William Reynolds—felt very differently, and he now went to work on putting together a rough cut of the song. Blending each location seamlessly into the next, cutting precisely on the beats and changes of camera placement, he realized that the number was not just pleasant—it was sensational, a bona fide show stopper in the middle of a three-hour roadshow film. So beautifully did he finesse even the first cut of the song, that after a screening of the number in a small Austrian theater, seen-it-all pro Ted McCord's reaction was a simple but profound: "This is really going to be something."

What Ted McCord, and very soon the entire world realized, was that Reynolds had put together one of the all-time classic movie musical numbers.

Maria von Trapp was now starring in the world's first music video.

"Happy Campers"

What "Do-Re-Mi" revealed to everyone's delighted surprise was that although Andrews was, naturally enough, emerging as the movie's leading light, all seven of the children were delivering performances of greater effectiveness than anyone had anticipated.

Wise's ability to strike just the right tone with young actors was not unexpected, as evidenced by the performances he had drawn from children in films as diverse as *Curse of the Cat People* and *The Day the Earth Stood Still*. Like Steven Spielberg, who drew terrific performances from the children in *E.T.*,

Wise was neither bullying nor condescending in his approach. He understood the necessity of figuratively and literally working with the children on their own level, ofttimes kneeling down to explain the requirements of the scene. Directions were kept short and to the point, and in the recollection of Nicholas Hammond, cut to the bottom line instantly: "Remember, Nicky, your dad's here and you want to try and look strong in front of him."

Only once did Wise feel the need to chastise the children for not paying attention: "You're here to do a job. You can play on your own time. You don't play on my time." It was precisely because he had always spoken with kindness to the children that this atypical reprimand made a lasting impression: "We wanted his approval . . . because he was a sweetheart of a man." Said Georg Steinitz: "Robert Wise made sure certain words were not used on the set because of the presence of the children. He was great with them—very gentle. They were well behaved, disciplined. In fact I only saw Robert Wise get upset once, when he thought the little one had been kept up too late. He wanted to make sure they were well taken care of. They had a teacher on the set, did their homework, and were always prepared for scenes. It was only a few of the parents who were hanging around and grew bored who caused a few problems. But Mr. Wise was great with everyone. I have only the highest praise for him. He set the standard for the atmosphere on the set. There was never any shouting—yells of 'Quiet, please' were not part of the on-set atmosphere."

Thanks to Wise's inclusive, paternalistic approach, all seven children found the work exhilarating, and enjoyed themselves thoroughly, growing pains and all. Those growing pains were often literal: Debbie Turner's baby teeth fell out and dentists had to craft temporary false teeth to fill the gaps. For Nicholas Hammond, his growth spurt during filming from five three to five nine, required him to film his later scenes alongside Charmian Carr with the actress standing on boxes in order to appear taller than her onscreen younger brother. Hammond's growth spurt, in fact, proved an ironic counterpoint to Heather Menzies's pre-filming worries that she would not be cast because she was then three inches taller than Nicky.

While Charmian Carr remained at the Bristol Hotel where Plummer lodged (at twenty-one, Carr was closer in age to Julie Andrews's twenty-eight than she was to the other children, the oldest of whom was thirteen), the other six children (and Dan Truhitte) stayed at the Mirabell Hotel with their parents.

Although well-behaved for the most part, the youngsters did pull minor pranks; shoes left outside guest room doors for overnight polishing were randomly switched, and havoc was occasionally wreaked with room service orders, but boys and girls alike were having too good a time with their "work" to feel the need to make trouble.

Even the required four and a half hours per day of studying with tutor Jean Seaman did not prove tiresome, given that the hands-on geography and history lessons found the children touring all over Salzburg and the Austrian countryside. A geography lesson on the formation of the Alps and how they shaped European history? Forget the dusty textbook. These children were standing on the very mountain peaks in question.

The handwritten reports reproduced in *The Sound of Music Family Scrapbook* underscore the high spirits: Angela Cartwright's report on her visit to the ice caves is amusingly creative, as she determinedly tries, in her own words, to make her essay "as scary as possible." The kids even had a bit of cheeky fun with *The Sound of Music* itself, with the older children writing a parody version of "Edelweiss" that concluded with the words: "Bless my paycheck forever." (It's a parody the two youngest, Debbie Turner and Kym Karath, had never heard until their 2005 Fortieth Anniversary Reunion.)

So congenial a group were the children that when filming resumed in Los Angeles, the local board of education wrote to assistant director Reggie Callow to tell him that there had been fewer problems with *The Sound of Music* children than there had been on any other film in recent memory. Perhaps more astonishing was the testimony of script supervisor Betty Chaplin, who stated: "Even the parents were terrific."

Surrounded by a congenial crew, a director they desperately wanted to please, beautiful scenery, and a star they adored, these young actors were having the time of their lives. Young and inexperienced though they were, those who were old enough already held enough perspective to appreciate just how special the experience was. In Nicholas Hammond's evocative recollection with Charmian Carr about the filming of "Do Re-Mi": "We were all talking and laughing and Saul was telling stories about musicals and joking about the hard roll and cheese we had for breakfast, and I remember your laughter, and I just thought, 'I don't want this rain to ever stop. I just love this and these people and this world.' I still do."

The seven child actors were having the time of their lives, and thanks to Wise's firm but low-key leadership, the behind the scenes personnel were all enjoying Austria. Only one person was unhappy. Very unhappy.

Christopher Plummer.

An Unhappy Captain

It's not that Christopher Plummer was unhappy with Austria. It was his time on the set of *The Sound of Music* that he didn't like. Having carved out a justifiably first-rate reputation for his interpretations of Shakespeare and Ibsen, he was already worried about what the film might do to his reputation as a serious classical actor. But rather than suffer in silence, he made sure that everyone involved knew that playing the captain ranked miles below his usual standards, behaving, in his own words, like a "pampered, arrogant, young bastard spoiled by too many great theater roles." He decided that the world should know what an affront the role remained, and he made a point of reminding people that he was playing the role "under duress, that it had been forced upon me and that I certainly deserved better." Writing about the experience decades later he bluntly admitted: "My behavior was unconscionable."

This theoretically happy family musical was now being partially anchored by a noticeably unhappy actor, but a situation that could easily have degenerated into a pervasively unhappy set never did so. Because of his talent and his (admittedly well-hidden) genuinely appealing personality, he had two unquestioned allies on the set, and they happened to be the most important allies of all: director Robert Wise and leading lady Julie Andrews. Said Plummer: "The one person who seemed to understand my motives completely and acted as if there was nothing untoward was Julie, the busiest of us all. I was so grateful to her for that, but I never told her."

The necessary rapport between the two leads was present on the set from the start, and Plummer, a flinty, gimlet-eyed observer, realized it at once. Writing with genuine emotion about his costar in his autobiography, he simply stated: "She held us together and made us a team." The feeling was clearly mutual because Andrews used the same words regarding Plummer: "He was the wonderful glue that held us all together—his command, his presence, his great good looks." If, as Andrews has stated, she was in awe of Plummer at the start of the shooting, that awe quickly changed to mutual respect, and in her decades' later recollection: "We've been great friends ever since."

As the six weeks of location filming stretched to eleven, the basic personalities of these key players were thrown into bold relief. Uniquely placed to observe all participants, Charmian Carr found that Julie Andrews never complained, Christopher Plummer cursed, and "Bob (Wise), who knew what was on the line as each minute ticked by, never lost his cool."

Swearing and fuming, Plummer's behavior affected his relationship with his onscreen children. If Julie Andrews was the glue that held the family together, bonding with the youngsters to such an extent that many of the seven openly idolized her, no such rapport existed between the children and Plummer. That real-life distance actually ended up helping the film, the remove between leading man and young actors coming to reflect and inform the onscreen distance between Captain von Trapp and his children; in the recall of Heather Menzies, during the seven months of shooting, Plummer "never said a single word to me off camera. Not one." Even when the script called for the children to reconcile with their father while singing "The Sound of Music," she recalled that she simply "didn't trust him. It wasn't until the premiere when he put his arm around me and said 'Good to see you' that he showed me any affection." (A slightly different take on Plummer's friendliness is offered by Duane Chase, who received a photograph of a shared comic moment off camera with Plummer, inscribed by the actor: "To the two laughing boys.")

Menzies did admit that part of such standoff behavior may have been Plummer behaving in character, while another portion of it simply arose from his own humorously sardonic point of view that "There needed to be a cynic of some kind around to stop it from getting too saccharine." What the children presumably did not hear, however, was the fact that he later admitted to calling the film "S and M."

It may just be, however, that the biggest reason for his ofttimes ornery disposition resulted from his general dislike of, or at best indifference to, children. Whatever the cause, it all increased the film's effectiveness, his view of children made plain in his own intentionally hilarious commentary: "I loathe them. I always find that they are a total nuisance; just when you're ready to work there's some union rule that you can't work these little monsters for more than five minutes at a time, so I enjoyed being the Nazi martinet during these scenes and treating them like cattle."

Speaking with his tongue lodged at least halfway in his cheek he did go on to state: "I got to like them enormously. I'm not all Peck's Bad Boy. Of course they still had to go to school, damn their hides." In his twenty-first-century recollection, Plummer seemed to hold a particularly bemused spot for Kym Karath: "The little one turned into a drop-dead knockout—gorgeous. Of course at the time we would become impatient with her because she was really a naughty girl but when you see her now you forgive her everything."

With the passage of time has come Plummer's affection toward the children, but at the time of shooting, he remained irritated and irritating, to the point that even the eternally genial Saul Chaplin found fault with the actor's behavior. Zeroing in on Plummer's self-admitted condescending behavior toward those on the film, Chaplin harrumphed: "He behaved as though he were a distinguished legendary actor who had agreed to grace this small amateur company with his presence. He sometimes wore a cape, which made him look like an escapee from Transylvania."

It wasn't just Plummer's inability to connect with the source material that displeased him. It was the musical component of the movie as well. Never having sung on film, Plummer very much wanted to supply all of his character's vocals himself, and he obstinately refused to let his admittedly untrained voice be dubbed. After lengthy discussions/disagreements with Wise, Chaplin, and Irwin Kostal, a compromise was reached: Plummer would work on his singing, and after recording his vocals at the end of shooting, he would acquiesce to being dubbed if the creative team felt that his singing was not up to the levels they all deemed necessary. Plummer worked diligently on his vocal technique throughout filming, and while the final results were certainly not substandard, they were also not inspiring, especially when placed in conjunction with Andrews's flawless soprano. Their vocal pairing, Plummer admitted, left something to be desired, and his own verdict was straightforward: "It's just not musical enough. . . . When our voices were put together, my long sustained notes were simply not good enough beside hers."

Plummer was right. Even a casual listen to his vocals reveals that while the notes are all in place, there is a lack of ease to his singing. The strain to hold notes is evident, and the audience can never quite relax while listening. Tension permeates the air, as if the audience needs to collectively root on the actor in his attempt. In the end, Plummer was ably dubbed by Bill Lee, whose wife Ada Beth Lee was portraying Sister Catherine in the film; the male version of Marni Nixon, Lee had also provided the singing voice of John Kerr in the 1958 film version of *South Pacific*.

Finding that he was not needed every day on set—"I was in Salzburg for nine or ten weeks but I worked for only a week or two"—Plummer took time to enjoy the sights and sounds of Salzburg. He grew very fond of his home base, the small and personal Bristol Hotel, where he particularly enjoyed playing the lounge piano into the early hours of the morning. (Saul Chaplin's disdain for the actor's behavior even extended to Plummer's piano playing. Although Plummer had trained as a classical pianist, Chaplin had no use for his playing, describing his style as "florid, with incessant, meaningless arpeggios.") Like Frank Sinatra, who demanded company from his friends during his boozy wee-small-hours revels, Plummer would, in the recollection of Charmian Carr, become angry if the other bar regulars—Breaux, Wood, and Betty Levin—tried to leave the bar and actually go to bed: "He complained about having to get up early and go through makeup when the rain would mean we wouldn't be shooting. He would get angry if we would leave the bar to go to bed." (Said Georg Steinitz: "Tricks were played on Plummer to get him out of the bar. Sometimes Reggie Callow—the first assistant director—would put him on the call sheet one day before he was needed. When he found out what was going on, he was mad. Really mad.")

Pleasure for Plummer came in the form of schnapps and pastries, which he happily consumed to the point where his costumes had to be let out. The actor eventually grew to love Salzburg so much that he has returned many times since, for the music, the scenery, and to visit friends. Although Julie Andrews has stated that Austria "is indelibly printed on my mind—the colors, the feeling, the fresh, fresh air in the Alps—so beautiful," she has actually only returned three times, the most recent visit taking place in September 2014 for the purposes of filming a documentary included with the film's 50th Anniversary DVD release.

In Carr's fond recollection, under Plummer's tutelage she enjoyed her first ever tastes of champagne, white wine, red wine, and whiskey. Not quite old enough to be Carr's father, Plummer seemed to occupy the role of favorite uncle, filling part of the void left by a father who had vanished. As it was, between a father who had disappeared and a mother who had started to drink excessively, Carr had begun to fit the classic pattern of children in unhappy homes who believe that they are the cause of all family problems. It was no wonder, then, that while making *The Sound of Music,* the young actress was happy to find herself surrounded by a new, much less complicated family circle. Flourishing in the glamorously foreign environs, she affected no world-weary airs, embracing her experiences with a wholesome enthusiasm. In a letter written to her mother while on location, she exudes a love for Austria reminiscent of Maria von Trapp herself, and in the process offers a clue as to why all seven children seemed as genuinely happy offscreen as on: "I wish I could stay here forever. It is almost like being in Heaven. The river is so inspiring and the trees are tall and green—all pointing up to God."

While Plummer's light schedule allowed him to enjoy the sights of the Austrian countryside, weather delays caused the film to fall further and further behind schedule. With damp and cold conditions prevailing, the daily call sheets soon evolved into three possibilities: sunny, overcast, and indoors at Durer studio. The weather remained so changeable that even scenes deemed weather-safe for outdoor filming ran into problems. It was all too symbolic of the rain-plagued shoot that just when the cameras rolled for Lehman's newly written "blueberry picking scene" on the terrace, a light drizzle began to fall. As the children began to speak of missing Maria, singing in rather dispirited fashion (and the audience knows things are bad when the von Trapps sound out of energy), the occasional raindrop increased to a consistent drip, before morphing into a steady rainfall. Rather than fall even further behind schedule, Ted McCord hung a tarp, adjusted the lighting on the terrace, and the scene proceeded without incident. Said Robert Wise: "Ted had to artificially light the scene to match what's under the tarp with what's not under the tarp—he did a great job." In the end, so skillfully relit was the scene that even eagle-eyed viewers of the Blu Ray reissue will have a tough time finding the hint of a shower.

With rainy conditions predominating almost from the start, beginning on May 14 Wise utilized the cover set of the Mother Superior's office, which had been constructed in Los Angeles and shipped to Austria's Durer studios, in order to film "Climb Ev'ry Mountain." The director at last had environs in Austria that he could totally control, and he knew how large the emotional import of "Climb Ev'ry Mountain" loomed in the message of *The Sound of Music*: faith, uplift—it all went right to the heart of the movie. He liked the setup for the song with the Mother Abbess urging Maria to face new possibilities of freedom by leaving the comfort of the Abbey behind, but what he couldn't shake was the feeling of embarrassment he had experienced listening to the song as presented onstage. If he felt manipulated by the song's onstage presentation as a stentorian showstopper, what would the song be like on a thirty-foot screen? How was he going to make this possible schmaltz-fest of a tune work? For that matter, how was he going to complete the outdoor staging of "So Long, Farewell," the film-concluding mountain climb, and the song itself?

By remembering what any great film director would do—let the camera tell the story.

Then break all the rules.

14

SONG AND DANCE

"CLIMB EV'RY MOUNTAIN"

Utterly stymied by what he considered to be the song's over-the-top emotion, and searching for a solution, Wise talked to Ted McCord about filming the scene from a side angle, thereby avoiding the cringe-inducing spectacle of Peggy Wood's Reverend Mother singing directly into the camera. Nobody wanted a thirty-foot-tall Mother Superior appearing to hector the audience in song, so Wise and McCord made the daring choice to begin the number with Wood's back to the camera. Instead of the soft focus look that dominates much of the film, McCord would here utilize deep shadows; even after Wood turns around, her face would often appear in half light. The anthemic power of the song would now be toned down by the scene's visual reserve, the song registering as the Mother Abbess's advice to a questioning Maria.

As her words to Maria moved from dialogue into song, Wood walked to the window, the camera panning with her as she began to sing while still in shadow. Finishing the song while standing at the window, she was no longer in full shadow, yet could still be seen only in partial light. Darkness to light—for the Reverend Mother, the song, and Maria alike.

Wood's superior acting ability managed to infuse the song with a gravitas leavened by nobility, her natural warmth combining with the music and deliberately subdued atmosphere to provide a genuinely memorable moment in the film. The sequence unfolded in such moving fashion that even Julie Andrews found herself affected in the playing: "It was so easy—I loved her speaking voice. The scene went very easily thanks to her. . . . When I first started to film the scene I became very teary—the song, the orchestra, a very moving moment for my character."

"SO LONG, FAREWELL—PART II"

With "Climb Ev'ry Mountain" completed, the next problems to be solved re-
volved around the complications posed by the frigid nighttime shoot for the
von Trapps' farewell concert. It wasn't the location that caused the difficulties;
Boris Leven and Maurice Zuberano had found the ideal setting for the concert
in the atmospheric Rock Riding Academy outdoor theater. Originally used as
the Archbishops' stables, the setting provided just the right dramatic, forbidding atmosphere for the climax to the film, although screenwriter Lehman's
original idea for a chase in which soldiers jumped down from the arches and
pursued the von Trapps through the forest had been discarded as impractical.

Instead, having spent several days preparing the lighting in advance of the
actual shooting, Ted McCord realized that his deliberately harsh photographic
approach could fully express the sense of danger simply via the sight of silent
storm troopers silhouetted in the more than one hundred natural arches of
the ampitheater. (One does wonder why the Nazis didn't just hurry the Captain along to his new position in the Navy of the Third Reich by shooting off
a few rounds to stop "So Long, Farewell" mid-chorus, but if they did that,
we'd never have had Gretl's solo. . . .)

Filming of the song was first delayed when the filmmakers realized that
contrary to their assumptions, none of the one thousand period-clad extras in
the outdoor theater knew the words to "Edelweiss." Said assistant director
Georg Steinetz: "My assignment was to tell the crowd to join in the singing of
'Edwelweiss'—but I had to teach them the song first! I think Robert Wise
thought the song was the Austrian national anthem and I had to say 'No—
it's by Rodgers and Hammerstein.' We arranged it that members of a chorus
sat in the first rows to sing and lip-synch to the action. It actually worked out
very well." This crash course in the lyrics of Oscar Hammerstein II caused
the filming to drag on into the early hours of the morning, the time enlivened
by the sight of five-year-old Kym Karath playing gin rummy with extras
dressed as Nazis.

What everyone remembers from those nights of shooting at the Rock
Riding Academy was the frigid May weather. Shooting consumed four
nights, and in Christopher Plummer's years' later recollection while watching

the film: "I don't think I'm totally sober there. We drank to keep warm and to keep our spirits up!"

With much of May occupied with the complicated and weather-delayed "Do-Re-Mi" montage, it wasn't until June 4 that the company filmed both a portion of the title song as well as the family's concluding climb over the Alps into freedom. Location scouting had turned up several mountains that would nicely frame the escape to Switzerland, but only one of them, Obersalzberg, possessed the roads essential for transporting all of the required personnel and equipment.

Once Julie Andrews had completed her twirl-spinning chores on "Maria's mountain," she journeyed to Obersalzberg to join the remainder of her on-screen family, all of whom were already ensconced at the location. Andrews remembers the set being miles from home base, with the trailers and food trucks parked at the bottom of the mountain, a very long way from the mountaintop. "We had to walk a very long way to get to this particular shot—and it was cold. But how fortunate we were to see that view!" A different recollection is offered by Georg Steinitz, who remembered that the location required no great effort, as the roads were wide, paved, and culminated in a parking lot situated close to the chosen location. Whichever remembrance is accurate, the stunning view proved to be the bottom line, a startling, panoramic expanse that would end the film just as it began—in the midst of the breathtaking scenery of the Alps.

This final scene, which would be scored to a full chorus urging the world to "Climb Ev'ry Mountain," did, however, prove more strenuous than anticipated due to a humorous-in-hindsight problem caused by five-year-old Kym Karath's starch-heavy diet. Having packed on more than a handful of pounds during shooting, Karath now proved such a cumbersome armful that Christopher Plummer insisted on a lighter double to carry on his back over the mountains. It was a wise move given that the mountain escape required twelve takes. (Plummer, in fact, was not alone in his surprise over Karath's heft during filming. As staged by Wood and Breaux, the "So Long, Farewell" number had required Charmian Carr to pick up youngest "sister" Karath at the climax of the song. After multiple takes, Carr's reaction was an emphatic: "My God! This kid is very heavy!") Extra poundage and all, after the twelfth and final take, the von Trapps

were judged successfully launched on their way to freedom in Switzerland.

When filming on "Do-Re-Mi" was completed on June 27, the children
(with the exception of Charmian Carr who stayed behind in Salzburg to
finish the shooting of a documentary entitled *Sights and Sounds of Salzburg*)
were sent back to Los Angeles to prepare for the resumption of interior filming on July 6. With Plummer and all of the supporting actors having already
left Salzburg, Julie Andrews alone remained in Austria. Saved for the last
day of location shooting in order to save the cost of housing extraneous cast
and crew, the completion of the title song remained the last big hurdle on
hand. All too predictably, the weather once again played havoc with the
schedule, and in the recall of Georg Steinitz, that continuing bad weather
pushed the filming of the song into several additional days of shooting.
"They put Julie Andrews in a hotel a few miles away and I was in charge of
bringing her to the set when we thought the sun would come out. It was a
delicate task to go to her hotel room and ask her to get out of bed and come
to the mountain but she was terrific about it. She was so nice, natural,
normal—great to work with. She'd say 'I know it won't clear up but I"ll
come anyway.' We all thought she was terrific."

The roads now a total washout that even jeeps could not penetrate, Julie
Andrews found herself loaded into an ox cart along with all of the camera
and sound equipment, rolling and heaving through boulders and mud while
bouncing along a very steep and extraordinarily bumpy path to the meadow.
At the end of an exhausting location shoot, the leading lady of this multimillion-
dollar musical was about to film the very famous title song, and found herself being transported to the location in a smelly ox cart, jostled by equipment
while wrapped in a fur coat. A fur coat? Not exactly the garment young postulant Maria Rainer would be wearing for her hillside warbling, but the never-
complaining Julie Andrews needed to keep warm. (Decades later, Andrews
would recall her wearing of the fur coat as a very strange choice, exclaiming
in wonder, "A mink coat of all dumb things!")

And now, just to complete the picture, as the fur-clad Andrews finally arrived at the green meadow, the farmer who owned the land ran outside and
began screaming obscenities at Andrews. In German. Andrews's dry comment? "Fortunately I couldn't understand him."

These Hollywood interlopers were disturbing his cows so much that they weren't producing milk. Hollywood be damned—"Get the hell off my land!" (Although not present for the filming of the song, Georg Steinitz casts some humorous doubt as to exactly what the farmer said: "Why would he yell and cause problems? He was being paid a lot of money!") As it was, Wise had made a deal for use of the meadow "as is," but when he arrived for shooting, the tall grass he thought would make the setting even more interesting had been cut down by the recalcitrant farmer. There was no time for a delay. Short, clipped grass it would be.

But for right now, there were further problems to be solved with that irate German farmer. How could the number include those famous Oscar Hammerstein II words: "To laugh like a brook as it trips and falls" when there was no brook to be found in this particular meadow? Veteran production designer Boris Leven thought he had solved the problem by creating and irrigating his own rubber-lined, highly realistic-looking brook, yet when the company arrived on July 1 for yet another weather-delayed day of filming, they discovered that the irritated farmer, pitchfork in hand, had purposefully opened holes in the rubber-lined brook and emptied it completely.

Two days later, with the brook now relined and refilled, that particular sequence within the number was ready for filming. Except—what about those birch trees through which the crystal clear mountain light would be oh-so-artfully filtered? Those "trees," brought in and planted for the shoot, actually looked more like tall stubs, but with McCord's careful use of angles, they'd photograph very nicely. As for the dappled lighting needed to create a sense of peaceful shade, the crew took care of that by hanging canvas directly overhead.

Shade—set.

Brook—filled.

Weather—not ready.

Waiting out another cloudburst, the filmmakers were finally rewarded with precisely twenty minutes of sunshine. With the camera at speed and sound in synch, Julie Andrews hopped onto the strategically placed stones in the brook, tossing pebbles in time with the prerecorded music and hitting her marks with unwavering precision. She smiled radiantly, completed the sequence, and prepared for the next shot, which would find her running toward the camera and cresting the hill just as she hit the phrase "I go to the hills . . ."

Effortlessly calibrating her energy and joyous demeanor so that they would blend seamlessly with the first half of the number filmed a full month earlier, Julie Andrews confidently strode through take after take, perfecting the musical number that would earn her a place in cinema history. A place in film history, however, was the furthest thing from Andrews's mind as one last take of the song was finally completed. What she wanted now was to hug her daughter Emma, soak the cold out of her bones in a long, hot bath, and prepare herself for the trip back to the United States.

Hollywood had never looked so good.

15.

BACK HOME: HOORAY FOR HOLLYWOOD

An exhausted but still game Andrews flew back to Hollywood to rejoin her cast mates, and with no further weather catastrophes to endure, the pace of filming picked up considerably as scene after scene unfolded smoothly on Fox soundstage fifteen.

At times the results were expected: it had become clear very early on in filming that Richard Haydn's impudent sarcasm would enliven every sequence in which Max appeared. At other times, scenes played out with layers and subtext that, if not a total surprise, landed with a grace and emotional depth that surpassed all expectations. First-rate as the work of Wood and Breaux had been in "Do- Re-Mi," their shining moment occurred when Maria and the captain danced "The Laendler" ("The Lonely Goatherd" played in waltz tempo) at the party that the captain throws in honor of the baroness.

For such a moving dance, the rehearsals actually started out on a highly humorous note. Fifty years later, the memory of Christopher Plummer's appearance at the start of dance rehearsal still makes Dee Dee Wood laugh. "On the first day Christopher appeared in ballet tights, black ballet slippers, and a T-shirt. I said: 'Mr. Plummer, you don't have to do that. You can wear your regular trousers and shoes. That'll be better—more in keeping with who you are when you're performing the dance.' Later on he told us that he deliberately planned that outfit!"

As for the dance itself, Maria first dances with Friedrich before the captain cuts in. Combining steps from several different Austrian folk dances, Wood and Breaux staged the dance in such an understated fashion that it allows the audience the chance to watch Maria and Georg fall in love while dancing. Hand outstretched, Maria hesitates mid-dance, and as she and the captain slowly spin while gazing into each others' eyes, they both understand that they are falling in love—a realization that stops them dead in their tracks. It's a lovely quiet moment, one ofttimes overlooked in discussions about the film's exuberance, and ranks as one of the key moments in which the full extent of Andrews's abilities as a musical actress became clear. Even Andrews herself was knocked out by the final dance: "There was romance in the air. There was a wonderful sort of skimming shot as we passed right in front of the camera with our arms crossed. It looked like we were floating." In the final analysis, said Dee Dee Wood: "I think it furthered the story of Maria and the captain more than anything else in the film. Once they started to dance—and then stopped while looking at each other—that was the key to the rest of the film. . . . I love the Laendler so much. The way they look at each other—as an audience member you feel so much and realize, 'Oh, boy, they are really in love.' They were both so marvelous in that sequence. When he danced Christopher was reserved, gentlemanly—a perfect fit for the character. And Julie—so very, very easy to work with. A total pro and a complete talent."

In fact, such was the extent of Andrews's abilities that her two most telling emotional moments in the film may well come in a pair of silent reactions. The first occurs when her seemingly unrequited love for the captain registers merely through the expression on her face as she watches him sing with his children. (Surprisingly, Wise at one point decided to film the scene without the captain joining the children in song, but he quickly came to realize that it was the captain's singing that provided the scene's emotional heft.)

Affecting as Andrews is in this moment, she was substantially aided by the work of Ted McCord. When, after joining his children in song, the captain realizes the error of his ways and quietly asks Maria to stay, his carefully phrased request—and for the first time it is a request, not a command—marks a turning point in his relationship with the governess. Maria pauses on the stairs to reply, and with the latticework of the staircase banister in the foreground and her shadow falling on the wall behind, the look of the scene lends additional texture by pinpointing Maria in a defined space and light at this crucial moment of change. McCord is not calling attention to himself with the shadows and light, but rather, simply serving the story itself. Here is the moment, in Julie Andrews's analysis, when the captain began to fall in love with Maria.

Andrews's second, and even more subtly crafted bit of acting, occurs when she returns to the von Trapp villa after running away to the abbey. Upon hearing that the captain is marrying the baroness—in Wise's words, the news represents a "blow to the pit of the stomach"—Maria's sadness and quiet resignation come silently to the fore through nothing more than Andrews's haunted and disappointed eyes. It's a beautifully modulated piece of acting that won her Wise's lasting admiration. In fact, it wasn't just his leading lady's energy and talent that bowled over the director. The seen-it-all veteran remained more than a bit in awe of Andrews's fierce work ethic, which landed her one of the highest compliments in the director's lexicon: "Julie wants to rehearse and rehearse and get it better and better. She's a delight to work with—how wonderfully well she works with the other actors in their scenes. Sometimes she'd say to me 'I can get it a little better' even after I thought it was a good take. . . ."

Andrews returned the compliment in full. It wasn't just Wise's ability to shape the overall arc of her performance that the star admired. She also paid him full credit for teaching her crucial film acting techniques: on what was only her third film, it was Wise who taught her how to gaze into someone's face by finding a single spot and never moving one's eyes, as well as how to hold still in a close-up. In short, she emphasized, it was Robert Wise who was responsible for "teaching me a great deal about film acting."

At the opposite end of the spectrum from the understated "Laendler" lay its musical twin, "The Lonely Goatherd," a number in which the participants' exuberance equaled that found in "Do-Re-Mi." In the stage show, Maria sang "The Lonely Goatherd" in order to cheer up children frightened by a thunderstorm, but Lehman had here invented a much improved setup for the song; Max has bought a marionette set as a means of showing the captain how such talented children should be allowed to sing in public—and make money. In this one stroke Lehman has explained cynical, money-hungry, yet somehow lovable Max. Even though he is always looking for the main chance, he still remains genuinely fond of the children.

It was the second change to the song, however, that made the number even more memorable: the use of actual marionettes to illustrate Hammerstein's cascade of rhyming lyrics:

Men on a road
With a load to tote heard

Once the decision had been made to utilize marionettes in the number, an offer went out to the world-famous Salzburg Marionette Theatre (founded 1913). They turned down the chance to participate in the film, a refusal that the present-day director of the theater Dr. Barbara Heuberger humorously analyzed by stating: "Perhaps they thought it was too American. Big mistake!" It was only at this point that an offer was put out to famed American puppeteers Bil and Cora Baird. Happily signing on, the Bairds worked for several weeks in tandem with Breaux and Wood to choreograph the puppets' every twitch of the strings in exact time to the music. Given the actors' uniform lack of experience with marionettes, the Bairds simplified the actors' required movements to a bare minimum, deciding to handle all of the intricate maneuvers by themselves. Wise framed one or two shots showing each of the five older children handling a marionette, assigned the two youngest, Debbie Turner and Kym Karath, the simple chore of moving the scenery, and trusted the Bairds to coordinate the more complex, breezy, polka-fueled movements.

Exhausting for the actors in its cramped intimacy, the number found Andrews and the children crammed close together under very hot lights, lipsynching to the prerecorded music while trying to synchronize their marionettes with the music. For Nicholas Hammond, however, the sequence proved one of sheer bliss; here, at last, he could stand next to Julie Andrews for hours on end. "My adoration for her was such that I couldn't have cared if there was any film in the camera."

The number itself is a high-spirited—and genuinely humorous—frolic, yet at the same time, by subtly showcasing the reactions of the captain and Elsa to the performance, serves as the real start of the love triangle between the captain, Maria, and the baroness. In its final form the number proved a bona fide audience pleaser, but whatever its dramatic utility, the last and funniest word on the subject of the marionettes belongs to Dee Dee Wood, who humorously queried: "Did you notice that those female marionettes were very well endowed? Did you notice that? In *The Sound of Music*!" She's right— and anyone who takes a second look at the number will never react in quite the same way again. All that clean country air . . .

Having successfully staged a production number with marionettes, for seven children no less, Maria now seems almost too good to be true—isn't there anything at which she's not adept? Twirling marionettes, whipping up seven matching outfits out of curtains, spreading unfailing good cheer—she's almost enough to bring out the cynic in even the most sympathetic viewer, which is precisely why Eleanor Parker's razor-sharp take on the baroness undercuts the sweetness so smoothly. Observing the exuberant singing and yodeling of Maria and the children as they deftly maneuver the marionettes, the baroness mutters to Max: "You should have told me to bring my harmonica." Baroness Elsa and Sister Berthe—acerbic sisters under the skin.

Even better is Parker's murmured reply to Maria's expression of concern that she's not sure she'll make a good nun: "If you need anything, I'd be happy to help you." In just this one abbreviated sequence lay the wisdom of Wise's instinct to cast Parker; in her sincerely insincere reading, she lands this choice line in a knowing, yet nonbitter fashion.

Parker seems to actually capture the essence of the real-life baroness, Princess Yvonne (called "Aunt Yvonne" by the von Trapp children). Reading Maria von Trapp's autobiographical description of her rival for the captain's affections, one can already hear Parker coolly delivering Yvonne's own words; upon meeting Maria for the first time, the princess dryly commented: "Well, well—the wonder girl of whom I have heard so much." After a little further bitchery in which Yvonne informs Maria that the captain "just likes you because you have been so congenial with the children," the essential difference between the two women was laid out in stark relief when Maria asked the princess why she was not going to include the children in her wedding to the captain: "My goodness, did you think I was marrying the children? What a queer little youngster you are!"

Parker's own performance seemed to grow in strength and skill throughout the course of filming, and one of the central reasons why the song "Something Good" succeeds so beautifully is because of Parker's performance in the immediately preceding sequence. In lesser hands, this scene in which the baroness releases the captain to go find Maria could have read as histrionic and false. Watching Parker's eyes throughout—her ability to silently convey Elsa's hurt, acceptance, and dawning realization that a marriage to the captain could never work—is to understand why her film career lasted four decades and brought her three Oscar nominations. Decades after the film's release Wise commented: "Every time I see the picture I respect and admire her for her performance." Wise's appreciation of Parker was echoed by the hard-to-please

Plummer, who extolled the actress's beauty, poise, and gentle elegance: "I nearly dumped Julie for her!"

As the filming neared conclusion, the seven children continued to have such a good time on the set that it came as a collective shock to them when, on August 10, right before singing the emotionally charged reprise of "The Sound of Music" with Christopher Plummer, they were informed by Robert Wise that this was to be the very last group scene they would film (only Charmian Carr's "Sixteen Going on Seventeen" remained). The thought of their journey together coming to an end, the prospect of returning to the black-and-white Kansas of their everyday lives after the magical Technicolor Oz experience of filmmaking, caused tears to flow and helped inform the scene. The combination of the inherent power of the material with a dawning realization that in real, as well as reel life, Plummer actually did care for them, unleashed a genuine emotional response in the children. In the recall of Charmian Carr, even director Wise was affected: "I think Robert Wise was crying when he directed it; I saw a few little tears in his eyes and those were genuine."

Production on the Fox lot wound down to the last few days, and the by-now thoroughly exhausted Andrews succumbed to a nonstop fit of laughter during "Something Good" that brought filming to a complete halt. Here was the emotional climax of the captain and Maria's love story, complete with a brand-new Richard Rodgers song, and Julie Andrews's laughter threatened to derail the entire scene. Five grueling months into the shoot, Andrews had passed the point of total exhaustion, and by her own admission, whenever tired, she becomes "wobbly" and starts to laugh.

Redoubling her efforts not to break up caused her to fall apart all over again, and Plummer soon joined her in uncontrollable fits of giggles. The inadvertent culprit? Cinematographer Ted McCord.

In lighting the set, McCord found that the hectagonal gazebo utilized for the number taxed even his ingenuity, with the multiple panes of glass, all set at different angles, refracting the light and causing it to bounce at complex angles. Couple that geometry with the background cyclorama utilized to convey the nighttime ambience, and McCord found it necessary to flood the set with light from oversized arc lamps. Pointed straight down, the lamps provided a powerful light by means of the carbon filters within the lights rubbing together. When the carbons in those old-fashioned lamps brushed against each other, they emitted a sound remarkably similar to that of someone passing gas—very loudly. In Andrews's impeccable enunciation, the arc lights emitted a "raspberry sound." Pronounced "Raaaasbery." Only Julie Andrews, it seems, could make a euphemism for farting sound like a fit topic for teatime discussion with the queen.

With the pressure mounting, and time/money wasting, Andrews and Plummer continued to laugh their way through their ballad of yearning and love. Wise called for a retake. Then another. And another. Nothing helped. Plummer, who had already announced he found it ridiculous to sing to his beloved while standing two inches in front of her face, fell apart as badly as did Andrews. Wise, in the recollection of Dee Dee Wood, "kept looking at his watch—but he never yelled. That was not his style." Instead, he ordered his two stars to take a lunch break. The unthinkable had occurred: the impeccably behaved and professional Andrews had caused a delay in production.

Lunch break over, the stars returned and promptly dissolved into giggles yet again. Finally, Wise came up with the idea of shooting the scene in silhouette: faces would be seen only in profile, and the goofy grins and chortles could skim by unnoticed. Hours later, the scene was finally completed. Ironically, the jerry-rigged solution now provided the perfect cap to the scene, the entire sequence flowing in seamless stages from McCord's day-for-night location shot of Maria wandering toward the water, into the captain and Maria's heart-to-heart chat on the waterside bench. When the duo finally enter the gazebo and sing of their love, McCord even managed to effect a heart-shaped pool of light between them as the visual capstone to the song. (On that last day of filming, Ted McCord informed Andrews: "I've been meaning to tell you that you have a slight bump on your nose and if you do fix it, it would make life a lot easier for all of us." In Andrews's smiling recollection: "I never did anything about it.")

After months of filming filled with rain, frustration—and very often exhilaration—only one scene remained to be filmed: "Sixteen Going on Seventeen." Wood and Breaux purposefully designed the number so that the movements seemed organic to teenagers, not professional dancers. Said Wood: "That number was so much fun. We staged it so that the circular bench in the gazebo elevated their movement, they could leap from bench to bench—the meeting in the center, the kiss—all great fun." Fifty years later, the recollection of working with Wood and Breaux floods Dan Truhitte with a similar enthusiasm: "They were the kindest, nicest people. We rehearsed that dance for six months! It was fifty years ago but it seems like yesterday to me."

Having been drilled incessantly by Breaux and Wood, Carr and Truhitte were raring to go through their paces. With the playback readied, the cameras rolled, and seventeen-year-old budding Nazi Rolfe and naive sixteen-year-old Liesl began to sing of their adolescent love. Leaping from one bench to another, Dorothy Jeakins's flowing dress for Carr enhancing the sense of movement, the number unfolded beautifully as the two actors expressed the sheer joy of being alive, young, and in love. Music and dance increased in tempo, swirling toward its conclusion—until the slippery sole of Carr's shoes caused her to crash right through one of the gazebo's plate-glass panels.

"Cut!"

Ankle sprained but not lacerated, Carr forged ahead with an ace bandage, adrenaline, and newly rubbed soles on her shoes. Additional takes completed, the crew burst into approving applause, providing Carr with her favorite memory from the entire seven months of production, and Fox executives with the welcome knowledge that with the exception of a few days of pickup shots, shooting of their eight-million-dollar, months-over-schedule, Technicolor musical had finally finished.

Now all that Wise and his team had to do was edit hundreds of thousands of feet of film, lay in the proper underscoring, supervise color levels on prints, please Richard Rodgers, make the studio happy—and complete every last one of these tasks in the five months remaining before the film's first sneak preview.

William Reynolds immediately went to work.

Seeking the right balance between acting choices, pace, and directorial intent, and armed with the safety net of Wise's multiple takes and varied angles, Reynolds found himself happily ensconced in the editing room throughout August and September with a plethora of choices. With his inherent musicality, he succeeded in cutting the film in synch with the rhythms—here faster, there slower, adding first, deleting later: "Do-Re-Mi" now pulsated in ever-increasing beats—as the montage assumed its final form, first Reynolds and then Wise grew more and more excited. Image after image popped onscreen until, as Ted Chapin points out, "You realize that ninety percent of the iconic images from the movie—everything we're most familiar with—come from 'Do-Re-Mi.' "

Paring away the excess, tightening the crosscuts and close-ups, Reynolds and Wise realized that the film would time out at approximately three hours; given the traditional model of twenty-four frames in a movie second, the film's final edit of exactly two hours and fifty-four minutes meant utilizing 200,000-plus frames—over 32,000 feet of 65 mm film.

The Sound of Music, it seemed, was beginning to assume epic proportions.

Concurrently with the editing, all music department employees began minutely calibrated work sessions aimed at heightening the effectiveness of the extensive underscoring, down to the last fraction of a second. Sound effects were painstakingly laid in: a library of tolling bells was scoured for just the right sound of wedding bells. The rustle of wind, the chirping of birds—all were carefully analyzed for maximum effect when heard over the opening credits. Irwin Kostal spent weeks experimenting with music, adding and deleting snippets of sound, trying to balance the desired dramatic effect while sticking to the contractual proviso that only the music of Richard Rodgers could be heard. Kostal's greatest challenge lay in scoring the graveyard escape confrontations with the Nazis: "The most difficult but also most rewarding were the scenes with the Nazis and the nuns at the end of the picture. That called for the greatest amount of originality on my part—I had to stick to Richard Rodgers but still be creative without changing anything."

Each department forged ahead, and when a rough cut was screened for Richard Rodgers in October of 1964 he pronounced himself very happy. Inevitably, however, the filmmakers began to question themselves. Was their excitement justified? Had they really succeeded in creating a fresh new film musical, one ready to take its place alongside the MGM Freed Unit classics such as *An American in Paris*? Or were they losing the forest for the trees, misguidedly thinking they had triumphed when all they were reacting to was relief that filming was over and a complete movie actually existed? Would they be laughed out of town or hailed as the saviors of 20th Century-Fox?

With one sneak preview, they were about to find out.

16.

SNEAK PREVIEW

⌐∿⌐

As the first public preview on January 15, 1965, at the Mann Theatre in Minneapolis loomed, buzz on the 20th Century-Fox lot began to grow. Word was leaking out from the editing room that Robert Wise might just have pulled off the unthinkable: a new screen musical that appealed to children and adults alike.

Like Richard Zanuck, Wise believed in the efficacy of previews as the true indicator of a film's potential. Listening to the audience—where they laughed, when they grew restless—would tell him what fine-tuning remained. Wise wanted a sneak preview, but only in the heartland of America. Let the cynics in Los Angeles and New York sneer. This was a family film, and the middle-class citizens of Minnesota, where the first preview of *West Side Story* had been held, represented the exact audience everyone involved desired.

Wise, Zanuck, and *The Sound of Music* publicity team arrived in Minneapolis in the midst of weather conditions that made rainy Salzburg seem idyllic. The temperature had not even reached freezing during the daytime hours, and was now dropping rapidly as the sun set. Would anyone show up?

By the time the screening began, enough hardy Midwesterners showed up to pack the theater to capacity. As the opening sequences unfolded on the big screen, viewers seemed so engrossed by the overwhelming natural beauty on display that no one paid the slightest bit of attention to the somewhat unfortunate choice of scene-setting words that scrolled across the bottom of the screen: "Salzburg, Austria, in the last golden days of the 1930s." Golden? One might rightly ask what was so golden about a worldwide depression and the simultaneous rise of Adolf Hitler. The intention of locating the film in a fairy-tale setting was apt, but the choice of words represented one of Lehman's few missteps, their lack of nuance rivaled only by those which float across the screen at the beginning of the legendary *Gone With the Wind*:

> There was a land of cavaliers and cotton fields called the old South
> Here in this pretty world gallantry took its last bow.

Those words might, just might, not find much favor within the African American community. . . .

But in that mid-winter Minneapolis audience, no one cared about a late-1930s history lesson. Wise and the Fox executives could instantly tell how much the audience liked Julie Andrews—no, it was more than liking. As evidenced by the sighs of pleasure after she finished singing each song, they were falling in love with her. Her singing didn't just please—it thrilled. It was akin to watching Fred Astaire or Gene Kelly dance onscreen. When those two masters danced they were not just making love to women through dance, they were portraying dance as the solution to life's problems. When Julie Andrews sang, whether it was the title song, "I Have Confidence," or "Do-Re-Mi," the audience felt that exact same way: everything would turn out just right in the end.

Julie Andrews was portraying a living, famous personality but it was Andrews herself the audience fell in love with, not the more obviously flawed real-life Maria von Trapp. Such a reaction, of course, was a part of any first-rate movie biography. It's Julia Roberts the audience loves, not the real Erin Brockovich. Barbra Streisand is the object of adoration, not Fanny Brice. The sun-washed *Sound of Music* was presenting Maria in the best possible light and audiences loved Julie Andrews for it, but it wasn't only Andrews the audience was falling for. They loved the kids, chuckling as they put a pinecone on Maria's seat at the table and *aww*-ing in unison over everything little Gretl did onscreen.

The audience was laughing in all the right spots, and seemed unusually attentive for a musical. There were no rustling sounds of boredom during the scenes of dialogue, no quick exits for a smoke, and they seemed particularly delighted by "Do-Re-Mi." As intermission approached and Maria packed her satchel to leave the von Trapps, utter silence descended. Had they miscalculated the pace? Wise and Zanuck braced themselves as the lights went up— and then the unexpected occurred.

The audience stood. Not to stretch, not to buy popcorn, not to head to the restroom, but to applaud the film. At intermission. In 1965. Long before standing ovations at Broadway shows became a pro forma means of audiences reassuring themselves that they had experienced a good time no matter how mediocre the expensive product. No, this was an audience so happy—thrilled even—with what they were experiencing that they stood to express their pleasure. Here on the screen in 65 millimeter, glorious Technicolor complete with stereophonic sound, was life as the audience wanted it to be. Even better—the film was based on a true story. This was more than Mary Poppins dropping out of the sky with an umbrella: here was a magically nice, real-life woman, carpet bag in hand, who was reuniting father and children into one big happy family.

Best and perhaps most unexpectedly of all, the audience had grown fully absorbed in the love story between Maria and the captain. It was only now, in the fully scored and edited version of the film that the full extent of Plummer's remarkable contribution to the movie could be glimpsed. Given little with which to work, Plummer had created a flesh-and-blood character, a naval hero whose tough exterior hid a decided tenderness for his children.

The measure of his performance didn't lie in the sarcastic putdowns so nicely timed to undercut the sweetness. Rather, it could be glimpsed in his quiet moments; gently declaring his love for Maria with a murmured "Oh, my love." In those three short syllables he managed to evoke an entire world of pent-up emotion. For all the troubles that moonlit declaration of love had given Wise, McCord, Andrews, and Plummer, there was no trace of the uncontrollable laughter onscreen. Instead, the sequence possessed a dreamlike quality that fit in perfectly with the fairy-tale atmosphere, and the audience fell—hook, line, and sinker. Even for Ernest Lehman, this moonlit gazebo declaration of love remained the one scene in the film guaranteed to make him cry: "There's something about that scene that gets me right in the heart."

As the film reached its climax, the audience's pleasure grew ever more palpable. A nanny who sang like a dream, turned her charges into singing stars, married their war hero father, outwitted the evil Nazis, and led the entire family on to a happily-ever-after life? Yes, oh yes: the audience willed itself to believe in this nigh-onto-perfect version of life. Maybe life really could turn out happily. After all, they had just watched it happen onscreen to a real-life family. What could be better than that? In a word: nothing.

Their preview scorecards proved the point: 223 rated the film "excellent," 3 "good," and 0 "fair."

When a second preview in Tulsa, Oklahoma, the next evening proved to be just as big an audience pleaser, Fox executives allowed themselves to believe they might actually have a winner on their hands. With all those parents starved for wholesome family entertainment, this movie might just gross—oh, say—forty million. Who knew—maybe fifty million when you added in all of the foreign territories. Okay, that might be too much to ask for, but still. . . .

With the February 2, 1965, press screening looming, Reynolds and Wise still worked on the film, chipping away at any extraneous moments: an encounter between Rolfe and Liesl in the midst of the "Do-Re-Mi" montage slowed the pace of the sequence—gone!

Dramatic scenes were shortened or cut entirely. When a scene of Maria praying in her room after arriving late for evening prayers proved cumbersome, that, too, was instantly deleted.

So, too, was a scene between Elsa and Max talking about the party at which she would meet Georg's friends. As originally planned, that dialogue would have been juxtaposed with scenes of Georg on the terrace pensively thinking about Maria, while Maria wistfully gazed out of her window, lost in thought about her growing attraction to the captain. In the end, both sequences were excised by order of Wise: "We seemed to be planting something too heavily at this point—it was all too early."

Successful previews in hand, and with dreams of multimillion-dollar grosses spreading throughout the Fox executive suites, the question now became one of how best to start spreading the word before the film's official world premiere in March. Fox publicists, led by Mike Kaplan, were about to begin earning their pay.

17

PUBLICITY

᯼

Even before the two previews, Fox had decided to spend substantial sums on publicizing their family-friendly film, but after the sensational response at both screenings, the studio granted Kaplan and his team of publicists a very healthy advertising budget of $3,000,000. There was to be no question of a wide release. Instead, there would be a carefully calibrated slow roll out for the film: a small number of theaters—131 to be precise; reserved seats; and a limited number of shows each day. *The Sound of Music* would be positioned as a bona fide moviegoing event.

The strategy was set, but the advertising artwork remained unfinished. Where was the one piece of art that captured the film's appeal at a glance? Version after version was drafted only to be summarily rejected. Nothing seemed to precisely capture the film's high spirits and tale of redemptive family love. One after another, twelve versions were nixed until everyone agreed that the answer had finally been found: Julie Andrews—front and center cresting the top of a hill, smile in place, feet off the ground in happiness—guitar and carpetbag swinging freely in the foreground. Christopher Plummer— off to the side, stern, forceful, hands on hips, handsome. Seven grinning children in matching yellow outfits running up the hill behind Julie Andrews. Music, scenery, and smiles. Happily ever after. Or, as the tagline would have it: "The Happiest Sound in All the World."

Sold.

Next. How to custom tailor the publicity for each of the film's limited number of markets? Kaplan began working overtime, personalizing the publicity by crafting separate stories for each city where the film would be released.

Basic strategy: let the word of mouth build so that people would actually travel some distance to see the film. Make *The Sound of Music* an event guaranteed to propel middle-American families out of the house.

The Sound of Music would not be shown in small theaters with screens positioned uncomfortably close to the projection booths. The 1920s movie palaces with outlandish yet secretly thrilling Moorish design may have all but vanished, but enough stand-alone single-screen theaters remained to comfortably house the widescreen release and make this moviegoing experience a throwback to the days of ushers in uniforms.

Kaplan wrote up the actual technical specifications of Todd-AO widescreen projection, even if few really understood the detailed jargon. Anything to make *The Sound of Music* seem unique. Todd-AO projection, which had been developed under the aegis of producer Mike Todd, in conjunction with the American Optical Company, utilized film stock 65 millimeters wide; the width of the projected image, not the depth of field, would prove the key, the end result being a movie projected in a 2:35:1 aspect ratio—an image over two times wider than high. Providing theaters with a simpler format than that of three-strip Cinerama, featuring a brighter and steadier image than that produced with CinemaScope, and with speakers placed behind the screen and throughout the theater, Todd-AO utilized six magnetic stereo tracks rather than the standard four. (With the six tracks requiring an additional five millimeters of film stock width, only the resulting 70 millimeter prints of *The Sound of Music* would be advertised as featuring "Todd-AO.")

Kaplan wrote up all of this technical wizardry, but it wasn't the detailed mumbo jumbo of Todd-AO that mattered to him. He wanted audiences munching on popcorn in their comfortable padded chairs to feel like they were surrounded by the very Alps themselves, as if they were escaping into the hills along with Maria. Their minds filled with newspaper stories about the film's technical wonders, audiences would enter the theater expecting an out-of-the-ordinary visual experience.

With color television having only been introduced in the United States two years earlier, and separate Academy Awards for black-and-white and color cinematography still the norm, the striking color composition found in *Sound of Music* could still gain the attention of moviegoers. And, just to make sure that potential audiences understood what they'd be seeing, there it was on the poster, plopped right between the figures of Charmian Carr and Christopher Plummer in letters nearly as big as Robert Wise's credit:

COLOR

BY DELUXE

With artwork finalized, 131 prints of the film were struck, and the press campaign rolled out across the United States. The public was primed. It was almost time for *The Sound of Music* to face the world.

But first, Wise and the studio wanted to successfully pass two tough critical tests: winning the approval of both composer Richard Rodgers and the entire von Trapp family. Calling the film "wonderful" and pronouncing himself thrilled with the end product, old pro Rodgers singled out the title number for special praise and in the end forthrightly stated, "I thought they did everything well."

Still, Rodgers could not help pointing out the different level of his involvement in Hollywood versus Broadway: he was no longer the producer of his own creation. Couching his explanation in language that must have resonated with Maria von Trapp and her own complicated reaction to Hollywood's version of her life story, he proclaimed: "Being the composer of a musical that has been transferred to the screen is a little like being the father of the bride. You try to think that she's still your baby, but the harsh truth keeps intruding."

As for the von Trapps, 20th Century-Fox arranged a private screening for family and close friends in New York City right before the official opening. All family members with the exception of Johannes attended, but at the time of the screening Johannes found himself enduring basic training at Fort Dix, New Jersey. Asking for leave to attend the screening, he was turned down flat. His solution? One friend loaned him a car for the trip to New York, while another slept in his bunk on the night of the screening so that he would not be marked absent. After a few minutes on the road out of Fort Dix he realized that he did not have enough money to travel on the New Jersey Turnpike and pass through the Holland Tunnel into Manhattan. Instead, he drove the entire distance up Route 1, checked into the Hotel Wellington, "walked into the dining room and charged my dinner to the room. Compared to the

Army it was all absolutely terrific." Like the majority of the family, he enjoyed the screening and was never caught by the Army. (In just the same vein,
Dan Truhitte could not attend the premiere because he was in the Marines.
"I didn't make it to the premiere and when I finally saw the film I was in
uniform—received permission and got leave to see the film.")

Maria's own reaction to the film? According to daughter Lorli, the film
so carried Maria away that "the wedding scene just enveloped her—she actually got out of her seat and walked down the aisle as if she was going to
marry my father again." Wrote Maria to Robert Wise in a telegram dated
February 24, 1965: "You are a much greater artist than I could ever have
thought. . . . in the name of my family and myself I thank you. Your friend,
Maria Trapp."

Richard Rodgers had pronounced himself pleased. The von Trapp family
was happy. Like the executives at 20th Century-Fox, they all sat back to
await the public's response. The verdict was at hand.

18.

WORLD PREMIERE

"It's as close to perfection as any movie musical I've ever seen. . . .
I know Oscar would have loved it."

—MRS. OSCAR HAMMERSTEIN II

March 2, 1965. The Rivoli Theatre, in the heart of Manhattan's theater district, Broadway and Forty-ninth Street:

Robert Wise and 20th Century-Fox felt confident. Sneak preview audiences had loved the film. Advance word of mouth was great. Revising their estimates upward, the studio heads now felt that the film might even gross as much as sixty million dollars. Jack Warner may have refused to cast Andrews in *My Fair Lady* because she was not a box office name, but so confident was Wise of Andrews's star quality that on the very eve of the premiere, he smilingly stated: "Jack Warner's loss turned out to be my gain."

Six months had now elapsed since the entire cast had seen one another, and all involved were happily reunited for what proved to be one of the last big studio premieres in the style of golden-age Hollywood: klieg lights, fancy dress, and a soundtrack accompaniment of screaming fans in bleachers. Only one notable name was absent: Maria von Trapp herself, inexplicably excluded from the invitation list by the Fox publicists.

Flashbulbs popped and fans bellowed approval as the cast arrived. For Charmian Carr, the entire evening seemed to speed by in a series of impressionistic jump cuts from overture to curtain calls: "I can remember exactly how it felt: it was as if I was inside an enchanted fairy tale, living in a dream. I wished that night could go on forever." Basking in the excitement of it all, her head turning round in surprise at the roar of welcome that greeted Julie Andrews, Carr realized the seismic turn her life had taken: "Little more than a year earlier, I'd been testing urine samples in a doctor's office. Now, I was singing to people coast to coast."

Settling into their seats, the audience filled the auditorium with a palpable sense of expectation. Forget the Rivoli's recent tenant, the disastrous *Cleopatra*. Word within the industry on *The Sound of Music* was great and the "show me" sophisticated New York City crowd was hopeful but wary. Could Robert Wise really have succeeded in cutting out the schmaltz?

The houselights dimmed, the curtain rose, and as the opening shots unfolded, even the tough New York City audience seemed to hold its collective breath. There on the big screen, courtesy of Wise, McCord, and second unit director Maurice Zuberano, was a series of breathtaking opening shots from the Salzkammergut lake district: a bird's-eye view that floated in leisurely fashion over the picture-postcard scenery of snowcapped mountains, quiet lakes, and verdant meadows. The countryside onscreen seemed a model of old-world grace, suspended in time and space. The images glided by accompanied only by the sound of the wind—even the 20th Century-Fox logo displayed at the start of the film was silent.

The faint chirps of birds mixed in with the wind, the layered sounds of nature increasing in volume until the sixty-piece orchestra slid in underneath and a solitary figure appeared in the distance. A mere speck on the horizon, the figure grew larger as the camera gathered speed, zoomed closer, then closer still, and the smiling figure of Julie Andrews in a striped novice's vestment, twirled, faced forward, and burst forth with a full-throated cry of "The hills are alive" directed right to the heavens—arms spread wide as if embracing nature and everyone in the world. There was no introductory verse as there had been on the Broadway stage, no sound of Maria pensively confiding, "My day in the hills has come to an end, I know." Instead Julie Andrews strode confidently toward the camera and twirled into the audience's collective sight and heart. The audience exhaled. And fell a little bit in love. It was all going to be okay.

So skillfully composed and edited was the sequence, the camera hurtling in for that close-up of Andrews's radiant smile, that it only became evident upon repeated viewings that the seamless sequence actually did contain a single cut, one which covered Julie Andrews just as she twirled into sight. It didn't matter in the slightest.

With this opening sequence Wise had both placed the audience inside the musical and at the same time staged the song in the expansive outdoors where Maria thrived. With his inherent understanding of camera placement he had opened up the entire musical so effortlessly that the audience capitulated without even thinking. In precisely three minutes Wise and others had actually captured Maria von Trapp's own words about her time in the mountains: "When you are a child of the mountains yourself, you really belong to them. You need them. They become the faithful guardians of your life." Andrews's swirl and wide-open arms embraced that entire natural world, the perfect visualization of Hammerstein's own heartfelt belief in the healing power of nature that is found in nearly every one of his shows: "The hills are alive," "Oh, what a beautiful mornin' . . . ," "June is bustin' out all over."

INTERMISSION

Marni Nixon: "The premiere was the first time I saw the completed film. I still remember the excitement of that night, being a part of it. I hadn't experienced anything like it before and I remember thinking, 'Wow, this is a great film.' It was a most glorious experience in every way. It brought back memories of the actual filming—you knew you were doing something worthwhile. Everyone worked to help make you better—to be the best you could be. All those tech, set, and lighting people working together as a great team led by Robert Wise. They had served the play well, yet every decision they made for translating the property to film kept the difference in the mediums in mind. It was all so well done. Just a great night."

Nicholas Hammond: Although arrival at the theater in a fiacre like that used in "Do-Re-Mi" would wait for the Hollywood premiere, Hammond, excited by the lights, the crowds, and the chance to be reunited with his fellow cast mates for the first time in six months, realized that what had felt like a private movie being shot in exotic locations was now being shared with the world. At intermission, as crowds of admiring strangers showered the cast with words of praise, he felt nothing less than "a tectonic shift in our lives and nothing would ever be the same for any of us."

It never was.

A New Fan

Julie Andrews: Although by now a Golden Globe and BAFTA award winner, and only one month shy of winning the Academy Award for *Mary Poppins,* Julie was still a relative neophyte when it came to the movie industry. *The Sound of Music* was only her third film, and she retained enough of the youngster inside to recall, decades later, the thrill of meeting Bette Davis at the premiere: "At the New York City premiere a lady came up to me and it was Bette Davis. She'd just seen it and she said, 'You are going to be a very big star!' which was such a huge compliment! I was kind of gobsmacked. I didn't know what to say!" (Davis, in fact, was echoing Lillian Gish, who had told Peggy Wood: "I think Julie Andrews will be our great coming motion picture star!")

The audience was happy. Bette Davis was thrilled. What Wise and Zanuck did not yet know was that the New York City critics felt differently. Very differently.

19

CRITICS ON THE WARPATH

Terrific advance reviews from *Variety* and *The Hollywood Reporter* had left Wise and Zanuck feeling confident about the critical reception that awaited the film from the big-city critics. *Variety* had printed an all-out rave, calling the film "a superb screen adaptation . . . a warmly pulsating, captivating drama, magnificently mounted and with a brilliant cast." Of even more note, *The Hollywood Reporter* raved in language that presciently crystallized why fans would soon find themselves returning to the film over and over: "It restores your faith in movies. If you sit quietly and let it take, it may also restore your faith in humanity." *Life* magazine's cover story on Julie Andrews cut right to the chase: "Julie's radiance floods the screen."

So it was that with a quiet confidence Wise and Saul Chaplin opened up an advance copy of the next day's *New York Times*—and blanched. Chief movie critic Bosley Crowther had bashed the film with condescending sarcasm, praising only Julie Andrews's "serenely controlled self-confidence." Dismissing the basic source material as operetta kitsch that was unworthy of Rodgers and Hammerstein, he reserved his harshest words for Christopher Plummer, writing, "The adults are fairly horrendous, especially Christopher Plummer as Captain von Trapp. Looking as handsome and phony as a store-window alpine guide . . ."

Definitely not what those in charge expected. A few quibbles seemed inevitable, but outright hostility? Would these widely read pans damn the film's chances at the box office? It was a distinct possibility, but a last sentence acknowledgment of the material's inherent appeal inadvertently pointed the way toward the film's success: "Its sentiments are abundant. Businesswise, Mr. Wise is no fool."

Perhaps Wise and Zanuck shouldn't have been surprised. By the mid-1960s, *The Sound of Music* seemed to have acquired status as critical shorthand for hokey, old-fashioned middle-class entertainment. When Robert Benton and David Newman's highly publicized *Esquire* cover story on "The New Sentimentality" saw the light of day in July 1964, the coauthors decreed that Michelangelo Antonioni and Malcolm X were in; *The Sound of Music*, Gene Kelly, and John Wayne decidedly out. The import of the article lay not so much in the authors' highly selective opinion making, but rather in its status as bellwether of a 1960s public dialogue about American culture that was about to become frantic, high decibel, and shrill.

Benton and Newman would go on to write the terrific screenplay for *Bonnie and Clyde,* but the irony of the article's baby-thrown-out-with-the-bathwater approach lies in the fact that the very artifacts they deemed hopelessly passé have actually thrived in the ensuing fifty years. *The Sound of Music* remains beloved around the world a full half century after the film's premiere, the 1974 release of *That's Entertainment* confirmed Gene Kelly's unquestioned status as one of the true auteurs of musical films, and John Wayne, shorn of his controversial Vietnam-era conservative politics, has remained a subject of critical reappraisal, rightly acclaimed for his terrific performances in John Ford Westerns ranging from *She Wore a Yellow Ribbon* and *The Searchers* to *The Man Who Shot Liberty Valance.*

At the time of the film's premiere, however, Zanuck and Wise were to discover that Benton and Newman were not alone in their intellectual disdain for *The Sound of Music.* Opening up further reviews, the duo realized that many big-city critics did more than dislike the film: they hated it, mounting scathingly worded indictments that treated the film as a personal affront. Stanley Kauffmann in the *New Republic* deemed the R&H songs "sickening" and dubbed Julie Andrews the woman destined to become "the most revolting refreshing actress in films."

It's not just the nature of such slash-and-burn Internet-style appraisals that startles; it's that Kauffmann felt martyred by having to endure the film, rhetorically asking in rather smug fashion, "Is there a special heaven for film critics? I feel confident of it, after enduring all of *The Sound of Music.* At that, heaven is small enough compensation for sitting through this Rodgers and Hammerstein atrocity."

Trying to find a quotable sentence, Wise scanned the Crowther review a

second time and realized that it was even worse than he thought. In condescending fashion, Crowther wrote that "the movie is staged by Mr. Wise in a
cosy-cum-corny fashion that even theater people know is old hat." In just one
sentence, Crowther had managed to look down upon Wise as well as the
entire theater community ("even theater people know . . ."). Yes, Wise could
rationalize that people had been complaining about Crowther's reviews for
years; one couldn't be sure exactly what Crowther would find first-rate at the
cinema, and, two years later, he famously missed the point of *Bonnie and
Clyde,* dismissing it simply as a glorification of violence. But for now, a pan
from *The New York Times* hurt—big time.

Newsweek got in on the act as well, issuing only a backhanded compliment
that praised Julie Andrews for triumphing over the film itself, but the heaviest artillery was unleashed from two of the highest-profile critics on the East
Coast, Pauline Kael and Judith Crist.

The Sound of Music was not congenial territory for Crist, whose taste ran
more to the wised-up cynicism of Billy Wilder (writing about his Oscar-
winning film *The Apartment,* she bluntly stated: "With that film we became
grown-ups."). Instead, although Crist may have liked Andrews, calling her
"the most enchanting and complete performer to come to the screen in years,"
when it came to the film itself, she abruptly reversed course, calling it, in her
New York Herald Tribune review of March 3, the "sound of marshmallows";
Crist's attack on the film—"Calorie-counters, diabetics, and grown-ups from
eight to eighty had best beware . . ."—seemed written in fiery prose purposely
designed to generate controversy rather than a reasoned consideration of screen
musicals. More than any other single film, *The Sound of Music* put the already
famous Crist at the vanguard of the popular cultural debates.

Leading off with the headline "If You Have Diabetes, Stay Away from
This Movie," Crist excoriated the film from start to finish: "There is nothing
like a supersized screen to convert seven darling little kids in no time at all
into all that W. C. Fields indicated little kids are—which is pure loathsome."
Utilizing her position as film critic for NBC television's *The Today Show,* Crist
went on to bash the film on television as well, and completed her trifecta of
slams with the review's reprint in *The Paris Herald.* That review, she laughingly noted, garnered her "hate mail from all over the world!"

Crist had plenty of company in terms of her critical contempt for *The
Sound of Music,* but a small but elite number of critics struck a more sober

tone in their disdain. In that very middle ground lay the esteemed Kenneth Tynan, who allowed that he was "mostly bored but intermittently, unexpectedly touched." Like most others he parceled out genuine praise for Andrews, whose "soaring voice and thrice-scrubbed innocence make me, even in guarded moments, catch my breath." In a similar vein, legendary director George Cukor spoke of the movie's "true innocence. In spite of its naivete, you find yourself caught up; there's a tug at the heart." Cukor had hit the nail on the head: Wise had successfully navigated the thin line between true sweetness and mawkish sentimentality, and the entire cast, led by Julie Andrews's incandescent performance, had pulled off a depiction of genuine innocence.

Genuine innocence? Big-city critics didn't care and weren't buying any of it. *The New Yorker*'s Brendan Gill delivered a decidedly over-the-top assessment capped by his opinion that the "handful of authentic location shots have a hokey studio sheen," an assertion that managed to both misread exactly how much of the film featured location shots—far more than a handful—and negates Ted McCord's smartly crafted cinematography. As it was, even the most famous critic of *Sound of Music*—Christopher Plummer—had praised McCord's extraordinary work, calling him "brilliant" and crediting him with inventing a scrim that allowed the Austrian countryside to appear in its natural splendor, without a storybook picture-postcard veneer: "It made the hills more natural because if he used the Technicolor effect the hills would have been so Schlag. He should have received an award." Gill, however, wouldn't allow a single such acknowledgment.

Never one to shy away from grand assessments, Gill called the acting of Andrews, Plummer, and Parker "well under ordinary high school level," an assessment that, whether one likes the film or not, ignores just how much skill was displayed by Andrews in the leading role. Safe to say, there was not a high schooler alive in 1965 or 2015 who possessed anywhere near the acting skills of these three award-winning actors, but so strong were the passions aroused by the film that hyperbole trumped common sense.

Joining Crist and Gill in the bash *The Sound of Music* sweepstakes, the brilliant and combative Pauline Kael found the movie phony—all faux "happy family" sentiments without acknowledgment of personality quirks or unfulfilled desires. Redoubling her efforts, she struck the pose of a world-weary upholder of artistic standards; *The Sound of Music*, she sighed, made it "even more difficult for anyone to try to do anything worth doing, anything relevant to the modern world, anything inventive or expressive."

In the face of the public's enthusiasm for the film, Kael pressed the attack even further. Thriving on attention, she boldly insisted that a film of such "luxuriant falseness" was "probably going to be the single most repressive influence on artistic freedom in movies for the next few years." It was Kael, more than anyone else, who seemed to lay the "blame" for the film at the door of a supposedly foolish American public who believed the "big lie, the sugarcoated lies that people seem to want to eat."

What exactly were these lies she thought so powerful that they would repress artistic freedom? True, the film compressed events, but all dramas based upon real events do: Ben Affleck's Academy Award–winning *Argo* is based on actual incidents, but the hostages in question did not escape from Iran while militants barreled down the runway in pursuit of their plane. That scene was simply inserted in order to heighten the dramatic climax. For her part, Maria von Trapp really did enter Nonnberg Abbey, leave to teach one of the von Trapp children, gain the trust and love of seven youngsters, marry a captain in the Austrian Navy, organize the family into a professional singing group, and escape the Nazis. Facts were facts: it was all a matter of presentation. Director Wise addressed the controversy head on by simply stating: "You're not telling untruths—you're just compressing events."

More than anything else, Kael, like Crist, seemed downright irritated by what she perceived as the sheer middle-class appeal of the film, treating the movie as ground zero of a middle-class culture she wanted to distance herself from with alacrity. Writing in her famous *McCall's* magazine review of the film, one so negative that it cost her the job as the magazine's film critic, she rhetorically asked: "Whom could it offend? Only those of us who, despite the fact that we may respond, loathe being manipulated." (The perceived air of manipulation caused more than critics to grow vitriolic. A growing number of college students also grew to dislike the film, with undergraduates in Moorehead, Minnesota, launching a public protest over the movie's monopoly on the town's one movie screen: "Forty weeks of schmaltz is enough.")

Indeed, at its most strident, Kael's criticism of the film's appeal seemed the quintessential manifestation of "popular with the masses equals bad," but the erudite critic could be just as over the top when she fell head over heels for a film, likening the release of Bernardo Bertolucci's *Last Tango in Paris* in 1973 to the premiere of Stravinsky's "Rites of Spring." Whatever the merits of Bertolucci's epic, Kael's critical judgment has not been well served by the passage of four decades since *Tango*'s premiere.

As it was, Kael reserved her heaviest ammunition for director Wise, hammering home her belief that *The Sound of Music* "makes a critic feel that maybe it's all hopeless. Why not just send the director, Robert Wise, a wire: 'You win. I give up' or rather, 'We both lose, we all lose'?" In her sneering put-down, Kael, like many critics, revealed her disdain for old-school directors such as Wise, whose wide-ranging skill sets had been honed during the studio system, in which assignments ranging across a wide variety of genres obviated the development of an instantaneously identifiable personal style. It was this lack of stylistic signature that seemed to truly rankle the intellectuals, and Andrew Sarris, the key American figure in spreading the "auteur" theory positioning the director as true author of the film, simply called Wise a "technician without a strong personality."

For all the beating he endured at the hands of the critical elite over a lack of style, Wise never grew particularly vexed by the criticism. The more outspoken Sidney Lumet, however, shot back that style is simply "the way you tell a particular story," adding that the director should always serve the material, not vice versa. Never one to shy away from a controversy, Lumet went on to underscore a distinction between true stylists and what he calls "decorators": "Critics talk about style as something apart from the movie because they need the style to be obvious. The reason they need it to be obvious is that they don't really see. . . . The decorators are easy to recognize. That's why the critics love them so."

As it was, no less an authority than Martin Scorsese said of Wise: "His films became increasingly fascinating to me because of the editing style, a very crisp, clear style of editing that kind of points the audience toward where to look in a scene." The fact that Wise's films earned a total of sixty-seven Academy Award nominations, winning nineteen, and that he himself was nominated seven times, winning four Oscars, speaks to the consistent quality of his work.

Whether the critics were attacking Wise, the screenplay, the children, or the actual nature of the story, the problem with their over-the-top criticism was that it tended to obscure a more reasoned analysis of the real flaws found in the film, an examination that could have led to an interesting exploration of how and why the film managed to overcome its own actual shortcomings:

1. Although musical numbers in the film are well staged, the conclusion of "So Long, Farewell" topples into camp when the assembled party guests wave and sing good-bye to the children in unison and perfect pitch. The concluding thirty seconds of the number seem nothing so much as silly.

Given the nature of that family sing-along entertainment for the assembled party guests, what Kael did get right was her humorous comment that she wondered if there wasn't in fact just one little von Trapp who didn't much feel like singing for the guests. (There's no question that there's a funny skit waiting to be written in which the von Trapp children pop beers, belch, smoke cigarettes, and listen to rap music.) Didn't they ever rebel, those too-good-to-be-true von Trapp kids? How could they be so consistently good-natured, with nary a sullen adolescent emotion in sight?

2. The nuns—serious, intelligent, hardworking women of faith living in a 1,200-year-old nunnery—are presented mostly as comic foils for a Maria who seems suspiciously irrepressible. Surely Maria's antics were met with as much impatience as bemusement on the part of the nuns.

3. The one brief shot of Nazis marching across the plaza works well, but nowhere is a sense of the true horrors represented by the Nazis to be found. Even in this one brief sequence, none of the Germans are shown carrying weapons. It's almost as if the Germans simply represented a pesky problem that could be overcome by Maria's energy and can-do spirit, with a nifty assist from nuns who steal carburetors from Nazi automobiles. There are no Jews glimpsed in the film, certainly no minorities, and no sign of the disconcertingly warm welcome Austrians gave to Hitler at the time of the Anschluss.

Then again, *The Sound of Music* was hardly designed as a polemic, and a history lesson was never intended; by their very nature, musicals—with the

notable exceptions of Stephen Sondheim's *Assassins* and *Pacific Overtures*—
are not designed to seriously delve into political problems except as background
to the story. Even *Evita,* in which the fascist Perons of Argentina command
center stage throughout, tends to feature the Cinderella-like climb of Eva Du-
arte Peron from peasant to first lady, at the expense of any meaningful political discourse.

It's ironic that those who most disliked *The Sound of Music* seemed to make a
leap in their criticism from dislike of the material to an assumption that those
who liked the film believed its "lie" in which everything in life turns out happily
ever after. It's an erroneous assumption, one akin to assuming that movie viewers
in the 1930s believed that life turned out just as it did in Andy Hardy movies.

This stream of modern-day feelings of cultural superiority is similarly exemplified by new millennium audiences making fun of Shirley Temple's popularity in the 1930s. In their sneering attitude of "we know better," such cultural
critics erroneously assume that Depression-era moviegoers were naifs. The
truth is that far from being dumb, those audiences liked Shirley Temple precisely because as a child star she was sensational, a preternaturally gifted singing, dancing mini-dynamo. Fans of *The Sound of Music* understood that their
own lives wouldn't work out as perfectly as those of the onscreen von Trapps.
Instead, just as happened with Shirley Temple, the movie provided a tuneful, smoothly professional uplifting form of wish fulfillment.

Even the decidedly inferior *Sound of Music* knockoffs such as *The Singing
Nun* and *Doctor Doolittle* never inspired the same level of vitriol as did *The
Sound of Music.* That state of affairs is likely the result of the fact that while
those imitations unfold in every bit as "saccharine" a fashion as does *The
Sound of Music,* they also were not nearly as skillfully composed, shot, or
performed, and proved decidedly less memorable. It was the sheer effectiveness of *The Sound of Music* that seemed to most enrage the critics.

It was not, of course, only *The Sound of Music* that inspired vitriol in the
mid- and late 1960s. Reviews from that sour era of upheaval reveal that critics
were writing in a particularly acerbic and ofttimes nasty fashion. If in the
twenty-first-century age of the Internet all criticism appears to be shot through
the prism of irony, critics in the mid-sixties simply grew mean, as if the more
vicious the attacks, the more firmly they established their bona fides. Former
favorites such as Doris Day were not just criticized, but actually ridiculed. As
pointed out by Mark Harris in his first-rate study of late 1960s Hollywood,

Pictures at a Revolution, Time magazine didn't just dislike Charlie Chaplin's *Countess from Hong Kong,* but eviscerated it with a headline that screamed: "Time to Retire." *Countess from Hong Kong* may not have been a great film—and it wasn't—but the film involved three certifiable legends in Charlie Chaplin, Marlon Brando, and Sophia Loren, and as such was worthy of even-handed consideration. By the mid- and late 1960s, if the film in question carried even a hint of sentiment, let alone sentimentality, the knives were drawn and shots fired. Explaining why a film didn't work was less of a priority than wit at the expense of others.

What seemed to particularly confound the critics was the fact that *The Sound of Music* represented a return to old-fashioned, "saccharine" fare they thought had finally disappeared. Gone from the slate of Hollywood studios were lighter-than-air confections like Astaire/Rogers musicals and screwball comedies. In fact, it had been Hollywood stalwart Alfred Hitchcock who hurled the first and most decisive bomb at the cinema of sentimentality with his 1960 masterpiece *Psycho.* In the wake of *Psycho,* Hollywood films had begun to trade in ambiguity and irony on a scale heretofore unthinkable. Satire and alienation increasingly constituted the bill of fare, from *The Misfits* with Monroe and Gable in 1961, to fears of nuclear destruction found in *Fail-Safe* and *Dr. Strangelove* (both 1964), yet here was *The Sound of Music* personifying old-school filmmaking in which narrative and dramatic continuity superseded all. Resolutely old-fashioned, *The Sound of Music* opened and quickly became the most popular film on the planet. Not just in America, but on every single continent where it played, *The Sound of Music* set one box office record after another, inspiring devotion and ardent fervor that led its most severe critics to ask one key question:

Had audiences all around the world lost their collective minds?

The von Trapp Family, 1941

December 1959: Mary Martin, Broadway's Maria von Trapp, flanked by The Sound of Music's *creative team. Left to right: Richard Rodgers, Oscar Hammerstein II, Howard Lindsay, and Russel Crouse.*

The family lineup: from Broadway (1959) . . .

... *to Hollywood (1965)*

The Trapp Family, *1960 English-language version of* Die Trapp Family *and* Die Trapp Family en Amerika. *Starring Ruth Eluwerik and Hans Holt as Maria and Georg, the film flopped at the box office.*

Screenwriter Ernest Lehman

Oscar-winning director Robert Wise (shown here on the set of his 1963 horror classic The Haunting) was everyone's choice to replace disgruntled original director William Wyler.

Wardrobe test shot with cast. Front row, L to R: Kym Karath, Debbie Turner, Angela Cartwright, Duane Chase, Heather Menzies, Nicholas Hammond, Charmian Carr; back row: Julie Andrews, Christopher Plummer.

From Dorothy Jeakins sketch to world-famous twirl

Prerecording with the children. Music supervisor Irwin Kostal augmented the sound with additional vocalists.

"My Favorite Things." The first scene filmed with Julie Andrews and the children—the bond between star and youngsters formed instantly.

Rushing to the abbey—late as usual

Wedding Day. Oscar-nominated Peggy Wood (Mother Abbess) is at the far left.
Said Julie Andrews of the wedding gown: "I've never felt prettier, before or since."

Maria arriving at the von Trapp villa with guitar, carpet bag, and an outfit the poor didn't want

Maria von Trapp visits the set, films a cameo, and then announces her retirement from screen acting, all in one day.

Shown here with Christopher Plummer, Eleanor Parker (Elsa) and Richard Haydn (Max) were favorites with their fellow cast members.

Waiting out the rain delays and cold temperatures during the filming of "Do-Re-Mi"

The "Do-Re-Mi" montage, starring Julie Andrews, seven children, and the city of Salzburg

An acerbic presence on the set, who in his own words "loathes the guitar"!

*Dripping wet and checking
her makeup before the terrace
confrontation with the captain*

*Cinematographer Ted
McCord's detailed
lighting—and the
moment when the
Captain begins to fall
in love with Maria*

"The Lonely Goatherd."
Said choreographer
Dee Dee Wood: "Those
female marionettes were
very well-endowed!"

Falling in love with
the Captain while
dancing the Laendler

A rare light moment with Christopher Plummer on set. Here with Duane Chase (Kurt).

Nonstop laughter from Andrews and Plummer caused Wise to shoot the scene in silhouette.

Dan Truhitte and Charmian Carr in "Sixteen Going on Seventeen," the last scene filmed

World Premiere, March 2, 1965.
Composer Richard Rodgers first
worked with Julie Andrews on
the 1957 television production of
Cinderella.

Thirteenth—and final—version of the art work, which featured new and amusing titles overseas. Here, in Spain: The Rebel Novice.

The sing-along phenomenon at the Hollywood Bowl

Reunited in 2005 for the 40th anniversary. Shown from left, back row: Charmian Carr, Nicholas Hammond, Heather Menzies, Duane Chase; front row: Angela Cartwright, Debbie Turner, Kym Karath.

Forty years later, and still great friends

20

THE ONE-BILLION-DOLLAR QUESTION

"When Mrs. Myra Franklin of Wales was asked why she had seen the
film nine hundred times, sitting in the same seat at a Monday matinee
every single week, she replied simply: 'It makes me feel happy.' "
—CHARMIAN CARR IN *FOREVER LIESL*

Contrary to accepted wisdom, initial business at the road show price of $3.50 per ticket was solid but far from an instantaneous sellout. As the wildly favorable word of mouth spread, however, the box office receipts began to soar. First, fans of musicals came. Then the ever-growing cadre of Julie Andrews devotees. Finally, those longing for a happy ending—anywhere—began to turn out in droves. At which point the oddest thing of all happened: all these fans of the movie returned to see it again. And then once more. And then once again—until the phenomenon eventually resulted in a record-setting first release run of four and a half years. Audiences couldn't let go of the film, proving once again that in obsession, closure is rare. Not wanting to accept that the film was over, that the three hours spent with the von Trapps had vanished, these men and women simply returned to the theater and entered into the von Trapp universe for yet another fix.

In fact, reason number one for the film's overwhelming popularity, and one almost lost in all of the discussions of the movie's success was the brilliance of the Rodgers and Hammerstein score. Rock revolution and all, the music of R&H spoke to fans of all ages, and besides the target audience of parents who held the purse strings, many younger fans of the film came to embrace the musical world of the von Trapps just as strongly.

As the 20,000,000 copies sold of the film's soundtrack attest, people of all ages responded to R&H's understanding of the most primal of emotions: family, heartbreak, and love. People embraced the score because in a very clever fashion, it featured one love song after another, but with each one cast in a slightly different form: "The Sound of Music" is a love song to nature straight from Maria's heart; "Do-Re-Mi" is a bridge of emotion between Maria and the children; "Edelweiss" is the bond between patriot and country; and "Climb Ev'ry Mountain" is the ultimate anthemic love song of faith. So wide ranging are these love songs that "Something Good," the sweetly romantic duet between Maria and the captain, may stand as the only traditional love song in the entire score. Whatever the form, audiences grabbed on to these declarations of love—and held tight.

Masters like Rodgers and Hammerstein, Irving Berlin, and Cole Porter understood where the heart strings lay and how to pluck them. They may have been businessmen, but they also happened to genuinely believe in what they were writing, and therein lay a key to their great success. When the critical potshots were flying at the film version of *The Sound of Music,* Rodgers did not hesitate to wade in, taking particular aim at those who criticized the film for being sentimental. Rodgers believed in the world of Maria von Trapp, and mused that the critics seemed to harbor resentment toward any iteration of straightforward emotion. Why, he asked, make an apology for the depiction of good triumphing over evil? Why be cynical? To his mind, the studied disapproval of critics ignored a basic fact of life—that "most of us live on sentiment." Four years down the road, he took time to throw a few further potshots at the supposedly "hip" new musicals in town: "(To reject sentiment) I think is ridiculous. And this is what they're doing. They will accept something that doesn't even make sense, much less sentiment, like *Hair.*"

Rodgers was, it seems, at least partially correct; *Hair*'s inventive score has retained its glow in the forty-plus years since its premiere, but it's still anyone's guess as to exactly what is going on in the book scenes—one reason why the show is not consistently revived in first-class productions. In the world of Rodgers and Hammerstein, character, music, and lyric were inextricably wed, and as a result, their songs and those of other golden-age composers and lyricists provided the background soundtrack for momentous events in everyday lives: anniversary celebrations—"Isn't It Romantic"; bar mitzvahs—"Sunrise, Sunset"; bridal processionals—"*The Sound of Music* Wedding Preludium"; funerals and post–9-11 declarations of solidarity—"You'll Never Walk Alone."

Just like their audience, Rodgers and Hammerstein believed that the von Trapps could sing their way to Switzerland, that Billy Bigelow in *Carousel* could redeem himself, that, in fact, none of us will ever walk alone again. In this worldview, faith endures, and when, to the accompaniment of swelling background chorus and orchestral uplift, the audience is told to persevere and climb ev'ry mountain, most surrender willingly. They want to believe.

At the time of the film's initial release, the turn away from sentiment had not yet approached the heights it would in the new millennium, but the rules of the game were rapidly changing, and there in the midst of an increasingly loud cultural tug-of-war rose the proudly retro *The Sound of Music.* There was no ambiguity in *The Sound of Music.* The good were not just good—they were godly. The bad were found in the form of the greatest villains of all, the Nazis. This black-and-white universe was safe, secure, and above all reassuring. Its bedrock appeal lay in the fact that the pain experienced in real life, the knowledge that coincidence and catastrophe could instantaneously snap the veneer of stability and peace of mind, simply did not exist in the universe of Maria von Trapp.

The moral certainty found in *The Sound of Music,* one that caused fans of the film to so embrace the look, sound, and feel of the onscreen world that their repeated viewings came to represent a form of wish fulfillment, seemed to represent nothing less than an attempt to live inside the movie and become von Trapps themselves. Audience members knew there was a distance between their own lives and what was on screen, but they wanted to be inside that world nonetheless. It's a notion Woody Allen plays with beautifully throughout *The Purple Rose of Cairo* (1985), in which Cecilia (Mia Farrow), married to an abusive man and drowning in a dead-end job, depends on the movies for her escape. She sees the movie *The Purple Rose of Cairo* so often that the film's star walks off the screen, into her life, and falls in love with her. For all the women who dreamed of marrying Captain von Trapp, and all the children who wished for a governess or mother just like Maria, the notion struck home. Whether naive or savvy, these super fans shared one overriding desire: to dive into the screen and live in the world of *The Sound of Music.* Only total immersion in that world would suffice. In the words of Nicholas Hammond: "Everyone in the world wants to be in our home movie— you show it to your kids."

In the words of Rosie O'Donnell: "After my mother died, I dreamed of

Julie Andrews becoming my mother. I had a recurring fantasy that Julie Andrews would show up at my house and fall in love with my dad and somehow the nanny/babysitter angle comes in and transforms the entire family. So for me it was a dream, a hope, a wish, a fantasy, something to sort of pin my sadness on, that elevated it." Rosie O'Donnell is far from alone among celebrities who revere *The Sound of Music*. When tennis legend Chris Evert was going through a difficult divorce, her fairy-tale life upended, she was asked "When are you happy?" Her swift reply: "For the three hours when I am watching *The Sound of Music*." A retreat for Chris Evert. A restoration for Rosie O'Donnell.

The film was not, of course, a touchstone only for women, celebrity or not. In what may rank as the most moving testimonial of all, on Oprah's 2010 *Sound of Music* reunion show, a Vietnam War combat veteran related how his wife "dragged" him to see the film in 1966. After deployment to Vietnam seven months later, he ended up watching the film a staggering 127 times: "I could go to another world for three hours. I could go to that part of me that was free. That part of me that had no worries, no woes, no concerns. For three hours, it was just wonderful, splendid peace."

In the watershed year of 1965, when the counterculture gained force and the United States seemed split down the middle, America's self-image ceased to be centered in the togetherness found in World War II and the immediate post-war era. Against the background of the Vietnam War and racial unrest, *The Sound of Music* represented the first, biggest, and most sustained pop cultural monument erected by traditional audiences as a fortress against all they found most disturbing in their too rapidly changing society.

As anti-war and civil rights protests roiled the nation, all of the old social standards—short hair on men, clean-cut appearance, attendance at church, automatic respect for all authority, unquestioning allegiance to the U.S. government—seemed, in the eyes of the vast middle class, to have been turned upside down. Large portions of those men and women, those famously characterized as the "silent majority," felt stranded by the cultural revolution flashing by. These were the men and women who elected Richard Nixon in 1968, who yearned for a unity and law-and-order society they felt was receding quickly into the rearview mirror. And there, standing tall in the foreground, loomed *The Sound of Music* as the best and most famous example of tradition and family stability.

Robert Wise himself zeroed in on the family unit as the central reason for "the enduring quality of this story," and it is not a big stretch to posit that a yearning for stability and family was an essential component underlying the diametrically opposed, but equally popular universe of Don Corleone in the seven-years-later *The Godfather*. Both *The Sound of Music* and *The Godfather* (each edited by William Reynolds) embrace the concept of family as refuge from a difficult world, a place of acceptance providing unquestioned love, support, and sense of belonging. Maria and Don Corleone, the original odd couple, both respect the eternal verities, secure in the knowledge that family trumps every other aspect of life. For the Corleones and the von Trapps alike, care, attention, and understanding provided by and for the family prove the order of the day. (Of course, one family provides care with machine guns, the other by singing show tunes. . . .)

On the fortieth anniversary of the film's release, Julie Andrews told *Today Show* host Ann Curry that she felt the continuing success of the film was a result of its "joy and decency and goodness. There was integrity running through the film." When all was said and done, the film provided the most precious human commodity of all: hope. In the words of Heidegger, "The possible ranks higher than the actual."

In that light, *The Sound of Music* represented an oasis amid the ongoing fear that a more decent and civilized past was now forever lost. It's as if return visits with the von Trapps allowed the audience to return to a place and state of mind where something peaceful, what F. Scott Fitzgerald termed "the golden hour," once existed; the mere act of returning allowed viewers to once again live in hope that the old feelings of innocence, certainty, and safety could be experienced just one more time.

Such nostalgia, an approach to life based upon emotion, not fact, flourishes whenever times are particularly tough precisely because it improves upon reality. Experiences and relationships are viewed through rose-colored glasses, resulting in a view of the past as being without pain or melancholia. The end product lies in the sought-after happy ending, or better yet, a story that never ends, the neatly tied up solutions flowing ever onward.

The world, of course, had never been as simple as those entranced by nostalgia would have it; in the apt lyric of Stephen Sondheim, one sung by a disillusioned yet worldly wise woman surveying the landscape of broken friendships in *Merrily We Roll Along*:

Why can't it be like it was? . . .
That's what everyone does:
Blames the way it is
On the way it was,
On the way it never ever was.

With *The Sound of Music*, however, it actually could be like it never ever was—and in Technicolor to boot.

The von Trapps touched a universal chord then and now by presenting viewers with a wounded family the general audience believed mirrored their own. The typical moviegoer feasting on popcorn at the local theater may not have lived with captains, nuns, or a gilded ballroom, but she did live in a family simply trying its best to make it through each day. The tale of an unhappy family healed by an outsider represented both familiarity and wish fulfillment.

That sense of familiarity proved so intense that fifty years later, part of the film's continued appeal lies in the fact that the mere mention of the title conjures up audience members' memories of watching the film for the first time. It's not just the film itself that is remembered, but the remembrance of watching it as a child.

For those who liked *The Sound of Music,* the film engendered feelings akin to those found in that wished-for happy childhood: safety, love, and a certainty that life would always unfold in a secure comforting fashion. Wrongs could always be righted, fair play would prevail, and a benign deity watched over all. Presenting parent-child reconciliation front and center, the film's happy ending allowed audiences to rewrite their own personal history, and they held fast to the idea that perhaps underneath their own father's uncommunicative exterior lay another version of the pre-Maria Captain von Trapp, a soul ready to be set free. Audiences knew that their own families weren't ideal, but in the words of the Carly Simon song, *The Sound of Music* exemplified the feeling "That's the way I've always heard it should be."

Which is precisely why, when Pauline Kael sneered that *The Sound of Music* pretends that we all live in the best of all possible worlds, she missed the key point many in the audience understood: that in their acquiescence, they, too, were pretending. Audiences wished life were like what they saw on the screen—a fairy tale come to life. But they knew the difference, and in that context, it's worth remembering that the first words they read in the film's popular souvenir program were "Once upon a time." As Agathe von Trapp mused, "It does not matter to people whether or not the story is true, but that it is a beautiful wholesome story that appeals to the emotions of the viewers."

In its own subtextual way, *The Sound of Music* even provided older middle-of-the-road audiences a vicarious, safe sense of rebellion; for men and women watching Maria chafe against both the rules of the convent and the autocratic rule of the captain, her triumphant display of individuality proved satisfying precisely because in the end it also managed to affirm the old-school values of God and country. *The Sound of Music* seemed to fulfill exactly what film historian David Thomson so memorably characterized as "an audience's yearning for the belief and transcendence that once existed in cinema."

That very yearning for belief and transcendence was translating into much more than box office gold. Small-town critics, industry approval, and mass heartland appeal overrode the disdain of the sophisticated, and when the Academy Award nominations for films released in 1965 were announced, the conservative motion picture academy had made its viewpoint crystal clear: *The Sound of Music* received no fewer than ten Oscar nominations, including the most coveted prize of all: Best Picture. Let everyone make as much fun as they wanted; the ultimate validation in the form of shiny gold statues might just be lying dead ahead.

21

THE ACADEMY AWARDS

As soon as the Oscar nominations were announced early in 1966, it became clear that the awards were shaping up as a horse race between two block-buster films: both *The Sound of Music* and *Doctor Zhivago* had each garnered a total of ten nominations. *The Sound of Music* scored nominations for: Best Picture, Best Director (Wise), Best Actress (Julie Andrews), Best Supporting Actress (Peggy Wood), Best Art Direction (Boris Leven with set decorators Walter Scott and Ruby Levitt), Best Cinematography (Ted McCord), Best Costume Design (Dorothy Jeakins), Best Musical Adaptation (Irwin Kostal), Best Sound (James Corcoran and Fred Hynes), and Best Editing (William Reynolds). Great news all around except for one glaring omission: Ernest Lehman had been overlooked for Best Screenplay adapted from another medium. Instead, the five nominees in that category consisted of *Cat Ballou, The Collector, Doctor Zhivago* (Robert Bolt's screenplay went on to win the Oscar), *Ship of Fools,* and *A Thousand Clowns.*

Why the omission? Perhaps the reasoning ran that *Sound of Music* was "just a musical," that Lehman had simply transferred a rather two-dimensional stage play into a simplistic screen musical. As it was, when the nominations were announced, Robert Wise, then on location directing *The Sand Pebbles* in Asia, cabled Lehman with a succinct "You wuz robbed." Although nursing his ego, Lehman appreciated his friend's cable, and the tetchy screenwriter ultimately took a more nuanced view of the omission; knowing that he had played an important part in the film's success, made it, he said, "very difficult for me to have any unhappy feelings about anything connected with this picture."

As it was, Lehman was not alone in being overlooked. Although the list of Best Song nominees did included two songs of great popularity and lasting appeal in "The Shadow of Your Smile" and "What's New Pussycat?" Richard Rodgers's two new songs for the film were completely overlooked. Just as incredibly, all of the songs written by the Beatles for *Help* were similarly ignored. Or, put another way, "The Ballad of Cat Ballou," "I Will Wait for You," and "The Sweetheart Tree" nabbed nominations over "Something Good," "Help," "Ticket to Ride," and "You've Got to Hide Your Love Away."

As the Academy Award campaign season revved up into high gear, publicist Mike Kaplan devised a particularly canny maneuver to help *Sound of Music*'s standing among the voters. Given the relatively small size of the 1965 Academy membership—only half the size of the twenty-first-century membership—Kaplan opened up the Saturday-morning screenings of the film on the Fox lot; it wasn't just Academy members and one guest who were invited, but the member's entire family as well. A family-friendly atmosphere, Kaplan rationalized, would generate enormous goodwill among the members. It did.

In the roll up to the Oscars, numerous second-tier award shows stoked the fires of anticipation among 20th Century-Fox executives and *The Sound of Music* team. With the Hollywood Foreign Press Association (Golden Globes) splitting its prizes into separate categories for drama and musical/comedy, *The Sound of Music* scored nominations for both Robert Wise and Peggy Wood, and won Golden Globes for Best Picture (Musical or Comedy) and Julie Andrews—Best Actress (Musical or Comedy). At the same time, Wise received additional honors as both Producer of the Year (the prestigious David O. Selznick Producer's Guild Award) and Best Director from the Directors Guild of America.

Momentum on behalf of the musical appeared to be building as key members of *The Sound of Music* team racked up the top awards bestowed by their own unions: William Reynolds won the American Cinema Editors "Eddie Award" as Editor of the Year, and Ernest Lehman happily received the Writers Guild of America Award for Best Written American Musical. Julie Andrews won the David di Donatello Award as Best Foreign Actress as well as a Golden Laurel Award, and was nominated for the BAFTA Best British Actress Award. More surprisingly, she finished second in the voting for Best Actress with the New York Film Critics Circle.

The Sound of Music itself was voted one of the top ten films of the year by the National Board of Review, yet all of these kudos paled in prestige next to the Oscars themselves. Would Julie Andrews become the first actress ever to win back-to-back Best Actress Oscars for performances in musical films? Could such an old-fashioned popular success actually win the top prize in a rapidly changing film industry?

With husband Tony Walton working elsewhere, Andrews attended the April 18, 1966, awards ceremony with friend and associate producer Saul Chaplin. As the night unfolded, *The Sound of Music* quickly won three technical awards: Best Scoring (Kostal), Best Sound (Corcoran and Hynes), and Best Editor (Reynolds). It was Reynolds who turned in the wittiest and most graceful speech of the evening, the always gentlemanly editor clutching his Oscar and telling the assembled crowd: "This picture was a joy to edit because whenever I got in trouble I would cut to Julie."

It soon became clear that the evening was shaping up into the anticipated horse race between *Sound of Music* and *Doctor Zhivago,* because mixed in with *Sound of Music*'s three wins were three losses to *Zhivago* in additional technical categories: Ted McCord lost the color cinematography award to Freddie Young's vibrant work on *Doctor Zhivago*, and production designer Boris Leven was overlooked in favor of John Box, Terry Marsh, and Dario Simoni for their depiction of revolutionary-era Russia. When Dorothy Jeakins lost the Best Costume Award to *Zhivago*'s Phyllis Dalton, unease began to set in among the *Sound of Music* personnel.

That anxiety was heightened when Peggy Wood lost the Best Supporting Actress Award to Shelley Winters for *A Patch of Blue*. After Martin Balsam won a Best Supporting Oscar for his turn in *A Thousand Clowns,* the attention turned to the biggest awards of the night. Forget Best Sound. People wanted to know if Wise, absent from the proceedings because of location shooting on *The Sand Pebbles,* would triumph over David Lean. Or would the biggest irony of all occur: might William Wyler win for directing *The Collector,* thereby vindicating his decision to quit the very film for which Wise was nominated? (Wyler did receive the prestigious Irving Thalberg Award that night, and when asked if his version of *The Sound of Music* would have been different, Wyler had laughingly replied: "Yes, mine might have been a failure. This one was a big success; mine could have been a flop. . . . Bob Wise became a rich man with it and I'm delighted.")

After nearly three hours of protracted tension, when presenter Shirley

MacLaine unsealed the envelope and called out Robert Wise's name as Best Director, Julie Andrews walked to the podium to accept the award on his behalf, and in the process received a long, roaring ovation. In those pre–cell phone, pre-Internet days, the news of Wise's award was relayed to him in stages: a newspaper in Hong Kong telephoned *Sand Pebbles* crew members on shore, who then radioed the results to the boat on which Wise was directing a scene. Unbeknownst to the director, the crew had smuggled firecrackers and Chinese dragon dancers onto the boat in anticipation of his possible victory, and when the news arrived, the ensuing thunderous display of sound and light caught a delighted Wise completely by surprise.

When the moment for the Best Actress Award arrived, the suspense in the air proved palpable. Would Academy voters reward Andrews two years in a row for playing nannies? She was the hottest new star in town, well liked, and Academy members had loved her witty acceptance speech upon receiving the Oscar for *Mary Poppins*: "I know you Americans are famous for your hospitality, but this is really ridiculous!" Golden Globe voters had followed up her win for *Mary Poppins* with another statuette for *Sound of Music,* so her chances looked promising. Prognosticators did not put much stock in the possibility of a win by Samantha Eggar (*The Collector*), Elizabeth Hartman (*A Patch of Blue*), or Simone Signoret (*Ship of Fools*). Instead, they touted the contest for Best Actress as a horse race between the two British Julies: Andrews and Christie, the latter having received rave reviews for her role as a disillusioned fashion model in *Darling.* Andrews and Christie were friendly "rivals" who had joked about attending the ceremony together. With Andrews having just presented the Best Actor award to Lee Marvin for "Cat Ballou," she did not have time to return to her seat before the announcement of Best Actress, so she waited in the wings, the suspense heightened by the fact that the Best Actress winner was to be announced by the previous year's winner for Best Actor: Andrews's Broadway *My Fair Lady* costar Rex Harrison. Milking the moment for all its worth, Harrison opened the envelope and cheekily announced the winner as: "Julie (long pause) . . . Christie for *Darling.*"

Perhaps the voters felt that Andrews had already been more than amply rewarded, and may have asked themselves: "How difficult can it be to play a singing nanny again?" The answer: very. Andrews's extraordinary skills may actually have worked against her, as her seamless combination of singing, dancing, and acting made it all look oh-so-easy—perhaps too easy. Like the great

Fred Astaire with his unearthly ability to make the most complex dance routine appear a mere trifle he just dashed off, Andrews's performance was meticulously thought out and executed, yet none of the effort showed. (So convincing was her performance that even her own daughter fell under its persuasive spell. When the very young Emma Walton watched the film, she would become so wrapped up in the story that when Maria temporarily leaves the von Trapps, a saddened Emma would, in Andrews's smiling recall, quickly tell her mother, " 'Well, I just have to go now, Mummy!' Because she didn't want to see me being unhappy.")

The moment had finally arrived for Best Picture of the Year. Jack Lemmon carefully read the list of nominees in alphabetical order: *Darling, Doctor Zhivago, Ship of Fools, The Sound of Music,* and *A Thousand Clowns.* When he ripped the envelope open and called out "*The Sound of Music,*" associate producer Saul Chaplin bounded to the stage to accept the award on behalf of producer Wise. *The Sound of Music* had triumphed, marking two years in a row that a musical had won the award as Best Picture; along with the previous year's winner, *My Fair Lady, The Sound of Music* had now become one of only two musicals to have won both Broadway's Tony Award as Best Musical and the Academy Award as Best Film.

Critics rolled their eyes, audiences felt vindicated, and best of all from the standpoint of 20th Century-Fox, the box office leaped forward yet again. In Salt Lake City, more than half a million admissions had now been clocked— a figure three times the local population. Whether in Salt Lake City, Des Moines, Houston, or Slippery Rock, *The Sound of Music* triumphed wherever it played, and as the phenomenon grew, its success was repeated all around the world: Asia, Australia, Africa, the Caribbean. It was dubbed into foreign languages and equipped with strange new titles. None of it mattered. One Austrian nun, in the very appealing persona of Julie Andrews, was now conquering the entire world.

22.

THE INTERNATIONAL PHENOMENON

"The thing that's most important about films, the aspect that has really caught me up as much as anything, is the universality of the language of film. . . . It's one of the pluses of the motion picture . . . getting the message over, getting it all around the world."

—ROBERT WISE

Just how popular was *The Sound of Music* around the world? Consider the fact that at the time of the film's initial release in the Philippines, crowds grew so unruly in their demand for holiday tickets that the police had to be called in to quell the mounting furor. No need for police to monitor *Bonnie and Clyde* or *The Godfather,* but for those wild and crazy *Sound of Music* fans? Call out the reinforcements.

Country by country, continent by continent, *The Sound of Music* juggernaut rolled on, pleasing millions, frustrating critics (although foreign critics ultimately proved kinder than those in the United States), and consistently setting box office records. The film's extended road show first-run release around the world proved such a resounding and continuing success that at the Fox stockholders meeting in 1967, the profits generated by *The Sound of Music* allowed the board to vote a one-third increase in quarterly dividends from thirty to forty cents per share. (The *New York Times* account of this stockholders' meeting at the Waldorf Astoria does include the rather startling news that one of the stockholders, Evelyn Y. Davis, asked questions of the executives while clad in a Batman costume.)

Everywhere the film opened it turned into an unprecedented success, the months' long runs etched in the record books from Italy and Australia to the

UK and Thailand (where marquees spelled out the title "Charms of the Heaven-Sound"). Wise himself credited part of the success to timing: "The world was hungry for this kind of warm, emotional family entertainment. It seemed to happen all over the world. . . . I saw the picture play in Japan, I saw it in Hong Kong—and it broke all records. It was wonderful to sit there and see the same kind of response from those Japanese audiences toward the things of the heart. . . . Timing is something you can't write in—it's just there if you're lucky."

Yes, the timing helped, but in this case only served to underscore the first-rate work on display. *The Sound of Music* succeeded overseas because family love is universal and talents like Robert Wise's and Julie Andrews's know no boundaries.

Except in Germany and Austria.

It's not that the film meandered along in Germany and Austria. The cold hard fact was that it flopped outright. Big time.

On the surface, of course, the reasons given for the film's flop were not political. Austrians and Germans seemed to feel that *The Sound of Music* trod on the territory of the very popular *Die Trapp-Familie* films; German in origin and language, those two films downplayed the political content of the von Trapps' flight from Austria, and resonated with the natives in a far more congenial fashion than did a Hollywood-produced, English-language musical.

It wasn't just the content of the film: Austrians proved rather vociferous in their criticism of *The Sound of Music*'s Hollywoodized version of Austrian dress. Said Georg Steinitz: "We thought that the Austrian costumes looked phony, that they didn't look Austrian enough. But in retrospect, I realize that they were more correct than I thought at the time. I've seen photos of the Trapp Family Choir and the film clothes are fairly close—well, not the curtains!" (In a similar vein, during filming, Christopher Plummer argued that his own wardrobe was inaccurate, desperately pleading to wear the dark-hued clothes he saw displayed in Salzburg stores. Ultimately, however, he admitted that Wise and Dorothy Jeakins were correct in their choice of lighter colors, which "lifted the movie from a morass of goo into a much lighter vein—a more positive look. It was right for the rest of the world but Austria still hated the clothes!")

And yet, the real reason for the film's failure may still have lain in the fact that the Nazi-era setting of the movie seemed to remind the population of an era that they would rather totally forget. The movie's depiction of Captain von Trapp's principled refusal to serve in the Reich's Navy only served to remind Austrians that masses of their fellow citizens had eagerly welcomed Hitler. Speaking in 2012, Marko Feingold, the president of the Jewish Community of Salzburg, bluntly stated: "Even today, the Austrian people claim that they had very little to do with it. They hide behind the claim that they were invaded but it's a false claim. There was no violent invasion. Ninety-eight percent of the population wanted the Anschluss. They have not come to terms with their past and they deny everything. They don't want to hear about it."

This view is contradicted, however, by Georg Steinitz. At the time of the film's premiere, Steinitz was not living in Austria, but instead working in the film department at Florida State University, yet he maintains that the film's unpopularity was due to its Hollywood-centric version of Austrian history. "It had nothing to do with politics. Other films have dealt with the subject and they attracted big crowds. Remember, before the annexation, Austria was a dictatorship with an outlawed socialist party: conservatives had one third of the power, the Nazis one third, and the outlawed socialists one third. When Hitler threatened, he had comparatively little opposition—the opposition was already in jail or in concentration camps—not as bad as what the Nazis did, but still camps." Offering a rueful laugh about the film's lack of success in his native Salzburg, he recalls that "the first run in Salzburg lasted only three days. All the extras from the movie came to see it—and that was it!"

As it was, when Wolfgang Wolf, branch manager of the Munich office of 20th Century-Fox, took it upon himself to cut a full one third of the movie, he deleted the entire last hour of the film, so that it now ended after Captain von Trapp and Maria marry. No shots of Nazis marching across the plaza. No swastika banners. No menacing searchlights. Just a total whitewash. When word of his unauthorized editing reached the Fox studios in Los Angeles, he was promptly fired and the film restored to its original length. (Ironically, Wise judged that audiences in foreign territories often grew bored with "Climb Ev'ry Mountain" and allowed the song to be cut in some countries. Cuts for political reasons, however, he would not countenance.)

Even after the film was restored to its full running time in Germany, however, it still bombed, the business so poor that from a total of seventy-one theaters, the distributor's share amounted to only $22,000. In the face of such overwhelming failure, an additional 229 scheduled bookings were canceled.

How did the cast feel about the failure of the movie in Germany and Austria? With her innate British sense of propriety, Julie Andrews is loathe to ever publicly criticize others, but perhaps with knowledge of the $900,000 Fox spent on filming in Salzburg in mind, at the time she did murmur: "It's really rather nasty of them." Andrews made that comment in 1966, but with *The Sound of Music* now a popular twenty-first-century presentation by the world famous Salzburg marionettes, and the stage musical successfully presented at Salzburg's Landestheater, one suspects that her opinion is now markedly different.

As it was, *The Sound of Music* had made Julie Andrews the most popular movie star in the world. Did she still love the film? Absolutely. Did she love all of the attention and expectations?

Well . . .

23.

JULIE ANDREWS: QUEEN OF HOLLYWOOD

"There's niceness where it can seem treacly, and there's just plain old being nice, and that's what Julie is. She can be very bawdy . . . but in the good sense of that thought. Julie's the whole ball of wax. To top it off, she can sing 'Spoonful of Sugar' and you don't get diabetes."

—CAROL BURNETT

As grosses for *The Sound of Music* grew into the stratosphere, whatever controversy attended the film, one fact had become crystal clear: Julie Andrews was the hottest movie star on the planet, riding the crest of a tidal wave. Worldwide adoration—the stuff of dreams. And a simultaneous blessing and curse.

It has become a somewhat accepted, though inaccurate, view that Julie Andrews rose to superstardom with the one-two punch of *Mary Poppins* and *The Sound of Music* and then instantly lost her perch at the top of the charts with a series of big flops. Such a view ignores the fact that Andrews extended her reign as the queen of the box office with her late sixties run of *Hawaii, Torn Curtain,* and *Thoroughly Modern Millie* (the last named playing like a substitute for her first Broadway success, *The Boy Friend.*)

From 1965 through 1967 Julie Andrews reigned as the biggest box office star in the world, male or female, and in the aftermath of *The Sound of Music*'s release, there was no one hotter in the entire world of show business. Through sheer force of talent, and the remarkable confluence of suitable roles and her own star personality, Julie Andrews had succeeded in making the world fall in love with her. In her own typically understated and well-considered fashion, she later acknowledged: "It did kind of knock me sideways

for a while. It was so much, so fast." Thanks to her own extraordinary performances in *Mary Poppins* and *The Sound of Music,* Andrews now had to
live up to an impossible standard: ever smiling, always warm, pristine, un-
touchable yet approachable. Complicating the situation, she had to live up to
that standard with the entire world watching.

As focus of both worship and aspiration, Andrews found herself in a daunt-
ing position. To the ordinary citizen searching for a suitable object of devotion in hopes of filling a void, Julie Andrews seemed just like the girl next
door. She wasn't, of course—the girl next door didn't sing with a four-octave
range and command stage and screen with equal finesse. But in the midst
of growing concerns over societal upheaval, she diverted beautifully. It wasn't
Andrews who invited the public to think that they could be just like her; the
public decided that for themselves.

The supreme irony of her popularity lay in the fact that the seemingly approachable Julie Andrews succeeded by leaving everyone else far behind her. As
the social unrest of the 1960s gathered force and life seemed to make less sense
by the day, Andrews, like all celebrities, came to assume an ever more important place in the public imagination. As faith in churches, banks, civic organiza-
tions, and the American Dream began to fade, the celebrity age began in
earnest. This increasing worship of celebrity provided a lifeline to those who
sensed that beneath the surface of everyday life, firm ground had disappeared.
Well, the reasoning ran, "those actors are rich and famous—so they must be
happy." And who was more famous—or nicer—than Julie Andrews? No one.

She was the national golden girl—at least for the next three years—which
makes it particularly interesting to place the squeaky clean image Andrews
found so constricting in relief against the goody-two-shoes persona of Doris
Day, the all-American girl next door whom Andrews replaced as the biggest
box office star in the world. For all of their monumental success, both women,
not surprisingly, grew to detest the word "image."

Although neither Andrews nor Day were well educated in terms of
schooling, both were very bright, self-demanding women who triumphed on
recordings as well as on film.

Day maintained a more successful solo recording career than did Andrews,
her years as a solo artist with Columbia resulting in seven number-one singles, twenty-one singles in the top ten, and well over a dozen gold albums.

By way of contrast, all of Andrews's success with records came with sound tracks and cast albums; *My Fair Lady, Camelot, Mary Poppins,* and *The Sound of Music* were all platinum successes, but her solo studio fare sold decidedly less well. It may be that Andrews's polished voice never suggested the intimacy and vulnerability that Day managed so beautifully, nor the larger-than-life romantic über drama that Streisand brought into the recording booth. Andrews always sounded in control, as if a lost love could be dealt with simply by means of a bit of can-do, stiff-upper-lip control.

Day never appeared in any single film that approached the titanic success of *Sound of Music*—few actresses ever did—but she acquitted herself successfully over a broader range of material than did Andrews, and in artistic terms, handled the universe of Alfred Hitchcock in the first rate *The Man Who Knew Too Much* (1956) with more nuance and appropriate neuroticism than Andrews did in the only partially successful *Torn Curtain* (1967). What the two women shared, however, in their girl-next-door persona, was a seemingly centered quality, the ability to make the moviegoing public believe that they were part of the audience's very own family. (There was, by way of contrast, nothing "girl next door" about Joan Crawford or Bette Davis; Crawford once famously remarked: "If you want the girl next door, go next door." Both Crawford and Davis thrived as divas who seemed to exist in an atmosphere of perpetual drama.) Such audience identification with Andrews and Day did carry great costs for the two actresses, however, resulting in a proprietary sense of ownership on the part of fans worldwide. It all constituted a possessiveness that caused Andrews, beneath her seeming friendliness, to remain perpetually, if never noticeably, on guard, and Day to retreat completely from all public life.

Both Andrews and Day were tagged as "the girl next door," but there was an essential difference at work here; Day really did read onscreen as the all-American girl next door—well, if the girl next door could act, sing like a million bucks, dance, and exude an understated sex appeal that managed the neat trick of appearing appropriate for both nighttime fun and a trip home to meet Mom. Andrews, with a similar scrubbed appearance, read more like the poised, pretty fun cousin visiting from Europe—a model of decorum with a subdued but detectable heat rising from just underneath the surface. At its most hyperbolic, Andrews's then adoring press coverage found *Time* magazine in December of 1966 all but eulogizing her as "Christmas carols in the snow, a companion by the fire, a laughing clown at charades, a girl to read poetry to on a cold winter's night." It was all more than a bit over the top, but *Time* was onto something here. For just this one moment in time, Julie Andrews did indeed seem capable of being all things to all people.

Andrews's star persona read best in musicals, where she turned larger than life while singing—not only because she was a sensational singer, but also because her musicality defined her very being, serving as both her ticket to fame and the essence of her stardom. For all her success with *Hawaii, Torn Curtain,* and *Princess Diaries,* she seemed a bit diminished when appearing in nonmusicals. Ironically, the opposite proved true of Day, a terrific singer who, for all of her success in musicals like *Love Me or Leave Me* and *The Pajama Game,* hit her box office peak with a series of non-musical romantic comedies costarring Rock Hudson, Cary Grant, and James Garner. (Garner, who starred with Andrews in *The Americanization of Emily* and with Day in *The Thrill of It All* and *Move Over Darling* called them two of the sexiest women with whom he had ever worked, saying of Day, "She exuded sex but made you smile about it.")

Unlike Day, Andrews never really struck a wifelike pose in her most popular pictures: not in *Mary Poppins, Victor/Victoria,* or *The Princess Diaries.* Even in *The Sound of Music,* the marriage takes place three quarters of the way through the film. She's never a fashion plate, unlike Day in her early-sixties sex comedies with Rock Hudson and Cary Grant, but what she manages to do beautifully is layer Maria von Trapp and all of her most well-known characters with a firm practicality. She speaks her mind, has spirit, and in *The Sound of Music* even criticizes her employer with verve. She is sui generis— unlike any other screen goddess we've seen, before or since.

Because of their similar good-girl personas, it therefore made a certain kind of sense that in mid-1960s America, Julie Andrews replaced Doris Day as queen of the box office. Day's tumble from her perch atop the box office rankings accelerated because of an increasingly dismal series of sex "comedies" like *Do Not Disturb* (1965) and *Where Were You When the Lights Went Out?* (1968), films that she knew were awful but that her husband/agent Marty Melcher had insisted she make for the money he desperately needed. At the same time, thanks to *Mary Poppins* and *The Sound of Music,* Julie Andrews began her meteoric rise to the top. The turnabout was quick: in the *Motion Picture Herald* poll of January 1966, Andrews ranked as the fourth biggest star of the preceding year, after Sean Connery, John Wayne, and Day. One year later, the same poll found Andrews perched at the very top of the box office list. The one-two-three punch of *Sound of Music, Hawaii,* and *Torn Curtain* in 1965 through 1967 had made Julie Andrews a bona fide movie star, one who had starred in the highest-grossing film of the year for three successive years. (At the time, so great was the Andrews star power that she, more than Paul Newman or Alfred Hitchcock, propelled *Torn Curtain* to the highest grosses of Hitchcock's entire career.)

She followed up this trifecta of number-one hits with *Thoroughly Modern Millie,* and although overly long, and running out of steam in its second half, the film grew into a smash hit for Universal. Audiences couldn't seem to get enough of a singing/dancing Julie Andrews, and she had reached a peak of stardom that made its own rules: anything was tolerated, even accepted, if Andrews was attached. In *Thoroughly Modern Millie* we're told that Millie hails from the heartland of America, yet she speaks with a decided English accent. The audience response was simple—who cares? Just let Andrews sing. Millie overcame any obstacle lying in her way through singing, dancing, and old-fashioned pluck: an American version of Maria von Trapp and Mary Poppins.

The overwhelming success of these musicals presented Andrews not only with worldwide acclaim but also with several extra hurdles to jump. She was clearly an intelligent, well-spoken, talented actress and singer, but the public responded so strongly to her portrayals of these virginal good women that they demanded she be like the women depicted onscreen: kind, firm yet gentle, the mother figure who solves all problems and arranges happy endings. In other words—flawless.

Andrews was only thirty-two by the time all of these musicals had been released, still defining herself as actress, singer, and young mother. Having worked since the age of ten, she was a lot more confident professionally than personally, and as the object of public worship, was now stuck between the opposite poles of world's biggest movie star and idealized girl next door. She had a lot of growing up to do and she had to do it in public, with the shadow of perfect Maria trailing her throughout. Like everyone else, Julie Andrews evolved as she grew older, losing her status at the top of the box office charts, but deepening as an actress, enduring public bumps as wife and mother, maturing—changing.

Everyone involved in *The Sound of Music* was undergoing transformation, whether the public wanted them to or not. Which led to one overwhelming question: how could anyone involved top *The Sound of Music*? Was it even possible?

The answer was "no"—but the efforts to do so proved fascinating.

24.

LIFE AFTER *THE SOUND OF MUSIC*

CHRISTOPHER PLUMMER

"I ended up very much liking the children . . . in the last analysis."
—CHRISTOPHER PLUMMER

For a period of time after the release of *The Sound of Music,* Christopher Plummer's worst career nightmare appeared to be coming true. Possessed of an impeccable theatrical résumé featuring starring roles in classic plays, he still came in for the sort of critical scorn he feared he'd receive for his participation in the film. *Esquire* magazine, in its withering August 1966 put down of the actor, simply referred to him as a "former actor who has become a Hollywood leading man."

For decades after the release of the movie, Plummer engaged in a constant bout of shadowboxing with the film's ever-lengthening shadow. No matter how brilliant his performance in Shakespeare or Pinter, he remained known to the public as Captain von Trapp. Just as he had feared, the "cardboard" figure of the captain turned out to cast the longest shadow of all.

Plummer's feelings about the film remained famously complicated. He admitted to calling the film "The Sound of Mucus," and at one point claimed everyone else, including Julie Andrews, did as well. It is a charge she flat-out denies, even stating that while she knows Plummer referred to the film by that derogatory term, she herself never heard him use it. Speaking at the time of the film's fortieth anniversary, Andrews mused: "I think he's terribly proud now to be part of the movie. And he's told me 'I was a very different young man then.' "

It's actually the decidedly unsentimental Plummer who uttered the exact words audiences worldwide most wanted to hear about his costar: "*The Sound of Music* was the actual Julie Andrews on the screen. If you know her as I do, she's just exactly like that." Andrews returned the favor, albeit in slightly different terms: "He's an adorable curmudgeon. He's very loving actually. He just doesn't want you to know that."

Fifty years after the release of the film, Plummer is now able to put aside his youthful arrogance regarding the material ("if anyone gave a chocolate soldier performance it was me. I should have been kicked in the ass for that."). Now he can simply enjoy the craftsmanship on display: "I think it's sentimental in the proper way." Watching the film in 2007 at a children's Easter party in his home state of Connecticut, he gracefully acknowledged: "Here was I, cynical old sod that I am, being totally seduced by the damn thing—and what's more, I felt a sudden surge of pride that I'd been a part of it."

As the decades passed, a mutual rapprochement seemed to have finally occurred between Plummer and the public regarding *The Sound of Music*: practically speaking, he understood how it kept his name current with each succeeding generation of youngsters, but more important, he finally came to understand and appreciate how much the film meant to people. At the same time, the public began to fully comprehend the breadth and depth of his career, realizing that Plummer's protean talent encompassed a host of challenging roles that brought him far beyond the shadow of Captain von Trapp.

Working nonstop in both film and theater with the energy of a man half his age, Plummer appeared onstage in everything from Neil Simon's *The Good Doctor* to his Tony Award–winning turn as Best Actor in a Musical for *Cyrano* (1974). Singing live eight times per week on the stage of Broadway's fabled Palace Theatre, with no Bill Lee in sight to dub his voice, Plummer charmed critics and audiences alike. From Harold Pinter's *No Man's Land* to another Tony Award–winning turn in the one-man play *Barrymore* (1997), from *Othello* to *Macbeth*, the sheer range of his talent began to make an impact on the public's consciousness in a manner totally unrelated to *The Sound of Music*. (The press, however, never fully let go; when, in 2004, Plummer triumphantly returned to New York City with his acclaimed portrayal of King Lear, the *New York Times* headlined a profile of the actor by trumpeting: "The Legend and the Other Guy; a Leering King Lear Exercises the Curse of Captain von Trapp.")

Seemingly at ease, and almost, if not quite, mellow, his continued good health and graceful aging kept him as busy as ever. When he wasn't onstage he churned out one film after another, and if not every one was a classic for the ages (*Dreamscape*—1984, *The Boss's Wife*—1986) there were first-rate films aplenty, ranging from John Huston's *The Man Who Would Be King* (1975) to his Academy Award–nominated turn as newsman Mike Wallace in *The Insider* (1999). Fourth billed in the 2001 Best Picture *A Beautiful Mind,* he finally claimed his own Oscar with his performance as an elderly gay father in *Beginners* (2010). An Academy Award winner at age eighty-two, he smilingly acknowledged: "It kind of rejuvenates your career, makes you feel very young." The worldwide success of *The Sound of Music* had lifted Plummer to an unexpected level of public recognition, but while the shadow of the captain lingered, it no longer felt oppressive: Christopher Plummer von Trapp had finally been fully replaced by Christopher Plummer, actor.

RICHARD RODGERS

The film version of *The Sound of Music* provided Rodgers with his last—and greatest—popular success. After the film's release, however, the joy he had found in the act of composing began to prove increasingly elusive, and his last shows proved unsuccessful with critics and public alike. Although his 1965 pairing with Hammerstein protégé Stephen Sondheim (*Do I Hear a Waltz?*) had proved a minor success, their temperaments clashed, and in the years following the release of *The Sound of Music,* he worked with other lyricists: with Martin Charnin on *Two by Two* (1970) and *I Remember Mama* (1979), and with Sheldon Harnick on *Rex* (1976). His astonishing gift for melody appeared to be intermittently intact, but all three of those productions were plagued by problems, and none lasted a full year on Broadway.

As he entered the last years of his life, the lifetime achievement awards began to proliferate with increasing speed, and in 1978, one year before his death from cancer and heart problems, Barnard College awarded him its greatest honor, the Barnard Medal of Distinction. Most fitting of all, however, in that same year he was selected to be among the first class of honorees for the Kennedy Center Honors, a fully justified tribute that found him included in the company of four of the greatest artists of the twentieth century: Marian Anderson, Fred Astaire, George Balanchine, and Arthur Rubinstein.

ROBERT WISE

"I'm very grateful that the film is so popular. It reminds us that film is a
medium more powerful than we are capable of understanding."
—ROBERT WISE

The year after *The Sound of Music* swept the Oscars, Robert Wise received
yet another Academy Award, the honorary and highly prestigious Irving Thalberg Award given to "creative producers whose body of work reflect a consistently high quality of motion picture production." Inevitably, however, he
never again struck box office gold on the same scale as *The Sound of Music*.

He did return to top form with *The Andromeda Strain* (1971), which featured a dazzling Oscar-nominated production design by Boris Leven, and *The
Hindenburg* (1975) found some success amid the mid-1970s vogue for "disaster films," but 1977's *Audrey Rose,* a tale of reincarnation, fared less well. He
spent a portion of the seventies working on a tantalizing property: a proposed
filming of Jack Finney's (*Invasion of the Body Snatchers*) beloved time travel
novel *Time and Again*. It represents the biggest "if only" of Wise's career, with
the book's expert blend of mystery, romance, and science fiction ranging across
three genres in which Wise had already triumphed (*The Haunting, Until They
Sail, The Day the Earth Stood Still*). What stimulated Wise about *Time and
Again*—the chance to re-create New York City in the late 1800s—is what ultimately proved the film's downfall: money men were scared off by the size
of the budget. Voted one of the five best mysteries of all time in a poll of Murder Ink readers, the book has remained unfilmed.

Although the highly anticipated *Star Trek* (1979) found success at the box
office, it also proved a frustrating experience for Wise; post-production editing was rushed in order to meet a Christmas release date, and the finished
film was not the movie Wise envisioned. Following *Star Trek,* he worked on
developing a number of projects during the 1980s, the most interesting of
which would have reunited him with Saul Chaplin and Ernest Lehman for
a film version of the Broadway musical *Zorba*. With Anthony Quinn tapped
to return in his most famous role, and the then wildly popular John Travolta
cast as the young man Zorba tutors, the musical seemed poised for production. After Wise spent ten months developing the property, however, he ran
into a stonewall of ever-increasing budget cuts, which rendered his vision

impossible. As a result, a ten-year gap ensued before he directed again, on the interesting, albeit not altogether satisfying, small-scale urban drama *Rooftops* (1989).

Maintaining a busy schedule off the set as well as on, in the post–*Sound of Music* years he served as president of both the Director's Guild (from 1971 to 1975) and the Motion Picture Academy (elected in 1985, he held the position for three terms). A board member of the American Film Institute (AFI) as well as chairman of the AFI Center for Advanced Film Studies, he lived long enough to observe the critical reevaluation of his six-decade career begin as he received one prestigious arts award after another: the D.W. Griffith Lifetime Achievement Award from the DGA in 1988, the National Medal of the Arts in 1992, and thanks to *The Sound of Music,* the Grand Decoration of Honor for Services to the Republic of Austria.

Interested in helping the next generation of filmmakers, Wise continued to advise young directors, and proved instrumental in facilitating production of the one-hour 1992 film "I Remember," a reconstruction of the life of Hungarian Jews during the Holocaust. Funding for the film had proven very difficult to obtain for the unknown filmmakers until Wise took a personal interest in the film. Said producer Anthony O. Roth: "Wise's name opens every door in town."

Fittingly, in 1998 he was chosen as the twenty-sixth recipient of the American Film Institute Lifetime Achievement Award. In an evening hosted by a very youthful-looking Julie Andrews, radiant in a black sequined gown with plunging neckline, Wise typically spent much of his AFI acceptance speech thanking his collaborators, particularly Ernest Lehman and "my special associate Saul Chaplin." It was Wise's humble references to his Indiana roots and his explanation of his filmmaking philosophy that resonated most strongly at the AFI gala, speaking as they did to his affinity for films like *The Sound of Music*: "Good movies speak to the great reach of human lives and the wonderful things we can accomplish in our best, our shining moments. . . . All good movies contain a single basic message—that human dignity is always worth preserving."

As the years passed, he expressed admiration for the leading directors of the younger generation, singling out Steven Spielberg and Martin Scorsese for special praise. It was, in fact, Scorsese who had pushed for Wise's selection for the AFI Award, publicly praising the range of Wise's work—from director of RKO B-movies in the 1940s to producer/director of multimillion-dollar Hollywood extravaganzas in the 1960s and '70s.

Eleven years after the release of *Rooftops,* Wise directed one final film, the Rod Serling scripted 2000 television movie *A Storm in Summer.* Starring Peter Falk as an elderly Jewish shop owner suddenly responsible for the care of a young African American boy, the film may have been a bit predictable in its outcome, but it proved a touching, thoroughly professional valedictory to Wise's seven-decade career, winning the Daytime Emmy Award as Outstanding Children's Special. For the eighty-six-year-old Wise, it proved a fitting way to end his career. Touching, heartfelt, and sentimental in equal measure, the film proved reflective of Wise's professional credo to the very end: story above all.

Throughout the decades Wise did stay in touch with many members of the *Sound of Music* cast, both out of genuine affection and as a means of extending the lingering glow of a particularly happy company. It wasn't just the children and the stars with whom he stayed in touch; having enjoyed Richard Haydn's sense of humor throughout shooting, Wise maintained his friendship with the actor for decades more, with the two men making a point of seeing each other every six or eight months. Wise also kept in contact with Peggy Wood for years after the film, and when he read of her death, admitted, "It gave me quite a tug—she was such a delightful person."

His closest professional *Sound of Music* ties remained with Julie Andrews, and the unexpected failure of their reunion on 1968's highly anticipated *Star!*—all a-glitter on its dazzling surface, the film sorely lacked a coherent score and rang hollow at its core—did not diminish their friendship. Although the two did not see each other regularly after *Star!*, they touched base several times every year and continued to exchange birthday cards through the decades. Wise was not one given to overstatement—something about those rock-ribbed Midwestern values made him mistrust Hollywood gush and over-the-top vows of eternal love—but the relationship between Wise and Andrews was the real thing. In the director's heartfelt assessment: "She's a marvelous lady. I love her." Andrews returned the compliment: "Robert Wise was my rock. To see him do his homework—his mind—you realize why he became the great director he is."

Wise stayed in touch with many members of the crew as well, and although he lost contact with Boris Leven, his friendship with Ernest Lehman endured.

After working together on *Executive Suite, Somebody Up There Likes Me,* and *West Side Story, The Sound of Music* had cemented their friendship for good. The same held true for his relationship with Saul and Betty Chaplin, about whom Wise enthused: "We're very good friends and see each other frequently." Editor Bill Reynolds and storyboard artist Maurice Zuberano remained close pals as well; having first worked with Zuberano on the 1949 film noir *The Set-Up,* Wise continued having "Zubie" storyboard all of his films; in the post–*Sound of Music* years, the duo worked together on *Sand Pebbles, Star!, Audrey Rose,* and *Star Trek,* their association continuing right up to Zuberano's death in 1994 at age eighty-two.

Wanting to keep his congenial team of A-listers together, Wise had also hoped to work again with Ted McCord on *The Sand Pebbles,* but McCord had by then fallen ill with heart problems, and after taking a reconnaissance trip to scout locations, he reluctantly informed Wise that the work would prove too strenuous for him. McCord shot only one other film after *The Sound of Music,* 1966's *A Fine Madness* starring Sean Connery. Declaring himself retired, McCord lived another ten years until his death in 1976 at age seventy-five.

If, through the years, *West Side Story* retained pride of place in Wise's personal career overview, then *Sound of Music* held his emotional center; the director continued as a second father figure to the seven children who had acted in the film, and also grew into a trusted friend. He stayed in particularly close touch with Charmian Carr, who lived near him in California. Speaking at the time of the Blu-ray reissue of the film, Wise made it clear that he had kept in contact with all of the children, and in his still gentlemanly manner happily rattled off personal information: Kym Karath "lives in New York City, just had her first child and married a French banker"; "Angela still lives here and has three darling children"; "Debbie is married with three children and lives in Minneapolis"; "Nicky lives in Australia and continues to act on stage and film"; "Duane Chase went into science. Over the years we've all had occasion to get together—we all went to London to do promotion—Nicky was there—that relationship with the children has continued to this very day."

By the time Wise died at age ninety-one in September 2005, the fact that he had never achieved a place in the auteur pantheon seemed utterly irrelevant: with his multiple Oscars and AFI Lifetime Achievement Award, a lack of critical approval seemed beside the point. The director of several blockbuster films cherished around the globe, his death garnered worldwide coverage. With his demise, old Hollywood had lost not just one of its few remaining legends, but a universally regarded, soft-spoken gentleman who understood every aspect of filmmaking, from sound effects and scoring to editing and direction. It seemed only fitting, then, that the film that made him a household name around the world led off every one of his obituaries: "Robert Wise, Oscar-winning director of *The Sound of Music* and *West Side Story* . . . "

FROZEN IN TIME: THROUGH THE YEARS WITH THE ONSCREEN VON TRAPP CHILDREN

The genuine camaraderie that existed and continues to this day among the seven onscreen von Trapp children would seem cloying if it weren't so grounded in real emotion. The 2010 cast reunion on the *Oprah* television show may have represented the first time that the seven children had all been together with Julie Andrews and Christopher Plummer since the Hollywood premiere in March of 1965, but the children had remained in constant touch with one another ever since filming ended. (Contrary to published reports, although Dan Truhitte was not invited to the reunion by the *Oprah* producers, he was not upset over the exclusion: "I never expected to be part of that. I would have liked it, but I certainly didn't get mad about it.")

In the smiling recall of Ted Chapin, the cast held a rather impromptu reunion dinner the night before the *Oprah* taping: "It was just great to see the 'children' reacting to Julie and Chris after all those years. Julie organized everyone by having them pull all the tables together so that they could really sit close to each other and talk. It was very sweet. There was a row of windows facing out onto the street—imagine if anyone had really looked in and seen the von Trapp family together again!"

Nicholas Hammond summed up the unique bond among the seven in his statement: "Having been there at each other's weddings, divorces, deaths in families, and moments of triumph and tragedy has created a bond of trust . . . no one else truly understands what we have lived with all these years and it has created some extremely close emotional and physical ties." Even the spouses of the actors became friendly, to the point where, as noted in the *Sound of Music Family Scrapbook,* the husbands of the actresses took to calling themselves "*The Sound of Music* Husbands' Club." At its deepest, the bond found Angela Cartwright staying with Heather Menzies for several days when Heather's husband, actor Robert Urich, lay dying from cancer. During that difficult time, Duane Chase flew in from Seattle to see Heather. Through good times and bad, the bond endured.

It wasn't just the affection and friendship shared with one another that kept the seven close. It was their shared sense of loyalty to the film itself, with all of the actors feeling protective of the film and their part in its legacy. In the words of Charmian Carr: "None of us ever wanted to let the fans of the film down." It was, Nick Hammond mused, "pretty rare to have your entire life spent having people coming up and thank you for the film and what it has meant to them."

To be sure, the overwhelming success of the film did in fact bring unanticipated problems to the young actors. For Kym Karath, who was in first grade when the film was released, the film's success caused difficulties at school. Bullied because of her onscreen renown, she suffered from both asthma and myopia, and worst of all in terms of fitting in, actually proved to be a good student. When her parents told her that the other students treated her badly only because they were jealous of her, Karath, realistically enough, found the words "small consolation."

Whatever the differences in their lives, the seven actors all shared one overwhelming burden: as the years passed, they remained frozen in people's minds as the children glimpsed onscreen. No matter the fan's age, *The Sound of Music* continued to make him or her feel young, serving as a direct connection to their own childhood. In its own showbiz way, *The Sound of Music* had become as potent a talisman as Proust's madeleines, an extra layer of poignancy added when fans all but murmured: "How could the von Trapp children get old?" The public seemed surprised, even disappointed, to meet actors who had moved not only past adolescence, but into gray-haired middle age.

Perhaps the fact of the actors' aging, no matter how graceful the process, rankled simply because the sight of middle-aged von Trapp children served as a reminder of how old the viewers themselves were; in the words of *Chicago*'s Roxie Hart, such a viewer was now "older than I ever intended to be . . ."

Those same fans desperately wanted to believe that the actors were just as much a family offscreen as on, and of all the questions the seven have answered for decades, the most frequent has been the simple yet all encompassing: "What is Julie Andrews really like?" The subtext of the question of course is: "Please tell me she's as wonderful as she seems onscreen in *The Sound of Music*— please!" To the delight of fans, for the most part that is precisely the answer that the seven actors continued to provide without hesitation.

Interestingly, it is Charmian Carr, a mere seven years younger than Andrews, who delivers the one qualified response to the frequent question. Asked what Andrews is like, she simply states: "She's a pro." Andrews, carrying the weight of the film on her shoulders, focused on the work, and Carr felt the lack of a genuine personal relationship: "But though close relationships happened between many of us. Julie chose to move on. I don't know why."

In truth, when Andrews's career took off into the stratosphere upon the film's release, it would have been nigh unto impossible for her to stay in touch with the seven children, but perhaps the remove Carr felt was reinforced by Andrews's natural British sense of propriety, the same remove which frustrated many interviewers through the years. At the twenty-fifth anniversary celebration in 1990, after not having seen Andrews for many years, Carr found the actress "as always, polite and cordial." Not warm, certainly not fuzzy, but polite. And a pro down to her toes.

Perhaps with time, however, Carr found Andrews to be more open, or, perhaps now that she was nearly seventy herself, Charmian could better understand the pressures upon Andrews. Whatever the reason, when Andrews and the children were reunited on the *Today Show* in November 2010, the emotion expressed by all eight appeared genuine, with the word "family" stressed by all of the participants. Carr's appraisal of the film? An openhearted declaration that "It gave us a second family."

True to form, when Andrews recorded a commentary for the fortieth anniversary DVD of the film, she took time to bestow an accolade on each of the seven children: "I remember Charmian's grace and beauty. Nicholas was kind of shy and a little stiff and awkward and it became endearing. Heather had a freckle-faced beauty. She too was rather shy. Duane I adored—he had such a great face. You want to pinch his cheeks. Angela Cartwright is such a beauty and you knew even then she was special. Little Debbie was losing her teeth and had a sweet lisp—there was something about her I wanted to hug. And then there was Kim—her sweetness—she was always somehow at my side hanging on to my thigh."

Only occasionally did the onscreen seven express displeasure with *The*

Sound of Music, and when they did, the frustrations centered around money. With tens of millions of units sold, *The Sound of Music* soundtrack has proved to be the most successful soundtrack ever released, but aside from Julie Andrews, no one who sang on the soundtrack ever received any money from it. Disappointed by their lack of compensation for the soundtrack or any anniversary publicity efforts, the "children" expressed their displeasure, with the contretemps coming to a head with the twenty-fifth anniversary celebration of the film's release in London: the seven refused to promote the film on any further anniversaries or milestones until they were compensated for their time. So surprising was their discontent that Robert Wise said "no" to further recompense, all but calling the actors ungrateful. In Wise's view, the seven were children in 1964, children who had been paid for a job.

All seven liked and respected Wise, but were aware of the fact that the director had grown extremely rich from the film: ten percent of the film's profits flowed to Wise and his company, Argyle Enterprises. The director shared in film and merchandising income, with his profit participation kicking in when rentals reached 2.5 times the negative cost, or roughly twenty million dollars. That break-even figure, reached by the end of summer in 1965, meant that millions of dollars in profit continued to flow to Wise through the decades (Saul Chaplin's share of the profits as associate producer came out of Wise's percentage).

No one involved with the film begrudged Wise his money—as producer and director the film's success was largely attributed to his vision. The fact that millions now flowed to the musical's original book writers, Lindsay and Crouse met with similar understanding; Lindsay and Crouse had structured the material to begin with, and thanks to Swifty Lazar's foresight, as the film's gross grew ever larger, the twelve million in net profits that would trigger the book writers' participation was quickly passed. Said Russel Crouse's decidedly happy widow Anna: "All I can say today is, thank God for Swifty!"

Wise, Lindsay, and Crouse aside, however, the onscreen children now took the view that they had also contributed greatly to the film's success, had continued to promote the film without any further compensation for decades, and deserved to share in the financial rewards. As adults, the seven actors realized that they did, in fact, maintain some power simply by virtue of audiences' collective memories: fans of the movie came to *Sound of Music* events wanting to see a modern-day version of the iconic family lineup. In the end, a compromise was reached, and in the words of Charmian Carr: "Ultimately, it got resolved like any family squabble. . . . It worked out. Future promotion would be compensated." Order had been restored and Wise's friendships with the actors extended throughout the reminder of his life, the director always speaking proudly of the fact that all of the children had led solid, hardworking, professional and personal lives that lacked even the hint of scandal.

CHARMIAN CARR Although Carr owed her fame and performing identity to *The Sound of Music,* she admits that "for a brief time Liesl began to feel like my evil twin, the perfect one, the one that everybody really loved." What the young actress had to figure out was how to coexist with such larger-than-life onscreen perfection that never changed through the decades. Though her occasional feelings of discontent disappeared over time, Carr confessed that she went through periods when she "resented Liesl as if she were a real person."

The film's most tireless ambassador after its release in 1965, she traveled around the world for two full years promoting the movie in foreign countries. Her most notable credit after *The Sound of Music* was her leading role in the Stephen Sondheim television musical *Evening Primrose* (1966). Twice married, she raised two daughters and is now a grandmother of two.

An interior decorator of note, her clients included both Ernest Lehman and Michael Jackson, for whom she decorated his Neverland Ranch. A lifelong fan of *The Sound of Music,* Jackson not only hired Carr as his decorator, but purposefully located the ranch in Encino where Carr lived. Decorator and superstar client collaborated happily in fulfilling Jackson's whimsical, often outré vision, growing close until a falling out over Jackson's never-ending plastic surgeries. Explained Carr: "I took him there when he had his skin bleached. . . . And I took him there when he had his first nose job." Charmian tried to talk Jackson out of undergoing yet another nose job, but he ignored her protestations, and the two drifted apart. Little dents the reflexive cast-iron good cheer of the *Sound of Music* children, but speaking in 2000, Carr dropped her bonhomie to bluntly recount her reaction to Jackson's post-surgery photos: "It's a terrible thing to say, but he had such an adorable face, he was so adorable. That he could have done to himself what he has done makes me sick to my stomach."

Although she never again appeared in a major motion picture, Charmian continued to work on behalf of the film at anniversary celebrations and sing-along *Sound of Music* screenings. The sing-along celebrations gained the film an enormous, fervent gay following, and when asked how it felt to be a gay icon, Carr smilingly explained: "I feel great. I think of Judy Garland and I think of Bette Midler and then I think 'Gee, that's good company to be in.' "

NICHOLAS HAMMOND After *The Sound of Music,* Hammond appeared on Broadway in the play *Conduct Unbecoming* (1970) and starred as the title character in the 1970s CBS television series *The Amazing Spider-Man.*

Having fallen in love with Australia after appearing in a television mini-series there in the mid-1980s, he decided to stay on and eventually acquired Australian citizenship. Still busy as screenwriter and actor, he has appeared in more than 150 television shows. In 2013, he hosted "An Evening with Julie Andrews" at theaters in Australia; a guided tour of Andrews's six-decade career, the show reunited the two *Sound of Music* actors to the delight of the aging, capacity crowds.

HEATHER MENZIES Menzies worked a second time with Julie Andrews two years after *The Sound of Music,* portraying the actress's younger sister in *Hawaii.* Like Andrews, Menzies felt confined by her wholesome image, but even her 1973 attempt to loosen up her image by posing nude for *Playboy* (a pictorial entitled "Tender Trapp") could not dent her lifelong association with the wholesome *Sound of Music.* In her own blunt assessment of the *Playboy* pictorial: "It didn't work."

After meeting Robert Urich while filming a Libby's Corned Beef television commercial, the two married in 1975, appearing together in the television series *Spenser, Vega$,* and *S.W.A.T.* In a 1990 interview with *Us* magazine, Menzies summed up her desire to move on from *The Sound of Music* with a succinct: "I had the time of my life, but it's a chapter in my life that's over."

After Urich died in 2002 from synovial sarcoma, Menzies, a mother of three and grandmother of two, and an ovarian cancer survivor herself, began spending much of her time working with the Urich Fund for Sarcoma Research at the University of Michigan Cancer Center.

ANGELA CARTWRIGHT Following *The Sound of Music,* Cartwright continued to work in television, most notably with a three-year run on the popular series *Lost in Space* (1965–1968). She reunited with Danny Thomas and

Marjorie Lord on *Make Room for Grandaddy,* but the series was quickly can-celed. Having married in 1976 and wanting to stay home with her two chil-dren, she spent the majority of her time raising her children while operating a clothing store called Rubber Boots. An artist and photographer with a gal-lery in Studio City, California, she has maintained a presence in show busi-ness by forming a production company with Heather Menzies and in 2004 she coauthored (with Tom McLaren) the book *Styling the Stars.*

DUANE CHASE No longer involved with show business aside from *Sound of Music* reunions, Chase graduated from the University of California Santa Barbara in 1976 with a B.S. in geology. He now lives in Seattle with his wife and children, designing software for geologists and geophysicists. In a nice bit of irony, Chase's wife, Petra, once worked as a nanny in Austria.

DEBBIE TURNER Married in 1980, she runs her own successful floral and event design company entitled Debbie Turner Originals. Although Turner relocated with her husband and four children to Minneapolis in the mid-1980s, she continues to maintain a business presence in Los Angeles and Park City, Utah, as well. One of her four daughters is named Angela, in honor of Angela Cartwright.

KYM KARATH After making guest appearances on numerous television shows such as *My Three Sons,* Karath attended the University of Southern Cal-ifornia and eventually moved to Paris in order to study art history. She con-tinues to act part-time, but after marriage to an investment banker, she has devoted the greater portion of her time to raising her son, Eric (born 1991).

DAN TRUHITTE Married, with six children and six grandchildren, Truhitte named two of his sons Tomas Rolfe and Rolfe Peter. He has contin-ued to mine *The Sound of Music* connection throughout the years, both out of affection for the film as well as for practical career purposes. He has taken groups on tours of Salzburg and has self-released the CD *Gazebo Love.* His post–*Sound of Music* career found him portraying Gene Kelly and Fred Astaire in the Las Vegas extravaganza *Hallelujah Hollywood* and he has per-formed in dozens of stage productions, including a turn as Captain von Trapp in a North Carolina dinner theater. He laughingly states: "I may be the olderst person to ever play the captain—but I'm doing it again in 2015, just in time for the fiftieth anniversary of the film."

He remains grateful and aware of the film's long shadow, sharply noting that the film has granted all participants a measure of immortality: "Our dance in the gazebo will be here long after we're both gone. I'll be forever grateful for that. . . . I don't watch the film all the time, but when I do, I marvel again at what a wonderfully made movie it is. . . . As long as we have family, we will have *The Sound of Music,* which uplifts the family. It has the music, the conflict, the love, and the principles, and those are things that hold our society together."

ELEANOR PARKER After four forgettable films in the two years following the release of *Sound of Music,* Parker turned her attention to television, guest-starring on many of the most popular series of the '60s, '70s, and '80s: *Man from U.N.C.L.E., Bracken's World, Hawaii 5-0, Vegas, Love Boat, Fantasy Island, Murder She Wrote.* Still beautiful, her talent intact, Parker, it seemed, was a victim of the dearth of suitable roles written for mature women in Hollywood, and turned in her final performance in the 1991 television film *Dead on the Money.*

She lived out the final decades of her life quietly, and died in Palm Springs, California, in December of 2013.

ERNEST LEHMAN

"The Sound of Music is a fairy tale that's almost real. It gives people hope. I have a hunch this picture may be watched in some way, shape, or form a thousand years from now."

Even as far back as 1963–64 when he was writing *The Sound of Music,* Lehman had received numerous phone calls from Abe Lastfogel, the president of the William Morris Agency, asking him to adapt Edward Albee's award-winning play *Who's Afraid of Virginia Woolf?* for the screen. Lehman agreed to take on the job with one proviso: he insisted upon serving not only as screenwriter, but also as producer of the black-and-white, etched-in-acid portrayal of marriage. Lehman had learned a key lesson by observing Wise's dual role as director and producer of both *West Side Story* and *The Sound of Music*: "If you're only the screenwriter, you have no control over who directs it, who's in it, who rewrites it, or who doesn't rewrite it."

When Lehman had once been asked about the best possible work environment for a screenwriter, he answered that it occurred when a producer "makes me feel safe and encouraged and enthusiastic . . . come hell or high water, this picture is going to be made." In that light, wearing dual hats as writer and producer of *Virginia Woolf* should have made the experience a highly enjoyable one for Lehman, but although the film proved an artistic and commercial success, it was not a happy experience for him and he quarreled repeatedly with first-time director Mike Nichols.

Even his Academy Award nomination as producer of Best Picture nominee *Virginia Woolf* could not offset the lingering memories of an unpleasant experience, and thirty-four years later, *Talk* magazine printed "Diary of Ernest Lehman," in which the screenwriter's detailed entries described his experiences on the film; in the process he portrayed Nichols as a demanding, heavy drinker. Publication of the diary resulted in angry letters from Nichols, Elizabeth Taylor, and George Segal, with Nichols calling Lehman's original script "unusable" and his actions as producer those of a man desiring to include himself "in a group that in fact had little to do with him." A chastened Lehman responded with "a deep apology for all the pettiness and inaccuracies made by my diary thirty-five years ago."

Lehman followed up *Virginia Woolf* with a return to musicals, writing and producing 1969's *Hello, Dolly!* The film won an Academy Award nomination for Best Picture, but despite many fine moments, it ultimately registered as an overblown rendering of a slight if tuneful story, and the then record-shattering budget of $20,000,000 meant that despite respectable business, the film did not recoup its cost. Three years later he directed for the first time, adapting Philip Roth's controversial *Portnoy's Complaint* for the screen. The film failed to win either critical approval or box office success, but Lehman kept working, closing out his writing career with Alfred Hitchcock's enjoyable *Family Plot* (1976), the Super Bowl thriller *Black Sunday* (1977), and the television miniseries *The French Atlantic Affair* (1979).

The passage of time served to highlight the extraordinary range of Lehman's work, and awards and honors began to flow his way. He was awarded the Writers Guild of America Screen Laurel Award in 1972, served as the president of the Writers Guild from 1983 to 1985, and in 1995 finally received the recognition he had so long craved in the form of the Lifetime Achieve-ment Award from the Writers Guild. The singular nature of his achievement—the extraordinary screenplays for *Sweet Smell of Success*, *North by Northwest*, *West Side Story*, *Sound of Music,* and *Virginia Woolf*—finally registered with the industry, and in 2001, Lehman, a four-time nominee for Best Screenplay, won the first honorary Oscar ever granted to a screenwriter. Considering that *The Sound of Music* remained, for Lehman, "a miracle that comes only to a very few, once in a lifetime," it seemed perfectly fitting that the award was presented to him by Julie Andrews, whom Lehman called his "fair lady."

Awards and all, to the end of his life, Lehman still carried a grievance against directors who slighted the screenwriter's contribution: "Somehow the mere fact that the director didn't write the picture—he's only directing it—is very difficult for him to take, and some of them have never learned to take it. The director knows that the script he is carrying around on the set every day was written by someone, and that's just not something that all directors eas-ily digest." Robert Wise, he felt, was the exception to the rule—for the most part: "My most easygoing relationship was with Robert Wise, with whom I did four pictures, though even with him I had my moments here and there."

In fact, age had not mellowed Lehman's edgy pride in his work, and woe to anyone who didn't remember that preeminent place held by the screenplay. When one interviewer at an AFI seminar asked Lehman about the crop dust-ing sequence in *North by Northwest*—"It's such a visual scene that it doesn't seem the kind of scene a writer would choose"—Lehman lowered the boom. "It seems visual, therefore, the writer has nothing to do with it. Is that what you're trying to say? That is utter nonsense. Let me tell you something as long as I'm sitting up here on this high horse. Read the first page of the screenplay of *The Sound of Music,* which describes the opening of the film. It was the first time I used the first-person singular in a screenplay. I just said, 'Here's what I want to see on the screen. Here's the effect I want.' *I want.* And you know what? I got it." Forty years had passed and Lehman cared as much as ever. No wonder he went on record declaring his gratitude to Wise for show-ing "considerable openness of mind toward suggestions written into the screen-play by this screenwriter."

It seemed fitting that Lehman came full circle professionally by helping to produce an interesting, albeit unsuccessful, Broadway musical version of his classic *Sweet Smell of Success* in 2002. Having jump-started his career with his screenplay for the film, he now ended it with a new iteration of the same material. Teaming again with his longtime friend and occasional adversary David Brown, Lehman proved physically frail but still game for the contest. In a 2002 *New Yorker* profile that captured the two lions in winter as they prepared for their final hurrah, Lehman revealed a highly strung nature that had now accelerated to the point where, in order to fall asleep at night, he would take "three Ambien, two trazodones, and a strong Halcion." Just to make sure people knew what pain he was in, he related to journalist Andrew Goldman that he had "a long-standing, incurable pain at the base of the penis, where a lot of nerves converge." Oh.

Lehman's quartet of films with Robert Wise remained among his career high points and it proved fitting that screenwriter David Freeman, referring to Lehman's mastery of multiple genres, called Lehman "The Robert Wise of screenwriters." (It's a compliment that author Sam Wasson refers to as "probably the greatest remark anyone has ever made or will ever make about Lehman.") By the time he died at age eighty-nine in 2005, he was routinely referred to as "the legendary Ernest Lehman," words that did not seem hyperbolic for a nine-time nominated, five-time winner of the WGA Award.

A director and producer he was as well, but when all was said and done, he remained a screenwriter first and last; asked his idea of a great working day, he defined it as one afternoon in 1956 that found him working on *Sweet Smell of Success*, writing additional dialogue for *Somebody Up There Likes Me,* and providing a polish with bits of dialogue on *The King and I*: That, he said, "was a good day."

SAUL CHAPLIN Once *The Sound of Music* premiered in 1965, Saul Chaplin emerged as the hands-down busiest member of the production team, supervising the musical dubbing of the film for foreign territories—a job that grew ever larger as the international demand for the film continued to grow.

With foreign vocalists re-recording the songs in their own language, Chaplin oversaw the dubbing of songs and dialogue in Paris, Barcelona, Rome, and Berlin, with separate soundtracks released by RCA in Spanish, German, French, and Italian. An enterprise never before tried on this scale, the multiple foreign language recordings generated enormous continuing profits for both 20th Century-Fox and RCA Records.

Even as the appetite for screen musicals dwindled in the years following the release of *The Sound of Music,* Chaplin continued to work on the biggest remaining exemplars of the genre, producing *Star!* with Wise, serving as associate producer of the unfortunate *Man of La Mancha* (1972), and assuming the role of producer on the more successful *That's Entertainment, Part II* (1976). His most well-known musical compositions, "Please Be Kind" and "Bei Mir Bist Du Schoen," continued to be used in television shows throughout the decades, and the latter popped up in almost every feature film set in the '30s or '40s, featuring prominently in *Swing Kids* (1993), *Angela's Ashes* (1999), *Being Julia* (2004), and *Memoirs of a Geisha* (2005).

With screen musicals nearly defunct by the end of the '70s, *That's Entertainment, Part II* proved to be Chaplin's last film. Without ever formally announcing his retirement, he was, at age sixty-four, finished with his producing career. Song royalties provided him with a nice income, as did his share of profits from *The Sound of Music,* and in 1994 he published his autobiography: *The Golden Age of Movie Musicals and Me.* It's a graceful memoir, full of stories about working with the greatest musical talents in Hollywood history: Fred Astaire, Gene Kelly, Judy Garland, Frank Sinatra, and Julie Andrews. The genial Chaplin's only words of criticism were reserved for Christopher Plummer's behavior on *The Sound of Music,* although it seems likely that Plummer's rapprochement with the film would have resulted in a similar peace with Chaplin. In a career that included *Les Girls, Can-Can, An American in Paris,* and *West Side Story, The Sound of Music* represented Chaplin's most glittering success of all. By the time he died on November 15, 1997, as a result of injuries sustained in a bad fall, the four-time Academy Award winner's stature within the industry had been certified for posterity.

BORIS LEVEN

After his Oscar nomination for *The Sound of Music,* Leven continued his collaboration with Robert Wise on *The Sand Pebbles* (1966), *Star!* (1968), and *The Andromeda Strain* (1971), earning Oscar nominations for all three films. His fascinating, multistoried underground laboratory for *The Andromeda Strain* exhibited his flair for combining eye-popping visuals with a sense of verisimilitude, and the meticulous set for the sci-fi epic managed the extraordinary feat of functioning as an additional character in a film about scientists racing to contain a deadly virus.

Leven's career rolled on into the 1970s and '80s with such films as *Jonathan Livingston Seagull* (1973), *Matilda* (1978), and *Fletch* (1985), but the last stage of his career was highlighted by a four-film collaboration with the hottest director of the era, Martin Scorsese: *New York, New York* (1977), *The Last Waltz* (1978), the cult classic *The King of Comedy* (1982), and *The Color of Money* (1986—and a final Oscar nomination). Working right up until his death in 1986, Leven designed both *The Color of Money* and the Goldie Hawn comedy *Wildcats* in the last year of his life.

In a career studded with every conceivable award known to the film industry, Leven received one last award in 2003 when he was elected posthumously to the Art Directors Hall of Fame. Given his stature as both designer and artist, it seemed appropriate that his legacy lives on not just in the films he designed, but also in his film renderings and paintings, which his widow, Vera, donated to both the University of Southern California and New York City's Museum of Modern Art.

MARC BREAUX AND DEE DEE WOOD

In some ways, choreographers Breaux and Wood were, like many of their *Sound of Music* collaborators, a victim of changing audience tastes; as musicals fell out of favor, the work opportunities grew increasingly scarce. After scoring back-to-back worldwide triumphs with *Mary Poppins* and *The Sound of Music,* Wood and Breaux went on to choreograph the decidedly less successful 1967 Disney musical *The Happiest Millionaire,* although they rebounded the next year by providing the musical staging for another beloved family musical, 1968's *Chitty Chitty Bang Bang,*

After their divorce, both choreographers continued to work steadily, although neither ever again reached the heights of *Poppins* and *Sound of Music*. Wood most notably choreographed for Cher's television series in 1975, as well as for both the 1984 Olympic Games and the Bette Midler movie *Beaches* (1988). Breaux turned his attention to a television reunion with *Poppins* star Dick Van Dyke, providing choreography for *The New Dick Van Dyke Show,* and also collaborating with the greatest dancer of all on the television special *Fred Astaire Salutes Fox Musicals*. He choreographed the 1976 feature film version of the Cinderella story entitled *The Slipper and the Rose,* as well as Mae West's surreal farewell to films, *Sextette* (1978).

Before Breaux died in 2013, the duo received the Life Achievement Award from the American Choreography Awards, the award being presented to the team by their *Bye Bye Birdie* friends Chita Rivera and Dick Van Dyke. The only previous recipients of the award represented the cream of Hollywood choreographers—Bob Fosse, Jack Cole, Herb Ross, and Breaux and Wood's mentor Michael Kidd—proof positive that their work on *Poppins* and *Sound of Music* had assured their place in Hollywood musical history. Said Wood: "*Poppins* and *Sound of Music* were so early in our careers. At the time I didn't fully understand how unique they were—I just thought 'That's the way it happens.' Now, when I think about those films and watch them, I just can't get over how very special they are."

WILLIAM REYNOLDS

Following his work on *The Sound of Music,* Reynolds went on to edit dozens of A-list Hollywood films, all of them characterized by a seamless low-key style. He worked with Robert Wise again on *The Sand Pebbles* (1966—Oscar nomination), *Star!,* and *Rooftops,* and established further proof of his cross-genre talent by editing the intense racial boxing drama *The Great White Hope. The Sting* (1973), deliberately edited in the style of the 1930s, won him a second Oscar, and he followed that triumph with the popular *The Great Waldo Pepper* (1975), *The Turning Point* (1977), and *A Little Romance* (1979). Reynolds, in fact, may be the one person who subsequently equaled, and in some ways surpassed, his work on *The Sound of Music,* thanks to his brilliant, Academy Award–nominated work on *The Godfather,* which he edited in tandem with Peter Zinner: Reynolds edited the first half of the film and Zinner the second.

Continuing to work steadily through the 1980s and 1990s, even Reynolds's flop films proved legendary, as he valiantly tried to edit sense from the hopelessly confused *Heaven's Gate* (1980) and *Ishtar* (1987). His skills remained undiminished as he entered the fifth decade of his career, turning in his customary smooth job on the television film version of *Gypsy,* starring Bette Midler (1993). By the time he edited his last film—*Carpool*—in 1996, he had won every award available to editors: two Academy Awards (seven total nominations), three American Cinema Editors (ACE) Awards, and the coveted ACE Career Achievement Award. In the end, it was one further tribute—this one from his peers—that summed up Reynolds's unparalleled place within the industry; in a poll conducted by *Film Comment,* Reynolds was selected as one of the three greatest film editors in the history of Hollywood.

DOROTHY JEAKINS

Throughout a career that eventually garnered her twelve Oscar nominations, Jeakins's own gentle style and mantra of always serving the script allowed her to work successfully with temperaments ranging from Streisand on *The Way We Were* to Katharine Hepburn in *On Golden Pond*. Stars enjoyed collaborating with the soft-spoken Jeakins, yet actors were not the designer's primary focus: "I was always a director's designer more than an actor's designer. My work was literary."

It's that very sensibility of serving the dictates of the script, rather than the actor, which made the compliment she received from Sean Connery mean all the more to her; after costuming *The Molly Maguires*, the 1970 Martin Ritt drama about nineteenth-century Pennsylvania coal miners, Connery wrote Jeakins a note that she called "the only fan letter" she ever received from an actor. Said the no-nonsense Connery: "Your clothes made me feel like a coal miner." It was, in Jeakins's view, the ultimate compliment any designer could receive.

The passing years only broadened Jeakins's range, from the 1969 Oscar-winning John Wayne western *True Grit,* to the World War II settings found in *The Way We Were* (1973—Oscar nomination). She costumed Julie Andrews once again for *Hawaii* (1966) and worked with Robert Wise on both *The Hindenburg* (1975) and *Audrey Rose* (1977). Whether it was the inspired black-and-white silliness of Mel Brooks's *Young Frankenstein* (1974—Oscar nomination), a monumental epic like 1956's *The Ten Commandments,* or a small family drama like *On Golden Pond* (1981), the films Jeakins costumed reflected her devotion to craft.

Jeakins retired from design in 1990, living five more years until her death on November 21, 1995. In a life characterized by a tumultuous private life, work remained an oasis of serenity. Obsessively re-creating the past on film, this most self-aware of designers had found her lifelong raison d'être: "In the middle of the night, I can put my world down to two words. 'Make beauty.' It's my cure and my private passion."

JULIE ANDREWS

"I think The Sound of Music *is a marvelous commercial*
for life—a plea for life."
—JULIE ANDREWS, 1973

Whatever the hurdles faced by the various *Sound of Music* designers and cast members in the wake of the film's success, no one else faced challenges of the magnitude confronting Julie Andrews. What can one do for an encore after starring in the most popular movie musical of all time and seemingly causing the entire world to fall in love with you?

Like any actor worth her salt, Julie Andrews attempted to step out of *The Sound of Music*'s enormous shadow by playing a completely different sort of woman—one even more famous than the pre–*Sound of Music* Maria von Trapp—theater legend Gertrude Lawrence. It seemed like an inspired idea in the planning stage: Andrews would be fulfilling her two-picture contract with Fox by reteaming with director Robert Wise on the Lawrence biopic *Star!,* the studio would land a new Julie Andrews musical, and this time there'd be even more Julie Andrews on display. If she sang seven songs in *The Sound of Music,* then this time she'd sing no fewer than sixteen. By her own admission, she worked even harder on *Star!* than she did on *The Sound of Music,* looked like a million dollars, sounded terrific—and the film went nowhere. Why?

The first and biggest reason was that in the midst of the turbulent 1960s, the audience at large, those who regarded Julie Andrews as the ideal mother, wife, and camp counselor, did not particularly want to see her play the brittle, caustic, somewhat forgotten and ofttimes bitchy Gertrude Lawrence. Even Andrews's vaunted onscreen warmth could not cut through the surface of this tough dame.

Granted, there were terrific songs by Cole Porter and the Gershwins, cherry-picked by Wise, Irwin Kostal, and Saul Chaplin, but in fact this mining of the masters' catalogue caused problem number two: what Julie Andrews missed in *Star!* was the dramatic framework provided by Rodgers and Hammerstein, Lindsay and Crouse, and Ernest Lehman. *The Sound of Music* contained terrific songs but the songs always served story and character development. In *Star!,* Andrews sang a succession of standards—"Do, Do, Do,"

"My Ship," "Limehouse Blues"—but they were songs Lawrence had sung in various shows, not songs that helped audiences understand her character. With the songs not imparting any particular information about the woman on hand, the audience reaction quickly morphed into "Heard one, heard them all." Julie Andrews was front and center in dozens of dazzling costumes, bedecked in million-dollar jewels and singing her heart out—and Daniel Massey as Noel Coward stole the show outright. Not burdened with the same musical potpourri as Andrews, Massey had the freedom to sing Coward's own compositions, which helped him deliver a full-bodied portrait of a charming, interesting, show business icon, warts and all.

Released upon a tidal wave of hype in October 1968, the very costly *Star!* landed with a thud at the box office. Even when recut, the shortened film, now entitled *Those Were the Happy Times!,* did not prove any more successful. The Julie Andrews/20th Century-Fox musical film connection had come full circle: *The Sound of Music* had rescued Fox from bankruptcy, and now, a mere three years later, *Star!* almost pushed the studio back into financial insolvency. It wasn't Andrews's fault—she didn't write *Star!*—but she was blamed nonetheless. Those jealous of her worldwide success and cynically tired of her genuinely nice personality, almost seemed to gloat at her new box office woes. Just as everyone from Ernest Lehman to Richard Zanuck, and even William Wyler, had claimed credit for casting the untested Andrews in *Sound of Music,* everyone now tried to distance themselves from the debacle of *Star!*

Julie Andrews was no longer considered invincible. In three short years she had dropped from biggest star in the world to a giant question mark at the box office. The Hollywood gossip mill went into overdrive, falling back on its basic business premise: you're only as good as your last credit. Claims of "I knew it all along" quickly led to questions of whether any star had ever fallen so quickly from her perch atop the box office.

As for Julie herself, having amicably divorced Tony Walton in 1967, she married writer/director Blake Edwards (*Days of Wine and Roses*, *Breakfast at Tiffany's*) two years later. Their long-term marriage, which lasted until Edwards's death in 2010, proved solid and a genuine case of opposites attracting: Edwards loosened Andrews up, and Andrews's optimistic outlook provided a welcome antidote to Edwards's sardonic, black-humored approach to life. Just how humorously aware they each were of their respective public images is revealed in a story both told throughout the years; shortly before they met, Edwards sardonically analyzed Andrews's extraordinary appeal by stating: "I know exactly what it is. She has lilacs for pubic hairs." Far from being put off when he told her the story, Andrews instantly replied: "Well, how did you ever guess?" Each subsequent year on their anniversary, they celebrated with a cake decorated with lilacs.

Edwards felt that Andrews compensated for her difficult childhood and attendant sad memories with a "tremendous struggle to overcome that by taking care of people. Me. The children. The cast and crew. Everybody." As he further acknowledged, everyone may laugh about the sugar overload in *Poppins* and *The Sound of Music,* but Andrews's warmth and sincerity constitute the real thing: "You watch her in a room full of children who don't know *Mary Poppins* or *The Sound of Music* and, I mean, she's like a magnet. They just go right to her." If, in fact, every star of consequence plays variations on their own nature—think John Wayne as the Western hero, Streisand in *Funny Girl,* Doris Day in *The Pajama Game*—then Andrews had indeed found her ideal roles in *Mary Poppins* and *The Sound of Music,* a perfect confluence of talent and timing.

Edwards acknowledged that his wife was not an easy person to get to know; a professional since childhood, and the possessor of an inner core of British reticence, she had, he felt, developed a self-protective nature because of having been "hurt a lot in the past." Theirs was a marriage between adults—not necessarily easy, but one that worked. They fought and loved, and in Andrews's own words: "Marriage is the hardest work you're ever going to do . . . (but) I love him more deeply because of the foibles and the fights."

After the failure of *Star!,* Andrews's career was dealt a further blow with the paltry box office returns for Edwards's multimillion-dollar musical valentine to his wife—1970's *Darling Lili.* Andrews looked sensational throughout, and the film does contain one moment that ranks among the greatest of her career, equal to anything found in *The Sound of Music.* On a darkened stage, she stands alone singing the terrific new Henry Mancini/Johnny Mercer ballad "Whistling Away the Dark." Her voice as pure as ever, she glides into Mercer's haunting lyric:

Often I think this sad, old world
Is whistling in the dark

Just like a child, who, late from school
Walks bravely home through the park

As Lili spins, the camera begins to whirl with her, rapturously circling her like a lover. Finally, the number ends and as the camera retreats back to its starting position, the screen turns to black and theater lights come up to show Lili onstage. The effect is dizzying—and dazzling. Standing alone, singing, Julie Andrews represents the essence of stardom.

Unfortunately none of the rest of the film approached this spectacular sequence and the audience left the theater two hours later utterly perplexed. Why did this musical set during World War I show Julie Andrews performing a striptease? Was Lili a good woman or bad? No one seemed to know exactly what the film was supposed to be: A musical? A World War I spy story? Tale of adventure or winking spoof? Word of mouth sank the film, and although it subsequently acquired a cult reputation, the box office returns remained dismal.

In fact, *Darling Lili* was only one of the spectacular disasters emanating from the massive success of *The Sound of Music*: as the worldwide box office grosses for the R&H musical continued to soar, every studio in town jumped on the musicals bandwagon in an increasingly desperate attempt to duplicate *The Sound of Music*'s triumph. The result was millions of dollars spent on ill-conceived films such as *Darling Lili*.

Darling Lili represented Paramount Pictures' disaster, just as 20th Century-Fox came a cropper with the extremely expensive *Doctor Doolittle* (1967), a charm-free adaptation of the Hugh Lofting children's stories that proved a monumental stiff, and a catastrophe narrowly avoided by Christopher Plummer. A rolling disaster from pre-production to its world premiere, the film starred Rex Harrison, who, for all of his talent, proved a temperamental performer even at the best of times. Consistently threatening to abandon filming, Harrison carried on in such increasingly unreasonable fashion that Christopher Plummer was offered the then sizable sum of $250,000 to take over the role. Fortunately for Plummer's career, Harrison returned to the movie.

With Hollywood's herd instinct functioning at its worst, studio after studio rushed to transfer Broadway musicals onto the screen, without anyone asking the most basic of questions: will this musical's story actually translate to the screen? Which musical stars will help to tell the story in entertaining fashion? Instead, Warner Brothers' *Camelot* (1967) sank under the combined weight of a lumbering screenplay, a King Arthur (Richard Harris) who for unfathomable reasons sported eyeshadow, and stagebound direction by Joshua Logan. The leaden *Paint Your Wagon* at Paramount (1970) starred Jean Seberg, Clint Eastwood (a knowledgeable jazz aficianado but decidedly not a singer), and the very nonmusical Lee Marvin. Even a truly great director like Francis Ford Coppola did not seem to fully understand the structure of musical films when attempting to adapt *Finian's Rainbow* (1968), but the musical owing the largest debt to *The Sound of Music,* 1970's *Song of Norway,* starring one-time Maria von Trapp, Florence Henderson, also registered as one of the worst. The purported story of Edvard Grieg, the torpid film did nothing so much as leave its few viewers humming the scenery.

Only *Thoroughly Modern Millie* (1967), the Academy Award—winning Best Picture *Oliver* (1968), and *Funny Girl,* directed by the great William Wyler, and featuring Streisand's electrifying film debut, came out clear winners. But for every *Funny Girl* there was *The Happiest Millionare* (1967) or *Goodbye, Mr. Chips*, (1969), poorly executed ventures featuring the wrong combination of score, director, and star.

No one seemed to pay attention to the fact that *The Sound of Music* featured a compelling story, a terrific score, an Oscar-winning director, and a sensational musical actress at the peak of her powers. The post—*Sound of Music* musicals failed because they took the "more is more" approach: throw more money at the production, add more stars, feature more locations—and hope for the best. It never worked.

By 1970, with musicals falling out of favor and the megamillion-dollar box office failures of *Star!* and *Darling Lili* attributed to her, Andrews fell out of favor, too. What was going on here? She certainly had not lost her talent, singing as beautifully as ever well into the 1970s; her acting range increased in breadth, and she matured into a middle-aged woman of unquestionable beauty. Why did the American public turn?

Part of it, of course, lay in the nature of the rapidly changing times. As the '60s turned into the early '70s and beyond, the enormous and ofttimes overwhelming social and political unrest sweeping not just the United States but the rest of the world changed the outlook of what people were interested in seeing on the big screen. A certain wildness permeated the culture onscreen and off, and whatever else she was, Julie Andrews was not wild. Clean-cut, yes, and able to radiate wholesomeness and great energy, but even more so, with her preternatural poise and beautifully modulated speaking and singing voices, she exuded a sense of refinement, one so strong that even her topless appearance in the 1981 film *S.O.B.* failed to dent her good-girl image.

The very assets that underlay Andrews's phenomenal appeal—the perfect enunciation, the brisk confidence, the every-problem-can-be-solved-with-good-cheer-and-hard-work approach, came to seem anachronistic. In the increasingly "real" world of personal films, those purposely devoid of studio gloss, her flawless elocution and rounded vowels seemed to smack more than a bit of a teacher giving a lesson. *Star!* and *Darling Lili* also shared the misfortune of being released five years too late and were light-years removed from the new world of *Bonnie and Clyde* and *Mean Streets.* Julie Andrews read as reliable, understanding, and exactly the woman you'd want with you in the trenches when tough times arrived; the problem was that in the post–*Bonnie and Clyde* era, the film culture centered around *Raging Bull*s and *Easy Rider*s, not refinement.

The world had changed and Andrews had, too, but not in the same way or at the same speed, which meant that the public simply could not, perhaps would not, perceive the change in her. Said Andrews: "I can't be what I was before I came to Hollywood. You can't be bending over backward to show everybody you haven't changed. I'm growing up late, that's all, desperately late."

All major stars have their moment in the sun followed by an inevitable falling off—it's inherent in the nature of stardom and the audience's unceasing quest for something new. In that light, Andrews's *Sound of Music*–fueled meteoric rise to superstardom and subsequent tumble at the box office can be placed in perspective by considering the career of the actor who replaced her as the most popular box office attraction in the world beginning in 1968: Sidney Poitier. Complicated as Andrews's saintly image proved to be for her, Poitier's standing as the sole bankable movie star of color proved even more complex, forced as he was into the straitjacket of movie star as role model.

Like Andrews, Poitier won an Oscar in the early 1960s (*Lilies of the Field* 1963), possessed a first-rate talent, and leaped to the top of the box office polls with a one-two-three-punch of successes: *A Patch of Blue* (1965), *To Sir, with Love* (1967), and *Guess Who's Coming to Dinner* (1967). The newly crowned King of Hollywood, Poitier was trapped by the very image that brought him stardom. Playing faultless, saintlike men who radiated kindness, generosity, and in the case of *Guess Who's Coming to Dinner*, a mensa-like intelligence to boot, the onscreen Poitier was often forced to present a man who seemed too good to be true.

Both Poitier and Andrews proved to be more popular with audiences than with critics, the two actors victims of critical disdain for their purported cinema of sentimentality. Time has, in fact, revealed all of the well-meaning liberal weaknesses inherent in *Guess Who's Coming to Dinner*'s sanitized brotherhood of man "message," and the film has, like many of director Stanley Kramer's polemics, not aged well. Yes, the sermonizing found therein did in fact tend to simplify complex problems to the point of triviality, but when Poitier became the most popular star in the world, it seemed as if big-city critics, almost always Caucasian, stood in line to take potshots at the actor. Such was the tenor of the unsettled late 1960s that the reviewer for the *National Review* felt no compunction about revealing the fact that he had walked out of *Guess Who's Coming to Dinner* after twenty minutes, yet still filed a review.

These mostly white critics considered the roles Poitier played—the saintly teacher in *To Sir, with Love* (1967), the near-perfect doctor in *Guess Who's Coming to Dinner*—as hopelessly unrealistic and dated. There was, of course, some truth to the charges, but in an era when actors of color remained marginalized or invisible, Poitier felt an obligation to present the best possible image of his race onscreen.

In truth, the more dated attitude actually emanated from a critic such as *The New Yorker*'s Brendan Gill, who zealously took it upon himself to declare his certainty that the "American Negro" must find Poitier's gentlemanly role in *A Patch of Blue* "extremely irritating." Gill's pipeline to the national African American community seems suspect, to say the least, but for men like Gill, or anyone eager to show their cultural bona fides, there could be no better targets than the too-perfect-for-words and decidedly uncool Julie Andrews and Sidney Poitier.

Poitier capped his remarkable run in these popular films with a first-rate turn that same year in the Oscar-winning Best Picture *In the Heat of the Night*, at which point, like Julie Andrews one year before, he had nowhere to go but down. Black militants, not Martin Luther King, dominated the headlines, and Poitier received increasing criticism for accepting roles that read onscreen as devoid of all sexuality. The radical cultural shift that seemed to coalesce with the assassinations of Robert Kennedy and Martin Luther King in the tumultuous year of 1968 seemed to change the very way in which the public regarded its movie stars. A larger-than-life, handsome presence now seemed to mean that the star in question was not a "real"—i.e., serious—actor. Instead, artistic kudos were reserved for actors with everyman looks. Tyrone Power and Sidney Poitier were out. Dustin Hoffman and Gene Hackman were in. After increasingly muddled turns in *The Lost Man* (1969), *Brother John* (1971), and *A Warm December* (1973), Poitier's reign at the top was over.

The precipitous drops of Andrews and Poitier from sought-after megastar to box office question mark were also a function of the studio system's disintegration. In the days of the studio system, when stars were protected and consistently employed in one film after another because of their seven-year contracts, *Star!* and *Darling Lili* would not have derailed Julie Andrews's standing so thoroughly. She simply would have been placed into another packaged studio production, one whose screenplay brought her closer to her essential star persona. By the late '60s, however, with stars functioning as free agents without studio protection, flops like *Star!* and *Darling Lili* mattered a great deal more. The stakes were greater: the highs were higher and the lows much lower, as well as more dangerous.

With the plum film roles having dried up, Andrews shifted her attention toward television. Having signed a very lucrative deal with ABC television for a weekly variety series, Andrews began her series in the fall of 1972. She looked great on the small screen, and her musicianship remained irreproachable, but the show never caught fire. Just as her great friend Carol Burnett conquered television but never became a film star, Andrews never succeeded with a weekly television series. In that failure, she followed in the long line of Hollywood legends who failed to gain a toehold with weekly series on the small screen: Frank Sinatra, Shirley MacLaine, and Henry Fonda all tried and flopped.

Andrews's series won a number of Emmy Awards but it may just be that the star's brisk personality never quite warmed the home screen. By way of contrast, Doris Day experienced great success with her weekly sitcom; if Day was a comfortable old friend who could be welcomed in for a friendly chat, Andrews's efficiency and lingering aura of British reserve kept the living room audiences at a slight, but decided remove.

After the failure of her television series, Andrews returned to films and her career continued at a steady pace. While she maintained her own performing ambitions, she nonetheless seemed to place her career in service to that of her husband, and over the following decades they would collaborate together on many films. *The Tamarind Seed* (1974), the very popular *10* (1979), and the scathing *S.O.B.* (1981), were interspersed with flops such as *The Man Who Loved Women,* but the one film whose success could be directly attributed to Andrews's presence was the funny, musical gender bending *Victor-Victoria* (1982) for which she received a third Academy Award nomination as Best Actress. To watch a peak-form Andrews playing a woman impersonating a man impersonating a woman, all the while belting out great showstoppers like "Le Jazz Hot," was to be reminded once again of what an extraordinary musical talent she remained.

Oddly enough, her best performance may have come in the small-scale, low-key, and truthful *That's Life!* (1986), a semi-autobiographical tale of life in the Edwards/Andrews household that was actually filmed in their home. Letting down her guard, she stashed her trademark crispness, appearing on-screen with a palpable vulnerability. The film represented her best dramatic performance since *The Americanization of Emily* in 1964, but although the film received several admiring notices, it attracted little interest at the box office. (Both *That's Life!* and the same year's *Duet for One* may have done little business, but Andrews did receive Golden Globe Best Actress nominations for both films.) Andrews may actually have been just a little ahead of her time with such diverse roles; audiences were slowly starting to adjust to the sight of stars stretching their acting muscles in different types of vehicles, but wholesale acceptance of that practice lay several decades down the road. In the words of film historian Jeanine Basinger: "Audiences in the twenty-first century now go see what they still think of as *my* George Clooney—but in a different sort of role. The diversity is more accepted if it's very well done—and not too far out of their narrow comfort zone."

At the time of *That's Life!*'s release, interviewers found the star speaking in remarkably forthright language about the emotional difficulties experienced by her two Vietnamese daughters, Amy and Joanna, whom she and Edwards had adopted in the 1970s. Julie Andrews, worldwide icon, now forged another bond with her legions of fans by sounding like every other overworked, stressed-out mother discussing the seemingly impossible task of finding the balance between motherhood and work: "It isn't easy. There's always guilt. I try to make quality time with my kids rather than quantity."

Andrews was now raising five children: Emma Kate Walton, Jennifer and Geoffrey Edwards—Blake's two children from his previous marriage to Patricia Walker—and daughters Amy and Joanna. She, more than anyone, was aware of the dichotomy between her image as perfect nanny and the reality of dealing with the everyday problems of her own family in California. Did she have a case of famous mother guilt? "I could give you chapter and verse on this. If I was a mommy that stayed home and was a plain, old comfy, easygoing lady that was there for the kids all the time . . . It's been hell for them."

While raising her children she continued to work on selected projects, scaling down her level of activity because of the children. She finally did return to Salzburg, this time with Plácido Domingo and John Denver, for a 1987 Emmy-nominated Christmas television special, parts of which were filmed at both Mondsee Cathedral and Leopoldskron Castle. It proved to be an agreeable one-hour special, perhaps most noteworthy for its welcome reminder that the Austrian countryside looked as beautiful at Christmas as it did in the summertime settings found in "Do-Re-Mi."

Extending her connection with Rodgers and Hammerstein into a fifth decade with a 1992 studio recording of *The King and I,* she finally made her long-awaited return to live theater, first in Sondheim's *Putting It Together* (1993) and then by starring in a Broadway version of *Victor/Victoria* directed by Edwards in 1995. Andrews received raves but declined her Tony Award nomination as Best Actress—and an all but certain win—in order to protest the fact that no one else involved with the show had received a single nomination; in the star's memorable phrase that made front-page news, her coworkers had been "egregiously overlooked." Andrews dutifully stayed with the show in order to try and help the producers recoup their investment, but the most difficult chapter of her professional life lay straight ahead.

After the discovery of noncancerous throat nodules brought about by singing eight shows per week in *Victor/Victoria,* Andrews underwent surgery for their removal in 1997. Unfortunately, after the initial healing period had passed, it became clear that far from helping, the operation had actually damaged her vocal chords and left her with permanent hoarseness. A suit filed in U.S. District Court in Manhattan on December 14, 1999, accused Dr. Scott Kessler and Dr. Jeffrey Libin of operating on both sides of her vocal chords when the right side did not require surgery. The lawsuit was settled out of court in September 2000, but the terms of the settlement remain confidential. Thanking her attorneys Peter Parcher and Orin Snyder "for representing me with such compassion and excellence," the star expressed her happiness at having "settled the case in a favorable manner," and cited her relief at closing "this chapter, an event which was unfortunate for all concerned." The lawsuit was settled, but the damage had been done. Julie Andrews's professional career as a singer was over.

She reunited with Christopher Plummer for a television version of *On Golden Pond* (2001), and if it did not prove to be particularly memorable, the two-hour film passed pleasantly enough. Further proof of their mutual devotion lay in their decision to tour a "Royal Christmas" show the next year, with Andrews and Plummer narrating while the young Charlotte Church handled the bulk of the singing. Plummer read poems and Julie, damaged voice and all, did manage to talk/sing one song. Audiences responded in great numbers at the box office, happy to be reunited with Maria and Captain von Trapp, their emotional attachment to the stars undiminished by the passage of forty years.

It was the ability to sing that had formed the core of Andrews's personality—in the star's own words, "I would have been a very lost soul if I hadn't had that gift (of singing). I would have been a very, very sad little girl. Thank God I had an identity"—and she now felt adrift. When that loss was combined with the death of favorite aunt Joan Morris, she experienced a profound depression that caused her to check into a Sierra Tucson (Arizona) facility for "guidance and management of emotional issues related to grief." In typical fashion she refused to dwell on the loss of her voice, choosing instead to focus on what she perceived as a positive, namely the opportunity to continue writing the children's books she had begun in 1971 with the publication of *Mandy*: "I'm so fortunate to have found all these other stimulating things to do, things if I had not had these problems with my voice I might not have embraced." Such rock-ribbed cheer would have made Maria and Mary Poppins themselves proud. Redoubling her literary efforts, Andrews churned out ever more stories with daughter Emma (twenty-seven books and counting by 2014), branching out further by publishing a highly regarded and candid number-one bestselling memoir of her pre-Hollywood years simply entitled *Home*.

With the passing years, the scope of Andrews's achievements loomed ever larger, and with critics no longer taking potshots at the icon, her popularity soared for a second time. There were, to be sure, detractors, and in a vivid picture painted by Andrews's biographer Richard Stirling, he utilized barbed prose to describe her appearance at a fortieth anniversary screening of *The Sound of Music* at the National Film Theatre in London. Andrews arrived in a protective bubble of security, the lobbies purposefully cleared of people as she exited the building, leaving Stirling to ask: "I wondered why she should put herself through such a schedule, if it required so much mental and physical disassociation."

Andrews still never failed to be less than polite to public and press alike, and if her behavior was perceived as remote, a reason for the remove still existed. Forty years earlier when *The Sound of Music* hit moviegoers worldwide with such titanic force, Julie Andrews had needed to protect herself from the onslaught of demands and worship. She didn't disappear from the public, like Streisand, but instead created a shell around herself, a means of preserving and protecting her private authentic self. It was a necessary move but one that caused Sheilah Graham, F. Scott Fitzgerald's onetime paramour and a longtime observer of the Hollywood scene, to write in her essay "The Iron Butterfly": "Miss Andrews is the woman nobody knows. She is encased in an iron sheath of charm that is impossible to penetrate."

She remained a professional down to her toes, and in responding to the fact that she had, like so many women in the arts, been called an "iron butterfly" she issued a clipped: "I'm resilient and I'm professional. If that's iron, then so be it." The problem wasn't one of iron will—it was one of image limiting the attempts to expand her range: "People forget that *Mary Poppins* was just a role, too. I'm more complex than that." Like any actress, she found it frustrating—"irritating and annoying" in her own words—that the image prevented directors from thinking of her for different sorts of roles, but she remained grateful for the audiences *Mary Poppins* and *The Sound of Music* continued to bring her with each new generation of children.

If the press still occasionally balked, the public never really deserted Andrews. They may not have liked some of her films, but they still loved Andrews herself. Her brisk professionalism may have limited her public acceptance in a wide variety of roles, but that same unwavering work ethic also underlay part of her appeal: given that knowledge of offscreen behavior inevitably informs part of an audience's response to a particular star, audiences sensed that the goodness displayed onscreen by Julie Andrews was reflected in her everyday life. They felt confident that their beloved star treated others kindly, never threw temper tantrums, and always gave her all. As Andrews herself declared: "I never want to disappoint an audience; I want to be fresh and great."

As the new millennium began, she settled in to a run of highly successful supporting roles, beginning with a turn as Queen Clarisse Renaldi in *The Princess Diaries* (2001). In both that film and its three-years-later sequel *The Princess Diaries 2: Royal Engagements,* she plays a royal grandmother, aristocratic but kind, who tutors awkward granddaughter Anne Hathaway in appropriate royal demeanor. Both films played out as a reversal of *My Fair Lady*; this time around it was Andrews who took on the Henry Higgins Svengali-like role of royal professor. The films found her returning to Disney Studios for the first time since the nearly forty-years-earlier *Mary Poppins,* and in their great popularity, brought her yet another generation of tweener fans.

Princess Diaries 2 found Andrews singing again for the first time since the botched surgery, but her singing of "Your Crowning Glory" was really a mix of singing and talking, and in Andrews's own words, utilized the "five bass notes" that her severely diminished range could now accommodate. If Mary Poppins and Maria had made her everyone's favorite pal, she had now morphed into another iteration of the ideal woman—this time as grandmother: Queen Clarisse, a kind of supernanny and a royal one at that, and a role that proved that with or without her singing voice, Andrews's star quality remained undiminished.

Secure in her top-tier placement in Hollywood history, and riding the crest of renewed popularity after the first *Princess Diaries* film, Andrews even managed to have the last laugh on her starchy persona with two 2003 television films based upon the evergreen Eloise books for children. In both films (*Eloise at the Plaza* and *Eloise at Christmastime*) Andrews once again played a nanny, but this time a gin-swilling, wide-bottomed harridan. She seemed to enjoy every last minute of the romp.

Combining these films with voice-over work as the queen in a hugely successful trio of *Shrek* films (2004, 2007, and 2010), as well as a voice-over role as Gru's Mom in the popular *Despicable Me* (2010), Andrews, it was becoming increasingly clear, had moved into new territory as a beloved national treasure. In her native England she received the Order of the British Empire from Queen Elizabeth in 2000, and in the United States, her home for more than fifty years, the lifetime achievement awards tumbled in one after the other: Disney Legend in Film Award (1991), Women in Film Crystal Award (1993), and in 2001, the Kennedy Center Honors. Honored for both her singing and her acting, she received the highest awards in both fields: The Pittsburgh Civic Light Opera Richard Rodgers Award for Excellence in Musical Theater (1989), The Society of Singers Lifetime Achievement Award (2001), The Screen Actors Guild Lifetime Achievement Award (2006), George and Ira Gershwin Lifetime Musical Achievement Award (2009), Grammy Lifetime Achievement Award (2011), the Prince Rainier Award, and most recently yet another Grammy, this time for Best Spoken Word Children's Album (2011). Andrews, it seemed, had once again achieved universal popularity and acclaim.

She has devoted time to a host of charities, primarily her work as goodwill ambassador for the United Nations Development Fund for Women, and after the death of Blake Edwards in 2010, continued her efforts on behalf of Operation USA, a privately funded worldwide relief organization that the couple helped found. Her increasing frankness in interviews about her throat surgery, the stark admission that she had received grief counseling, and especially the beautifully written, candid memoir *Home* finally allowed audiences to peek beneath the always friendly but guarded exterior. Julie Andrews was now part of everyone's family.

25.

SORRY-GRATEFUL: THE REAL-LIFE VON TRAPPS

"Our story has been told so many times that you began to confuse reality and fiction." Johannes von Trapp

When Georg von Trapp died on May 30, 1947, Maria did not falter in her determination that the family keep singing. (Indeed, although she missed Georg greatly, the ever-practical Maria had him buried without shoes on, in order that all of his shoes could be sent to Austria as part of the post-war aid effort she had started.) Concert tours continued after his death, but Maria could no longer keep the children isolated through work and constant touring. Rupert was practicing medicine, Martina had died, and Johanna and Lorli had married. When Johanna announced she was getting married, Maria, upset that she had compromised the family's ability to make a living, locked Johanna in her room. Johanna's solution? Climbing out her window and eloping.

Non-family members were hired to fill the gaps in the singing group, but these non-family members had to be paid a salary—a practice Maria called "Christian communism"—and the family decided that the end had been reached. Although Maria herself would have happily continued touring, her now-grown children had reached their limit and the last family concert was given on January 26, 1956, in Concord, New Hampshire. Having toured from shortly after their arrival in the United States in 1938 until 1956, by the end of those nearly two decades the family had given an astounding two thousand concerts in thirty different countries and every one of the then forty-eight states.

In effect, the family's great strength—togetherness—had, with the passage of time, turned into its weakness. When the family arrived penniless in

America in 1938, their survival lay in unity; the entire family committed to the musical tours and, beginning in 1942, to the building of the von Trapp Lodge and its satellite farm and music camp. By the time touring actually stopped in 1956, the older children were nearing forty, and even in Stowe had never had the opportunity to fully put down roots. School, dating, sports, and community activities had all taken second place to touring. Staying true to the dynamic of family togetherness had proven all consuming. In Johannes's analysis: "When we stopped, for most of the family it was a relief to stop traveling. We had been living her dream—through the kids. My mother loved contact with the public. She was like a politician who draws nourishment from this contact with the public."

That drive did not always make for an entirely easy family life, and although Johannes has spoken of his mother "cutting through" the formality of the house rather quickly, he detailed a life of discipline and lingering formality: "When we first moved here to Vermont—at the end of four miles of dirt road—if I was going down to the village, I had to wear a coat and tie. . . . Now of course I understand the issue of the clothes—it was a crutch for appropriate behavior—dress a certain way and you will act a certain way."

Although the family's profile increased with the success of *The Sound of Music* on Broadway in 1959, it was only with the worldwide success of the film in 1965 that the expectations foisted upon the von Trapp family increased exponentially, the entire family now forced to live up to the impossibly high standards of family life set by the film. Bad tempers? Normal family squabbles and human frailty? The public didn't want to hear of it. How, in fact, could the real-life von Trapps, a genuinely loving and close-knit family, ever hope to compete with the film's overwhelming image. There on the screen, thirty feet high and in Todd-AO stereophonic sound, resided the world's happiest family. In the words of Charmian Carr: "There isn't that ideal family. It doesn't exist."

Millions of people worldwide wanted, indeed needed, that perfect family to exist, the demands leading even Maria herself to acknowledge that she had grown "quite fed up" with the incessant publicity. Maria was a genuinely compassionate person, but she was a driven woman, experienced moments of doubt and worry, and could prove difficult. Said Johannes: "My mother had tremendous strengths but she had characteristics that also made her very difficult." In later years, daughter Rosmarie put it more bluntly: "She wasn't happy all the time—she could be up and down. My bipolar friend reminded me of my mother. She tried to be nice with the public but she had to let go—and was cross with us."

And yet, *The Sound of Music* legend came to affect even Maria herself. She may have occasionally grown exasperated with the public, but after experiencing a rather life-altering moment with visitors to the von Trapp Lodge in 1978, her perspective changed radically: "The father of a young family told (me), 'This is the highlight of our vacation. We saved for a whole year; now you have made the whole trip.' If I can bring real joy just by stopping and smiling, it is a privilege."

Of course, one person's family matriarch is another's tough dame, and in a scene reported by a Stowe acquaintance, Maria threatened the town of Stowe that if they didn't plow her roads instantly, she'd give her land to the Catholic Church and thereby deny the town any tax revenue from the land. She could be forceful, indeed tough, and in a revealing comment by a Stowe village resident, was painted as someone who "didn't care if anyone liked her; she was here to do her business and take care of her family." Whether striking a business deal, or simply driving her Karmann Ghia around Stowe "like a maniac . . . tires squealing," Maria barreled through life with a loving yet steamrolling personality. Skipping across a brook singing "like a lark who is learning to pray" she didn't.

Although resentment toward Maria had begun to grow after the touring stopped—almost as if the normal frustrations children feel toward parents in adolescence and early adulthood had been kept tamped down for decades and now could finally burst through—while she was alive Maria succeeded in squelching family discontent by sheer force of personality. No one dared to cross the family matriarch. Johannes himself analyzed the problem as extending back through the decades to Maria's philosophy of fostering family togetherness over everything else: "Any influence that might lead off to an individual life was sternly suppressed by my mother. It was like bottling up a volcano. Eventually it blows. But at the same time there was that discipline which made us all function together. . . . She was a very complex person. Incredibly strong with a formidable will, literally an indomitable will, and sometimes running into that will was not so pleasant. We could have our head-to-heads. She had a very unhappy childhood. Someone with her background either becomes a very strong person or becomes a homeless person. She became very strong."

So dominant had Maria's personality been, that in Rosmarie's straightforward explanation: "After my mother's death, everyone started looking for their own identity." It took Maria's death for the grievances to come to light; even if the children had been inclined to air grievances with their mother, it's highly unlikely that they would have made any headway. As Johannes admitted: "My mother never paid attention to it (the unrest). She just sort of said, 'Be quiet.' " It's no surprise then, that a business psychologist hired to help sort out various family business problems concluded that the children, never having confronted their mother with any of their discontent while she was alive, had "unresolved business with Maria."

As a result, just as the seven youngsters who portrayed the von Trapp children on film have struggled to escape the shadow of an identity frozen in time fifty years ago, so, too, did the real-life von Trapp children spend much of the twentieth century forging their individual identities while continuing to function as members of the world-famous von Trapp family. Coping with both a larger-than-life mother as well as a wildly successful film, the children found their own ways of dealing, in manners both public and private:

RUPERT Born in 1911, the oldest child and the doctor whose defiance of the German Reich had played such a key role in the family's journey to America, Rupert became a U.S. citizen through his service in World War II, established a busy and successful medical practice in Rhode Island, and fathered six children. Yet it wasn't the demands of a medical career that he remembered as difficult, it was the four hours of singing practice every day, which he characterized as "hard work." And yet for Rupert, who returned to Vermont after retiring, the family's musical roots never vanished. In a 1978 *Washington Post* profile of the family, the reporter noted that Rupert "grew misty eyed when listening to a record of the family singing sixteenth- and seventeenth-century madrigals." After his death in 1992, Rupert was buried in the family's Stowe, Vermont, plot.

AGATHE Born in 1913, she applied for U.S. citizenship after the family emigrated, never married, and spent her professional life as a kindergarten teacher, first in Stowe, Vermont, and then, until her retirement in 1993, in Baltimore, Maryland. Shy and a talented sketch artist, she exhibited her watercolors at the Austrian Embassy in Washington, D.C., and illustrated the *Trapp Family Book of Christmas Carols* as well as her own autobiography.

Never fully comfortable with the Stowe family home having been turned into a lodge, Agathe felt that the house was too small a dwelling to hold dozens of guests, and after the Lodge burned to the ground on December 20, 1980, she stated: "I was not sorry to hear that our first home in the United States was destroyed. . . . For Mother, however, it was a terrible blow to see her life's work disappear. She never quite recovered from the shock. . . . Strong in her beliefs, Mother lived her life passionately without compromise. Although she was not always easy to live with, I am grateful that she seized the opportunities that made it possible for us to share our musical talents with the world."

Her bemused thoughts on *The Sound of Music* seemed to sum up the entire family's mixed feelings: "A very nice story but not our story. If they hadn't used our name, I probably would have enjoyed it." After her death in Baltimore in 2010, Agathe was buried in the family cemetery at the Lodge.

MARIA Born in 1914 and the second oldest von Trapp daughter, Maria was twenty-three years old when the family emigrated to America. Having toured with the family singing group for decades (as second soprano), she took up her life's work as a missionary at age forty-two—"I felt such a pull"—after meeting a priest from Papua New Guinea in Sydney, Australia. Following in the footsteps of her stepmother, she traveled around the world as a lay missionary for thirty-two years, with only two brief interruptions for vacations in Vermont. Working primarily in Papua New Guinea, she taught English, formed a choir with schoolchildren for church services, and adopted a young boy, Kikuli Mwanukuzi, long before such international cross-cultural adoptions had gained any currency.

After retirement in 1987, she returned to Vermont where she lived in a small house on the lodge property, played the accordion, and taught Austrian dance with half sister Rosmarie; the last surviving child of Georg's marriage to Agathe, she lived until age ninety-nine, dying in February of 2014. She remained a von Trapp to the very end, and touching footage from the British television documentary *Climb'd Ev'ry Mountain* shows that while the very elderly Maria had forgotten how to speak in English, she could still play the accordion.

Like her siblings, Maria both liked the film for its positive portrayal of the family, yet simultaneously resented its distortions: "I always say they took raisins out of the dough and made a new dough." She cited the film's portrayal of her father as an unrelenting martinet as a particularly unwanted liberty with the truth: "We were all pretty shocked at how they portrayed our father, he was so completely different. He always looked after us a lot, especially after our mother died. You have to separate yourself from all that, and you have to get used to it. It is something you simply cannot avoid." Maria's view was wholeheartedly echoed by Johannes, who stated: "My father was very congenial, far more so than depicted in the film. Then again, that portrayal started with the stage production, which was built around Mary Martin, so the role of the captain certainly became less important."

In the summer of 2008 Maria returned to Austria to see her childhood home in Salzburg just before it opened as a bed and breakfast. Visiting the house for the first time since the 1930s, she was overwhelmed by memories: "Our whole life is in here, in this house. Especially here in the stairwell, where we always used to slide down the railings." Very much at peace with the decades-long spotlight the film shone on the family, she remained, in her own words, "grateful to *The Sound of Music* because people don't forget us."

WERNER Born in 1915, Werner, like his brother Rupert, became a U.S. citizen by serving in the United States Armed Forces during World War II. Grateful for his safe return from the war, he built the stone chapel that still exists on the grounds of the Lodge, married, raised six children, shed his Catholic roots, and emerged as a born-again Christian who ran a dairy farm in the town of Waitsfield, Vermont.

Although living relatively close by the Lodge, Werner deliberately chose not to be involved in the running of the Lodge in any way. In 1978, twenty years before a family squabble dissolved into lawsuits that were ultimately settled, and while Maria herself was still alive, he bluntly stated: "I'm glad I'm thirty miles from Stowe and not drawn into it. I'd speak against it if I had a chance." Seemingly the most disenchanted of the ten children regarding the family's public profile, in a 1978 interview he emphasized his born-again outlook and his conviction that he now had "a peace of mind I never had before because of my personal relationship with Christ." Until his death in 1992, the same year in which his older brother Rupert died, Werner maintained his distance from the family enterprise. Returned to the family fold in death, he is buried in the family plot in Stowe.

HEDWIG Born in 1917 Hedwig was the second of the children to die, predeceased only by Martina. A skilled photographer, she worked as a teacher after the family stopped touring, becoming a naturalized American citizen in 1948. Hedwig maintained a nuanced perspective on life with stepmother Maria, and in an observation that cut to the core of the family's storied public journey, matter-of-factly told her brother: "You know, Johannes, if it weren't for mother, we'd all have been cooks and maids." Instead, she taught handicrafts and singing for many years at St. Anthony's School in Kailua, Hawaii, and directed the children's choir.

Only fifty-five at the time of her death in 1972, she suffered a fatal asthma attack while living with her Aunt Joan ("Tante Joan") on the shores of Lake Zell am See, and is now buried in the family plot in Stowe.

JOHANNA Born in 1919, Johanna become a naturalized American citizen in 1948, after which she married Ernst Winter and had seven children (four boys and three girls). She kept the greatest distance from the lodge by moving permanently back to Austria, where she died at age seventy-five in Vienna in 1994. She is buried in Austria, alongside her oldest son. With her passing, there were no longer any von Trapps living in Austria.

MARTINA Born in 1921, Martina followed in the footsteps of her sisters by acquiring U.S. citizenship in 1948. She married the French Canadian Jean Dupiere in 1949, and after becoming pregnant, stayed home from the family's tour in 1951 in order to prepare for the birth of her first child. She gave premature birth to a daughter, and died from complications relating to her cesarean section in 1951. The first of the children to die, she survived her father by only four years, and is buried in the family cemetery along with her daughter, father, stepmother, and siblings Werner, Rupert, and Hedwig. Ever the unrelenting professionals, the family continued their concert tour at the time of her death, with only Maria attending the funeral.

ROSMARIE Born in 1929, Rosmarie had been the first to refuse any further touring after the death of her father in 1947. "I was not happy onstage at all. I was made to do it. I don't know what my mother believed in except the Lord. She tried to get everyone to go into the convent. I knew I'd be in prison."

She was, by her own admission, very shy, suffered from stage fright, and after the death of Georg, had a nervous breakdown. "I depended a lot on him. He was always in the background in the concerts. When he died I couldn't handle being at home. . . . One night I just ran out to try to find relief." Three days later she was spotted wandering across a farmer's field, and when she was brought back home, Maria saw only two alternative treatments: life in a convent or in a mental hospital. Rosmarie was given electric shock treatments. "They gave me electric shock treatment. It was too much." Frustrated, upset, and depressed, Rosmarie changed course: "I got rebellious. I smoked."

The firstborn of Maria's three children with Georg, Rosmarie, surprisingly stated in later years that she felt neglected by Maria in favor of her half siblings: "My mother concentrated on the older children—the ones in the movie." Rosmarie faced the toughest emotional times of any of the von Trapps, experiences about which she speaks forthrightly but with difficulty: "From age twenty to age forty, I had a tough growing-up period. . . . Most of the time I lived in Vermont. In my adult life, I didn't work outside the farm. There was one year that I studied to be a nurse and after that I had another nervous breakdown and spent a year in the hospital. I made mistakes all the time."

There were thoughts of marriage and boyfriends, but the relationships never fully developed: "I didn't hang out with boys—I was scared of boys. My mother didn't foster us getting involved with boys. . . . I began relationships with men at a somewhat older age and when I had a boyfriend he started using drugs and the relationship eventually ended. . . . If I could have done anything with my life, I would have gotten married. I wanted to but then I got scared. My ideal husband: I would have wanted one like my Dad. . . . I made some wrong choices in life, and afterward I never married. I had two serious car accidents that required a real effort to recover from."

Her thoughts on the film of *The Sound of Music* echo those of her siblings: "When we saw the movie we saw a story that was a bit different from our life story. *The Sound of Music* is not the real story of my family. . . . First of all, we never went out running to the field and singing songs like that. We never sang those songs. The movie tells about the period that we were in Salzburg. Our life in America isn't depicted at all. You could say that our life wasn't so glamorous like in the movie. We had a very hard life for the most part. It was a struggle. We lived in a struggle and coped with the hardships of survival."

Rosmarie worked as a missionary in New Guinea from 1956 to 1959, and then joined the Community of the Crucified One, gaining membership in a branch of the community in Vermont. Like several of her siblings, she found peace in a renewed relationship with God. "At age forty I told myself that I don't know how to live my life and decided to give my life to God. That was the turning point. Before that I didn't have my own faith in God. I always lived like my family, I was their shadow, I followed them, I did what they did. Since I didn't have my own personal faith in God, I also didn't have faith in myself. One day when I was feeling very desperate I listened to the radio and the man who was talking said, 'If you're in despair, go talk with God, talk with Jesus about your problem. Tell him that you want to start over, that you need help.' This was when I was forty."

Recounting her decision to turn her life over to God, Rosmarie spoke of an instantaneous change in her life: "I went to bed and when I got up in the morning my depression was gone. Everything changed in one night." The peace she found with God also allowed her to repair her sometimes troubled relationship with her mother: "We had a special connection. I was her eldest daughter and I looked a lot like her. It was hard for her to raise me within the unique sort of life we were living, so she let my big sisters raise me." It was, in fact, Rosmarie who nursed Maria through several strokes before her death on March 28, 1987. "For many years I blamed her for my problems and didn't know how to repair our relationship. Thankfully, we were able to reconcile before she died."

Rosmarie now spends half of the year in Vermont (where she gives recorder lessons and conducts sing-alongs with guests at the lodge), and the other half of the year near Jerusalem, in the isolated community of Ir Ovot in the northern Arava region. In a 2006 interview, she spoke of the appeal the desert holds for her: "This place brings me quiet . . . I came here for the first time in 2001, and ever since then I've divided my year in half: six months here and six months in America. But here I feel closest to God."

ELEONORE Born in 1931, and nicknamed Lorli, she sang first soprano in the family chorus; after the von Trapps stopped touring she was asked to join other groups, an invitation she responded to with a simple "I can't. I just can't. It was unique—what we had."

She has raised seven daughters with her husband Hugh Campbell, and lives in Waitsfield, Vermont, the same town in which brother Werner lived; just like Werner, she "accepted the Lord" as her savior, calling herself born-again. According to sister Agathe, Lorli has remained "active with groups working to restore traditional family values in Vermont." An energetic gardener, like her sister Rosmarie, Lorli is a fervent supporter of the state of Israel.

Lorli's evenhanded assessment of the film indicates a somewhat loving acceptance of liberties taken as weighed against overall effectivness: "(For instance) they completely invented the scene of nuns taking away the distributor caps—yet it's a lovely scene and the film has wonderful moments. . . . God used our singing to touch people's hearts."

When Maria died in March of 1987, it was Lorli who was by her bedside: "She had a very peaceful death."

JOHANNES Born in 1939 and markedly younger than all of his siblings except Rosmarie and Lorli, Johannes had the advantage of distance from the mythical life in Austria, as well as the ability to attend college (Dartmouth) without interruptions for touring. Although mostly homeschooled as a youngster, he did spend time in boarding school, and his time at Dartmouth, as well as at Yale University graduate school, gave him scientific training and an ability to bring an "evenhanded scientific assessment" to bear on matters regarding the lodge. Figuring that since he and his Dartmouth roommate had enjoyed cross-country skiing others would as well, Johannes utilized his master's in forestry from Yale to design and build trails; when those trails opened to the public in 1968, they made the Lodge the first cross-country ski resort in the United States.

Running the lodge was not the career Johannes had necessarily planned on, but when the family finances appeared to be fast approaching collapse, he stepped in to run the business, taking over the day-to-day operations from his mother. His assumption of responsibility caused new problems within the family, however, and after Maria's death, the business psychologist called in to help with family problems concluded that both children and grandchildren alike had transferred their discontent from Maria to Johannes.

One reason why Maria felt comfortable handing over the reins to Johannes was that he possessed a temperament that was in many ways similar to his mother's. One outside observer found the mother-son duo to be remarkably similar: "Johannes is charismatic, smart, tough, and disciplined, very Maria-like." Acknowledged by others as "Maria's favorite," Johannes was single-minded in his determination, the only one of the ten children who consistently dared to forcibly disagree with her. A reporter for a 1973 interview quoted Maria as delineating the yin-yang of temperament she shared with Johannes: "She believes that she is known for her tendency to exaggerate, her son Johannes to understate." Forty-two years later Johannes's bemused reaction to the quote was: "It may be that I exaggerate on the downside—maybe it's a genetic problem. Of course now I'm not reacting to my mother's excessive enthusiasm. . . . Everything she did was larger, louder, bigger, faster."

In the end, any clashes between mother and son did not hinder their closeness and Johannes quickly points out the multitude of areas where Maria's genuinely loving personality more than met the storybook version found in *The Sound of Music*: "She loved to make people happy. She would read about someone in trouble and invite the widow and six children for Christmas."

The ever-shining spotlight of the film has given Johannes the same personal hurdles to overcome as his siblings. He has noted on more than one occasion that when members of the public meet him, they want to know who portrayed him in the movie; explaining that he wasn't born until the family arrived in America, their disappointment grows. When told by Nicholas Hammond that his situation is better than Nick's own, because he's an actual von Trapp and not a celluloid imitation, Johannes, with more than a touch of smiling irony, murmured, "They want me to be you."

Both grateful to and somewhat frustrated by *The Sound of Music* for its portrayal of his family, Johannes nonetheless understands the appeal of the film and how it has made the survival of the Lodge possible. An astute businessman, he now oversees a Trapp farm, a Trapp brewery, and needless to say, a Trapp family gift shop. Thanks in part to the film, he has created a successful, very public position as keeper of the flame/family business. Drawing a bead on the film's Hollywoodization of Austrian culture, he pondered his discovery that the Lodge's gift shop had been selling an eight-inch stuffed goat that sings "The Lonely Goatherd." "Isn't that awful? . . . My staff hid it from me for months. But it does sell. The bottom line is that we don't want to dumb down, which can make it difficult at times. I refuse to have a television in the bar!"

The problem, he feels, lies in the fact that he refuses to change the actual von Trapp culture to conform with Hollywood's version. "At the lodge, people want to walk in and hear the *Sound of Music*. The answer is no—you'll hear classical music. I don't let them play songs from the *Sound of Music* when I'm at the lodge, partly because I've heard it enough—and because it's not who we were. We sang classical music and Austrian folk songs—it had a different aura to it. The von Trapps were serious musicians, raised in an old-world, aristocratic manner that required performance at a certain high level at all times. I don't mean that to sound superior—not at all. It's just who we were. . . . We're about environmental sensitivity, artistic sensitivity . . ." It's not that Johannes objects to his sister Rosmarie leading sing-alongs two times per week at the Lodge; it's that the sing-alongs include songs from *The Sound of Music*—"much to my irritation . . . *The Sound of Music* simplifies everything. I think perhaps reality is at the same time less glamorous but more interesting than the myth."

In actuality, *The Sound of Music* is screened occasionally at the Lodge, but in Johannes's own words, it's the location and scenery that remain the focus of the Lodge's appeal: "We want to maximize the advantages of the beautiful Vermont landscape and location. That's our selling point and what we're very proud of. There really are many people who come to the lodge without having much knowledge about the film."

And yet the film remains an unquestioned part of the Lodge's appeal, and the fact that such a hugely popular movie cuts across all social and economic classes is both part of the Lodge's success and simultaneously makes it difficult to run. As related by Johannes, some years back when he was arranging a financing deal with CitiCorp after the Lodge burned: "I said to the bankers, 'Look around the room. There are young people and old. Whites and minorities. Rich and less well-off—that's what makes it difficult to operate. We want to appeal to the sophisticated traveler but also to the mass market.' "

Having turned seventy-five in 2014, Johannes has put the all-consuming business of *The Sound of Music* in perspective, arriving at a point where he simply states: "I can appreciate and enjoy the film, and see what it has meant to people. It's a humbling experience. Early in 2014 I watched five minutes of the film and was struck all over again by how well made it is. Extraordinary." In this acceptance of the film, he has begun to understand the throngs who, as one observer noted, "come to the Trapp family lodge and treat it as a place of pilgrimage. Mecca with melodies. Lourdes with lullabyes."

In the twenty-first century, just as Austrians made peace with the film's place in the worldwide culture, so, too, have multiple generations of the Trapps arrived at a rapprochement with the film. A full generation removed from the events depicted in the film, Maria's grandchildren maintain a detachment impossible for the original children to achieve. In Johannes's view, the younger generation "finds the historical and cultural differences and inaccuracies in the film less jarring. It's easier for them to deal with." As stated in bemused fashion by Maria's granddaughter Elisabeth (Werner and Erika's second daughter, and the one grandchild who has maintained a consistent solo musical career): "Seeing the film was surreal. You're looking at these kids but we're thinking those kids are our older aunts and uncles. Totally surreal."

The family's relationship with the film has now come full circle; Johannes's son Sam is now the operational manager of the Lodge in tandem with Johannes's son-in-law, and he has emphasized and embraced the resort's connection to the film more fully than did his father, even starring in a television commercial for the Lodge that was purposefully shown during the film's annual broadcast on United States television. For Sam, the "burden" is now gratefully borne: "When we were growing up, we had a sense of holding the movie at arm's length. Out of humility but at the same time, because of the degree of disappointment we had that our grandfather was portrayed as so stern and that our aunts and uncles' names and birth orders had been changed. Then, over time, seeing how much the movie meant to people, we have come around to making peace with the film."

Spoken like a true von Trapp.

26

FIFTY YEARS OF STATISTICS

❧

1965: The bald statistics—at the time of the film's soundtrack's release in 1965, it was not only nominated for a Grammy Award as album of the year, but also proved to be the quickest ever (two weeks) gold certified soundtrack in the history of the Recording Industry Association of America. The recording remained number one on the Billboard charts for fourteen weeks, a longer period of time than that of any album released by Elvis Presley or the Beatles.

1968: The soundtrack recording proved to be the source of the first major squabble over money derived from the film, when the musical's Broadway producers, Leland Hayward and Richard Halliday, brought suit against Richard Rodgers and the estate of Oscar Hammerstein. At the heart of the complaint lay the plaintiffs' claim that Rodgers and Hammerstein had made a separate arrangement with Fox regarding royalties accruing from the soundtrack album, and had not informed their original coproducers, Hayward and Halliday, of the arrangement. In fact, Rodgers and Hammerstein's lawyers had negotiated ownership of the soundtrack recording on behalf of their clients, just as they had for the original Broadway recordings of *Sound of Music* and *Flower Drum Song*.

By the time of the lawsuit in 1968, the soundtrack had sold upward of five million units, and when the American Arbitration Association handed down an award of $1,076,795.21 in favor of Hayward and Halliday, it ranked as the largest ever arbitration award granted to date. In the language of Justice John M. Murtagh, Hayward and Halliday had "gone out of their way to avoid smearing anyone with the 'tarbrush of fraud' " (but) the "plain fact of the matter" is that Rodgers and the executors of Hammerstein's estate were "guilty of willful misconduct." R&H appealed, but five months later, the appellate division upheld Hayward and Halliday's victory to the tune of $1.6 million. For such a high-stakes lawsuit, the proceedings unfolded in a remarkably civilized fashion, with Hayward claiming that before the arbitration began, Richard Rodgers said to him "Let the lawyers fight but we'll remain friends."

DECEMBER 1969: *The Sound of Music* ends its initial run in movie theaters, a record-shattering five years and nine months after its release.

1970: As U.S. involvement in Southeast Asia escalated into Laos and Cambodia and students were murdered at Kent State, sales of *The Sound of Music* soundtrack surpassed 12,000,000 units.

1973: Only three years after the *Sound of Music* ends its first-run release, it is rereleased in movie theaters around the world.

1974–1976: Nixon resigns, Ford stumbles into the White House, inflation rises, and on February 29, 1976, *The Sound of Music* appears on television for the first time. Even when edited to fit the three-hour prime-time broadcast slot, the film still proves a ratings bonanza. Such is the power of broadcast television in those pre-cable days, and so high the ratings, that this first televised showing results in the sale of some 500,000 additional copies of the soundtrack, bringing the total sold, as of 1976, to 15,500,000.

1978: Basking in the success of the 1976 broadcast of the film, NBC pays $21.5 million for the rights to broadcast the film for twenty years; shortly thereafter, the BBC pays $4 million for the right to run the film ten times.

1983: The afternoon of May 27, the day before the opening of the G-7 summit meeting in Williamsburg, Virginia, where the United States is hosting the only conference held in America during the eight years of the Reagan presidency. Concerned that the president has not adequately prepared for the complicated talks, James Baker, the White House chief of staff compiles a thick book of facts, figures, and talking points, presented in a digestible format playing to Reagan's strengths as "The Great Communicator." Returning to check in with the president the next day, an agitated Baker realizes that the book has not been opened. The president's explanation for his failure to read any of the material? "Well, Jim, *The Sound of Music* was on last night."

1987: As the number of amateur productions of *The Sound of Music* continues to grow each year, making it, along with *Oklahoma!,* the most popular show in the entire Rodgers and Hammerstein catalogue, new recordings of the score arrive on the scene. Most notable of all: a 1987 studio recording starring opera diva Frederica von Stade as Maria. "Flicka" turns in an earnest, diligent, talented performance—and makes no one forget Julie Andrews.

1990: *The Sound of Music* is reissued in theaters for a second time.

1995: In commemoration of the film's thirtieth anniversary, a special four-hour Easter television broadcast is hosted by Julie Andrews.

2001: *The Sound of Music* finally achieves formal recognition by the elite when the Library of Congress chooses the film for preservation in its film registry, finding that it meets the criteria of being "culturally, historically, or aesthetically significant." Somewhere Pauline Kael and Judith Crist were gnashing their teeth, but there it was—according to the Library of Congress, *The Sound of Music* was now aesthetically significant. (To which the film's continuing detractors would retort: "And the French think Jerry Lewis is a genius.")

2005: Box office–wise, in inflation-adjusted dollars, *The Sound of Music* now ranks as the third-highest-grossing film of all time. With its cumulative worldwide gross of $1,162,109,500, Maria von Trapp trails only *Gone With the Wind* and *Star Wars*.

Around the World in the New Millennium

The explosion of the home video market in the 1980s may have derailed the positioning of *The Sound of Music* as a once-a-year family-viewing phenomenon along the lines of the 1950s and '60s annual network broadcast of *The Wizard of Oz*, but early in the new millennium the popularity of Maria von Trapp grew in a different direction, with sales of the video propelling the film to new heights of popularity. *The Sound of Music* was now ready for family-friendly viewing all around the world, 365 days of the year. First released on video in 1979, *The Sound of Music* remained the record holder for the greatest number of weeks spent on the chart of bestselling home videos and DVDs.

It wasn't just in America that the film's profile grew ever larger; the worldwide revolution of the home video market caused the global appeal of the film to skyrocket just as much. The movie continued to prove wildly popular in Russia, where the stage version, amusingly titled *Zwucky Musicky* also proved a substantial hit. (The Italians, true to form, translated the film's title as *All Together with Passion*.) In the huge new market of China, the film remained "easily the most well-known Western musical in China." The Chinese government might have looked upon the film as harmless, but for millions of Chinese, the story of determined individuals standing up to an oppressive regime struck a deep chord. There's nary an Asian person in sight, and certainly not a single person of color, but Maria and the children remained just as popular in Asia as in the United States.

Johannes von Trapp experienced the film's popularity in China firsthand while working on an economic benefit financing project with the Chinese. Planning to build a brewery on the von Trapp property, and with hopes of creating a regional brand of "Trapp Lager," Johannes made three trips to China for discussions regarding the appropriate financing. Accompanied by his son Sam on two of the trips, he realized that *The Sound of Music* was familiar to virtually all adults in China because it rated as one of only five films that Mao permitted to be shown: "Everyone had seen the film many, many times."

Given the Chinese government's policy of one child per family, Johannes found that many Chinese parents felt their children were lacking the traditional Chinese sense of extended family, and solved the problem by gathering groups of friends for food and entertainment. At one such gathering, after a young child had played an emotional version of Beethoven's "Apassionata," the hosts looked at Johannes and in heavily accented English asked him for "Something from *Sound of Music*." Johannes responded with a solo version of "Edelweiss," the "one song from the score I will sing. . . . The power of the film to cross all cultural and national boundaries is astonishing. They really love that music."

The film may not have been quite as popular in Austria as in China, but Austrians remain grateful for the decades' long boon to tourism fostered by its worldwide appeal. It's not just because Frommer's *Budget Travel Magazine* named Salzburg the number-one movie-related travel site in the world—after all, where exactly was the big competition? *Gone With the Wind*'s Tara existed only in bits and pieces stored in a barn, and *The Godfather*'s Corleone compound is a private home on Staten Island. Instead, it's the sheer number of *Sound of Music* tourists that astounds, with both David Brenner, the Austrian minister of arts and culture, and Laurence Maslon in his *Sound of Music Companion* noting that "out of one million annual tourists (to Austria), more than 300,000 people journey there specifically because of *The Sound of Music*."

Salzberg may be the home of Mozart, but *The Sound of Music* locations appear to have surpassed Wolfgang Amadeus's birthplace as the "go to" Salzburg destinations. Says city native Georg Steinitz: "It took the city and country more than forty years to realize the impact of the film and what it has meant to people around the world. People in Salzburg may want visitors to come to the city because of Mozart, but *The Sound of Music* draws even more people. The film has become a myth—in a category of its own."

Thanks to the official *Sound of Music* tour presented by Panorama Tours and the That's Entertourment company, visitors are now ferried on three-hour, sixty-five-mile bus tours to the sites made famous by the film. Panorama, the very first of the *Sound of Music* tour companies, and the firm that actually drove cast and crew around Salzburg during the location shooting in 1964, claims to have served 30,000 people per year since the film's premiere. Fifty years after the film's initial release, at the height of the summer tourist season the tours still attract two hundred paying customers per day. (Steinitz has taken one of the bus tours as a lark, reporting, "The guides seem to have little idea of what really happened on the set, but people have a good time—their memories of the film take over.") And when the tourists disembark from the bus, there is now the option of extending the experience by taking in the Salzburg Marionettes own production of *The Sound of Music*. Said Ted Chapin: "Those who valued the tourist trade realized that after getting off the bus, those tourists would want something *Sound of Music* related to do—attending the marionette production was a perfect way to extend the experience, and proves lucrative for all involved."

One particularly popular attraction for the tourists has been the Boris Leven–designed "Sixteen Going on Seventeen" gazebo. Figuring that the gazebo fit in nicely with the grounds at Leopoldskronit, at the completion of filming 20th Century-Fox decided to leave the gazebo by the lake as a present to the city. It seemed like a good idea at the time, but given the film's overwhelming popularity, an unanticipated problem ensued: so great was the demand to see the gazebo that trespassers at the secluded property began showing up with alarming frequency. The solution devised by the city of Salzburg was to relocate the gazebo to the Hellbrunn Palace Park; redesigned for its new home, the gazebo was now bigger, but maintained the same essential look and romantic aura beloved by fans.

Popular as the gazebo remains, however, its popularity is topped by one other *Sound of Music* setting: the stairs at the block-long Mirabell Gardens featured at the finale of "Do-Re-Mi." Summer tourists flock to re-create the stair-hopping climax of the song in such large numbers that the manager of the onsite Sheraton Hotel has laughingly commented that visitors don't ask for their room number when checking in—they only want to make a bee-line for the iconic steps where they hop up and down in time to music. Life imitating art imitating life. . . .

For audiences around the world, it has all devolved into a simple mathematical equation: Alps equals *Sound of Music* equals Julie Andrews singing and twirling equals happily ever after. No one is more aware of the association than Andrews herself, and she has laughingly related the story of preparing for a concert at the London Palladium by walking the hills near her home in Switzerland in order to build up her stamina; given the solitude of the hills, after she trekked some distance she thought she'd start to sing. In fact, she told herself, why not start with "The hills are alive . . . " Casting a quick glance to make sure she was alone, Julie Andrews began a lusty version of her signature song, only to turn a corner and come upon an entire group of Japanese tourists just then cresting a hill. A startled Julie Andrews looked at a group of equally startled and happy Japanese tourists. The star's bemused reaction: "They must have thought that I did that sort of thing all the time." If only she did.

27

THE SING-ALONG PHENOMENON

"This is like the Rocky Horror Picture Show *for dorks."*
—VICTORIA REMOND, INVESTMENT BANKER

A s a bemused Robert Wise looked out at 18,000 costumed fans in the Hollywood Bowl gleefully singing along with every word of *The Sound of Music,* as he fully took in the sight of grown men and women dressed up as von Trapp children, "rays of golden sun," and carburetors, he could definitely have been forgiven for wondering: "What exactly is going on here? Is this the same movie I made forty years ago? How on earth did *The Sound of Music* become a mass costumed sing-along?"

As it turned out, the *Sound of Music* sing-along had morphed from a one-night screening to an international phenomenon in a remarkably short period of time, having begun life as a simple one-night event at the London Gay and Lesbian Film Festival in 1999. Inspired by a visit to his grandmother at a Scottish nursing home, where the residents had been given lyric sheets so that they could sing along at a screening of *Seven Brides for Seven Brothers,* the sing-along organizer figured that the idea might just translate to *The Sound of Music.* At the least, he thought, some chuckles would ensue for a few dozen people, and a onetime sing-along screening was arranged.

The quick sellout success of that one night led producer David Johnson to book a return sing-along engagement at London's Prince Charles Cinema in August 1999. Inspired by the decades' long midnight screening success of *The Rocky Horror Picture Show, The Sound of Music* sing-along unfolded just like that audience participation fest—but without the attitude. With the song lyrics scrolling across the bottom of the screen, the hundreds in attendance lustily joined in, channeling their inner von Trapp by talking back to the screen, booing the Nazis, and singing at the top of their lungs.

The success of the sing-along in London led to further packed screenings around the world: Holland, Sweden, Norway, Belgium, Switzerland, and Malaysia followed in quick succession, until the emerging phenomenon finally hit the United States at New York City's Ziegfeld Theater in September 2000. The last traditional single-screen movie palace still standing in Manhattan, the Ziegfeld was filled to capacity, with Dan Truhitte and all seven of the on-screen von Trapp children in attendance much to the crowd's delight.

Julie Andrews and Christopher Plummer did not attend, but Mary Rodgers Guettel, the talented composer daughter of Richard Rodgers, bestowed her stamp of approval, stating, "I think it's a very affectionate and sweet tribute." Bemused but approving, Guettel, according to the *Newsday* reporter who interviewed her, sounded a "bit like Julie Andrews's Maria . . . imparting a good-natured dignity to the raucous proceedings with her understated though heavily pearled presence."

As news of the phenomenon gained worldwide attention, the funniest comment of all came from Christopher Plummer, whose good-natured assessment of the costume-wearing fans was a laughing: "I just hope all those people wearing lederhosen are as uncomfortable as I was." Like Caesar advancing upon Gaul, the sing-along then conquered Chicago before landing at the Hollywood Bowl for an outdoor screening complete with the seven children, Ernest Lehman, Robert Wise, and 18,000 costumed fans. Over the years, sing-along at the Bowl went on to sell out no fewer than six showings—with more to follow. What exactly was going on here? A pop culture version of the Messiah sing-along?

In truth, what was going on turned out to be part revival meeting, part camp fest, and total "come out of the closet of musical comedy geekdom and declare your love for the *Sound of Music*." Each screening featured a host who led the audience in vocal warm-ups, as well as a costume competition complete with prizes. With interactive fun packs, headscarfs, and small foam rubber nuns available for purchase at concession stands, audience members were encouraged to "Wave your edelweiss" and "Open your von Trapp and sing." In other words, the screenings provided a chance to let loose, act silly, and admit to loving *The Sound of Music* without fear of ridicule. Men dressed as nuns, and women as "wild geese with the moon on their wings." (Anyone who ever doubted the iconic appeal of the *Sound of Music* costumes need only look at the money fetched when several items were auctioned in July of 2013 at a Profiles in History auction in California. A selection of costumes, including the floral lederhosen worn by the onscreen children, as well as Maria's (seemingly) homemade dress—described in the auction handbook as "a heavy brown homespun Austrian-style dress with a wheat-colored homespun blouse"—sold for an extraordinary $1.3 million.)

Just before each sing-along screening began, the host for the evening would instruct the audience that they actually held the power of the film in their hands. In fact, the host explained, once the film started, if everyone would just call Julie Andrews's name long enough, she'd hear them, twirl and start to sing. Sure enough, as the camera zoomed in on what Rodgers and Hammerstein VP Bert Fink humorously and accurately dubbed "the most famous meadow in the world," the audience would begin to call out "Hi, Julie," "Over here, Julie!," "Sing, girl—twirl, twirl, twirl!"

Boos greeted the baroness, with the most vociferous abuse heaped upon the Nazis. Adults sang "So Long, Farewell" right along with all seven children. This time around everyone pretended to be in on the joke.

And yet.

At each and every sing-along, as the film unfolded, the irony slowly diminished until the audience participation, even if always carrying a touch of humor, proved genuinely heartfelt. Here was a communal iteration of E. M. Forster's dictum "Only connect." Audience members who arrived under the protective cloak of irony, as if by dressing up and seeming to make fun of the film they could still revel in that which they secretly adored, eventually dropped the mask. Underneath all the layers of self-protection lay a childhood wish for happily ever after.

The audience knew better now, but still wished it didn't, and "knowing" remained the key word when it came to the sing-along. The now-adult audiences know that the world isn't black and white and, by dint of tough experience, understand that all families face unhappiness that at times can prove overwhelming. But for the three hours of the sing-along, all can secretly wish it weren't so, and can actually pretend that they aren't any wiser.

In the three hours of the sing-along lay a collective wish to retain part of childhood's magic, and more to the point, *The Sound of Music* now took audience members back to their own childhood, both the one actually lived and the one always desired. Seeing the film decades after their first viewing al-lowed audiences who had already seen the movie dozens of times to tell them-selves that they were looking at the film in a new, ironic way, while actually reliving a secret version of themselves and their longed-for happiness. For most, that which had never been obtained loomed larger than all that had actually been acquired.

Okay, the audience told itself, singing a song in the face of the Nazis would likely have resulted in death, not a pictorially stunning mountain escape. And yes, we're all wised up now, as Stephen Sondheim wrote so accurately in *Merrily We Roll Along*:

Now you know
Now you know that life is shitty and full of pain.

But the sing-along phenomenon proved potent precisely because it allowed the audience to drop the corrosive veneer of cynicism and enter into the fun wholeheartedly. Irony is on display, and it's abundant, but it lies in the home-made costumes; for all of the hilarious comments aimed at the screen (surely no one involved in the filming could have anticipated the lascivious comments that ensue when Christopher Plummer's Captain von Trapp appears with a riding crop), sing-along audiences around the globe unabashedly and joyfully enter into the process. (It's no accident that sing-along *Mary Poppins* never re-ally caught on in the same way, because *Poppins* is a little too brisk and effi-cient. As much fun as the film is, it doesn't provide the audience with the same sense of freedom and happily ever after. After all, Mary Poppins disappears at the end of the film, flying off to presumably help another family. Maria's magic remained unique.)

Andrews herself has never attended a sing-along screening, knowing full well that she would be mobbed if ever spotted, although she did muse about attending while wearing "my Elizabeth Taylor wig." The phenomenon both amuses and intrigues the star; with her dry British sense of humor, what she really pondered was "who gets the residuals, that's all I can think of. Certainly not me . . . " She even admitted, in a December 2001 interview with *The Irish Times,* to being flabbergasted that her own doctor in New York told her he had attended one of the sing-alongs. "For heaven's sake," she asked. Why did he—a doctor!—feel compelled to join the mass silliness? His simple answer could serve as the primer for the tens of thousands of his fellow attendees: "Julie, I can't tell you; it is such a catharsis to get up and yell and scream and sing." Which is another way of saying that all social inhibitions about appearing uncool are jettisoned for three hours, and even for a doctor, a happy return to childhood proves the order of the day. And if that return occurs while wearing outlandish costumes fashioned to represent the carburetors clipped from the Nazi automobiles, so much the better. It's like being an eight-year-old on Halloween night again—with a magical belief in an unending future and limitless possibilities still intact.

NEW ITERATIONS

⌇

As *The Sound of Music* entered the twenty-first century, one new production gained instant nationwide attention: a live television version of the stage play starring country/pop singer Carrie Underwood, which aired on NBC television in December 2013.

When famed musical producers Craig Zadan and Neil Meron (*Chicago*) decided to present a live television musical, their instantaneous first choice was the family-friendly *Sound of Music*. On the day after the production aired, critics were once again harsh in their assessments, taking a "this is neither fish nor fowl" approach in their reviews: here was a stage production without an audience, one filmed not in a theater, but on television sets. Was it a stage production? A film? A special television hybrid? What exactly was going on here?

The difference in the criticism this time around lay in the fact that it centered less on *The Sound of Music*'s perceived sentimentality, and much more on the fact that this one-night television event could not hold a candle to either the Robert Wise film or the great Julie Andrews. (Interestingly, at a question-and-answer appearance in honor of the film's fortieth anniversary, Andrews had stated that if the film were ever remade, she felt Cameron Diaz would be the perfect choice to play Maria.) Just as London critics received the 2006 Andrew Lloyd Webber–produced stage revival with much more respect than they had the original West End production, even critics of the television version granted the underlying property its due. Time, it seemed, had granted critics a renewed respect for the sheer professionalism of the basic material.

Instead, the negative critical response this time around lay more with the production than the show itself. Carrie Underwood was praised for her singing while pilloried for her rudimentary acting skills, but R&H president Ted

Chapin, who approved the production, had high words of praise for the star: "What a great work ethic. She worked like a demon and gained everybody's respect. It was a huge risk for her. She's a great singer but not a trained or experienced actress. All credit to her for taking the leap."

Whatever the critical reservations, audiences did not care. The musical proved a ratings smash, with more than twenty million viewers tuning in, and so popular was the broadcast that it was re-aired within two weeks. The instantaneous release of the DVD proved just as popular and within days soared to the top of the sales charts.

As it turned out, it wasn't even the critics who stirred up the most controversy about the production: it was the very public comments of Kym Karath and Charmian Carr, both of whom spoke out against the television version. Watching the show with costars Charmian Carr and Angela Cartwright, Karath pronounced herself "mystified and disappointed," tweeting, "Must admit some scenes are actually painful to watch." Carr's take on Carrie Underwood? "She is not a very good actress."

It was not every fifty-five-year-old musical that could still possess cultural currency in the ever exploding electronic entertainment universe of the twenty-first century, but of ultimately more importance than the live television version was the musical's continued power as a touchstone for artists who parody, pay tribute to, and utilize the film as a springboard for their own cross-cultural explorations.

Rock diva Kylie Minogue not only sang "The Sound of Music" in the genre-busting Baz Luhrmann film *Moulin Rouge,* but also used the recording in her subsequent tours. Even more noticeably, rocker Gwen Stefani sampled Julie Andrews's yodeling of "The Lonely Goatherd" in her music video "Wind It Up," happily admitting to a lifelong obsession with the film. Putting her own decidedly different spin on the totemic items associated with the film, Stefani's version of a nun's habit was a minidress, while the visual motif of her video featured a cubist interpretation of the film's opening scene: green blocks represented the mountainside. Uncool to sample "The Sound of Music?" Stefani couldn't care less and thought just the opposite: "It was a dream of mine to put *The Sound of Music* to a beat because it's my favorite movie. It's one of my biggest inspirations."

By now, some forty feature films have contained references to the movie, ranging from the comedic mid-1960s Woody Allen film *What's Up, Tiger Lily?*

to the decidedly darker *Opposite of Sex* and *Dancer in the Dark*. Imitation, it seems, really is the sincerest form of flattery, because it's the same situation on television, where some thirty shows have referenced the musical, from *Lonely Guy* to the hilarious *Will and Grace* episode where, at a *Sound of Music* sing-along screening, Grace sings so terribly that she scares the children.

Even the nontraditional music scene has horned in on the act, with the Brooklyn Rundfunk Orkestrata, led by producer/arranger Peter Kiesewalter, releasing a *Sound of Music* tribute CD that featured twelve songs radically reinterpreted through the filter of folk, rock, heavy metal, jazz, and funk; in the most clever mash-up of all, the Orkestrata combined "Do-Re-Mi" with the Jackson Five's "ABC." When the ever-vigilant Rodgers and Hammerstein organization first heard about the album, they feared a mockery of the score, and a cease-and-desist order was issued. After meeting with Kiesewalter, however, R&H president Ted Chapin and VP Bert Fink realized that far from parodying *The Sound of Music,* Kiesewalter was simply having fun and reinterpreting music he liked and cared about. The resulting CD actually rendered the score fresh—if occasionally unrecognizable. The von Trapp family itself approved of the Orkestrata's CD, even inviting the group to play at the opening of the new performing arts center at the family lodge. It's an oddball reading of the score, to be certain, but in its overall effect certainly no stranger than the 1959 recording featuring the von Trapps themselves singing selections from the musical, the ultimate case of life imitating art imitating life, and one that leaves the listener inside a dizzying hall of mirrors.

With such multimedia interest in the score, it seemed just a matter of time before *The Sound of Music* would hit the world of dance, which it did in the form of "Fräulein Maria" a first-rate dance tribute created by choreographer Doug Elkins. True to the film's status as touchstone of family restoration, Elkins's inspiration to create the piece came after his divorce in 2003. Having watched the movie repeatedly with his son Liam and daughter Gigi, he looked upon the dance as a means of honoring his children. With the blessing of the Rodgers and Hammerstein Organization, Elkins created a dance/performance art piece that featured three Marias dancing to the score, one of whom was an overweight man in a pink dress. While definitely chuckle-inducing, "Fäulein Maria" functioned not just as parody, but also as heartfelt tribute, the choreography emphasizing the yearning subtext that infuses the film: Maria's search for love and personal freedom combined with the children's wish to reconnect with their father.

Debuting at the hip New York club Joe's Pub in December 2006, Elkins's piece mixed dance styles ranging from hip-hop to Martha Graham, all of them set to the songs "The Sound of Music," "Do-Re-Mi," "So Long, Farewell," and "Climb Ev'ry Mountain." In Elkins's cleverly, and subtly wrought piece, it all comes through clearly, right down to the "Climb Ev'ry Mountain" solo danced by a man in a hoodie. Named one of the top-ten dance performances of 2008 by Joan Acocella in the *New Yorker* magazine, this puppet-filled, gender-bending performance piece proved a great popular success and nabbed a New York Dance and Performance Bessie Award.

Rock videos, funk orchestras, modern dance pieces: successes all, but the most eye-catching new iteration proved to be *Sound of Music*–inspired flash mobs, in which hundreds of men and women begin dancing in choreographed precision to the film's soundtrack. The best known of the flash mobs was filmed in Antwerp's train station, which in and of itself is strikingly reminiscent of the von Trapp villa's interior. As the music started, hundreds of seemingly unconnected men and women began to dance to "Do-Re-Mi." As Julie Andrews's vocal took off, a rap-inspired riff was laid in, a cheering crowd gathered, and the dancers accelerated their pace until the entire piece ended in wavelike rows of precision collapse. Antwerp's flash mob may have started as a television stunt to cast the lead in a local production of *The Sound of Music,* but it has lived on in YouTube popularity—29,000,000 hits and counting—long after the local production shut. Goofy, fun, and most of all infectious, the video is still replayed endlessly on computer screens around the world, introducing the score to a young Web audience undreamed of by Rodgers, Hammerstein, and Wise.

29

FULL CIRCLE

REPRISE ON BROADWAY

As the stock and amateur productions of this most profitable show in the entire Rodgers and Hammerstein catalogue continued to proliferate (including two productions in which Maria's granddaughter Elisabeth von Trapp-Hall portrayed her grandmother), momentum began to grow for the musical's first major Broadway revival since the original production closed in June of 1963.

In the conservative, revival happy atmosphere of late-twentieth-century Broadway, the abnormally long wait appeared to be the result of two overwhelming questions: How do you compete with the most beloved movie musical of all time? What can compare with Julie Andrews singing in the Alps?

It finally being judged that enough time had passed since the release of the movie, *The Sound of Music* returned to Broadway on March 12, 1998, the date of Agathe von Trapp's eighty-fifth birthday and the sixtieth anniversary of the Anschluss. Starring the talented Broadway stalwart Rebecca Luker as Maria and Australian Michael Siberry as Captain von Trapp, the production received mildly favorable reviews; time had mellowed some, but not all, of the critical antipathy toward the piece, and the show still remained an irresistible target for some. In his mixed review, Ben Brantley, the chief drama critic of *The New York Times,* praised certain elements but still managed to stick in the knife: "On one level, it will always nauseate." The show settled in for a pleasant fifteen-month run, which ultimately did not return its capitalization, but in some ways, it was the events that occurred nine months later on Wednesday, December 2, 1998, that proved almost more memorable than the run of the show itself.

When the von Trapp family was honored by the State of Salzburg with the Golden Decoration of Honor for its Family Relief Effort after World War II, and the seven movie children received the Mozart Medal for the part *The Sound of Music* played in bringing tourists to Salzburg, six of the von Trapps—Johannes the youngest at age sixty—stood up and sang together in public for the first time in forty years.

After years in which the von Trapps had regarded *The Sound of Music* like a nice relative who had overstayed her welcome, family members now embraced the musical with genuine affection. The family sang "Silent Night," first in German and then in English, after which Johannes announced that the family would close by singing one song they had never sung together in public: "Edelweiss." The crowd rose to its feet, everyone in the room singing along in heartfelt fashion. At the song's conclusion, Georg and Agathe's daughter Maria turned to the seven screen children, and as recounted by Charmian Carr, grasped their hands and smilingly proclaimed: "Now you are family."

COMING HOME

In the fifty years since the von Trapps had left their homeland, conflicted feelings about the family still abounded. Some felt a lingering resentment that the family had "abandoned" their homeland, yet many thousands more remained grateful for Maria's heroic post-war relief efforts. As her legend grew through the years, so, too, did the positive feelings about the family, and in 1967 Maria was awarded the highly prestigious Honorary Cross First Class for Science and Art Cultural Endeavors.

Respect for the family took another quantum leap forward when, exactly thirty years later, on the fiftieth anniversary of Georg's death, the Austrian Military Academy visited the Trapp Family Lodge to honor the captain with a full military graveside ceremony. Eighty-nine cadets from the Theresianum Military Academy, who had three years earlier chosen Baron von Trapp as their class patron, were invited by the family to spend the weekend at the Lodge. The highlight of the ceremonies was a morning Mass attended by members of the family, with the cadets standing watch during a performance of Franz Schubert's "German Mass." At the completion of Schubert's mass, the cadets lay a wreath at the grave of Maria and Georg. Granted, the choice of the "German Mass" seemed a strange one, given the baron's anti-German feelings at the time of the Anschluss, but the sentiment behind the performance proved genuine.

And so, after the graveside service and the revival of the musical on Broadway, it made a perfect kind of sense that the circle fully closed when, for the first time ever, *The Sound of Music* opened onstage in Salzburg, at the Landestheater on October 23, 2011. Seventy-three years had now passed since the family had fled Austria, and the theater's artistic director Carl Philip von Maldeghem sensed that the time was right for a production. The subject of the Nazis was no longer taboo and, von Maldeghem felt, the musical could help educate young twenty-first-century audiences whose grasp of history seemed shaky or nonexistent.

In the view of Johannes von Trapp: "The cultural and underlying elephant in the room was and remains the Nazis. We left the country and most Austrians didn't. Austria hasn't yet confronted that fully—many pretend they were invaded, and while that's true, the invaders were also welcome. . . . That defensiveness about the country's actual history endured in dismissing the play as American kitsch. . . . It was an Austrian cast—three different groups of children performed the roles of the von Trapps, lots of parents were involved—it was an Austrian production through and through. Seeing it performed by Austrians in Austria, and realizing how well received the play was, went a long way for me in resolving these issues."

The Salzburg production faced the issue of Hitler head on: with actors dressed in Nazi uniforms standing guard by each of the theater's exits during the climax of act two, there was no possibility that the audience at this production could escape Austria's Nazi-era past. Far from being upset by this reminder, the audience embraced the show wholeheartedly with a minutes-long standing ovation on opening night. At that opening-night curtain call, Nicholas Hammond and Johannes (with his children Sam and Kristina) walked on stage to a roaring welcome from the crowd. Reconciliation between Salzburg, the von Trapps, and *The Sound of Music* was complete.

Having made peace with *The Sound of Music*'s legacy, Salzburg now hosts *Sound of Music* concerts in Mirabell Gardens every summer, and *Sound of Music* postage stamps are sold at local post offices. Even those who previously criticized the film's ersatz version of Austrian culture now acknowledge the value of the film as a worldwide calling card for Austria, a help particularly welcome in the 1990s when Jörg Haider's anti-immigrant Freedom Party caused image problems for the country. Hollywood make-believe or not, *The Sound of Music* has lured hundreds of thousands of happy moviegoers to the Austrian locations so lovingly presented onscreen, and not so coincidentally, enticed them to spend a great deal of money around Salzburg in the process. Hearty capitalist Maria von Trapp would have approved.

30.

AND IN THE END . . .

⌇

It may be that the sheer weight of the film's popularity has simply worn down its detractors, or even more likely, that with the era of the 1960s cultural wars at an end the film is now evaluated on its own merits, but a full-scale critical reevaluation of *The Sound of Music* movie has begun to take place. In *The New York Times,* home of Bosley Crowther's scathing opening-night review in 1965, columnist Todd Purdum addressed the fortieth anniversary of the film's opening with lavish and genuine praise: "Forty years and a lot less innocence later, in the era of film as theme-park thrill ride and prepackaged comic-book sequel, a little artful manipulation seems a small enough price, and *The Sound of Music* a big enough blessing. Let it bloom and grow."

In a twenty-first century awash in a collective addiction to technology, isolation, and a mistrust of the sincere run rampant, and with seemingly the entire world approaching life as if guesting on David Letterman while exchanging ironic anecdotes with the host, the heart-on-its-sleeve emotion displayed by *The Sound of Music* now registers as nothing short of startling

Films like *The Sound of Music,* or a twenty-first-century feel-good equivalent such as the television series *Downton Abbey,* do more than take people away from their technology-obsessed lives. They provide safety, an actual refuge from lives that have grown both fragmented and increasingly absurd. Even when placed against the background of world wars, or perhaps especially when placed against the darkening atmosphere of 1930s Salzburg or post–World War I England, *The Sound of Music* and *Downton Abbey* restore order and a sense of decorum. In our overly frenetic lives, they give us breathing room, a break from today's onrushing relentless pace while simultaneously tapping into the yearning of millions for respect, civility, and manners.

Three hours with Maria, seven children, a dozen show tunes, and a passel of nuns, and for millions of viewers the universal fear of losing one's place in life is banished. The endless worries of our everyday lives—expired food, dangerous toys—seem puny next to the larger-than-life von Trapps conquering Nazis and the Alps alike. For men and women whose lives seem like an endless argument without any clear winner, the film is not a sugarcoated lie. The predictability of the plot and the inevitability of the happy ending are precisely what comfort.

What *The Sound of Music* does, in a first-rate old-school professional fashion, is reassure, telling us that our dreams are worthwhile, that any obstacles and fears can be overcome with hard work, a show tune or three, and most important of all, the love of family. In such a universe lies seemingly complete happiness, with edges squared off and each piece finding its mate like a completed jigsaw puzzle: brother to sister, husband to wife, parent to child. Family. In the universe of *The Sound of Music,* love conquers all, and in our collective connection to the innocence displayed onscreen lies a bridge to our own lost innocence, as well as the hope, faint but still beating, that goodness may just win out.

The personification of that goodness, for fifty years and counting, remains Julie Andrews, and when Andrews, Plummer, and all seven screen children reunited on Oprah Winfrey's television show in October of 2010, it felt in part like a passing of the torch; with the onscreen von Trapp family looking on, the great grandchildren of Georg von Trapp sang "Edelweiss" as footage of the film played behind them. (Having banded together to perform around the world as "The von Trapps," these four grandchildren of Werner von Trapp have enjoyed substantial success, singing American and Austrian folk songs and performing with major symphony orchestras. They have recorded six CDs, including "Dream a Little Dream of Me" with hipster multi-lingual group Pink Martini; that CD includes a rendition of "Edelweiss" complete with guest vocalist Chairman Carr.) The fourth generation of von Trapps were now a public part of *The Sound of Music* legacy, and Julie Andrews, the forever young Maria von Trapp onscreen, now reigned as the elder stateswoman of the gathering, a family/celluloid matriarch.

Andrews has referred to the film as "a very happy accident all around," but of course that modest statement couldn't be further from the truth. *The Sound of Music* worked because the most talented professionals in Hollywood were all working at the top of their games, led by the newest and brightest musical star in town, Julie Andrews. She made it all look so easy and natural that the audience collectively assumed Maria von Trapp really did sing a hymn to nature while striding the hills. Right over there—just beyond the crest of that mountain—right where the von Trapps fled to freedom. . . .

Let others try to appear hip. Julie, like *The Sound of Music* itself, presents herself as resolutely old school and makes no apologies for it. She remains herself, a woman with perfect diction and a voice for the ages who played a would-be nun with such skill that audiences around the world felt "This is the way it should be done—the way we wish we could do it ourselves. Effortless." If, as Schopenhauer said, "Talent is like a marksman who hits a target that the rest cannot reach," then in *The Sound of Music,* Julie Andrews hits the target while making it all look easy. Her performance remains a present for audiences, granting a heightened form of pleasure, the sort of pure joy found in an idealized world.

Yes, the image of the nearly perfect Maria von Trapp frozen in time onscreen may have felt more than occasionally constricting to Andrews, but those days are, for the most part, long past, and the actress is grateful for the joy the film has brought to millions. Zealously guarding the image of herself in that verdant Mehlweg meadow, twirling and singing for all the world, she remains a one-woman embodiment of life as even the most cynical of adults wishes it could be. Maria von Trapp a burden for Andrews? Not a chance. Secure in the knowledge that her work in *The Sound of Music* continues to enchant audiences around the world, she understands just how much of a gift to others her family films have been: "I just think it's a pretty nice cross that I just have to bear."

Once, when asked how she'd like to be remembered, Andrews, with a hint of tears in her eyes, came up with a response that managed to strike a note at once both appealing and slightly melancholy, but most of all, comforting. It is, in its own way, a fitting epitaph for *The Sound of Music* itself, a spot-on explanation of just why this musical film, mostly adored, occasionally reviled, but certainly a permanent part of our collective consciousness, has endured for half a century, and will continue to do so for half a century more:

"I guess it would be something along the lines of 'She had a capacity to make people happy, to make them feel warm.' . . . Look, I'm realistic enough to realize that life is horrible and brutish for most people, so that what we do as entertainers can sometimes seem fairly frivolous. But because there is so much out there that is harsh, maybe it's not such a bad idea if we can try to soften it in whatever way we can."

Old-fashioned? Yes. And timeless.

NOTES

1. A VERY GOOD PLACE TO START

3 "When you sing, you pray twice," Laurence Maslon, *The Sound of Music Companion* (New York: Simon and Schuster, 2006), 74.

3 "finally got so angry I yelled 'That's enough!," Julia Antopol Hirsch, *The Sound of Music: The Making of America's Favorite Movie* (Chicago: Contemporary Books, 1993), 150.

2. HOW DO YOU SOLVE A PROBLEM LIKE . . .

6 "insecurities that plagued her all of her life," "My Favorite Things: Julie Andrews Remembers," *The Sound of Music* 40th Anniversary Edition, Johannes von Trapp commentary, 20th Century Fox, 2005.

7 "suddenly it occurred to me," *Climbed Every Mountain: The Story Behind* The Sound of Music, BBC documentary with Sue Perkins, 2012 Northern Upstart productions.

7 "Now I had heard from my uncle," Ibid.

8 "She did everything 100 percent," *The von Trapp Family: Harmony and Discord*, Johannes von Trapp, A&E Biography, 2000, DVD.

8 "Who's Maria?," Julia Antopol Hirsch, *The Sound of Music: The Making of America's Favorite Movie* (Chicago: Contemporary Books, Inc., 1993), 33.

8 "a little strange," *Climbed Every Mountain: The Story Behind* The Sound of Music.

8 when the family traveled to Salzburg in 1950, *The Sound of Music* 30th Anniversary Edition, "*The Sound of Music* Gallery," researched, written, and assembled by Michael Matessino, 20th Century Fox 1995, DVD.

9 "My mother was absolutely unsuited," *The Sound of Music* 40th Anniversary Edition, "My Favorite Things: Julie Andrews Remembers," Johannes von Trapp.

9 "I had no manners," *Climbed Every Mountain: The Story Behind* The Sound of Music.

9 "an awfully strict person," Georg Steinitz interview with author, January 14, 2014.

10 "She needed, all the time," *Vanity Fair,* June 1998.

10 "My satchel looked exactly," Maria Augusta Trapp, *The Story of the Trapp Family Singers* (New York: Harper Collins, 1949), 15.

10 "She had a horrible dress on," *The von Trapp Family: Harmony and Discord*.

10 The captain executed a slight bow, *Climbed Every Mountain: The Story Behind* The Sound of Music.

10 "Led by a sober-faced young girl," Trapp, *The Story of the Trapp Family Singers*, 18.

11 "We loved our signals," Agathe von Trapp, *Memories Before and After* The Sound of Music (New York: Harper Collins, 2010), 75.

11 "I grew up without being kissed," Hirsch, *The Sound of Music: The Making of America's Favorite Movie*, 204.

11 "Only one thing is necessary," Trapp, *The Story of the Trapp Family Singers*, 311.

11 "Poppa says he will marry you," *Climbed Every Mountain: The Story Behind* The Sound of Music.

11 "Do you think I should marry Gustl?," Agathe von Trapp, *Memories Before and After* The Sound of Music, 188.

11 "I think if it is the will of God," Ibid.

12 "I can't say I know it or I don't know it," *Vanity Fair*, June 1998.

12 "When she first came it was heaven on Earth," *The von Trapp Family Harmony and Discord*.

12 "We just let it happen," Alex Witchel, "A Few Favorite Things the Musical Left Out," *New York Times*, January 1, 1998.

12 "All my happiness shattered," Trapp, *The Story of the Trapp Family Singers,* 59.

12 "They didn't sing. I couldn't understand this," *Climbed Every Mountain: The Story Behind* The Sound of Music.

12 "Sometimes our house must have sounded," "Maria von Trapp, *Sound of Music* Daughter Dies at 99," *New York Times,* February 23, 2014.

12 "Thanks to our father," Agathe von Trapp, *Memories Before and After* The Sound of Music, 198.

13 "That 'but' was the decision of our lives," *Climbed Every Mountain: The Story Behind* The Sound of Music.

13 "None of us knew then," Trapp, *The Story of the Trapp Family Singers*, 102.

14 "They both probably had unfulfilled dreams," *Climbed Every Mountain: The Story Behind* The Sound of Music.

14 "He slowly but surely molded us," Ibid.

14 "We were intoxicated with music," Trapp, *The Story of the Trapp Family Singers*, 104.

15 "You have gold in your throats," Mark Bortridge, "The Real Maria," *The Independent*, October 29, 2006.

15 "only the solemn family resolution," Trapp, *The Story of the Trapp Family Singers*, 106.

15 "He didn't like the idea," *The von Trapp Family: Harmony and Discord*.

15 "If one didn't know," Trapp, *The Story of the Trapp Family Singers,* 122.

16 "the love for your homeland comes even before the love for your family," Ibid., 116.

16 "He'd put ground glass," Ibid., 117–118.

16 "remembered with gratitude," Agathe von Trapp, *Memories Before and After* The Sound of Music, 133.

16 "We went from being rich," *The Julie Andrews Hour,* January 20, 1973.

17 "Don't they know geography," Hirsch, *The Sound of Music: The Making of America's Favorite Movie*, 75.

17 "In Hollywood you make your own geography," Ibid.

17 a private residence for Adolf Hitler when he visited, *The Sound of Music* 40th Anniversary, Johannes von Trapp commentary.

17 "I really believe everything was arranged by God," Witchel, *New York Times*.

18 "The Trapp Family Choir—sounds," Trapp, *The Story of the Trapp Family Singers*, 184.

18 "It was difficult," *Climbed Every Mountain: The Story Behind* The Sound of Music.

19 "Traveling with the family," Ibid.

19 "He said mass every day," Ibid.

19 beginning with the night a fly, *The von Trapp Family: Harmony and Discord.*

19 "If you can tell stories," *The Sound of Music* 30th Anniversary Edition, "*The Sound of Music*: From Fact to Phenomenon."

20 "My mother was the bundle of energy," Johannes von Trapp, in interview with author, January 9, 2014.

20 "She had a volatile temper," *The von Trapp Family: Harmony and Discord.*

20 "My grandfather didn't want to be in public," *Climbed Every Mountain: The Story Behind* The Sound of Music.

20 "starting to bubble up," Ibid.

20 "My father saw the house," *The Sound of Music* 30th Anniversary Edition, "*The Sound of Music*: From Fact to Phenomenon."

21 "we sort of eased into it," *The von Trapp Family: Harmony and Discord.*

21 "like a forest fire," Trapp, *The Story of the Trapp Family Singers*, 275.

21 "From then on only one thing matters," Maria von Trapp, *Yesterday, Today, and Forever* (Green Forest Arkansas: New Leaf Press, 1975), 103.

22 "Mother, remember the old saying," Trapp, *The Story of the Trapp Family Singers*, 218.

22 "No one can console like a mother," von Trapp, *Yesterday, Today, and Forever,* 151.

22 "After the seven fat years," Trapp, *The Story of the Trapp Family Singers,* 306.

22 "the memorable year," Ibid., 303.

22 "this (recovery) cannot be attributed to medicine," Ibid., 307.

23 "Mourning is a surrender to the illusion that death is final," Frederick Nolan, *The Sound of Their Music: The Story of Rodgers & Hammerstein* (New York: Applause Theatre & Cinema Books, 2002), 264.

23 "the complete absence," von Trapp, *Yesterday, Today, and Forever,* 167.

23 "One can go to hell," von Trapp, *Yesterday, Today, and Forever,* 168.

23 "My mother was never very good," *The von Trapp Family: Harmony and Discord.*

3. BROADWAY AND RODGERS AND HAMMERSTEIN

25 "The combined sales," Maslon, *The Sound of Music Companion*, 88.

26 "My mother had a bit," *Climbed Every Mountain: The Story Behind* The Sound of Music.

26 "She felt a religious mission," Johannes von Trapp, interview with author, January 9, 2014.

26 Richard Halliday finally hit upon, Max Wilk, *The Making of The Sound of Music* (London: Routledge Publishing, 2007).

27 because Loewe did not share his partner's enthusiasm, Meryle Secrest, *Somewhere for Me: A Biography of Richard Rodgers* (New York: Knopf, 2001), 277.

27 many of the show's fifty-two backers, *New York Times*, November 22, 1968.

28 ranking among the twenty most influential, Nolan, *The Sound of Their Music*, 265.

28 fifty percent of all Americans could be classified as middle class, Paul Monaco, *Ribbons in Time—Movies and Society Since 1945* (Bloomington: Indiana University Press, 1987), 94.

29 "My father believed," *The Sound of Music* 30th Anniversary Edition, "*The Sound of Music*: From Fact to Phenomenon."

29 "gave him the breath of life," Richard Rodgers, *Musical Stages: An Autobiography* (New York: Random House, 1975), 333.

29 "Chemically depressed is what we'd call it now," Ibid., 1995 edition, viii.

29 "He was never as happy as he wanted to be," Ibid., 333

29 "almost to the day he died," Ibid., 303.

30 "a grave, quiet, very tall," *Sound of Music* 40th Anniversary Edition, "My Favorite Things: Julie Andrews Remembers."

30 "He always looked at the positive," Secrest, *Somewhere for Me: A Biography of Richard Rodgers*, 352.

30 "We're very likely to get thrown off our balance," Ibid., 335.

31 "Much has been written of the success," Howard Lindsay, *New York Times*, December 4, 1966.

32 "the quickest job we've ever done," Nolan, *The Sound of Their Music: The Story of Rodgers & Hammerstein*, 249.

33 much to Rodgers's delight, *Sound of Music* Original Cast Recording Columbia Records, liner notes taken from Richard Rodgers, *Musical Stages*, 1959.

33 sketched in "sound of summer," Hugh Fordin, *Getting to Know Him: A Biography of Oscar Hammerstein II* (New York: Random House, 1977), 344.

34 "What does God want me to do," *The Sound of Music* 30th Anniversary Edition, "*The Sound of Music* Gallery."

34 "Climb Ev'ry Mountain/High Though it Seem," Nolan, *The Sound of Their Music: The Story of Rodgers & Hammerstein,* 256.

35 Maria taught Martin, Ibid., 249.

35 "Mary and my mother," *The Sound of Music* 40th Anniversary Edition, Johannes von Trapp Commentary.

35 "I knew that my part required," Wilk, *The Making of The Sound of Music,* 146.

36 "deceptive simplicity," Fordin, *Getting to Know Him: A Biography of Oscar Hammerstein II*, 353.

36 "The lyricist seems increasingly," Ibid.

36 "fit any homeland you are passionate about," *The Sound of Music* 40th Anniversary Edition, Julie Andrews commentary.

36 "I have only seen Oscar," Wilk, *The Making of The Sound of Music,* 144.

36 "It broke your heart," Ibid.

37 in the recollection of Anna Crouse, *The von Trapp Family Harmony and Discord.*

37 "I don't remember when the family wasn't well known," Johannes von Trapp, interview with author, January 9, 2014.

37 "not only too sweet for words," Walter Kerr, *New York Herald Tribune,* November 17, 1959.

37 "Practically anyone could write," Wilk, *The Making of The Sound of Music,* 183.

37 "I wonder why nobody ever did it?" Ibid.

37 "Rodgers and Hammerstein's Great Leap Backwards," Secrest, *Somewhere for Me: A Biography of Richard Rodgers*, 350.

38 "Anyone who can't, on occasion," *Sound of Music* Original Cast Recording, Columbia Records.

38 "would not pinch Johanna," Trapp, *The Story of the Trapp Famly Singers*, 68.

38 "It was very hard to convince her," Ibid.

38 the work of the Italian music theorists, *The Sound of Music* New Broadway Cast Recording, liner notes by Theodore S. Chapin, 1998.

39 when another famous Maria, Ibid.

39 "With better than two million dollars," Wilk, *The Making of The Sound of Music,* 149.

40 Rodgers and Hammerstein would receive the lion's share, Joan Barthel, "The Biggest Money Making Movie of All Time—How Come?" *New York Times*, November 20, 1966.

4. 20TH CENTURY-FOX—GOING, GOING, ALMOST GONE

42 "Today people go to see a movie," Monaco, *Ribbons in Time: Movies and Society Since 1945,* 43.

42 "During the second week of March 1960 alone," Ibid., 12.

42 "Their uncompromisingly sentimental," Wilk, *The Making of The Sound of Music,* 163.

43 *"You've got to be taught to be afraid" South Pacific,* music by Richard Rodgers, lyrics by Oscar Hammerstein, 1949.

5. THE SWEET SMELL OF ERNEST LEHMAN

46 "It would be unthinkable for a writer," American Film Institute: Seminar with Ernest Lehman (AFI: Beverly Hills, California), March 31, 1976.

47 "doctor's prescription for fourteen days without Billy Wilder," Sam Wasson, *Fifth Avenue, 5 A.M.: Audrey Hepburn, Breakfast at Tiffany's, and the Dawn of the Modern Woman* (New York: Harper Collins, 2010), 44.

47 "someday this show," *The Sound of Music* 30th Anniversary Edition, "Ernest Lehman: Master Storyteller."

47 It would, he felt, stand the test of time, Max Wilk, *Overture and Finale: Rodgers & Hammerstein and the Creation of Their Two Greatest Hits* (New York: Backstage Books, 1993) p. 163.

47 "wistful yearning," Ibid., 167.

48 "This is a situation," Jeanine Basinger, *Gene Kelly* (New York: Pyramid Books, 1976), 83.

49 "I think that much of good screenwriting," American Film Institute: Seminar with Ernest Lehman (AFI: Beverly Hills, California), March 31, 1976.

49 "Lehman later admitted," *The Sound of Music* 30th Anniversary Edition, "Ernest Lehman: Master Storyteller."

49 landed on the front pages, Barthel, *New York Times.*

49 "you must need the money," Wilk, *Overture and Finale: Rodgers & Hammerstein and the Creation of Their Two Greatest Hits,* 167.

49 "He led me out the front door," Ibid.

6. SIX CHARACTERS IN SEARCH OF A DIRECTOR

51 "What about the greatest director in the world," *The Sound of Music* 30th Anniversary Edition, "Ernest Lehman: Master Storyteller."

51 "Ernie, I hated the show," Wilk, *Overture and Finale: Rodgers & Hammerstein and the Creation of Their Two Greatest Hits,* 168–169.

52 "They want me to make this picture," Jan Herman, *William Wyler: A Talent for Trouble* (New York: Putnam, 1995), 432.

52 "I knew it would be a success," Ibid., 420.

52 "Lehman kept after me," William Wyler and Axel Madsen, *William Wyler: The Authorized Biography* (New York: Thomas Y. Crowell Company, 1973), 365.

52 "That's your job," *The Sound of Music* 30th Anniversary Edition, "Ernest Lehman: Master Storyteller."

52 'It is not to be a picture," Ibid.

53 "It was hilarious," Wyler and Madsen, *William Wyler: The Authorized Biography*, 366.

53 "We have a scene of the 1936 Anschluss," Ibid.

53 "We survived that," Ibid., 367.

53 "As soon as Wyler stated," Jan Herman, *William Wyler: A Talent for Trouble* (New York: Putnam, 1995), 420.

53 "I knew the movie wasn't really a political thing," Wyler and Madsen, *William Wyler: The Authorized Biography*, 366.

53 In the recollection of Maurice Zuberano, Hirsch, *The Sound of Music: The Making of America's Favorite Movie*, 78.

54 Wyler started a screaming match, *The Sound of Music* 30th Anniversary Edition, "Ernest Lehman: Master Storyteller."

54 "No musical with swastikas in it," Hirsch, *The Sound of Music: The Making of America's Favorite Movie*, 13.

54 "Willy had all but signed," Herman, *William Wyler: A Talent for Trouble*, 421.

54 "I can't bear to make a picture," Ibid.

54 "Go tell your client," *The Sound of Music* 30th Anniversary Edition, "Ernest Lehman: Master Storyteller."

54 "We all ranted and raved," Wilk, *Overture and Finale: Rodgers & Hammerstein and the Creation of Their Two Greatest Hits*, 172.

57 "What he did brilliantly," *The Sound of Music* 40th Anniversary Edition, "My Favorite Things: Julie Andrews Remembers."

57 Having conceived the opening number, Hirsch, *The Sound of Music: The Making of America's Favorite Movie*, 33.

58 "If you say yes," *The Sound of Music* 30th Anniversary Edition, "Ernest Lehman: Master Storyteller."

58 "You son of a bitch," Ibid.

58 "The best movies leave audiences feeling," Robert Wise, American Film Institute Lifetime Achievement Award acceptance speech, February 19, 1998.

59 "speed of the whip pans," Sergio Leemann, *Robert Wise on His Films: From Editing Room to Director's Chair* (Los Angeles: Silman-James Press, 1995), 21.

59 "I honestly believe," Georg Steinitz, interview with author, January 14, 2014.

60 "cut by the studio gardener," *New York Times,* September 15, 2005, "Robert Wise, Film Director, Dies at 91"

60 "If a scene seems a trifle slow," Leemann, *Robert Wise on His Films: From Editing Room to Director's Chair*, 8.

62 "Taken from the original," Ibid., 43.

63 "knee deep in snow," Saul Chaplin, *The Golden Age of Movie Musicals and Me* (Norman: University of Oklahoma Press, 1994), 211.

7. DESIGNING *THE SOUND OF MUSIC*

65 "Boris was a tremendous asset," *Sound of Music* 40th Anniversary Edition, Robert Wise commentary.

65 "master at putting reality," Ibid.

66 "no fewer than 750 Chinese figures," *New York Morning Telegraph*, December 19, 1941.

67 "I have always enjoyed a complete rapport," "Rene L. Ash Interviews Art Director Boris Leven," *Film Index*, 1972.

67 "Among his associates," *Variety*, January 28, 1976.

69 "I felt he could bring the right touch," *Sound of Music* 40th Anniversary Edition, Robert Wise commentary.

69 "The only time I watch the editing," *New York Post,* July 7, 1997.

70 "by feel, not by rote," Ibid.

70 "Try to make the best possible version," *New York Times,* July 22, 1997.

70 It was, he felt, Ibid.

70 "I valued Bill's judgment," *Sound of Music* 40th Anniversary Edition, Robert Wise commentary.

70 "Her special talent," Robert Wise, *New York Times*, March 13, 1981.

71 At one point, Deborah Nadoolman Landis, *Hollywood Sketchbook: A Century of Costume Illustration* (New York: Harper Design, 2012), 244.

71 "To this hour," *New York Times*, March 13, 1981.

71 "pathologically shy," Landis, *Hollywood Sketchbook: A Century of Costume Illustration*, 244.

71 "I learned to read and write," Ibid.

72 "an affinity for the past," *New York Times*, March 13, 1981.

72 "I was part of the costume congress," Ibid.

72 "DeMille was the most vicious man," Ibid.

73 "I'll let my imagination," Landis, *Hollywood Sketchbook: A Century of Costume Illustration*, 247.

73 "She very seldom tries to impose," *New York Times*, March 13, 1981.

73 "The canvas is the script," Ibid.

73 "Dorothy Jeakins avoided," *The Sound of Music*: 30th Anniversary Edition, "*The Sound of Music:* From Fact to Phenomenon."

8. JULIE DOOLITTLE POPPINS VON TRAPP

75 "*The Sound of Music* was the actual naked Julie Andrews on the screen," *The Sound of Music* 40th Anniversary Edition, "My Favorite Things: Julie Andrews Remembers."

76 "If you're asked to do that show," *The Sound of Music* 40th Anniversary Edition, Julie Andrews commentary.

77 "I think it was the most generous piece of advice," Ibid.

77 watched by an estimated 107 million people, Ethan Mordden, *Rodgers & Hammerstein* (New York: Harry N. Abrams, 1992).

77 "the greatest screen test ever," *The Sound of Music* 40th Anniversary Edition, "My Favorite Things: Julie Andrews Remembers."

77 "We thought we were so clever," *The Sound of Music* 40th Anniversary Edition, "My Favorite Things: Julie Andrews Remembers."

79 "Whether it's a man or woman," Wasson, *Fifth Avenue, 5 A.M.: Audrey Hepburn, Breakfast at Tiffany's, and the Dawn of the Modern Woman*, 21.

79 girls next door possessing, Tom Santopietro, *Considering Doris Day* (New York: St. Martin's Press, 2007).

80 "Let's go sign her right now," *The Sound of Music*: 30th Anniversary Edition, "*The Sound of Music:* From Fact to Phenomenon."

80 "I had seen her play in *My Fair Lady,*" Herman, *William Wyler: A Talent for Trouble,* 420.

80 "right through the camera," Richard Sterling, *Julie Andrews: An Intimate Biography* (New York: St. Martins Press, 2007), 5.

80 "never dreamed," *Rodgers and Hammerstein: The Sound of Movies,* Julie Andrews commentary, directed by Ken Burns, 20th Century Fox and Rodgers and Hammerstein Organization, 1995.

81 "Having done *The Americanization of Emily,*" *The Sound of Music:* 30th Anniversary Edition, "*The Sound of Music:* From Fact to Phenomenon."

81 "Now what are we going to do," Ibid.

81 "too mush," " Sterling, *Julie Andrews: An Intimate Biography,* 80.

81 "Bob Wise Will Curb Schmaltz," *Variety,* February 4, 1964.

81 "He was just the right man," Jeanine Basinger, interview with author, April 29, 2014.

82 "You must see the picture clearly," Sterling, *Julie Andrews: An Intimate Biography,* 145.

82 "That seventy-piece orchestra," *The Sound of Music* 40th Anniversary Edition, "My Favorite Things: Julie Andrews Remembers."

83 "learn music instantly," Chaplin, *The Golden Age of Movie Musicals and Me,* 219.

9. CAPTAIN GEORG VAN TRAPP

84 "I agree with W.C. Fields," *The Sound of Music* 40th Anniversary Edition, Christopher Plummer Commentary.

84 "I felt we must go," *The Sound of Music* 40th Anniversary Edition, Robert Wise commentary.

85 "I just knew he would give it an edge," *The Sound of Music* 30th Anniversary Edition. "*The Sound of Music:* From Fact to Phenomenon."

85 "I'm a good mimic," *Playbill,* November 2012.

85 "Sometimes being an actor," Radio interview, Christopher Plummer with Steve Gray from set of *The Sound of Music.*

86 "If you fly over to London," *The Sound of Music* 40th Anniversary Edition, Robert Wise commentary

86 Plummer recalled that Mary Martin, *The Sound of Music* 40th Anniversary Edition, "My Favorite Things: Julie Andrews Remembers."

86 "a tyrannical saint," *The Sound of Music,* 45th Anniversary Edition, "Maria and the Musical."

87 "Bob was the last of the gentleman directors," *The Sound of Music* 40th Anniversary Edition, Christopher Plummer commentary.

87 "I love the stage but movies," Radio interview, Christopher Plummer with Steve Gray from set of *The Sound of Music.*

87 "As long as von Trapp remains," Letter from Christopher Plummer to Robert Wise, 2/10/64, *The Sound of Music* 30th Anniversary Edition, "*The Sound of Music* Gallery."

88 "This guy was insisting," Wilk, *The Making of The Sound of Music,* 175.

88 "Ernie said many times," *The Sound of Music* 40th Anniversary Edition, Robert Wise commentary.

88 "Ernie Lehman listened to my suggestions," *The Sound of Music* 40th Anniversary Edition, Christopher Plummer commentary.

88 "camouflage with a sharp mind," Charmian Carr with Jean A. S. Strauss, *Forever Liesel* (New York: Viking Press, 2000), 61.

88 "The baroness had too much humor," *The Sound of Music* 30th Anniversary Edition, "*The Sound of Music:* From Fact to Phenomenon."

88 "the most boring man I ever met!," *The Sound of Music* 40th Anniversary Edition, Christopher Plummer commentary.

88 "It was much more of a story than in the play," *The Sound of Music* 40th Anniversary Edition, "Julie Andrews and Christopher Plummer: A Reminiscence," 20th Century Fox, 2005.

89 "I hope something can be done," Letter from Christopher Plummer to Robert Wise, *The Sound of Music* 30th Anniversary Edition.

89 "I suggested to him," *The Sound of Music* 40th Anniversary Edition, Christopher Plummer commentary.

89 " 'If you look at that,' " Ibid.

89 "We were in the middle—on that rope bridge," Ibid.

10. A CAPTAIN WITH SEVEN CHILDREN

90 "I selected those children," *The Sound of Music* 40th Anniversary Edition, Robert Wise commentary.

90 "I didn't worry so much," Ibid.

92 "We ultimately realized," Carr with Strauss, *Forever Liesl*, 50.

92 "solid professional," Dee Dee Wood, interview with author, May 8, 2014.

92 "Changing my last name," Carr with Strauss, *Forever Liesl*, 125.

92 "They felt my eyes were too blue," *The Sound of Music* 30th Anniversary Edition, "*The Sound of Music:* From Fact to Phenomenon."

92 "Every day at rehearsal," *The Sound of Music* 40th Anniversary Edition, "From Liesl to Gretl: A 40th Anniversay Reunion."

93 "it was something about musical instruments," Fred Bronson, *The Sound of Music Family Scrapbook* (Milwaukee: Applause Theatre & Cinema Books, 2011), 9.

94 "Lovely to work with," *The Sound of Music* 40th Anniversary Edition, Robert Wise commentary.

94 He would look over the lineup and then combine actors, *The Sound of Music* 40th Anniversary Edition, "From Liesl to Gretl: A 40th Anniversay Reunion."

95 "five going on twenty-five," Bronson, *The Sound of Music Family Scrapbook,* 11.

95 "If I had not hired her," Ibid.

95 "If it doesn't take too long," Ibid., 85.

11. COMPLETING THE CAST

97 "I loved Eleanor Parker," *The Sound of Music* 40th Anniversary Edition, "Julie Andrews and Christopher Plummer: A Reminiscence."

98 "came to mind right away," *The Sound of Music* 40th Anniversary Edition, Robert Wise commentary.

99 "Getting my voice back in shape," Radio interview, Peggy Wood with Steve Gray from set of *The Sound of Music.*

99 "I looked up her background," *The Sound of Music* 40th Anniversary Edition, Robert Wise commentary.

100 "professionalism," Graham Payn and Sheridan Morley, eds., *The Noel Coward Diaries.* (New York: Little Brown, 1982), 455.

100 "rotten Nazis and emotional juveniles," Wikipedia.com entry on Louis Nye.

101 "I'd be exhausted," *The Sound of Music* 40th Anniversary Edition, Julie Andrews commentary.

102 "We wanted to give Marni a chance," *The Sound of Music* 40th Anniversary Edition, Robert Wise commentary.

102 "They wanted those foreign singers," Marni Nixon, interview with author, April 8, 2014.

103 "My agent had sent me on a cattle call," Dan Truhitte, interview with author, May 7, 2014.

104 " 'You must be Dan Truhitte,' " Ibid.

104 "You need someone," "Sixteen Going on Seventeen" from *The Sound of Music,* music by Richard Rodgers, lyrics by Oscar Hammerstein II.

104 "Dan Truhitte handled the part," *The Sound of Music* 40th Anniversary Edition, Robert Wise commentary.

12. LET'S START AT THE VERY BEGINNING

106 "like a high diver," Hirsch, *The Sound of Music: The Making of America's Favorite Movie,* 104.

106 "All I could think of," Ibid., 117.

108 "I never saw her make a mistake," *The Sound of Music* 40th Anniversary Edition, "From Liesl to Gretl: A 40th Anniversay Reunion."

108 "Musical numbers are what," George Stevens, Jr., ed., *Conversations with the Great Moviemakers of Hollywood's Golden Age* (New York: Vintage Books, 2007), 491.

108 "Ernie did a marvelous job," *The Sound of Music* 40th Anniversary Edition, Robert Wise commentary.

109 "I tried to do that," Stevens, *Conversations with the Great Moviemakers of Hollywood's Golden Age*, 470.

109 "Robert Wise was one hundred percent," Dee Dee Woods, interview with author, May 8, 2014.

109 "We solved the problem," Ibid.

110 It was Andrews who came up with a neat bit of trickery, *The Sound of Music* 40th Anniversary Edition, Julie Andrews commentary.

110 "rather sulkily," Hirsch, *The Sound of Music: The Making of America's Favorite Movie,* 129.

110 "Playing the guitar," *The Sound of Music* 40th Anniversary Edition, Julie Andrews commentary.

110 "Julie is so musical," *The Sound of Music* 40th Anniversary Edition, Robert Wise commentary.

110 "I loathe the guitar," *The Sound of Music* 40th Anniversary Edition, Christopher Plummer commentary.

111 "Julie was so great with the kids," *The Sound of Music* 40th Anniversary Edition, Robert Wise commentary.

111 "a motherly hug," Bronson, *The Sound of Music Family Scrapbook,* 21.

111 "That love you see," Ibid.

111 " I couldn't have looked more adoring," *The Sound of Music* 40th Anniversary Edition, "From Liesl to Gretl: A 40th Anniversay Reunion."

111 "a magical way about her," Bronson, *The Sound of Music Family Scrapbook,* 4.

111 "Every one of the children," Ibid., 40.

111 "In the stage show Rolfe," *The Sound of Music* 40th Anniversary Edition, Robert Wise commentary.

111 "The tough part was," Dan Truhitte, interview with author, May 7, 2014.

112 "In fact the only time," *The Sound of Music* 30th Anniversary Edition, "A Telegram from Daniel Truhitte."

112 "He treated everyone," Dan Truhitte interview with author, May 7, 2014.

112 "I had very light lashes," Marni Nixon, interview with author, April 1, 2014.

112 "It was like a print," Ibid.

113 "It's amazing how real it all felt," *The Sound of Music* 40th Anniversary Edition, Julie Andrews commentary.

113 "This will sound like heresy," Sergio Leemann, *Robert Wise on His Films: From Editing Room to Director's Chair* (Los Angeles: Silman-James Press, 1995), 183.

113 "It's obviously not a dance number," Dee Dee Wood, interview with author, May 8, 2014.

114 "definitely no polyester," Marni Nixon, interview with author, April 1, 2014.

114 "without a lot of jiggling around," Ibid.

114 "'Marni, I'm such a fan of yours,'" Carr with Strauss, *Forever Liesel*, 59.

114 "I said to Julie that I was having trouble," Marni Nixon, interview with author, April 1, 2014.

115 "I'll never forget Julie," Ibid.

115 "Nobody told us when we went to Salzburg," *The Sound of Music* 40th Anniversary Edition, Julie Andrews commentary.

13. SALZBURG, RAIN, NATURE'S REVENGE

116 "I looked like Orson Welles," *The Sound of Music* 30th Anniversary Edition, "*The Sound of Music:* From Fact to Phenomenon."

116 "I really envied them," *The Sound of Music* 40th Anniversary Edition, Julie Andrews commentary.

117 "I was mad," Marni Nixon, interview with author, April 1, 2014

117 "I'm the man you're looking for," Georg Steinitz, interview with author, January 14, 2014.

117 "I was saved by the fact," Ibid.

117 "We all knew what each department was doing," Dee Dee Wood, interview with author, May 8, 2014.

118 "Unfortunately the lights had no regard," Chaplin, *The Golden Age of Movie Musicals and Me*, 221.

118 "I couldn't explain it," *The Sound of Music* 30th Anniversary Edition, "*The Sound of Music:* From Fact to Phenomenon."

118 "the beer, the quiche," Ibid.

118 "I lost myself in work, work, work," Stirling, *Julie Andrews: An Intimate Biography*, 123–124.

118 "hug Emma Kate," Ibid., 124–125.

119 "freezing . . . found myself in tears," Dee Dee Wood, interview with author, May 8, 2014.

120 "a little bit of a cool atmosphere," Georg Steinitz, interview with author, January 14, 2014.

120 With additional natural light flooding the cathedral, *American Cinematographer,* April 1965.

120 "was the bishop of the abbey," *The Sound of Music* 40th Anniversary Edition, Julie Andrews commentary.

120 "I've never felt as beautiful," Hirsch, *The Sound of Music: The Making of America's Favorite Movie,* 91.

120 "It was very simple," *The Sound of Music* 40th Anniversary Edition, Julie Andrews commentary.

121 "She became a great friend," Ibid.

121 "even more harrowing," *New York World Telegraph & Sun,* February 27, 1965.

121 the original plan for the sequence, Georg Steinitz, interview with author, January 14, 2014.

122 "No townspeople would watch," Dee Dee Wood, interview with author, May 8, 2014.

122 "The compromise seemed to be," Georg Steinitz, interview with author, January 14, 2014.

122 "Of course that caused a lot of controversy," Ibid.

122 "I liked the fact," Stevens, *Conversations with the Great Moviemakers of Hollywood's Golden Age,* 482.

123 The older nun holding her hand up, *The Sound of Music* 40th Anniversary Edition, Julie Andrews commentary.

123 "All told there were about fifty people," *The Sound of Music* 30th Anniversary Edition, *"The Sound of Music:* From Fact to Phenomenon."

124 a concluding twenty-five yard dolly shot, *Daily Telegraph,* June 24, 1964.

124 "Either he didn't want to write," Chaplin, *The Golden Age of Movie Musicals and Me,* 217.

124 "Prefer my version," Ibid., 218.

125 "deliberately appearing to be so nervous," *The Sound of Music* 40th Anniversary Edition, "My Favorite Things: Julie Andrews Remember."

125 "I tried to act dotty," *The Sound of Music* 40th Anniversary Edition, Julie Andrews commentary.

125 "based loosely," Hirsch, *The Sound of Music: The Making of America's Favorite Movie,* 40.

125 "My job was to translate that play," *The Sound of Music* 40th Anniversary Edition, Robert Wise commentary.

125 "She was bossy," *The Sound of Music* 40th Anniversary Edition, "My Favorite Things: Julie Andrews Remembers."

125 "My mother never quite accepted," Ibid.

125 "charming and lovely," *The Sound of Music* 40th Anniversary Edition, Robert Wise commentary.

125 "That's one ambition I'm giving up," *The Sound of Music* 20th Century-Fox original publicity production notes, 1965.

126 "You're so much more handsome," Carr with Strauss, *Forever Liesl,* 60.

126 "buxom . . . bouncy and bossy," Christopher Plummer, *In Spite of Myself: A Memoir,* (New York: Knopf, 2008), 399.

126 "We got on like a house afire," *The Sound of Music* 40th Anniversary Edition, "My Favorite Things: Julie Andrews Remembers."

126 "I absolutely adored her," Carr with Strauss, *Forever Liesl,* 60.

126 "I was kind of nervous," *The Sound of Music* 30th Anniversary Edition, *"The Sound of Music:* From Fact to Phenomenon."

126 "I'm delighted you're playing it as a tomboy," *The Sound of Music* 20th Century-Fox original publicity production notes, 1965.

126 "so slight by comparison," Hirsch, *The Sound of Music: The Making of America's Favorite Movie,* 133.

126 "too gentle," *Washington Post,* February 26, 1978.

127 "wanted to stay away from castles," *The Sound of Music* 40th Anniversary Edition, Robert Wise commentary.

127 "When Christopher Plummer tried to tear the flag," Georg Steinitz, interview with author, January 14, 2014.

127 "My family did live in a big house," *The Sound of Music* 40th Anniversary Edition, Johannes von Trapp commentary.

128 Leven re-created the setting at Bertelesmann, *The Sound of Music* 40th Anniversary Edition, Robert Wise commentary.

129 "Robert Wise definitely had a gift," Bronson, *The Sound of Music Family Scrapbook*, 36.

129 "My baby! My baby," Ibid., 37.

130 "key turning point in the story," *The Sound of Music* 40th Anniversary Edition, Robert Wise commentary.

130 "I was really pleased," Ibid.

130 "They asked what we were going to do," Dr. Steve Taft interview with Marc Breaux, University of Northern Idaho, June 1999. uni.edu./taft/breauxinterview

131 "When we got to Salzburg," *The Sound of Music* 40th Anniversary Edition, Charmian Carr commentary.

132 "Filming the montage was the quintessential moment," *The Sound of Music* 40th Anniversary Edition, Julie Andrews commentary.

132 "*South Pacific* is almost like three movies in one," Theodore S. Chapin, interview with author, May 14, 2014.

133 "A great song can take the place," *The Sound of Music* 45th Anniversary Edition, "Writing the Show."

133 inside of a cloud, Carr with Strauss, *Forever Liesl*, 75.

133 Julie Andrews would pick up the guitar, *The Sound of Music* 40th Anniversary Edition, "From Liesl to Gretl: A 40th Anniversay Reunion."

133 "Ted McCord would continually look through," *The Sound of Music* 40th Anniversary Edition, Julie Andrews commentary.

134 "I was a klutz," *The Sound of Music* 40th Anniversary Edition, "From Liesl to Gretl: A 40th Anniversay Reunion."

134 "They were all lovely," Julie Andrews on *The Ellen DeGeneres Show,* January 26, 2007.

135 "Saul worked with Julie," *The Sound of Music* 40th Anniversary Edition, Robert Wise commentary.

135 "Saul, Marc, Dee Dee, and myself," *The Sound of Music* 40th Anniversary Edition, Julie Andrews commentary.

135 "The song we sang the most," *The Sound of Music*, 30th Anniversary Edition, "*The Sound of Music:* From Fact to Phenomenon."

135 "There was candlelight," Ibid.

135 "Where else could you find," Ibid.

135 "a very nice gentleman," Georg Steinitz, interview with author, January 14, 2014.

135 "Part of the love that's evident," Carr with Strauss, *Forever Liesl*, 216.

135 "Saul was as great a gentleman as Robert Wise," Dan Truhitte, interview with author, May 7, 2014.

136 "I thought it would be fun," *The Sound of Music* 40th Anniversary Edition, Julie Andrews commentary.

136 "We had no sense that 'Do-Re-Mi,' " Georg Steinitz, interview with author, January 14, 2014.

136 "This is really going to be something," *The Sound of Music* 40th Anniversary Edition, "From Liesl to Gretl: A 40th Anniversay Reunion."

137 "Remember, Nicky," Bronson, *The Sound of Music Family Scrapbook*, 70.

137 "You're here to do a job," Ibid., 73.

137 "We wanted his approval," Ibid.

137 "Robert Wise made sure certain words," Georg Steinitz, interview with author, January 14, 2014.

138 "as scary as possible," Bronson, *The Sound of Music Family Scrapbook*, 67.

138 had never heard, *The Sound of Music* 40th Anniversary Edition, "From Liesl to Gretl: A 40th Anniversay Reunion."

138 fewer problems with, Hirsch, *The Sound of Music: The Making of America's Favorite Movie*, 140.

138 "even the parents were terrific," *The Sound of Music* 30th Anniversary Edition, "*The Sound of Music:* From Fact to Phenomenon."

138 "We were all talking and laughing," Carr with Strauss, *Forever Liesl*, 183–184.

139 "pampered arrogant," Plummer, *In Spite of Myself: A Memoir*, 394.

139 "under duress," Ibid.

139 "My behavior was unconscionable," Ibid.

139 "The one person who seemed to understand," Ibid, 395.

139 "She held us together," Ibid.

139 "He was the wonderful glue," *The Sound of Music* 40th Anniversary Edition, Julie Andrews commentary.

140 in awe of Plummer, Ibid.

140 "We've been great friends ever since," Ibid.

140 "Bob (Wise), who knew what was on the line," Carr with Strauss, *Forever Liesl*, 73.

140 "never said a single word to me," Ibid., 64.

140 "didn't trust him," Bronson, *The Sound of Music Family Scrapbook*, 41.

140 "To the two laughing boys," *The Sound of Music* 40th Anniversary Edition, "From Liesl to Gretl: A 40th Anniversay Reunion."

140 "There needed to be a cynic," *The Oprah Winfrey Show*, October 28, 2010.

140 he later admitted to calling the film, Plummer, *In Spite of Myself: A Memoir,* 392–393.

140 "I loathe them," *The Sound of Music* 40th Anniversary Edition, Christopher Plummer commentary.

141 "I got to like them enormously," Ibid.

141 "The little one," Ibid.

141 "He behaved as though," Chaplin, *The Golden Age of Movie Musicals and Me*, 213.

141 "It's just not musical enough," Hirsch, *The Sound of Music: The Making of America's Favorite Movie,* 160.

141 "When our voices," *The Sound of Music* 30th Anniversary Edition, "*The Sound of Music:* From Fact to Phenomenon."

142 "I was in Salzburg for nine or ten weeks," Ibid.

142 "florid, with incessant, meaningless," Chaplin, *The Golden Age of Movie Musicals and Me*, 213.

142 "He complained about having to get up early," *The Sound of Music* 40th Anniversary Edition, Charmian Carr commentary.

142 "Tricks were played on Plummer," Georg Steinitz, interview with author, January 14, 2014.

142 "indelibly printed on my mind," *The Sound of Music* 40th Anniversary Edition, "Julie Andrews and Christopher Plummer: A Reminiscence."

142 she has actually only returned twice, *The Sound of Music* 30th Anniversary Edition, "*The Sound of Music:* From Fact to Phenomenon."

143 "I wish I could stay here forever," Carr with Strauss, *Forever Liesl*, 70.

143 the daily call sheets, *The Sound of Music*, original publicity production notes.

143 "Ted had to artificially light," *The Sound of Music* 40th Anniversary Edition, Robert Wise commentary.

143 what he couldn't shake, Hirsch, *The Sound of Music: The Making of America's Favorite Movie,* 147.

14. SONG AND DANCE

145 "It was so easy," *The Sound of Music* 40th Anniversary Edition, Julie Andrews commentary.

146 "My assignment was to tell," Georg Steinitz, interview with author, January 14, 2014.

146 "I don't think I'm totally sober there," *The Sound of Music* 40th Anniversary Edition, "Julie Andrews and Christopher Plummer: A Reminiscence."

147 "We had to walk a very long way," *The Sound of Music* 40th Anniversary Edition, Julie Andrews commentary.

147 A different recollection, Georg Steinitz, interview with author, January 14, 2014.

147 "My God this kid is very heavy!," *The Sound of Music* 40th Anniversary Edition, Charmian Carr commentary.

148 "They put Julie Andrews in a hotel," Georg Steinitz, interview with author, January 14, 2014.

148 "A mink coat of all dumb things," *The Sound of Music* 40th Anniversary Edition, Julie Andrews commentary.

148 "Fortunately I couldn't understand him," Ibid.

148 "Why would he yell?," Georg Steinitz, interview with author, January 14, 2014.

149 purposefully opened holes, *The Sound of Music* 40th Anniversary Edition, Julie Andrews commentary.

15. BACK HOME

151 "On the first day Christopher appeared," Dee Dee Wood, interview with author, May 8, 2014.

152 "There was romance in the air," *The Sound of Music* 40th Anniversary Edition, Julie Andrews commentary.

152 "I think it furthered the story," *The Sound of Music* 40th Anniversary Edition, Dee Dee Wood commentary.

152 "I love the Laendler so much," Dee Dee Wood, interview with author, May 8, 2014.

152 Surprisingly, Wise at one point, Barthel, *New York Times*, November 20, 1966.

153 "blow to the pit of the stomach," *The Sound of Music* 40th Anniversary Edition, Robert Wise commentary.

153 "Julie wants to rehearse and rehearse," Ibid.

153 "teaching me a great deal," Hirsch, *The Sound of Music: The Making of America's Favorite Movie,* 117.

154 "Perhaps they thought," *Climbed Every Mountain: The Story Behind* The Sound of Music.

154 "My adoration for her was such," Bronson, *The Sound of Music Family Scrapbook*, 50.

154 "Did you notice," *The Sound of Music* 40th Anniversary Edition, Dee Dee Wood commentary.

155 "Well, well—the wonder girl," Trapp, *The Story of the Trapp Family Singers,* 49.

155 "just likes you," Ibid., 50.

155 "My goodness, did you think," Ibid., 51.

155 "Every time I see the picture," *The Sound of Music* 40th Anniversary Edition, Robert Wise commentary.

156 "I nearly dumped Julie," *The Sound of Music* 40th Anniversary Edition, Christopher Plummer commentary.

156 "I think Robert Wise was crying," *The Sound of Music* 40th Anniversary Edition, Charmian Carr commentary.

156 "'wobbly,'" *The Sound of Music* 40th Anniversary Edition, Julie Andrews commentary.

157 "kept looking at his watch," Dee Dee Wood, interview with author, May 8, 2014.

157 "I've been meaning to tell you," *The Today Show,* November 10, 2010.

157 "That number was so much fun," Dee Dee Wood, interview with author, May 8, 2014.

158 "They were the kindest, nicest people," Dan Truhitte, interview with author, May 7, 2014.

158 "You realize that 90 percent of the iconic images," Ted Chapin, interview with author, May 12, 2014.

159 "over 32,000 feet," *The Sound of Music* 45th Anniversary Edition, "Maria in the 21st Century."

159 "The most difficult," *The Sound of Music* 30th Anniversary Edition, "*The Sound of Music:* From Fact to Phenomenon."

16. SNEAK PREVIEW

162 "There's something about that scene," Carr with Strauss, *Forever Liesl*, 94.

163 223 rated the film, *The Sound of Music* 30th Anniversary Edition, "*The Sound of Music* Gallery."

163 "We seemed to be planting," *The Sound of Music* 40th Anniversary Edition, Robert Wise commentary.

17. PUBLICITY

166 "I thought they did everything well," Geoffrey Block, ed. *The Richard Rodgers Reader* (New York: Oxford University Press, 2002), 320.

166 "Being the composer of a musical that has been transferred," *New York World Telegraph and Sun*, February 27, 1966.

166 "walked into the dining room," Johannes von Trapp, interview with author, January 9, 2014.

167 "I didn't make it to the premiere," Dan Truhitte, interview with author, May 7, 2014.

167 "the wedding scene just enveloped her," *The von Trapp Family: Harmony and Discord*.

167 "You are a much greater artist," *The Sound of Music* 30th Anniversary Edition, "*The Sound of Music* Gallery."

18. WORLD PREMIERE

168 "It's as close to perfection," *The Sound of Music* 30th Anniversary Edition, "*The Sound of Music* Gallery."

168 "Jack Warner's loss," *New York Daily News*, February 27, 1965.

168 "I can remember exactly how it felt," Carr with Strauss, *Forever Liesl*, 110.

168 "Little more than a year earlier," Ibid., 120–121.

170 "When you are a child of the mountains," Trapp, *The Story of the Trapp Family Singers*, 21.

170 "The premiere was the first time," Marni Nixon, interview with author, April 1, 2014.

170 "a tectonic shift in our lives," Bronson, *The Sound of Music Family Scrapbook*, 83.

171 "At the New York City premiere," *Rachel Ray Show*, November 20, 2010.

171 "I think Julie Andrews will be," Peggy Wood, radio interview with Steve Gray on the set of *The Sound of Music*.

19. CRITICS ON THE WARPATH

172 " a superb screen adaptation," *Variety*, March 3, 1965.

172 "It restores your faith in movies," Stirling, *Julie Andrews: An Intimate Biography*, 163.

172 "Julie's radiance," Ibid., 154.

172 "serenely controlled self-confidence," Bosley Crowther, *New York Times*, March 3, 1965.

172 "The adults are fairly horrendous," Ibid.

172 "Its sentiments are abundant," Ibid.

173 "sickening . . . the most revolting refreshing actress in films," Stanley Kauffman, *The New Republic*, March 20, 1965.

173 "Is there a special heaven for film critics?," Ibid.

174 "the movie is staged by Mr. Wise," Bosley Crowther, *New York Times,* March 3, 1965.

174 praised Julie Andrews for triumphing over the film itself, *Newsweek*, March 12, 1965.

174 "With that film we became grown-ups," Wasson, *Fifth Avenue, 5 A.M.: Audrey Hepburn, Breakfast at Tiffany's, and the Dawn of the Modern Woman,* 11.

174 "the most enchanting and complete performer," Stirling, *Julie Andrews: An Intimate Biography*, 152.

174 "sound of marshmellows," Judith Crist, *New York Herald Tribune,* March 4, 1965.

174 "Calorie-counters, diabetics, and grown-ups," Ibid.

174 "There is nothing like a supersized screen," Ibid.

174 "hate mail from all over the world," Wilk, *The Making of The Sound of Music*, 78.

175 "mostly bored but intermittently touched," Stirling, *Julie Andrews: An Intimate Biography*, 154.

175 "soaring voice and thrice-scrubbed innocence," Ibid.

175 "true innocence," Joan Barthel, *New York Times*, November 20, 1966.

175 "handful of authentic location shots," Brendan Gill, *The New Yorker*, March 6, 1965.

175 "brilliant . . . It made the hills more natural," *The Sound of Music* 40th Anniversary Edition, "Julie Andrews and Christopher Plummer: A Reminiscence."

175 "well under ordinary high school level," Brendan Gill, *The New Yorker*, March 6, 1965.

175 "even more difficult for anyone to try," Pauline Kael, *Kiss Kiss, Bang Bang* (New York: Bantam, 1969), 214.

176 "luxuriant falseness . . . probably going to be the single most repressive," Ibid.

176 "big lie, the sugarcoated lies," Ibid.

176 "You're not telling untruths," *The Sound of Music* 40th Anniversary Edition, Robert Wise commentary.

176 "Whom could it offend," Pauline Kael, *McCall's Magazine*, March 1965.

176 "Forty weeks of schmaltz is enough," Joan Barthel, *New York Times*, November 20, 1966.

177 "makes a critic feel that maybe," Pauline Kael, *McCall's Magazine*, March 1965.

177 "a technician without a strong personality," Andrew Sarris, *The American Cinema: Director, and Directions 1929–1968* (New York: Dutton, 1968), 203.

177 "Critics talk about style," Sidney Lunnet, *Making Movies* (New York: Vintage Books, 1996), 51.

177 "His films became increasingly fascinating to me," Martin Scorsese, "Robert Wise, Film Director, Dies at 91," *New York Times*, September 15, 2005.

180 "Time to Retire," Mark Harris, *Pictures at a Revolution: Five Movies and the Birth of the New Hollywood* (New York: Penguin Press, 2008), 322.

20. THE ONE-BILLION-DOLLAR QUESTION

181 "When Mrs. Myra Franklin," Carr with Strauss, *Forever Liesl*, 11.

182 the critics seemed to harbor resentment, Block, ed., *The Richard Rodgers Reader*, 320.

182 "most of us live on sentiment," Ibid.

182 " . . . I think is ridiculous," Ibid.

183 "Everyone in the world," *The Sound of Music* 40th Anniversary Edition, "From Liesl to Gretl."

183 "After my mother died," *The Oprah Winfrey Show,* October 28, 2010.

184 "I could go to another world for three hours," Ibid.

185 "the enduring quality of this story," Leemann, *Robert Wise on His Films: From Editing Room to Director's Chair,* 184.

185 "joy and decency and goodness," *The Today Show,* November 9, 2005.

186 "Why can't it be like it was," *Merrily We Roll Along*, music and lyrics by Stephen Sondheim, 1981.

187 "It does not matter to people," Agathe von Trapp, *Memories Before and After The Sound of Music*, 197.

187 "an audience's yearning for belief and transcendence," David Thomson, *Moments That Made the Movies* (New York: Thames and Hudson, 2013), 19.

21. THE ACADEMY AWARDS

188 "You wuz robbed," *The Sound of Music* 30th Anniversary Edition, "*The Sound of Music* Gallery."

188 "very difficult for me," Wilk, *Overture and Finale: Rodgers & Hammerstein and the Creation of Their Two Greatest Hits,* 185.

189 wasn't just Academy members and one guest, Hirsch, *The Sound of Music: The Making of America's Favorite Movie,* 191.

190 "This picture was a joy to edit," *The Sound of Music* 30th Anniversary Edition, "From Fact to Phenomenon."

190 "Yes, mine might have been a failure," Gabriel Miller, *William Wyler: Interviews* (Jackson: University of Mississippi Press, 2010), 118.

192 " 'Well, I just have to go now, Mummy,' " *The Sound of Music* 40th Anniversary Edition, Julie Andrews commentary.

192 a figure three times the local population, Stirling, *Julie Andrews: An Intimate Biography,* 184.

22. THE INTERNATIONAL PHENOMENON

193 "The thing that's most important about films," Stevens, ed., *Conversations with the Great Moviemakers of Hollywood's Golden Age,* 483–484.

193 crowds grew so unruly, Barthel, *New York Times*, November 20, 1966.

193 while clad in a Batman costume, *New York Times,* May 17, 1967.

194 "The world was hungry," George Stevens, ed., *Conversations with the Great Moviemakers of Hollywood's Golden Age*, 483–484.

194 "Timing is something," Ibid., 475.

194 "We thought that the Austrian costumes," Georg Steinitz, interview with author, January 14, 2014.

194 "lifted the movie from a morass of goo," *The Sound of Music* 40th Anniversary Edition, Christopher Plummer commentary.

195 "Even today the Austrian people," *Climbed Every Mountain: The Story Behind* The Sound of Music.

195 "It had nothing to do with politics," Georg Steinitz, interview with author, January 14, 2014.

195 "the first run in Salzberg," Ibid.

196 an additional 229 scheduled bookings, *New York Times,* April 7, 1967.

196 "It's really rather nasty of them," Joan Barthel, *New York Times*, November 20, 1966.

23. JULIE ANDREWS

197 "There's niceness where it can seem treacly," Carol Burnett, *Backstage,* January 18–24, 2007.

197 "It did kind of knock me sideways," *The Sound of Music* 30th Anniversary Edition, "From Fact to Phenomenon."

199 "Christmas carols in the snow," *Time* magazine, December 23, 1966.

200 "She exuded sex," Santopietro, *Considering Doris Day*, 9.

24. LIFE AFTER *THE SOUND OF MUSIC*

202 "I ended up very much liking the children," *The Sound of Music* 40th Anniversary Edition, Christopher Plummer commentary.

202 "former actor," *Esquire* magazine, August 1966.

202 "I think he's terribly proud," *Newsday*, November 27, 2005.

203 "*The Sound of Music* was the actual Julie Andrews," Stirling, *Julie Andrews: An Intimate Biography*, 350.

203 "He's an adorable curmudgeon," *Newsday,* November 27, 2005.

203 "if anyone gave a chocolate soldier performance," *The Sound of Music* 40th Anniversary Edition, Christopher Plummer commentary.

203 "I think it's sentimental in the proper way," *The Sound of Music* 30th Anniversary Edition, *The Sound of Music:* From Fact to Phenomenon.

203 "Here was I, cynical old sod that I am," Plummer, *In Spite of Myself: A Memoir,* 408.

203 "The Legend and the Other Guy; a Leering King Lear Exorcises Captain von Trapp," *New York Times,* February 2, 2004.

204 "It kind of rejuvenates your career," *Playbill*, November 2010.

205 "I'm very grateful that the film is so popular," *The Sound of Music* 40th Anniversary Edition, Robert Wise commentary.

206 "Wise's name opens every door," *Variety,* April 13, 1992.

206 "Good movies speak to the great reach," Robert Wise, AFI acceptance speech, February 19, 1998.

207 "It gave me quite a tug," *The Sound of Music* 40th Anniversary Edition, Robert Wise commentary.

207 "She's a marvelous lady," Stirling, *Julie Andrews: An Intimate Biography,* 350.

207 "Robert Wise was my rock," *The Sound of Music* 40th Anniversary Edition, "My Favorite Things: Julie Andrews Remembers."

208 "We're very good friends," *The Sound of Music* 40th Anniversary Edition, Robert Wise commentary.

209 "I never expected to be part of that," Dan Truhitte, interview with author, May 7, 2014.

209 "It was just great to see," Ted Chapin, interview with author, May 14, 2014.

209 "Having been there," Bronson, *The Sound of Music Family Scrapbook,* 92.

210 "*The Sound of Music* Husband's Club," Ibid., 90.

210 "None of us ever wanted to let the fans," Carr with Strauss, *Forever Liesl,* 172.

210 "pretty rare to have your entire life," *Climbed Every Mountain: The Story Behind* The Sound of Music.

210 "small consolation," Bronson, *The Sound of Music Family Scrapbook,* 85.

210 "older than I ever intended to be," *Chicago,* music by John Kander, lyrics by Fred Ebb 1975.

211 "She's a pro," Carr with Strauss, *Forever Liesl,* 197.

211 "But though close relationships," Ibid., 195.

211 "as always, polite and cordial," Ibid., 197.

211 "It gave us a second family," *The Today Show,* November 10, 2010.

211 "I remember Charmian's grace and beauty," *The Sound of Music* 40th Anniversary Edition, Julie Andrews commentary.

212 reached by the end of summer in 1965, *Variety,* August 11, 1965.

212 "All I can say today," Wilk, *Overture and Finale: Rodgers & Hammerstein and the Creation of Their Two Greatest Hits,* 163.

213 "Ultimately, it got resolved like any family squabble," Carr with Strauss, *Forever Liesl,* 215.

213 "for a brief time Liesl began to feel," Carr with Strauss, *Forever Liesl,* 126.

213 "resented Liesl as if," Ibid.

213 "I took him there," *The London Observer,* November 12, 2000.

213 "It's a terrible thing to say," Ibid.

214 "I feel great," Ibid.

214 "It didn't work," *The Oprah Winfrey Show,* October 28, 2010.

214 "I had the time of my life," *Us Magazine,* March 5, 1990.

215 "I may be the oldest," Dan Truhitte, interview with author, May 7, 2014.

216 "Our dance in the gazebo," Carr with Strauss, *Forever Liesl,* 182.

216 "I don't watch the film all the time," Dan Truhitte, interview with author, May 7, 2014.

216 "As long as we have family," "Dan 'Rolfe' Truhitte Still Making Music," Jim Longworth, *Triad Today,* November 23, 2011.

216 "The Sound of Music is a fairy tale," *The Sound of Music* 30th Anniversary Edition, "Ernest Lehman: Master Storyteller."

216 "If you're only the screenwriter," Stevens, ed., *Conversations with the Great Moviemakers of Hollywood's Golden Age,* 502.

217 "makes me feel safe," Ibid., 510.

217 "a group that in fact had little to do," Liz Smith, *Newsday,* March 31, 2000.

217 "a deep apology," Ibid.

218 "a miracle that comes to only a very few," Wilk, *Overture and Finale: Rodgers & Hammerstein and the Creation of Their Two Greatest Hits*, 185.

218 "Somehow the mere fact," Stevens, ed., *Conversations with the Great Moviemakers of Hollywood's Golden Age*, 489.

218 "My most easygoing relationship," Ibid. 488.

218 "It's such a visual scene," Ibid., 491.

218 "It seems visual," Ibid., 495.

218 "considerable openness of mind," Ibid., 501.

219 "three Ambien," *The New Yorker*, March 4, 2002.

219 "a long-standing, incurable pain," Ibid.

219 "probably the greatest remark," Wasson, *Fifth Avenue, 5 A.M.: Audrey Hepburn, Breakfast at Tiffany's, and the Dawn of the Modern Woman*, 216.

219 "was a good day," *Variety*, March 5–11, 2011.

222 *Poppins* and *Sound of Music*, Dee Dee Wood, interview with author, May 8, 2014.

223 in a poll conducted by *Film Comment*, *Film Comment*, 1977.

223 "I was always a director's designer," *New York Times*, November 22, 1995.

223 "the only fan letter," *New York Times*, March 13, 1981.

223 "Your clothes made me feel," Ibid.

223 "In the middle of the night," Ibid.

224 "I think *The Sound of Music*," *The Sound of Music* 30th Anniversary Edition, "Broadcast Promotions and Interviews."

226 "I know exactly what it is," *Lear's*, September 1992.

226 "tremendous struggle to overcome," *Fanfare*, March 14, 1992.

226 "You watch her in a room full of children," *Vanity Fair*, October 1995.

226 "hurt a lot in the past," *Fanfare*, March 14, 1992.

226 "Marriage is the hardest work you're ever going to do," *Vanity Fair*, October 1995.

226 "*Often I think this sad old world*," *Darling Lili*, music by Henry Mancini, lyrics by Johnny Mercer, 1970.

229 "I can't be what I was," Stirling, *Julie Andrews: An Intimate Biography*, 215.

230 "extremely irritating," Harris, *Pictures at a Revolution: Five Movies and the Birth of the New Hollywood*, 160.

232 "Audiences in the twenty-first century," Jeanine Basinger, interview with author, April 26, 2014.

232 "It isn't easy," Stirling, *Julie Andrews: An Intimate Biography*, 292.

233 "I could give you chapter and verse," *Vanity Fair*, October 1995.

233 "representing me with such compassion," abcnews.go.com/9/7/2000.

233 "settled the case," Ibid.

233 "this chapter," Ibid.

234 "I would have been a very lost soul," *New York Times*, December 23, 2001.

234 "guidance and management," *Newsday*, August 4, 2003.

234 "I'm so fortunate to have found," Ibid.

235 "I wondered why she should," Stirling, *Julie Andrews: An Intimate Biography*, 351.

235 "Miss Andrews is the woman," Ibid., 353.

235 "I'm resilient and I'm professional," *Fanfare*, March 14, 1993.

235 "People forget that *Mary Poppins*," Ibid.

235 "irritating and annoying," *Vanity Fair*, October 1995.

235 "I never want to disappoint," John J. O'Connor, "Julie Andrews With Tough Edges," *New York Times*, October 25, 1995.

236 "five bass notes," *Daily Mail*, December 29, 2007.

25. SORRY-GRATEFUL

238 "Our story has been told," *Climbed Every Mountain: The Story Behind* The Sound of Music.

238 Climbing out her window, *Von Trapp Family: Harmony and Discord*.

238 "Christian communism," Agathe von Trapp, *Memories Before and After* The Sound of Music, 191.

239 "When we stopped," *Climbed Every Mountain: The Story Behind* The Sound of Music.

239 "When we first moved here," *The Sound of Music* 40th Anniversary Edition, Johannes von Trapp commentary.

239 "Now of course I understand the issue," interview with author, January 9, 2014.

239 "There isn't the ideal family," *London Observer*, April 1, 2000.

239 "My mother had tremendous strengths," Hirsch, *The Sound of Music: The Making of America's Favorite Movie*, 203.

239 "She wasn't happy all the time," *Climbed Every Mountain: The Story Behind* The Sound of Music.

240 "The father of a young family," *Washington Post*, February 26, 1978.

240 "didn't care if anyone," Suzanna Andrews, *Vanity Fair*, "The Sound of Money," June 1998.

240 "like a maniac," Ibid.

240 "Any influence that might lead," Alex Witchel, "A Few Favorite Things the Musical Left Out," *New York Times*, January 1, 1998.

240 "She was a very complex person," *Climbed Every Mountain: The Story Behind* The Sound of Music.

241 "After my mother's death," Ibid.

241 "My mother never paid attention to it," Suzanna Andrews, "The Sound of Money," *Vanity Fair*, June 1998.

241 "unresolved business," Ibid.

241 "hard work," *Washington Post*, February 26, 1978.

241 "grew misty eyed," Ibid.

242 "I was not sorry to hear," Agathe von Trapp, *Memories Before and After The Sound of Music*, 196.

242 "A very nice story," *AARP Bulletin*, quoted in *New York Times*, December 20, 2010.

242 "I felt such a pull," Witchel, *New York Times*, January 1, 1998.

243 "I always say they took the raisins," Ibid.

243 "We were all pretty shocked," *London Telegraph*, February 23, 2014.

243 "My father was very congenial," Johannes von Trapp, interview with author, January 9, 2014.

243 "Our whole life is in here," *London Telegraph*, February 23, 2014.

243 "grateful to *The Sound of Music*," *The Sound of Music* 45th Anniversary Edition, "Von Trapps in Vermont."

243 "I'm glad I'm thirty miles from Stowe," *Washington Post*, February 26, 1978.

243 "a peace of mind," Ibid.

244 "You know, Johannes," Antapol, *The Sound of Music: The Making of America's Favorite Movie*, 204.

245 "I was not happy onstage," *Climbed Every Mountain: The Story Behind* The Sound of Music.

245 "I depended a lot on him," Ibid.

245 "One night I just ran out," *The Von Trapp Family: Harmony and Discord*.

245 "They gave me electric shock treatment," *Climbed Every Mountain: The Story Behind* The Sound of Music.

245 "I got rebellious," Ibid.

245 "My mother concentrated," Ibid.

245 "I didn't hang out," Ibid.

245 "I began relationships with men," Rosmarie von Trapp, interview with Kobi Ben Sihon, buzzer17.proboards.com/ May 26, 2006.

245 "If I could have done anything with my life," *Climbed Every Mountain: The Story Behind The Sound of Music.*

246 "When we saw the movie," Rosmarie von Trapp, interview with Kobi Ben Sihon, buzzer17.proboards.com/ May 26, 2006.

246 "At age forty," Ibid.

246 "I went to bed," Ibid.

246 "We had a special connection," Ibid.

246 "For many years," Ibid.

247 "This place brings me quiet," Ibid.

247 "I can't, I just can't," *The Von Trapp Family: Harmony and Discord.*

247 "active with groups," Agathe von Trapp, *Memories Before and After The Sound of Music,* 205.

247 "they completely invented," *The Sound of Music* 30th Anniversary Edition, *The Sound of Music:* From Fact to Phenomenon."

247 "She had a very peaceful death," The *Von Trapp Family: Harmony and Discord.*

247 "evenhanded scientific assessment," Johannes von Trapp, interview with author, January 9, 2014.

247 made the Lodge the first, Ibid.

248 "Johannes is charismatic," Suzanna Andrews, "The Sound of Money," *Vanity Fair,* June 1998.

248 "Maria's favorite," Ibid.

248 "She believes that she is known," Archer Winsten, *New York Post,* "Rages and Outrages," April 16, 1973.

248 "It may be that I exaggerate," Johannes von Trapp, interview with author, January 9, 2014.

248 "Everything she did," Alex Witchel, "A Few Favorite Things the Musical Left Out," *New York Times,* January 1, 1998.

248 "She loved to make people happy," Ibid.

248 "They want me to be you," Carr with Strauss, *Forever Liesl,* 228.

249 "Isn't that awful?," Witchel, *New York Times.*

249 "The bottom line," Johannes von Trapp, interview with author, January 9, 2014.

249 "At the lodge," Ibid.

249 "We're about environmental sensitivity," Witchel, *New York Times.*

249 "much to my irritation," Ibid.

249 "We want to maximize the advantages," Johannes von Trapp, interview with author, January 9, 2014.

249 "I said to the bankers," Ibid.

250 "I can appreciate," Ibid.

250 "come to the Trapp family lodge," *Climbed Every Mountain: The Story Behind The Sound of Music.*

250 "finds the historical and cultural," Johannes von Trapp, interview with author, January 9, 2014.

250 "Seeing the film was surreal," *Climbs Every Mountain: The Story Behind The Sound of Music.*

250 "When we were growing up," Ibid.

26. FIFTY YEARS OF STATISTICS

251 "gone out of their way," *Newsweek*, April 29, 1968.

251 "plain fact of the matter," Ibid.

251 "guilty of willful misconduct," Ibid.

251 the appellate division upheld, *New York Times*, October 2, 1968.

252 "Let the lawyers fight," *New York Times*, November 22, 1968.

252 sale of some 500,000 additional copies, *Variety*, May 5, 1976.

252 the BBC pays $4 million, *Variety*, May 18, 1979.

252 "Well Jim, '*The Sound of Music*' " Adrian Woolridge, "The Great Delegator," *New York Times,* January 29, 2006.

253 With its cumulative worldwide gross, boxofficemojo.com.

253 remained the record holder, Todd Purdham, *Billboard* Top 40 charts, *New York Times*, May 30, 2005.

254 "easily the most well-known," Maslon, *The Sound of Music Companion*, 157.

254 "Everyone had seen the film," Johannes von Trapp, interview with author, January 9, 2014.

254 "one song from the score," Ibid.

254 "out of one million annual tourists," Maslon, *The Sound of Music Companion*, 172.

255 "go to" Salzburg destinations, *The Sound of Music* 40th Anniversary Edition, "The Sound of Music Tour—A Living Story."

255 "It took the city and country," Georg Steinitz, interview with author, January 14, 2014.

255 claims to have served, *The Sound of Music* 45th Anniversary Edition, "The Sound of Music Tour—A Living Story."

255 the tours still attract, *The Today Show*, November 10, 2005.

255 "The guides seem to have little idea," Georg Steinitz, interview with author, January 14, 2014.

255 "Those who valued the tourist trade," Ted Chapin, interview with author, May 14, 2014.

255 the gazebo was now bigger, *The Sound of Music* 40th Anniversary Edition, "On Location with the *Sound of Music*."

256 they only want to make a beeline, Ibid.

256 "They must have thought," *Theatre Week*, May 24, 1993.

27. THE SING-ALONG PHENOMENON

257 "This is like the Rocky Horror Picture Show," *New York Times*, September 24, 2000.

258 "I think it's a very affectionate," *Newsday*, September 8, 2000.

258 "bit like Julie Andrews' Maria," Ibid.

258 "I just hope all those people," *Christian Science Monitor,* June 29, 2001.

259 "a heavy brown homespun," Profiles in History auction catalogue, July 2013.

259 "the most famous meadow in the world," *The Sound of Music* 40th Anniversary Edition, "On Location with the *Sound of Music*."

260 "*Now you know*," *Merrily We Roll Along*, music and lyrics by Stephen Sondheim, 1981.

260 "my Elizabeth Taylor wig," Stirling, *Julie Andrews: An Intimate Biography*, 339.

260 "who gets the residuals," Ibid.

260 "For heaven's sake," Hugh Linehan, *The Irish Times,* "Supergalhasfragilethoraxbutis-stillloquacious," December 8, 2001.

261 "Julie, I can't tell you," Ibid.

28. NEW ITERATIONS

262 she felt Cameron Diaz, *AM New York*, November 29, 2005.

263 "What a great work ethic," Ted Chapin, interview with author, May 14, 2014.

263 "mystified and disappointed," *Daily Mail* online, December 6, 2013.

263 "Must admit some scenes," Ibid.

263 "She is not a very good actress," *vulture.com*, December 6, 2013.

263 "It was a dream of mine," *Wind It Up* video, Youtube.com.

263 some forty feature films," *New York Times*, July 27, 2000.

29. FULL CIRCLE

266 "On one level," Brantley, *New York Times*, March 13, 1998.

267 "Now you are family," Carr with Strauss, *Forever Liesl*, 236.

268 cadets lay a wreath, *New York Times,* July 14, 1997.

268 "The cultural and underlying elephant," Johannes von Trapp, interview with author, January 9, 2014.

30. AND IN THE END . . .

270 "Forty years and a lot less innocence," Todd Purdham, "The Hills Still Resonate," *New York Times*, May 30, 2005.

271 "a very happy accident all around," *Rosie O'Donnell Show,* January 23, 2000.

272 "Talent is like a marksman," Joseph Epstein, *Fred Astaire* (New Haven: Yale University Press, 2008).

272 "I just think," *Vanity Fair*, October 1995.

272 "I guess it would be," "Sunday Fanfare," *New York Daily News*, February 9, 1997.

BIBLIOGRAPHY

BOOKS

Basinger, Jeanine. *Gene Kelly*. New York: Pyramid Books, 1976.

Block, Geoffrey, ed. *The Richard Rodgers Reader*. New York: Oxford University Press, 2002.

Bronson, Fred. *The Sound of Music Family Scrapbook*. Milwaukee: Applause Theatre & Cinema Books, 2011.

Busch, Justin E. A. *Self and Society in the Films of Robert Wise*. Jefferson, North Carolina: McFarland & Company, 2010.

Carr, Charmian, with Jean A. S. Strauss. *Forever Liesl*. New York: Penguin, 2000.

Chaplin, Saul. *The Golden Age of Movie Musicals and Me*. Norman: University of Oklahoma Press, 1994.

Davis, Fred. *Yearning for Yesterday: A Sociology of Nostalgia*. New York: Free Press, 1979.

Epstein, Joseph. *Fred Astaire*. New Haven: Yale University Press, 2008.

Fordin, Hugh. *Getting to Know Him: A Biography of Oscar Hammerstein II*. New York: Random House, 1977.

Harris, Mark. *Pictures at a Revolution: Five Movies and the Birth of the New Hollywood*. New York: Penguin, 2008.

Herman, Jan. *William Wyler: A Talent for Trouble*. New York: Putnam, 1995.

Hirsch, Julia Antopol. *The Sound of Music: The Making of America's Favorite Movie*. Chicago: Contemporary Books, 1993.

Kael, Pauline. *Kiss Kiss Bang Bang*. New York: Bantam, 1969.

Keenan, Richard C. *The Films of Robert Wise*. Lanham, Maryland: The Scarecrow Press, 2007.

Landis, Deborah Nadoolman. *Hollywood Sketchbook: A Century of Costume Illustration*. New York: Harper Design, 2012.

Leemann, Sergio. *Robert Wise on His Films: From Editing Room to Director's Chair*. Los Angeles: Silman-James Press, 1995.

Lehman, Ernest. *Screening Sickness and Other Tales of Tinsel Town*. New York: Putnam, 1992.

Lumet, Sidney. *Making Movies*. New York: Vintage Books. 1996.

Martin, Mary. *My Heart Belongs*. New York: William Morrow, 1976.

Maslon, Laurence. *The Sound of Music Companion*. New York: Simon and Schuster, 2006.

Miller, Gabriel. *William Wyler Interviews*. Jackson: University of Mississippi Press, 2010.

Monaco, Paul. *History of the American Cinema: The Sixties: 1960–1969*. Los Angeles: University of California Press, 2001.

———. *Ribbons in Time—Movies and Society Since 1945*. Bloomington: Indiana University Press, 1987.

Mordden, Ethan. *Rodgers and Hammerstein*. New York: Harry N. Abrams, 1992.

Nolan, Frederick. *The Sound of Their Music: The Story of Rodgers & Hammerstein*. New York: Applause Theatre & Cinema Books, 2002.

Payn, Graham, and Sheridan Morley, eds. *The Noel Coward Diaries*. New York: Little Brown, 1982.

Peary, Danny, ed. *Close-Ups: The Movie Star Book*. New York: Workman Publishing Company, 1978.

Plummer, Christopher. *In Spite of Myself: A Memoir*. New York: Knopf, 2008.

Poitier, Sidney. *The Measure of a Man*. New York: Pocket Books, 2001.

Rodgers, Richard. *Musical Stages: An Autobiography*. New York: Random House, 1975.

Sackett, Susan. *The Hollywood Reporter Book of Box Office Hits*. New York: Billboard Books, 1990.

Sarris, Andrew. *The American Cinema: Directors and Directions 1929–1968*. New York: Dutton, 1968.

Secrest, Meryle. *Somewhere for Me: A Biography of Richard Rodgers*. New York: Knopf, 2001.

Stevens, George, Jr. *Conversations with the Great Moviemakers of Hollywood's Golden Age*. New York: Vintage Books, 2007.

Stirling, Richard. *Julie Andrews: An Intimate Biography*. New York: St. Martins Press, 2007.

Thomson, David. *Moments That Made the Movies*. New York: Thames & Hudson, 2013.

Trapp, Maria Augusta. *The Story of the Trapp Family Singers*. New York: Harper Collins, 1949.

von Trapp, Agathe. *Memories Before and After The Sound of Music*. New York: Harper Collins, 2010.

von Trapp, Maria. *Yesterday, Today, and Forever*. Green Forest, Arkansas: New Leaf Press, 1975.

Wasson, Sam. *Fifth Avenue, 5 A.M.? Audrey Hepburn, Breakfast at Tiffany's, and the Dawn of the Modern Woman*. New York: Harper Collins, 2010.

Wilk, Max. *Overture and Finale: Rodgers & Hammerstein and the Creation of Their Two Greatest Hits*. New York: Backstage Books, 1993.

———. *The Making of The Sound of Music*. London: Routledge Publishing, 2007.

Wyler, William and Axel Madsen. *William Wyler: The Authorized Biography*. New York: Thomas Y. Crowell Company, 1973.

MISCELLANEOUS

Seminar with Ernest Lehman, American Film Institute, Beverly Hills, California, March, 1976.

Production Notes, *The Sound of Music Film*, 20th Century-Fox, 1965.

RCA Victor Notes and Press Release, *The Sound of Music* soundtrack.

DVD

Climbed Every Mountain: The Story Behind The Sound of Music, with Sue Perkins, Northern Upstart productions, 2012.

Hollywood Screen tests: AMC, 1999

Julie and Carol at Carnegie Hall. CBS Television, 1962.

Rodgers and Hammerstein: The Sound of American Music, 1985.

Rodgers and Hammerstein: The Sound of Movies. Director Ken Burns. 20th Century Fox Film Corp and Rodgers and Hammerstein Organization, 1995.

Rodgers and Hammerstein's *The Sound of Music* 30th Anniversary Edition, 20th Century Fox, 1995.

DVD Extras:

"From Fact to Phenomenon," produced and directed by Michael Matessino.

"Ernest Lehman: Master Storyteller."

"Salzburg: Sight and Sound."

"The Sound of Music Gallery." Researched, written, and assembled by Michael Matessino.

"A Telegram from Daniel Truhitte."

Rodgers and Hammerstein's *The Sound of Music:* 40th Anniversary Edition, 20th Century Fox, 2005.

DVD extras:

Audio Commentaries with Julie Andrews, Christopher Plummer, Charmian Carr, Johannes von Trapp, Robert Wise, Dee Dee Wood.

"From Liesl to Gretl: A 40th Anniversary Reunion."

"Julie Andrews and Christopher Plummer: A Reminiscence."

"My Favorite Things: Julie Andrews Remembers"

"On Location with the Sound of Music"

"Screen Tests, Rare Treasures, Interviews, Photo Galleries"

Von Trapp Family: Harmony and Discord. A&E Biography, 2000.

"When You Know the Notes to Sing: Sing-A-Long Phenomenon"

Rodgers and Hammerstein's *The Sound of Music:* 45th Anniversary Edition, 20th Century Fox 2010

DVD extras:

"The Broadway Show"

"A City of Song: Filming Locations in Salzburg"

"Cutting Room Floor"

"A Generous Heart"

"Locations in Salzburg"

"Maria and the Musical"

"Maria in the 21st Century"

"Stage vs. Screen"

"Von Trapps Today"

"Von Trapps in Vermont"

"Writing the Show"

"The Sound of Music Tour: A Living Story"

"Musical Stages: Creating The Sound of Music"

"Shaping the Story"

CD

The Sound of Music. Original Cast Recording, Columbia Records, 1959, reissue 1998. (Liner notes from *Musical Stages* by Richard Rodgers 1973.)

The Sound of Music. Broadway Revival Cast Recording, 1998.

The Sound of Music 45th Anniversary Liner notes by Bert Fink, Movie Soundtrack, RCA Records, 2010.

PERIODICALS

AARP. September and October 2004.

Acocella, Joan. "Critics Notebook Favorite Things." *New Yorker.* December 8, 2008.

American Film. "Ernest Lehman: Dialogue on Film." October 1976.

Andrews, Suzanna. "The Sound of Money." *Vanity Fair.* June 1998.

Arthur Frommer's Budget Travel Magazine. "The 25 Movies that Literally Moved Us." December 2004–January 2005.

Backstage. "2006 SAG Life Achievement Award Recipient." January 18–24, 2007.

Barnes, Brooks. "The Sound of Music—The Blu Ray Treatment." *New York Times.* May 10, 2010.

Barthel, Joan. "The Biggest Money Making Movie of All-Time—How Come?" *New York Times.* November 20, 1966.

———— "The Sweet Smell of Ernie's Success." *New York Times.* November 24, 1968.

Bernard, Jami. "A New Favorite Thing." *New York Daily News.* September 8, 2000.

Bortridge, Mark. "The Real Maria." *The Independent.* October 29, 2006.

Cahill, Tim. "Poppins Picks Up the Pieces." *New York Daily News.* August 21, 1977.

Cameron, Kate. "The Sound of Music." *New York Daily News.* February 27, 1965.

Canby, Vincent. "Sound of Profits Resounds at Fox." *New York Times.* May 17, 1967.

Champlin, Charles. "Sound of Music—Hills are Alive Again." *Los Angeles Times.* March 14, 1973.

Chiarella, Chris. "Reinventing A Classic." *Video.* May 1995.

Christian Science Montior. "Hills Are Alive with Sound of Music." June 29, 2001.

————. August 3, 2001.

Clifford, Stephanie. "Von Trapps Reunited Without the Singing." *New York Times.* December 24, 2008.

Connor, Tracy. "Fair Julie May Never Sing Again." *New York Post.* November 19, 1998.

Copp, Jay. "Move Over Julie. We Search for the Real Sound of Music." *Christian Science Monitor.* June 24, 2003.

Crist, Judith. "If You Have Diabetes, Stay Away From This Movie." *New York Herald Tribune.* March 3, 1965.

Crowther, Bosley. "The Sound of Music." *New York Times.* March 3, 1965.

Current Biography. April 1994.

Daily Mail. December 29, 2007.

Dewan, Shaila. "The Rocky Horror Picture Show With Dirndls." *New York Times.* September 24, 2000.

Elle. November 2009.

Esquire. August 1966.

Film Comment. William Reynolds Interview with John A. Gallagher. March/April 1977.

Film Fan Monthly. October 1974.

Film Index. "Rene Lash Interviews Art Director Boris Leven." 1972.

Fitzsimmons, Emma. "Maria von Trapp, *Sound of Music* daughter, dies at 99." *New York Times.* February 23, 2014.

Flett, Kathryn. "Sixteen Going on Fifty Something." *London Observer.* April 1, 2001.

Gardella, Kay. "Fair Julie Lights Up ABC Television." *New York Daily News.* September 10, 1972.

Goldman, Andrew. "The Producers—Show Business." *New Yorker.* March 4, 2002.

Hammon, Sally. "A Talk with Julie Andrews." *New York Post.* July 25, 1970.

Harmetz, Aljean. "Designer with an Affinity for the Past." *New York Times.* March 13, 1981.

Heffernan, Virginia. "Poppins on the Loose: Lock Up Your Children." *New York Times.* December 24, 2004.

Heyman, Marshall. "Keeping Sound of Music Alive." *Wall Street Journal.* January 6, 2011.

Hohendel, Kristin. "All Together Now; The Hills Are Still Alive." *New York Times.* July 27, 2000.

Kafka, John. "Munich (Hitler's Hotbed) Slashes 20th's *Music,* Eliminating Nazis as Heavies." *Variety.* June 1, 1966.

Lane, Anthony. "Letter from London—The Maria Problem." *New Yorker.* February 14, 2000.

Lane, Harriet. "Ray, A Drop of Golden Nun." *London Observer.* October 3, 1999.

Lear's magazine. September 1992.

Life magazine. "Hollywood Discovers The Toast of Broadway." November 13, 1964.

London Observer. "Robert Wise Obituary." September 18, 2005.

London Telegraph. "Maria von Trapp Obituary." February 23, 2014.

Longworth, Jim. "Dan 'Rolfe' Truhitte Still Making Music." *Triad Today.* November 23, 2011.

Marowitz, Charles. "Bonnie & Clyde Symptom and Cause." *Village Voice.* December 23, 1967.

McBride, Joseph. "Wise Lends Hand to Holocaust Pic." *Variety.* April 13, 1992.

McCall's. April 1965.

McCarthy, Todd. "Lehman's Words Etched in Celluloid." *Variety.* March 5–11, 2001.

McCord, Ted. "How I Photographed the Sound of Music." *American Cinematographer.* April 1965, 223–225.

Mendolsohn, Daniel. "No, No Nobel." *New Yorker.* May 27, 1996.

New Republic. March 20, 1965.

Newsday. "The Hills Are Alive, All Right." September 8, 2000.

————. August 4, 2003.

————. November 27, 2005.

New York Daily News. "Andrews Tops Special Night." December 16, 1987.

New Yorker. March 6, 1965; February 1, 1967.

New York Morning Telegraph. December 19, 1941.

New York Post. December 19, 1997.

————. "Cutting-room King William Reynolds, 87." July 19, 1997.

New York Times. "Letters to the Editor." December 4, 1966.

————. "Where Music Sounded." June 1, 1975.

————. "Ted McCord Obituary." January 26, 1976.

————. "Dorothy Jeakins Obituary." November 30, 1995.

————. "Life's Medicine Without the Sugar." May 31, 1996.

————. "William Reynolds Dies at 87; Oscar Winner for Film Editing." July 22, 1997.

————. August 6, 2005.

————. "Robert Wise Obituary." September 15, 2005.

New York World Telegraph & Sun. "Sound of Movie Music: Richard Rodgers." February 27, 1965.

O'Connor, John J. "Julie Andrews with Tough Edges." *New York Times.* October 25, 1995.

Pacheco, Patrick. "Fanfare: Thoroughly Modern Julie." *New York Daily News*. March 14, 1993.
————. "Julie—Madly, Deeply." *New York Daily News*. February 9, 1997; May 4, 1999.

Page, Candace. "Trapp Family Lodge Survives Discord." *Vermont Homes and Towns*. January 2, 2001.

Parker, Heidi. "Actor who played Rolfe the Nazi Angry at Oprah for Leaving Him Out of the *Sound of Music* Reunion." *Daily Mail*. October 30, 2010.
————. "Kym Karath from Original Sound of Music Not Thrilled with Carrie Underwood Version." *Daily Mail*. December 6, 2013.

Playbill. November 2012.

Purdum, Todd S. "The Hills Still Resonate." *New York Times*. May 20, 2005.

Shinnick, Kevin G. "Hail to the Master: Robert Wise Interview." *Scarlett Street*. No. 25, 1997.

Slate, Libby. "25th Anniversary for Oscar Laden 'The Sound of Music'." *Los Angeles Times*. March 31, 1990.

Small, Jennifer. "Apparently Julie Andrews Was Too Tame to Do Her Justice." *Washington Post*. February 26, 1978.

Standford, Peter. "Caught in a von Trapp." *London Observer*. November 12, 2000.

Star Ledger. "25th Anniversary of The Sound of Music Should Produce Plenty of Dough-Re-Mi." September 2, 1990.

Stein, Herb. "Authentic Scenic Backgrounds Highlight Fox's *Sound of Music*." *Morning Telegraph*. June 24, 1964.

Theatre Week. May 24, 1993.

Thomson, David. "An Oscar for All the Ones He Should Have Got." *New York Times*. March 25, 2001.

Toronto Sun. "Julie Andrews's Sound of Music Costumes Sell for $1.3 Million at Auction." July 29, 2013.
————. "Christopher Plummer, Julie Andrews Honour Eleanor Parker." December 2013.

TV Guide. December 9–15, 1972.

Variety. "Bob Wise Will Curb Schmaitz." February 4, 1964.
————. "The Sound of Music." March 3, 1965.
————. "Music Nears Recouping Negative Cost as US Canada Rentals Hit 7,500,000." August 11, 1965.
————. "Ted McCord Obituary." January 28, 1976.
————. "In the Background." May 5, 1976.
————. "Wise Elected Prexy of Picture Academy." August 7, 1986.
————. "Boris Leven Obituary." October 22, 1986.
————. "Julie Andrews Resonates in Seventh Showbiz Decade." September 24-30, 2001.
————. "Ernest Lehman Obituary." July 11–17, 2005.
————. "Wise Crafted Oscar Winners (obituary)." September 19, 2005.

Ven Meter, Jonathan. "Victor/Victorious." *Vanity Fair*. October 1995.

Weinraub, Barnard. "A Life in Hollywood but Never a Niche." *New York Times*. Febuary 19, 1998.

Winsten, Archer. "Rages & Outrages." *New York Post*. April 16, 1973.

Witchel, Alex. "A Few Favorite Things the Musical Left Out." *New York Times*. January 1, 1998.

Wolff, Craig. "The Mysterious Gift of a Voice, Here and Then Gone." *New York Times*. December 23, 2001.

Woolridge, Adrian. "The Great Delegator." *New York Times*. January 29, 2006.

Zolotow, Sam. "Rodgers Loses Bid in Royalties Case." *New York Times*. November 22, 1968.

ORAL HISTORY
Interview with Marc Breaux, University of Northern Idaho, June 1999 as transcribed www.edu.taft Dr. Steve Taft, Chair, performing arts department.

RADIO
On-set interviews: Steve Gray with Julie Andrews, Christopher Plummer, and Peggy Wood, 1964.

TELEVISION
Julie Andrews Show. Episode 16, ABC: January 20, 1973.
Oprah Winfrey Show. ABC October 28, 2010.
Rosie O'Donnell Show. ABC January 21, 2000.
The Today Show NBC May 21, 2002.
The Today Show NBC: November 10, 2010.
Rachel Ray Show. November 10, 2010.
Ellen DeGeneries Show. CBS: January 26, 2007.

WEB SITES
ABCNews.go.com,
Boxofficemojo.com
Kobi Ben Sihon interview with Rosmarie von Trapp at http://buzzer17.proboards.com/ May 26, 2006.
Facebook.com: Sound of Music Facebook Page
International Movie Database: imdb.com
Rodgers and Hammerstein.com: www.rnh.com
www.Salzburg.sound-of-music.com
Screen Source: Top Grossing Movies, www.Amug.org/~scrnsrc
www.singalonga.net
www.trappfamily.com
Vulture.com, December 6, 2013
Wikipedia.com

INDEX